Alien Security

An Anthology for Human Freedom

Alien Security

An Anthology for Human Freedom

Your Own World Books
Nevada USA

www.AlienSecurity.info
www.Yowbooks.com
www.Yowusa.com

**Fiction is the safest place to hide a
terrible truth, so that all may find it.**
—Marshall Masters

Compilation Copyright Notices

Alien Security: An Anthology for Human Freedom
An Anthology Compilation of Public Domain and Copyrighted Material

Compilation Public Domain Works
Please Feel Free to Share With Others, As-Is and with Full Author Attribution
- *Alien Security, Maurice E. Osborn Author*
- *Alien Security (2nd Edition), Janice Manning, Editor*
- *Sagan Continuation Project (Appendix B), Marshall Masters*
- *The Hundredth Monkey (Battle Book Report #2), Ken Keyes, Jr.*
- *Twenty-Five Ways To Suppress Truth (Battle Book Report #3), H. Michael Sweeney*
- *The 8 Traits of A Disinformationalist (Battle Book Report #4), H. Michael Sweeney*

Compilation Copyrighted Material
2009 Your Own World, Inc., All Rights Reserved
- *Foreword by Marshall Masters*
- *Doing the Tell (Battle Book Report #1), Marshall Masters*
- *Cover Illustrations by Anthony Diecidue, artofant.com*

All other content and compilation rights are reserved by:
©2009 Your Own World, Inc., Nevada, USA

Trade Paperback
First Edition — November 2009
ISBN-10: 1-59772-100-X
ISBN-13: 978-1-59772-100-4

YOUR OWN WORLD BOOKS
an imprint of Your Own World, Inc.
Nevada USA
aliensecurity.info
yowbooks.com
yowusa.com
SAN: 256-1646

Notices

Every effort has been made to make this book as complete and as accurate as possible and no warranty or fitness is implied. All of the information provided in this book is provided on an "as is" basis. The authors and the publisher shall not be liable or responsible to any person or entity with respect to any loss or damages arising from the information contained herein.

Trademarks

All terms mentioned in this book that are known to be trademarks or service marking have been capitalized. Your Own World, Inc. cannot attest to the accuracy of this information and the use of any term in this book should not be regarded as affecting the validity of any trademark or service mark.

Table of Contents

Foreword by Marshall Masters..*xiii*

Alien Security..1

   Introduction..5

   Preface..9

First Contact...11

   7/3/47 Radar Station at White Sands Proving Ground..................11

   7/4/47 At Andrews Army Air Field, Washington D.C...................14

   7/4/47 In a Secure Briefing Room at Andrews A.A.F..................19

   7/4/47 At the Brazel Sheep Ranch in New Mexico.....................19

   7/4/47 The Plains of San Augustin, New Mexico......................20

   7/4/47 On the Runway of Condron Field, N.M........................20

   7/4/47 At the Site LZ-1 Near Corona, New Mexico...................21

   7/4/47 At the Home of Brazel's Nearest Neighbor...................24

Recovery..27

   7/5/47 At Site LZ-1 Near Corona, New Mexico......................27

   7/5/47 On Highway 54 in Corona, New Mexico........................28

   7/5/47 Near Oscura Peak, New Mexico...............................29

   7/5/47 At Site LZ-2 near Oscura Peak, N.M.........................30

   7/5/47 At the Home of Hollis Wilson in Corona, N.M................32

   7/6/47 The Plains of San Augustin, New Mexico.....................33

   7/6/47 Chaves County Sheriff's Office, Roswell, N.M...............34

   7/6/47 At Base Commander's Office of Roswell A.A.F................35

   7/6/47 At the Debris Field on Brazel's Ranch......................36

   7/6/47 At the Command Post of Site LZ-2...........................36

   7/7/47 At a Hangar of Alamogordo Army Air Field...................36

   7/7/47 In an Office at Alamogordo Army Air Field..................37

7/7/47 At the Debris Field on Brazel's Ranch...38

Crisis Management...41

7/8/47 At the Public Relations Office of Roswell A.A.F...............................41
7/8/47 At the Base Commander's Office of Roswell A.A.F..........................42
7/8/47 In the Control Tower at Muroc A.A.F...43
7/9/47 In the White House, Washington D.C...44
7/9/47 At the Base Commander's Office of Roswell A.A.F..........................45
7/9/47 In General Ramey's Office at Carswell A.A.F.................................46
7/10/47 In the Situation Room of the White House.....................................48
7/12/47 General Ramey's Office at Carswell A.A.F....................................51
7/14/47 At Military Police Headquarters, Roswell Base.............................52

Discovery...55

7/16/47 In Gen. Vandenberg's Office at the Pentagon..............................55
7/18/47 The Army Medical Corps Facility of Wright Field.........................56
8/25/47 In the Oval Office of the White House...58
9/19/47 In Gen. Vandenberg's Office at the Pentagon..............................59
9/24/47 In the Oval Office of the White House...60
9/26/47 The National Security Council, Washington D.C............................61
11/30/47 In a Conference Room at the Pentagon.......................................61
12/30/47 In a Briefing Room at Wright-Patterson A.F.B.............................62
1/18/48 In Gen. Vandenberg's Office at the Pentagon..............................63
7/28/48 In Evens' Office at Wright Field, Dayton, Ohio.............................64
12/16/48 In a Conference Room at the Pentagon.......................................66

Disinformation..67

2/12/49 In a Majestic-12 Meeting at the Pentagon.....................................67
5/22/49 Forrestal's Room at Bethesda Naval Hospital................................68
8/14/49 In Evens' Office at Wright Field, Dayton, Ohio.............................69
9/18/49 At White Sands Proving Ground, N.M...69
12/27/49 In the Press Room of the Pentagon..70
1/12/50 Facility YY-II at Los Alamos National Laboratories.......................71
4/18/50 Air Technical Intelligence Center, Wright Field.............................72
11/14/51 In a Majestic-12 Meeting at the Pentagon....................................73
7/27/52 The Aerial Phenomena Group at Wright Field...............................73
1/12/50 Facility YY-II at Los Alamos National Laboratories.......................74

11/18/52 In President-Elect Eisenhower's Office.................................75
12/14/52 In a Briefing Room at Wright-Patterson A.F.B...............................76

Formal Contact...79

3/27/53 In the Situation Room of the White House...............................79
5/2/53 In General Vandenberg's Office at the Pentagon..........................80
10/19/53 In the project Sigma Center at the Pentagon...........................80
12/7/53 At the Project Sigma Center in the Pentagon............................83
12/8/53 At the Project Sigma Center in the Pentagon............................85
2/20/54 On the Runway of Muroc Air Force Base..................................85
2/24/54/ In a Majestic-12 Meeting at the Pentagon..............................87
3/13/54 At the Project Sigma Center in the Pentagon............................88
4/25/54 On the Runway of Holloman Air Force Base...............................88

Aftermath...91

5/12/54 The Hotel de Bilderberg, Oostebeek, Holland............................91
4/1/55 At a Meeting of the Majestic-12 Members.................................92
7/1/55 In the Office of Lt. Col. Evens at the Pentagon.........................93
5/12/56 At White Sands Proving Ground, N.M...................................96
5/15/56 At White Sands Proving Ground, N.M...................................96
8/12/57 At a Meeting of the Majestic-12 Members...............................96
11/25/57 In General Twining's Office at the Pentagon..........................97
3/9/58 At Dreamland in Nevada...97

Insiders..103

11/29/60 The Office of the Secretary of Defense...............................103
12/12/60 In Colonel Evens' Office at the Pentagon.............................104
2/15/61 In the Oval Office of the White House.................................106
3/21/61 The Council on Foreign Relations Building.............................106
11/6/61 In Colonel Evens' Office at the Pentagon..............................108
12/7/61 In the Oval Office of the White House.................................109
3/3/62 At a Board of Directors' Meeting for the C.F.R.........................111

Coup d'Etat...113

3/16/62 At the Office of the National Security Adviser........................113
8/14/63 In the Oval Office of the White House.................................114
8/27/63 In the Intelligence Complex at Camp Perry, VA.........................115

9/9/63 In Defense Secretary McNamara's Office..118

9/15/63 In the Oval Office of the White House..118

11/21/63 In the President's Quarters of the White House..........................122

11/22/63 At Daley Plaza in Dallas, Texas..123

12/24/63 At a Bar in Washington, D.C..124

The Exchange..129

4/24/64 At White Sands Missile Range, New Mexico................................129

7/11/65 At the Nevada Test Site of Area 51..131

7/11/65 On Board the Alien Craft..134

First Day on Planet Serpo..140

Day 2 on Planet Serpo..143

Subsequent Days on Serpo..147

National Security..165

8/19/65 At the National Security Facility..165

4/23/66 At the Office of Congressman Gerald Ford................................167

8/30/66 At the National Security Agency Facility................................168

12/12/67 In Evens' Office at the N.S.A..169

5/30/68 In Evens' Office at the N.S.A..170

12/14/68 In the Oval Office at the White House................................170

12/19/69 In Evens' Office at the N.S.A..171

6/15/71 In Evens' Office at the N.S.A..171

9/19/72 At a Meeting of the Majestic-12..172

12/11/73 In Evens' Office at the N.S.A..173

12/22/74 In Evens' Office at the N.S.A..173

9/23/75 In Evens' Office at the N.S.A..173

11/23/75 At an Executive Meeting of the N.S.A................................173

11/29/75 In Evens' Office at the N.S.A..174

11/26/77 In the Communications Center at the N.S.A................................175

12/15/77 At the Dreamland Facility in Nevada................................177

6/19/78 In Evens' Office at the N.S.A..178

7/14/78 At White Sands Proving Grounds, New Mexico................................179

10/12/79 In Evens' Office at the N.S.A..180

10/15/79 At a Surveillance Detail in Baltimore, MD................................180

10/15/79 Inside Linda's Vehicle..181

10/15/79 With the Surveillance Detail..181

10/16/79 At a Meeting in the National Security Agency...............................182

10/18/79 On the Top Level of Dulce Base..182

10/21/79 On the Second Level of Dulce Base...184

10/22/79 On the Lower Levels of Dulce Base...185

10/22/79 On Level 7 of Dulce Base...188

Personal Contacts..193

5/18/80 In the Green Mountains of Vermont..193

5/20/80 At Evens' House in Baltimore, Maryland......................................199

5/20/80 Inside an Alien Spacecraft...200

5/21/80 At Evens' House in Baltimore, Maryland......................................202

Acclimation..203

12/22/80 Evens' Office at the National Security Agency..............................203

3/7/81 The Presidential Retreat at Camp David, MD...................................204

3/27/81 In the Oval Office of the White House.......................................209

4/9/81 At the Hotel Daniels in New York City..210

4/10/81 At an Apartment in New York City..211

4/11/81 At the Restaurant Adams in New York...212

4/14/81 In a Conference Room at the N.S.A...214

2/15/82 At a Parking Garage in Washington, D.C......................................216

2/23/82 Evens' Office at the N.S.A..218

2/23/82 At Evens' House in Baltimore, MD..219

2/27/82 In Evens' Office at the N.S.A...220

12/5/83 At a Parking Garage in Washington, D.C......................................220

5/22/88 In Evens' Office at the N.S.A...221

Captured..223

7/14/88 At an Apartment in Yelm, WA...223

7/30/88 At a Parking Lot in a Maryland Suburb.......................................223

7/30/88 In the Interrogation Section of the N.S.A...................................224

7/30/88 In a Forest Clearing...226

7/30/88 On Board a Pleiadian Spacecraft...227

Evens' Letter...231

Appendices...241

Appendix A — References...243

Chapter 1 – First Contact...244
Chapter 2 – Recovery...246
Chapter 3 – Crisis Management...248
Chapter 4 – Discovery...250
Chapter 5 – Disinformation...252
Chapter 6 – Formal Contact...254
Chapter 7 – Aftermath...256
Chapter 8 – Insiders...258
Chapter 9 – Coup d'Etat...260
Chapter 10 – The Exchange...262
Chapter 11 – National Security...264
Chapter 12 – Confrontation...267
Chapter 13 – Personal Contacts...268
Chapter 14 – Acclimation...270
Chapter 15 – Captured...272
Chapter 16 – Evens' Letter...273

Appendix B — The Sagan Continuation Project...275

Battle Book Reports...285

Report 1 — Doing the Tell...287
Report 2 —The Hundredth Monkey...297
Report 3 — Twenty-Five Ways to Suppress Truth...327
Report 4 — The 8 Traits of a Disinformationalist...343

Foreword by Marshall Masters

Fiction is the safest place to hide a terrible truth, so that all may find it.

The book you now hold in your hands is more than a good fiction read. It holds a key of awareness to your own future freedom, if not your very life. This is because it conveys a terrible truth. Simple in its origin, yet fraught with consequences for elites. It is why they fund an ongoing and highly organized onslaught of global disinformation.

Do not assume that this is just another cover-up. Rather, this disinformation effort represents the most horrific crimes against humanity since Hitler's minions were tried in Nuremberg, Germany (1945 to 1946) following WWII.

Of the 22 tried, over half were hung on the gallows, because as "good Nazis" they knew what they were doing. That they had "quietly" murdered millions of Jews, Jehovah's Witnesses, Disabled, Gays, Gypsies and others deemed to be undesirable.

Depending on how the numbers are tallied, between 11 million to 17 million people were murdered. What they did was known, but world leaders like American President Franklin Delano Roosevelt and Pope Pius XII allowed the Nazis to preserve a cloak of secrecy for their "Final Solution" as Hitler called it. For reasons of political expediency, of course.

On the heels of this 1946 realization, that aiding monsters with their crimes against humanity is to be on the wrong side of history, comes 1947 and Roswell. This is why the ongoing Roswell cover-up war of disinformation is not about "us" being unable to handle the truth. It is about our leaders once again aiding monsters with their crimes against humanity — yet again!

We Must Bear Witness or Perish in Silence

Today, we're watching as literally hundreds of Roswell witnesses are dying off from old age. Many such as Major Jesse Marcel Sr. simply grew tired of the government's broken promises. That the truth would be revealed some day.

Weary of the politically expedient reasons, Marcel came forward as a true hero to reveal the terrible truth. In can therefore be said that he was in it for the species. Not theirs. Ours.

Meanwhile, other Roswell witnesses have started coming forward with their own deathbed confessions. Though each only witnessed mere fragments of the overall event, they too were silenced by decades of brutal intimidation.

In light of these recent deathbed confessions, self-proclaimed debunkers and cynics are predictably quick with their simple sounding, "so what" jabs; but that's their job too. To assist disinformation operatives charged with burying the truth of what really happened and the reason why it is so important.

More interested in airing their 24/7 unfortunately dead white female news stories, the media dutifully reports the pronouncements of these debunkers as entertainment. Likewise, they go to great lengths to avoid vetting these sources and of course, they replay that hackneyed sound byte over and over. "It's that Roswell crap again!" Ask yourself, is that just bad reporting or is something else going on?

Consider this. When the day comes that the last Roswell witness dies, a true propaganda plum will drop into the waiting hands of the disinformation victors and their puppet media mavens. It will be a free and unhindered hand to bury the history of this event as they please.

That is... only if you let them and this in turn, begs a simple question. Why bother?

This Is Your Fight Too

If you're a simple person like Maurice Osborn, you know why. Furthermore, if you're an honest person too, you'll also have the courage to admit your knowing to yourself. Then, you'll know exactly what's at stake.

The most precious gift given to us by the creator. Even more precious than life itself, it the gift of free will. It is more than the right to peacefully express our lives as we see fit. It is the right to fight for our lives and to do that, we need the truth.

To let the disinformation operatives and their unpaid legions of arrogant debunkers and cynics convince you otherwise, is to willfully abandon your most precious possession. Your free will.

Worse yet, if we collectively abandon our free will as a species, we shall condemn both ourselves and future generations to a bitter slavery. One imposed upon us by off-world exploiters, and carried out by their inhuman vassals.

This is exactly what Maurice sees happening to humanity. It is why he wrote this book. So that this terrible truth could see the light of day, all around the world.

By conveying this terrible truth through fiction-based-on-fact, the worst criticism disinformation operatives and arrogant debunkers and cynics heap upon this book, is that it is fiction. Consequently, the more they attack it, the more it will grow.

This is why fiction is the safest place to hide a terrible truth, so that all may find it.

Spread the Word

Above and beyond the fiction plot, the essence of the facts behind this book is presented as a viral message. One that delivers a unique distillation of all that is known of this topic in the available literature so be sure to spend some time reading through the Bibliography (Appendix A.)

The end result of Maurice's effort is viral presentation is that it strips away decades of layered disinformation and propaganda ploys, with the precision of a surgical laser. Maurice's cuts are so clean and precise, they peel back the noisy layers of disinformation so as to finally lay bare, the terrible truth that hangs over each of us like a malevolent Sword of Damocles.

Now I will share it with you now, so that you can prepare yourself for a story that will forever change your worldview. Or at the very least, leave you with a future regret. One that may come to haunt you, with a disheartening realization. That you failed to look outside the news box created by our expertly, dumbed-down media.

Frankly, if ignorance is bliss, now is the time to stop reading.

The Terrible Truth

The terrible truth, Maurice unmasks in this book, is not what happened at Roswell. But rather, what happened after Roswell! A fateful turn for the worse that will be remembered as a dark turning point in the history of humankind.

That following Roswell, our leaders were received clandestine visits from various extraterrestrial races, both benign and exploitative. Each offered clear choices for our world and our relationship to the other civilizations that inhabit our galaxy.

Shortsighted, warlike and politically motivated in their thinking, they chose to ignore the more enlightened choices offered by benign races.

Rather, they chose to snatch the cosmic beads and blankets of a Faustian bargain with exploitative races. All in the naïve belief they could pry loose a bounty of war winning technologies and then cleverly "cheat the devils" of their due.

In their rush to judgment, our elites and leaders failed to grasp a simple fact. These very same malevolent races have played this exploitation game for millennia. Now the shame our leaders dread, is that they're winning and predictably so. Not because their better, but because we've been sold out as a species. That's the real terrible truth and they're as loath to admit it even to themselves, as you may be to accept it.

Like addicted gamblers who've already lost the family fortune on the gaming tables, elites continue hedging their bets with disinformation schemes, designed to keep us in the dark. With our right of free will thus suppressed, they can and continue to, recklessly pawn whatever remains of our future.

Who is the "our"? You, me and everyone else who has the God-given right to stand up and say "this is my planet too and I deserve the truth!" However, the point of Maurice's book is to go beyond "this is my planet too and I deserve the truth!"

This Is Our Planet and We Deserve the Truth

Given that we know we are besieged by extraterrestrial races bent on enslaving us with the help of their human minions, is humanity all alone in this crisis?

Did the benign races who approached our leaders after the 1947 incident at Roswell abandon us because our leaders made unfortunate choices. No! They remain as friends from afar and they're continually expressing their concerns for us. Likewise, they're also telling us that the situation is not hopeless. We can still turn it around.

Likewise, it must be noted that this precious candle of opportunity is burning at both ends. Therefore, let us not be easily lured into cheery mood of complacency. Rather, we as a species must collectively grasp this as a Carpe diem, "seize the day," moment. The time has come for us to collectively rise up to say in a chorus of defiance," this is our planet and disrespectful exploiters are not welcome. Go away."

When we do, the benign races who also wish to see us freedom as a peaceful species, will be able to come to our side. That is, provided, we're not threatening other races in the galaxy. This is pretty darn "big if" for us.

Think of the present day belligerent and dangerous antics of rogue nation leaders such as those in Iran and North Korea. This kind of reckless brinkmanship and hateful rhetoric, is most worrisome for much of the rest of the world. Now extend that out on a galactic scale.

Do we want the galaxy to see us as "nutters with nukes" and therefore better enslaved than left to their own devices? Assuming that all we're offing as a species is broader application of these dangerous antics, then who will want to ally with us? The exploiters, that's who and they're already here, ex post facto.

Conversely, if we are willing to co-exist peacefully in the galaxy as a noble species, we will be welcomed. Provided we can collectively rise up to say "NO" to these off-world exploiters and their human minions in clear, noble, consistent and unequivocal manner.

In other words, we cannot claim our right of free will unless we're prepared to defend it. There is no free lunch on Earth; nor is there one in the galaxy.

This is the message Maurice and others like him have found. Consequently, it propels his every step and as a simple man who knows this terrible truth, he will fight it any way he can, for as long as he draws breathe.

Maurice is but one of many with a simple message to us all. That if we have the courage and determination to express our free will with a moral purpose, we can and will prevail!

So is this superhero stuff? Nope and here is the good news. There are simple things you can do to make a difference starting today. It is called "doing the tell" and you'll be able to read all about it in Doing the Tell, by Marshall Masters, after you've finished reading Maurice's story. Here is some more good news. This friendly conversation of freedom has been ongoing with benign races since 1974!

They're Talking and Sometimes We Listen

Neither a saint nor a celebrity by temperament, Maurice is more like the geek who gets your PC working again. Or the honest mechanic who squeezes some extra life out of a tired engine or transmission so you can motor your way to a better situation. He's you. He's me. And yes, he's a shy hero one day and a cranky pain in the patootie the next. Sound familiar?

If not, here is a name you'll recognize. Carl Sagan (1934-1996), the author of the fiction title Contact, which later became the 1997 blockbuster film by the same title, and starred Jodie Foster.

This spectacular film presented us with the notion of benevolent life in the universe and featured a early scene at the Arecibo telescope. The world's largest single-dish radio telescope in Puerto Rico.

A key starting place for this story because in 1974, Sagan used this same telescope to broadcast a contact message into space. Then with NASA's Viking (1975) and the Voyager (1977) missions, he sent two more contact messages into space. The answers came in 1991 and 1992 as crop circles and they were both peaceful and respectful.

Carl Sagan Answered

The first crop circle formation appeared in a field adjacent to the Chilbolton Radio Telescope in Hampshire, England in 2001. It was a reply to Sagan's 1974 Arecibo contact message using Sagan's very own 1974 Arecibo communication protocol.

The second crop circle formation appeared in Crabwood England on August 15, 2002. Like the digital disc with the human drawings that was carried into space with the Voyager (1977) spacecraft, it also featured an alien face as well as a similar disc protocol as well.

To date, the only reliable translation of the digital message contained in the disc glyph of this 2002 formation was made by Maurice Osborn. Here is his translation:

Beware the bearers of FALSE gifts & their BROKEN PROMISES. Much PAIN but still time. BELIEVE. There is GOOD out there. We oppose DECEPTION. COnduit CLOSING,

Maurice's translation would set in motion the mutual interest we shared, and which prompted us to co-found The Sagan Continuation Project. The history of the project is contained in Appendix B - The Sagan Continuation Project.

For now, the two sentences in this message that need to be addressed immediately are.

Beware the bearers of FALSE gifts & their BROKEN PROMISES.

This message is a clarion call for awareness. It warns us that our governments are in league with the "bearers of FALSE gifts" and that "their BROKEN PROMISES" are clear evidence that they've been had. Likewise, so have we, except that we're the last to know.

We oppose DECEPTION.

Where the first sentence is a call to awareness, this sentence is a clear call to action. The benign creators of this formation are telling us that they are giving us what we need most – the truth. If we can handle it, then we also need to "oppose DECEPTION."

Are you wondering if it wouldn't be easier for all of us to sit this out, and let someone else handle the "oppose DECEPTION" chores for us?

This Is Everyone's Fight

Did you, or someone you know as a kid ever run across a schoolyard to watch a bully pummel some unfortunate kid?

Did you fall back or melt away when you heard the school principal coming to break up the altercation. Or perhaps when the bully starting looking at you the wrong way?

Wakey wakey. This is not about watching some other poor kid getting an undeserved whuppin' in the back corner of a schoolyard. It's about you, your life, your free will and this planet. If after reading this book you decide to fall back or melt away so that someone else can "oppose DECEPTION" for you, then what does that say about you?

It says that you're just as error-prone are our leaders, but with one big difference. Their unwise choice got us into this mess, whereas your timid reluctance to get involved, could be the final choice that seals humanity's fate.

Once that happens, you'll wear the same yoke of slavery as everyone else. Either that or you'll sellout to the PTB and start cracking a whip for better food and provisions. Assuming you're not a psychopath, try and sleep with that.

We're All In This Together

If as a species, we choose unwisely (or choose not to choose at all), we will continue to plod along on our present path of fear, hate and exploitation. At the end of this path will come the soul-crushing yoke of species slavery portended in this book.

Then, and only after countless generations have passed and our world has been fully raped of its resources and natural beauty, will our freedom be restored – for whatever time remains. This is why other races who have emerged from generations of slavery are trying to warn us about what happened to them.

Their motive is simple. Because all life in the universe is connected, it is important to them that we understand how dangerously close we are to suffering the same fate.

What they urge us to do through passive mediums, is to believe in our future and that if we chose wisely, and soon, we can follow an alternate path. One that offers us a bright future as a successful, enlightened and peaceful species.

Walking this path means that humanity overcome its violent differences and greet the future with compassion and integrity. It will be a difficult path, but it is the only one that leads to a future where we become an evolved species in the cosmic family of life.

This is the hope Maurice and others are offering you in this book and elsewhere. However, the real questions are what you, the reader want to believe and you are ready to stan-dalone in your knowing, if need be?

In Maurice's vision of the future, a brave few will initially answer the call; those willing and able to energize a new consciousness of free will for all humankind and a magnificent moment in our history. Then other will join and the exploiters who seek to enslave us will melt away, as benign species come to our aide. Assuming we have the will and the courage to fight for our creator-given right of free will.

If you are amongst the brave few, this book will show you what is at stake and what you can do. To help you start doing this today, read Doing the Tell, by Marshall Masters.

If you are amongst the many to follow, then this book will help you to listen for the call to action, so that you may know when to join the ranks in time to make a difference.

Above all, never forget. It's our world, and we're going to keep it. BELIEVE.

—*Marshall Masters, Publisher*

Marshall's Motto

Destiny finds those who listen,
and fate finds the rest.

So learn what you can learn,
do what you can do,
and never give up hope!

Alien Security

Maurice Osborn

Alien Security

2ⁿᵈ Edition – November 2009

First Edition Cover

Introduction

I began researching the UFO phenomenon extensively in 1985. This was a most remarkable period for revelations regarding the extraterrestrial presence here. Linda Moulton Howe was reporting on animal mutilations, Whitley Strieber was describing alien abductions in his book "Communion", and President Reagan was telling the world about how mankind would unite under a threat from outer space.

Government Involvement

I also researched the U.S. government's involvement with the extraterrestrial presence on Earth. This was a time when the "Majestic Documents" were being disclosed, the "Dulce Papers" revealed information about a joint human and alien underground base and John Lear reported on events at Area 51. In 1995, I wrote my first textbook regarding extraterrestrials, titled "Alien Life Forms". I also lectured and produced a video titled, "The U.S. and ETs" about my research into how the U.S. Government has handled the extraterrestrial presence here.

Crop Circles

In 2001, I became interested in the crop circle phenomenon when I realized the significance of a formation at Chilbolton, England in relation to a message that was created by Dr. Carl Sagan and broadcast into space back in 1995. This new formation described the appearance, home worlds, and method of communication of an extraterrestrial race of beings. This also described the composition of their bodies, their height, and their population.

In 2002 I produced a documentary video about the hidden messages discovered in crop circles, titled "Alien Messages". This described how I deciphered a digital message that was found in a crop formation in England at Crabwood Farmhouse. The formation appeared to be of an extraterrestrial entity that was holding out a disk with the message on it, which said, "Beware the bearers of false gifts and their broken promises. Much pain but still time. Believe. There is good out there. We oppose deception. Conduit closing."

As a computer programmer, I was able to write a software program that let anyone type a text message and have it transformed into the same format as in the previous crop formation. I then sought the assistance of people over the Internet to create an appropriate message in response to the prior crop circle message. It was Marshall Masters who answered the call and intuitively created what has come to be known as the "Sagan Continuation Message". It stated, "We welcome all who respect our free will. If you choose to help, then help us to help ourselves. There is good here too. We look for a reply."

In August of 2004, myself and five other people from England placed this message in a crop formation at Market Lavington, England with the farmer's permission. This event was documented in a video, titled "Human Messages". Although there has not been a reply to this message found in any subsequent crop circle formation, there has been a response. In September of 2008 at Avebury Down, England, an elaborate cross formation was discovered with a dot pattern next to it that spelled out the word "Believe" in the same way as before.

Malevolent Contacts

These messages of hope and concern have filled me with a desire to find the good "out there" and to become aware of the bad. Unfortunately, I became aware of a non-human evil presence in a very personal and disturbing way when I was abducted in 2005. I awoke one morning to find that I had a bloody nose. While attempting to blow out whatever was causing the bleeding, a small capsule was expelled into the sink and then it fell down the drain. I immediately realized that these were symptoms of an alien abduction experience from my many years of research.

I underwent regression therapy where I recalled the abduction experience by gray-skinned, large headed beings with big black eyes. I am now able to remember how this being held an instrument with its long fingers while a device was implanted deep into my brain through my nose. I resent this very much as a violation of my basic human rights. Unfortunately, I am not the only person to have been abducted and violated against their will.

A recent Roper poll revealed that millions of Americans exhibit symptoms associated with the abduction experience and they are completely oblivious to it. However, many people experience unexplained scars or bruises and live in constant terror of it happening to them again. I know of this horror and I care greatly about what is happening to them. As a result, I prepared two pamphlets, titled "Alien Abduction Resistance" and "Beware of the Grays" to help people cope with this intrusion in their lives. In addition, I also produced a video of a lecture that I gave on this subject titled, "Earth Freedom".

Benevolent Contacts

In order to obtain a fair and balanced perspective on this phenomenon, I also researched and reported on many benevolent appearing alien races and their contacts. The Meier case is one of the most famous amongst Ufologists, and with good reason. Despite its controversial nature and its problematic single-source drawbacks, the evidence is highly compelling. Consequently, I do not fully accept all that Meier has made public. Nonetheless, the body of work, on balance, is worthy of considered investigation.

For this reason, I decided to bring an independent, 3rd party voice to the Meier debate, and wrote a book "The Essence of the Notes". It documents the first 76 encounters that Mr. Meier has had with beings from the Pleiades, which were originally translated by Wendelle Stevens. Because that translation offered poor English-language readability, the more polished version offered in "The Essence of the Notes" makes the translations more accessible to a wider range of people.

Revelations

This current book, "Alien Security" is my way of bringing to light what the U.S. Government has been doing about the extraterrestrial presence here since the crash of a UFO near Roswell, New Mexico in 1947. This reveals how alien beings have been allowed to violate our airspace, conduct secret experiments in underground facilities, and abduct people against their will, as well as mutilate our animals completely unabated by those who are sworn to protect us.

Having personal experience with both benevolent and malevolent alien beings has given me a unique perspective on this whole phenomenon. While I welcome open and consensual contact with extraterrestrial races that respect our free will and are willing to help us to help ourselves, I also care about preserving freedom and self-determination for all mankind on Earth. This means exposing the atrocities being conducted against humanity so that we can rid our planet of these self-serving extraterrestrials and bring justice against those who permit this disgraceful and illegal conduct to continue.

This book attempts to show how malevolent alien beings have secretly conspired with wealthy and powerful people so that they can take control over our planet and cause humanity to serve them as their slaves. After reading this book, you will be faced with the decision to either stand up for our rights as free people and preserve our planet or remain divided until we are no longer free and our Earth is stripped of everything that we need to survive. It has happened on many other worlds. If you care that it could happen here, then stand up for your rights.—*Maurice Osborn*

Preface

This book reveals factual historical events regarding extraterrestrial contacts as seen through the eyes of fictional characters named Tom Evens, Stan Edwards and Linda Davis. This format enables the reader to obtain detailed information in a dramatic and highly entertaining way. The three fictitious characters interact with real people in this story. Their true names, titles, and accomplishments have been presented as revealed in the referenced source documentation of Appendix A. No attempt has been made to misrepresent or slander the people presented here.

Each scene is prefaced with a date and location. Although the exact dates of certain events may not be known, every effort has been made to depict the sequence of historical events accurately. Much of the information presented was derived from published non-fiction books pertaining to the subjects involved. However, other information from anonymous or unsubstantiated sources, such as with the "Majestic Documents", is also included.

Since the subject matter of this book has been officially dismissed as unimportant by military and government officials, documented proof about this subject has been difficult to obtain. In fact, there has been a massive, well-orchestrated effort to discredit the sources of this information and plant disinformation in order to discourage people from becoming aware of official misconduct related to the handling of extraterrestrial contacts.

The reader is encouraged to investigate the validity of the information provided in this book. Whenever the reader encounters a section of the book where the source of the information is of interest, he or she may use the References section in Appendix A. To derive the source for information presented in this book, it is necessary to take note of the chapter number and any reference number in square brackets at the end of a sentence.

Appendix A contains a list of reference numbers and description fields for every chapter of the book. The references are numbered in order of appearance in each chapter. The description field contains information about the source of the material that is located in the book, as indicated by the reference number. This information includes the title of the source material, author, publisher, date of publication, heading, and location of the material within the source.

Armed with the chapter and reference number of the information in question, the reader can turn to Appendix A of the book and find the heading that corresponds to the chapter where the statement is located. Next, they can look for the reference number in square brackets at the end of the appropriate sentence. The information in the corresponding description field in the Appendix provides a complete description of where the statement was derived.

It is hoped that the reader will find this story to be enlightening as well as entertaining. Since this is a depiction of little known, but important, historical events, it is also hoped that the reader will receive this information with an open mind. Much of this information will be found to be incredible and very disturbing. However, it is very important that the reader does not react to this out of fear, anger, or intolerance. Instead, it is hoped that this information will bring about enlightenment so that proper choices can be made with regard to extraterrestrial life on this planet.

First Contact

7/3/47 Radar Station at White Sands Proving Ground

"Alamogordo Tower, this is White Sands, over? ... Alamogordo Tower, this is White Sands. How do you read me, over?" the Army Radioman says into his headset. There is still no response.

An Army General shouts, "Sergeant, why haven't you made contact with Alamogordo Army Air Field yet?"

The Sergeant swallows hard and reports, "Sir, I do not know. I have made contact with Kirtland Field, but Alamogordo is not responding. They should be monitoring this frequency."

The General frowns and says, "Very well. I want to be notified just as soon as contact is established. Contact them by the land line if they do not respond by radio."

"Yes, Sir", the Radioman says and thinks, *Why me? That idiot can hear every word of radio communications, along with everyone else in the room, over the loud speaker system.* He glances over at the V.I.P. section and notices that all of the visiting Admirals, Generals, and civilian dignitaries are staring directly at him. He averts his attention to what is happening in the rest of this dimly lit room. The green florescent glow from the radar screens and the amber light of the electronic vacuum tubes cast strange looking shadows on the pale gray concrete walls.

White Sands Proving Ground, New Mexico, is where all of the newest and most advanced technology is tested in the United States. This is an Army facility with the Naval Research Laboratories located nearby. [1] Next to the Atomic Energy Commission facilities at Los Alamos, this is the most secure and isolated base in America, with miles of open desert. This Radar Station houses some of the most sophisticated electronic equipment known to mankind. The Control Room is kept dimly lit for better viewing of the large, round radar screens. There are several radar consoles along one wall. An operator mans each console, with junior officers and technicians busily checking every function.

Everyone is especially nervous with the big brass present to witness the launch of a German V-2 Rocket, which the U.S. Army recovered at the end of World War II. The V.I.P. section overlooks the launch pad through a large, reinforced window with the radar consoles and various plotting boards to the right of the window. The plotting boards show the position of all airborne aircraft around the center, which represents the Radar Station's location. There are men behind these panels who keep the displayed information current, as provided by the radar operators over intercom headsets.

Lieutenant General Nathan Twining, who is the Chief of Air Materiel Command, examines the panels closely. This is his show tonight. He has assembled representatives from the government, military, and civilian aircraft manufacturing companies to demonstrate the capabilities of the German V-2 rocket. At the end of the war, Germany's top scientists, engineers, and technicians were secretly transferred to the United States in a program known as Project Paperclip. And now, with their help, General Twining hopes to demonstrate the potential of rocket propulsion.

The time is 11:30 PM, Mountain Standard Time. The main plot shows an aircraft arriving over White Sands, from Alamogordo AAF. The loud speakers crackle to life with, "White Sands, this is Alamogordo Tower, over".

The Radioman grabs for the transmit switch and says, "Alamogordo, this is White Sands. How do you read me, over?"

"We read you loud and clear, over."

The Radioman says to General Twining, "Sir, communications have been established."

The General exhales and says, "Very well."

The Sergeant then radios, "Roger, Alamogordo. We read you same and now show Eagle One over the target area, over."

"Roger, White Sands, we concur. Out."

A telephone rings and an Army officer answers it with, "This is White Sands Radar Station 'Alpha'. This is Lieutenant Johnson speaking."

"Lieutenant Johnson, this is Captain Avery at the Signal Corps Engineering Laboratories at Fort Mammoth, New Jersey. Let me speak to General Twining."

The Lieutenant states "Very well, Captain" and motions to the General to take the call.

The General grabs the handset and says, "This is General Twining."

"Sir, this is Captain Avery at the Signal Corps Engineering Laboratories at Fort Mammoth, New Jersey. We have reports from multiple radar installations in East Texas indicating that two unidentified craft, flying at incredible speeds, have been tracked heading towards your location." [2]

The General grinds his teeth together, says "Thank you, Captain", and hangs up the telephone.

Just then, someone points at the plot board and asks, "What's that?"

Everyone is astonished to see two new targets traveling at high speed toward White Sands from the Southeast and then they stop just outside the base.

General Twining asks, "What is happening? Did the two new targets crash?"

The Lieutenant responds, "No sir, the unidentified objects are stationary in mid air at 3,400 feet." The General asks, "How is that possible?" There is no reply.

The Radioman is heard over the loudspeaker saying, "Eagle One, this is White Sands. Can you see other aircraft in your vicinity, over?"

"This is Eagle One. That's affirmative, White Sands. I see two very bright lights, which are hovering about a thousand feet above the ground. Wait a minute. Correction, White Sands, the lights are now directly above me, and they are matching my speed. It Ahhh!"

"Eagle One, this is Holloman. Say again, over … Eagle One, this is Holloman. What is your status? Over ..."

Everyone watches the plot board and notice that the three targets merge into one and then remain stationary.

General Twining stands and says, "What in hell is going on?"

The Facilities Commander says, "Sir, there appears to have been a midair collision of the three objects."

The General asks, "Then why are they still being detected by radar?"

"I don't know, Sir" is the reply.

Some time later, the plot board shows all objects disappearing from radar.

The Radioman states, "Alamogordo Tower, this is White Sands. We just lost radar contact with Eagle One and the unidentified flying objects. Are you tracking them, over?"

"White Sands, Alamogordo Tower. That's a negative."

"Roger, Alamogordo. We detected a surge in emissions just before the loss of the objects. Did you detect anything, over?"

"That is affirmative, White Sands. We detected the same." [3]

"Understood. This is White Sands. Out."

General Twining runs over to the Facilities Commander and asks, "What in the world just happened?"

The Commander says, "Sir, we just lost contact with all three objects. A last known position and bearing has been calculated for two of the contacts. One landing zone has been designated LZ-1 and is located near Corona, approximately 75 miles Northwest of Roswell, New Mexico. The site of the other contact has been designated LZ-2 and is located approximately

20 miles Southeast of Socorro, New Mexico. Excuse me, General. I have to call the Signal Corps Engineering Laboratories, at Fort Mammoth." [4]

The General asks, "But, what about the location of the third object?"

He is told, "I don't know, Sir. Perhaps aerial reconnaissance of the area will locate it in the morning."

7/4/47 At Andrews Army Air Field, Washington D.C.

A telephone rings and is answered with, "Detachment three of the ninety-three, ninety-third Technical Services Unit. This is Master Sergeant Murphy. May I help you?"

He hears, "Sergeant, this is Lieutenant General Hoyt Vandenberg at the Central Intelligence Group. I am placing your unit on alert for immediate deployment in response to an incident that has just happened. The orders are being sent from the Army Chief of Staff now. Wake up your people, Sergeant. Get them going."

"Yes, Sir!" Murphy says and hangs up the telephone. If the sergeant was bored and drowsy before, he is fully awake and alert now. *Holy smokes,* he says to himself, *This is it!* He grabs the telephone again and dials the unit commander's home telephone number.

It rings eleven times before he hears the Colonel shout, "Hello!"

"Sir, its Sergeant Murphy. General Vandenberg just called. Our unit has been put on alert for immediate departure in response to an incident." "Very well, Sergeant. I'll be there in thirty minutes. You'd better start waking everybody up. Oh, shit! We're still one man short. Has that Captain from Los Alamos reported in yet?"

"Yes sir. He arrived yesterday. He's staying over at the In-Transit barracks."

The unit commander thinks about this for a moment and says, "Okay. Send someone over there to wake him up. Have him report to my office at 0200 hours and have everyone in the unit meet in the secure conference room at 0300 hours." "Yes, sir!"

Colonel Steven V. Harbrough enters his office, followed by Sergeant Murphy, who says, "The men have been alerted and are getting themselves ready for the meeting now, Sir. [5] That Captain from Los Alamos has also been awakened and should be here shortly. Here are our orders."

The Colonel sits down at his desk, takes the sheet of paper from Murphy, and starts reading it.

T O P   S E C R E T

```
: : : : : : : : : : : : : : : : : : : : : : : : : : : : : : : : : : : : : :

: T O P   S E C R E T :
: AUTH: AC of S, G-2 :
: INIT:_C_:
: DATE: 04 Jul 47 :


: : : : : : : : : : : : : : : : : : : : : : : : : : : : : : : : : : : : : :
```

a. See current G-2 Per Rpt and Estimate of Situation, 03 Jul.

b. A Team depart Andrews AAF and proceed to Condron Field, N.M., must arrive no later than 1000 MST.

c. Make contact with OIC of 4th Army CIC for briefing prior to investigation. Rpt directly G-2. Auth to make any inquiry and are cleared for "need to know".

d. Comm by secure R/T when investigation is finished.

e. Depart via Alamogordo and proceed to Andrews AAF.

f. Expect Rpt and Summary no later than 25 Jul. [6]

The Colonel looks up from the paper and says, "Well, it's official. I sure hope we don't screw this up. Thank-you, Sergeant. That will be all. Have the Captain report here just as soon as he arrives."

Murphy says, "Yes, sir" as he leaves the office and closes the door behind him.

The Colonel spins the dial of the combination lock on his filing cabinet. When the file drawer opens, he pulls the Captain's personnel file folder out and starts reviewing it.

Captain Thomas L. Evens had been scheduled to be interviewed later today. But now, the Colonel will have to determine right away if this new guy has what is needed to be a part of his team. He looks up at the sparse surroundings of the room and wishes he could be meeting Evens in his regular office back at Alamogordo Field. This room was furnished with only a metal desk, wooden chairs, a file cabinet, and coat rack. The walls are bare and painted in a dirty brown color.

The Colonel is startled from these thoughts by a knock at the door. "Enter."

A tall, blond haired officer enters the office, dressed in a Class-A Dress Uniform. He stands at attention in front of the desk and says, "Captain Tom Evens, reporting as ordered, Sir."

"At ease, Captain. Have a seat." The Colonel gestures to a chair in front of his desk and Evens sits down.

The two men size each other up. Evens judges the Colonel to probably be in his late thirties. Although, he still appears to be in pretty good shape. Evens notices the ring on the Colonel's finger which identifies him as a West Point graduate. He is dressed in a stiffly starched fatigue uniform and appears to be under a great deal of pressure.

The Colonel thinks Evens looks awfully young to be a Captain. Then, he looks at the ribbons on his chest and sees that Evens was awarded the Bronze Star medal and that he served in the European theater of operations during the war. He appears to have a stocky build and is in good physical shape. The Colonel says, "Its unfortunate that we could not have met at a more reasonable hour. But, something has come up and there is not much time for us to get acquainted. Do you know why you are here?"

Evens clears his throat and says, "I believe that this may have something to do with the fact that I volunteered to be apart of a rapid deployment, aircraft crash response team. All I know is that I have been ordered to report here today."

The Colonel gestures to the folder before him and says, "I have been going over your file to see if you qualify to be apart of a new unit, which I command. I've asked you to come here to answer some questions, which I have about your background. First, I'm curious why you joined the Army at the young age of 17?"

Evens takes a deep breath, lets it out, and says, "Well Sir, it was right after the bombing of Pearl Harbor and I wanted to join along with my older brother."

Harbrough then asks, "How did you receive your battlefield commission?" Evens replies, "As an M.P., I was involved with traffic control for the Red Ball Express. That's what they called the supply line of trucks that were kept constantly moving to keep up with Patton's tank movements. Anyway, I just happened to overhear someone in one of the trucks say something in German. I alerted the officer in charge and a bunch of us surrounded the truck. A firefight began and our officer was killed. They made me a second lieutenant and put me in charge of the Military Police detail."

The Colonel asks, "Is that where you got that Bronze Star ribbon?"

Evens says, "Yes, Sir. It was all blind luck, really."

The Colonel leans forward and says, "Well, there had to be an element of skill somewhere inside of you, because you have been promoted twice since then. Let's see. After four months of being in charge of security for the Red Ball Express, you were reassigned to logistics, where you took on the task of insuring that supplies got through to the front lines in Germany. You must have done something right. Because you were promoted to First Lieutenant and reassigned again to G-2, Army Intelligence. Now, I know they don't let just any idiot off the street do that sort of work."

Evens smiles and says, "You'd be surprised, Sir."

The Colonel continues, "Well, whatever you did there, it caused you to be promoted again to the rank of Captain and be transferred back here to the States to work with the staff of the Manhattan Project. Where, as everyone now knows, the first atomic bombs were developed and tested. What did you do there?"

Evens wipes his sweaty palms on his pant legs and states, "I was involved in insuring security for the transportation of important materials in and out of the facilities at Los Alamos. But, once those procedures were established, my work generally evolved into just verifying the backgrounds of the personnel who worked there. And, that is what I have been doing ever since."

The Colonel asks, "Are you married?"

"I'm just recently divorced, Sir. After the war, I returned home on leave and married my childhood sweetheart. But, she didn't like the New Mexican desert and didn't care much for Army life. That's when I found out that 'till death do you part' really means, 'till you get a divorce'. When she left, I needed to get away from there. And, I wasn't really happy at my job of just shuffling papers. Which is why I volunteered to be part of your unit, Sir."

Harbrough says, "Yeah, I can tell. You're the kind of guy who likes to be out, doing things and not just sitting at a desk."

"That's true, Sir."

The Colonel leans back in his chair, thinks for a moment, and asks Evens, "What is your opinion about flying saucers?"

Evens grins and replies, "I don't think there is much of anything to the stories, Sir."

"Well", the Colonel says, "Signal Corps' radar stations have been tracking UFOs on-and-off for about a month now, over sensitive military installations. The UFOs would periodically remain stationary for minutes at a time and then resume their original course. [7] In light of these activities, Alpha Team was established to respond to any suspected contact that might arise. So you see, you have not volunteered for a crashed aircraft recovery team. You have volunteered to be a part of a UFO contact response unit. Nobody knows where they come from and there is a great deal of concern that these craft may be some new type of Russian surveillance aircraft. There is also speculation that they may even come from another planet entirely."

The Colonel is doing all that he can to keep from laughing at the expression on Evens' face. Evens has a look of amazement with his jaw hanging down. The Colonel says, "I am in command of Detachment 3 of the 9393rd Technical Services Unit assigned to Alamogordo AAF. My unit is known as Alpha Team and is comprised of myself, a sergeant, an aeronautical engineer, scientist, medical doctor, a radio biological team, and a security specialist."

This seems to have snapped Evens out of his shocked state. He asks, "Flying Saucers are real?"

The Colonel says, "Well, there is a great deal of evidence to that effect. But as I said, no one knows where they come from, who is inside of them, or what they are doing here."

Harbrough decides that Evens would probably be able to deal with what would be expected of him on his team. So, he says, "Captain, an incident has just occurred, and my unit has been ordered to investigate. However, we are one man short of having a full complement. I would like you to be the new security specialist assigned to this unit. Are you up to it?"

Evens thinks, *Wow! He's asking me to be a part of a team to investigate UFOs? This is great!* With a serious look on his face, Evens says, "Yes Colonel, you can count on me. What are my responsibilities?"

The Colonel tells Evens, "You will be in charge of Military Police details, which will be temporarily assigned to this unit from bases in the local area, where we will be responding. Upon arrival at the site, your initial responsibilities will include the capture of the UFO and any personnel from inside the craft. Then, you will establish a defensive perimeter around the landing site in order to prevent unauthorized personnel from gaining access to it. And lastly, you will detain all unauthorized personnel in the area that may have witnessed the event. Once that is accomplished, you are to make certain that the witnesses remain silent about what they have seen, insure the retrieval of all debris in the area and supervise the secure transportation of everything to the appropriate facilities." [8]

Evens thinks about this for awhile and then asks, "What if the personnel, from inside of the UFO, have some sort of weapons and do not want to be captured?"

The Colonel smiles and says, "Well, in that case Captain, it will be your responsibility to defend this country from all enemies, foreign and domestic."

Evens thinks, *Holy smokes! He's saying that I may have to go into battle with aliens from outer space.* With a grin on his face, the Captain says, "I understand, Colonel. You can rely on me to do my duty."

7/4/47 In a Secure Briefing Room at Andrews A.A.F.

After being dismissed from Colonel Harbrough's office, Captain Evens finds himself directed toward a small briefing room by Sergeant Murphy. There is a podium at one end and several rows of seats arranged in two sections in front of it. The room is brightly lit. Evens can see several Army, Navy, and civilian personnel talking, in small groups, along the front and center isle of the room.

At 0300 hours, Colonel Harbrough enters the room and calls the meeting to order by saying, "Good morning, gentlemen. Will everyone please take their seat. For those who may not know me, I am Colonel Harbrough, in command of Detachment 3 of the 9393rd Technical Services Unit. A situation occurred on 3 July, 1947 at 2332 hours MST, over White Sands Proving Ground, New Mexico. A midair collision is suspected to have occurred between two Unidentified Flying Objects and another object. A high altitude explosion was recorded by a Project MOGUL constant level balloon. Radars from White Sands Proving Ground and Holloman Field also detected a surge. The locations of both suspected crash sites have been calculated and made available to this team." [9]

The Colonel pauses for a moment and then says, "Alpha Team has been ordered to respond to this situation. We are to depart Andrews Field and arrive at Condron Field, New Mexico no later than 1000 hours MST. After meeting with the commander of 4th Army's Counter Intelligence Corps, for a briefing of the situation, this unit is ordered to proceed to the suspected crash sites and investigate. We have been authorized to make any inquiry and are cleared for "need to know". A full report and summary is expected no later than 25 July. Now, you have all been briefed on what your assignments are in situations like this. I want every member of this team to be assembled at the staging area in one hour, with all gear and provisions, for immediate departure. Are there any questions?" With no one responding, the Colonel dismisses the troops and everyone hurriedly exits the room.

7/4/47 At the Brazel Sheep Ranch in New Mexico

Rancher William (Mac) Brazel lives in a small house on a sheep ranch with no radio or telephone. The closest town is Corona, which is 30 miles Southeast of his ranch. His wife and children live in Tularosa, NM where the children attend school. Mr. Brazel had heard an odd explosion late in the evening, during an electrical storm. But, he paid no attention to it, thinking it was a part of the storm. The next morning, he finds wreckage scattered over a wide area of his ranch. [10]

7/4/47 The Plains of San Augustin, New Mexico

Grady Landon (Barney) Barnett, a civil engineer working for the U.S. Soil Conservation Service, is on assignment near Magdalena, NM, west of Socorro, when he sees light reflecting off of metal and goes to investigate. He sees a metallic, disc-shaped object about 30 feet across. Members of an archaeological research team from the University of Pennsylvania also come to investigate. [11]

Professor W. Curry Holden walks up to Barney and says, "Hi. I'm Professor Holden. My students and I were in the area when we noticed this object here. What happened?"

Barney says, "I don't know. I just got here myself. My name is Barney Barnett." They both shake hands and then look at the machine. It appears to have been split open by an explosion or impact. It seems to be made of a metal similar to dirty stainless steel. [12]

Professor Holden asks, "What in the world is that? It doesn't have any propellers, jet or rocket engines. How do you suppose that it got here?"

Barney says, "I have no idea. It must be something new that the Army is developing. Is there anyone inside?"

"I don't know." The professor walks up to the craft and shouts inside, "Hello! Is anyone in there?" There is no response. The professor says, "Well, whatever it is, someone is bound to want to know what happened to it. My students and I are going to head back into town and notify the authorities about what we found here. We will let them figure it out." [13]

7/4/47 On the Runway of Condron Field, N.M.

At about this same time, a transport plane lands at Condron Field and the members of Alpha Team disembark. They are met by the commander of 4th Army's Counter Intelligence Corps. The CIC officer tells the team leaders, including Colonel Harbrough and Captain Evens, "A Parachute recovery team from Holloman Air Field has been dispatched to Site LZ-1. [14] They radioed that they found what appears to be an escape module with five dead bodies and an aircraft that crashed nearby along with the pilot's body. But, they reported that the body had been dissected, as you would a frog. [15] Site LZ-2, where a UFO is suspected to have gone down, has been determined to be approximately twenty miles Southeast of Socorro, New Mexico. [16] Transportation has been arranged and is standing by along with a detachment of military police from Alamogordo Field."

The Colonel says, "Good. Then, we will get started right away. We will head to LZ-1 first, recover the bodies there, and then secure LZ-2." He orders the team leaders to have their people gather their gear and mount the vehicles for immediate departure. Everyone hurriedly begins preparations for their departure.

Captain Evens runs over to the detachment of Military Police, finds their leader, and says, "I am Captain Evens. I'm taking command of this unit."

The unit's officer, a Lieutenant, salutes and says, "Yes sir. We have been instructed to provide you with every assistance. Can you tell us what this is all about, Sir?"

Evens returns the salute and says, "I will have to tell you on the way because we are moving out right now. Get your men on board their vehicles. Right now, Lieutenant!" When everyone is ready, Evens and his unit, take their place within the military convoy of trucks heading out.

7/4/47 At the Site LZ-1 Near Corona, New Mexico

A few hours later, Alpha Team arrives at the site. Colonel Harbrough is the first to arrive in a jeep with a driver. He sees a severely damaged cylindrical-shaped module, the motionless bodies on the ground, and the paratroopers. When his jeep stops, a Lieutenant salutes and says, "Lieutenant Baxter of the 432nd parachute recovery team."

The Colonel returns his salute, gets out of the jeep, and says, "At ease, Lieutenant. What is the situation here?"

"Sir, the cylindrical unit over there appears to be some sort of escape module, which burst open upon impact with the Earth. We found two bodies inside and three others scattered a short distance away. They do not appear to be human. We also found a crashed aircraft and another body about fifty yards from here, which appears to have been surgically dissected." [17]

The Colonel thinks for a moment, thanks the lieutenant and tells him that he is relieved.

The team leaders gather around the Colonel. He tells them, "This vehicle is now the command post. Doctor, I want your medical team to look after the bodies. Stabilize them, if possible, and have them transported to the appropriate military facilities as soon as possible. Major, have your radio-biological team begin taking radiological measurements right away. Captain, have your men set up a defensive perimeter around this site and search the area for other bodies. As soon as the module is ready for transport, I want it hoisted onto a truck. Let's go, people."

The medical team members don their protective suits and examine the three alien bodies lying outside of the escape module. They appear to be human with certain anatomical differences in the head, eyes, hands, and feet. They have a slight build at about four feet tall with a grayish-pink skin color. They have no hair on their bodies and are clothed in tight fitting flight suits that appear to be fire proof. Some of the bodies appear to be burned on their head and hands. Their overall stature appears like young children. There appears to be both male and female genders, but this was difficult to distinguish since they all looked identical to one another. [18]

The doctor tells his team members, "These three appear to have suffered from sudden decompression and heat suffocation. I am calling the time of death as 1342 hours. Get these bodies into the lead lined body-bags right away. I want them taken, by ambulances, to the hospital at Roswell Army Air Field."

A medical technician says, "Yes, Sir" and then supervises the operation. He notices that one of the bodies appears to be secreting some sort of body fluids. He instructs two of the team members to clean up the fluids and place them in plastic bags.

Others of the medical team climb up onto the module and look inside through an open hatch. One of them shouts, "Doctor! There are two more bodies inside."

The doctor shouts back, "Very well. I am coming to investigate." The doctor enters the module through the hatch and finds one body sitting in a chair and the other one sprawled out on the floor. They are both dead. The Doctor orders his team to take the bodies outside, place them in body-bags, and take them, via ambulance, to the Los Alamos Medical Facility. [19]

As a medical technician carries a body out of the module, another team member helps him. But, before they are able to reach the ambulance, the technician is overcome and collapses. The Doctor rushes over to examine him and asks the other man what happened.

The man says, "I don't know, Sir. He was complaining of feeling sick and, to tell you the truth, I'm not feeling very well myself."

The Doctor orders his medical team to immediately transport both men to Los Alamos under strict quarantine measures. He also orders the fifth body to be taken to Randolph Field. Just then, the two medical personnel, who had been handling the body fluids from one of the dead bodies, also collapse and are rushed to Los Alamos for treatment. [20]

A soldier, standing guard next to the module, sees the sickly men being taken away in ambulances and he starts to panic. He says, "Oh God! It's an alien sickness. Oh no. I don't want to die."

Evens hears this and tries to calm the soldier by saying, "Don't worry. It's not contagious. You are okay, aren't you? Get a grip of yourself, soldier!"

But, the sentry becomes even more hysterical, saying, "You're wrong, Sir. I saw the medical team members get sick after taking the alien bodies away. They caught something from those creatures and now it's spreading. Did you see what those beings looked like? They're horrible and they're dead. They're all dead! Oh God, I don't want to die."

Evens grabs the soldier's rifle away from him, and says, "You are relieved of duty, soldier." Evens then calls for the medical team to take care of him and heads for the command post. [21]

Evens listens as the Doctor tells the Colonel, "We found a total of five dead bodies. I don't know where they came from. But, they are definitely not human. They have been taken to the medical facilities at Roswell, Randolph, and Los Alamos. However, four of my men have become ill and have been taken to Los Alamos for treatment. They appear to be suffering from some form of toxin or highly contagious disease. I believe that they were contaminated with the fluids from the dead alien bodies while they were being transported."

The Colonel asks, "These men were wearing their protective suits at the time, weren't they?"

"Yes Sir, they were. I believe that the suits are ineffective against whatever these men came in contact with."

The Colonel then asks, "Is there a danger of this thing spreading and contaminating anyone else?"

"I do not believe so. It appears to be a blood born disease and not airborne. We have contained all bodily fluids, and I have given special precautionary instructions for the treatment of the infected members of my team."

"Very well, Doctor. Thank you for your report."

The Colonel turns to Evens and asks, "What is your report, Captain?"

Evens says, "Sir, the perimeter is secure. But, something just happened that troubles me. One of the soldiers, which I had standing outside to guard the module, saw the medical personnel being taken away and became hysterical, thinking that an alien disease was spreading. He suffered a nervous breakdown and I had to relieve him from duty so that he could be treated. I am concerned that this situation could affect others of the security detail in the same way. They are performing under tremendous pressure to deal with situations which they are not prepared to handle."

The Colonel says, "Yes. I think you're right. But, we are just going to have to deal with this the best that we can. Be on the lookout for other instances like this. None of us were prepared to deal with what we've seen here today. Do you have anything else to report?"

"Yes sir. I would like the doctor and his team to examine the dead body near the crashed aircraft that we discovered to the South of here. There is something very strange about it."

The Colonel says, "Yes. Request approved. Doctor, I want a full report when you have finished."

The Colonel turns to Evens and says "Captain, it will be getting dark in another couple of hours. After you have shown the doctor where the body is laying, I want you to have your men eat some C-rations and be ready to stand watch tonight in shifts. I am going to supervise the hoisting of the module onto the lowboy truck. Once we have checked the area for any debris in the morning, I want you to insure that the module and any debris that we find has plenty of protection as it is transported across White Sands Proving Grounds to the storage facilities at the Naval Research Laboratory tomorrow. We will then head out for the other crash site by ten hundred hours. That is all." The men salute, acknowledge their orders and run off to insure that they are carried out.

After the doctor assembles his team, Evens leads them to where the pilot's body is laying. The doctor asks, "Is this how you found him?"

Evens nods his head and says, "Yep. It looks like the aircraft and body were just lowered to the ground."

The doctor notices that a portion of the pilot's jaw is missing along with some teeth and his tongue. There are no eyes in their sockets, the man is missing his genitals and his rectum has been cored out with surgical precision. But, most troubling of all is the fact that there is no blood in the body or anywhere on the ground. The doctor instructs his team to place the body in a black body bag, which they do and then they carry it away.

7/4/47 At the Home of Brazel's Nearest Neighbor

Later that same evening, Mr. Brazel collects some of the material that he found on his ranch and puts it in the back of his truck. He then drives over to the home of his neighbor, Floyd Proctor, in order to get a second opinion about what the materials might be.

Floyd comes over to greet Mr. Brazel, as he gets out of his truck, and says, "Howdy, Mac. What brings you out here this evening?"

"Hi Floyd. I woke up this morning to find a bunch of strange stuff scattered on my property. I brought some of it over in order to see if you might be able to help me figure out what it is."

Floyd says, "Well, I'll try." [22]

Mr. Brazel shows him what he has in the back of his truck. Floyd looks at some of the pieces and says, "Wow. You're right, Mac. This is really strange stuff. I have never seen anything like this before."

Mac hands him something that looks like a small beam of half an inch square and says, "Check out what's written on the side of this piece."

Floyd looks at it and says, "What is that? Some sort of hieroglyphics or something? I can't read that. It looks like it's made out of balsa wood. It seems very light, but it's very hard and flexible, as well."

They try to break it and it will not break. They then try to burn it and it will not burn. [23]

Next, Mac shows him a brown, parchment-like substance and says, "Here is another piece that has little numbers with symbols that look like they have been painted on in pink and purple colors. They are not all the same symbols, but they do have the same general pattern."

Floyd says, "What kind of writing is that? I can't read this stuff. But, it sure looks like it means something to somebody."

Mr. Brazel also shows Floyd several small pieces of a tinfoil-like material that is very light and thin. He then grabs a piece, which is about two feet long and one foot wide, and says, "let's just see how strong this stuff really is." He leans the piece against a wall and hits it, as hard as he can, with a sixteen-pound sledgehammer. There is no mark or dent of any kind on it anywhere.

They try everything they can do to bend it, tear it, and cut it without any success at all. They can flex it back and forth and even wrinkle it. But, they cannot put a crease in it that will stay. Finally, Floyd says, "I'm sorry, Mac. I'd like to help you. But, I got no idea what that stuff could be."

Brazel thanks his neighbor, gathers up all of the stuff, and heads back to his ranch, even more puzzled than before.

Recovery

7/5/47 At Site LZ-1 Near Corona, New Mexico

Some time before daybreak, Captain Evens wakes up to find himself lying in a very uncomfortable position on the front seat of a three-quarter ton truck. He sits up and tries to work out all of his sore muscles. Then, he switches on the cab light and looks at himself in the rear view mirror. *What a mess,* he says to himself. He splashes some water, from a canteen, on his face, wipes it off with his shirt sleeve, and runs a comb through his hair. He puts his coat on and notices that his new Class-A dress uniform is wrinkled and filthy dirty. *Not a very good example for a unit commander to make,* he realizes. But, it's the best that he can do, under the circumstances.

He gets out of the truck and goes to inspect his troops on the perimeter. He arranged the men into three-man groups, located every one hundred yards, in a circle around the craft. Each man was responsible for a three hour shift of guard duty so that they would all get six hours of sleep. It was easy to see who the smokers were from the glow of the cigarettes.

As he came upon each position, he noticed that the sentry would either come to attention and salute or challenge him by saying, "Halt! Who goes there." Then, he would have to identify himself and give the password. He was very impressed and didn't mind having to do this at all.

Then, Evens came up to a post where the sentry did not acknowledge him at all. *If this guy is sleeping, I'm going to make him wish that he were dead,* Evens thought. But, he saw that the soldier was trembling and deep in thought.

When he finally does see Evens, he says, "Oh, hello Captain, Sir."

It was a warm summer evening, so Evens asks him, "Are you cold?"

"No Sir, just scared."

Evens smiles and asks, "What are you frightened about, Soldier? Do you think a coyote is going to come and get you?"

"No, Sir. But, what if more of these creatures come by and want their friends and property back? What are we supposed to do then, Sir?"

Evens stops smiling. He hadn't thought about that possibility. But, he didn't want the soldier to know that he did not know the answer. So, he says, "I don't think there is much chance of that happening. Take it easy, Private. I'm more worried about word of this getting out and having the whole town of Socorro coming here to look around. Then, we would have real problems on our hands."

It was starting to get light out now. Evens finds the Lieutenant and tells him to wake the men, let them eat some C-rations, and have them be on the lookout for any inquisitive civilians. He also orders some patrols to be sent out into the surrounding area. And finally, he tells the Lieutenant to have the shivering Private relieved of duty so that he can receive treatment.

After the men had eaten and made themselves ready, Evens orders one man at each post to remain on guard duty and the rest of them to search the entire area for any debris that they may find from the crash. At the same time, a crane is used to hoist the module onto a lowboy trailer under the Colonel's close supervision. It is then covered with a tarp and fastened securely to the trailer. Evens then organizes a small convoy of military vehicles to transport the module and all debris from the area. Finally, the rest of Alpha Team depart for Site LZ-2.

7/5/47 On Highway 54 in Corona, New Mexico

Deputy Maynard Tolby of the Lincoln County Sheriff's department is at his regular spot, looking for speeders on their way to work, when he hears his radio speaker squawk and then, "Patrol 3, this is Dispatch".

The deputy reaches for his microphone and says, "This is Patrol 3. Go ahead, Mabel."

"Patrol 3, an archeology team discovered something that crashed South of Oscura Peak. The Sheriff wants you to check it out."

"Okay Dispatch, I'm on my way." The deputy thinks for a moment, switches frequencies on his radio, and says into his microphone, "State police 7, this is Lincoln County Patrol 3, over?"

State Police Officer Will Johnson responds with, "County Patrol 3, this is State police 7, over?"

"Will, I just got a call to check out something that crashed South of Oscura Peak. Could you give me a hand with this?"

"Sure thing, Maynard. I'm on my way."

The deputy says "Thanks, Will. I'll see you there" and heads out of town with his lights flashing and his siren wailing.

7/5/47 Near Oscura Peak, New Mexico

Approximately 45 minutes later, the deputy and State police officer park about 50 yards from something that had crashed and get out of their vehicles. The deputy asks, "What is that?"

The officer says, "Maybe it's a craft being developed by the Army, but it sure don't look like anything I've seen before. Let's go check for survivors."

The men rush over to the craft and look inside where it had split open on impact. They yell, "Hello! Is there anybody in there?" But, they don't see anyone or hear anything.

They look around and the Officer says, "Hey, look at these tracks. They appear to be heading out in that direction."

The Deputy looks closely and says, "Yeah, they look like a child's footprints, but they don't look like any footprints that I have ever seen before."

Both men's eyes become wide open as they realize what this could mean. They draw their pistols and follow the tracks around a large rock where they find a living alien being standing with its hands in front of it. The men are amazed to see a short slender humanoid body of about four feet high. Its body had a head, two arms, and two legs, but the skin was very different. The head was larger than normal and very distinctive with a neck that was long and slender. The eyes were large, the mouth and ears were small, and it had a turned up nose. The men holstered their weapons and escorted the being to the Deputy's car where it sat inside. The Officer offered the entity a drink from his canteen, which it accepted. But, it refused any food.

The deputy reached for his microphone and said, "Dispatch, this is Patrol 3."

"This is Dispatch. What is your situation, Patrol 3?"

"I am at the crash site of a flying saucer."

"Yeah right. Tell me another one."

The Deputy's face turns red as he yells in the microphone, "Damn it, this is no joke! I'm serious and I have an alien being from another world sitting in the back seat of my car. Now, what am I supposed to do with him?"

"Wait one." About two minutes later, the deputy hears, "Patrol 3, this is Dispatch. You are instructed to transport the being to the Los Alamos National Laboratories. They will be contacted and waiting for your arrival, over?"

The Deputy says, "Roger Dispatch. I will comply." The Officer provides an escort as they drive to Los Alamos.[1]

7/5/47 At Site LZ-2 near Oscura Peak, N.M.

About an hour later, Alpha Team arrives at the site. Colonel Harbrough is the first to see the disc-shaped craft and several civilians looking at everything. These are the students of the archeology team, along with their friends and relatives, here to look at everything. Even the Fire Brigade from the town of Roswell is here.

The Colonel immediately takes control and yells at the civilians, "Attention! The Army is taking over this site. All civilians must move away from the craft, at once!"

The team leaders gather around the Colonel. He tells them, "This is now the command post. Doctor, I want your medical team to look for any survivors. Captain, get a defensive perimeter set up and advise the civilians. Major, have your radio-biological team begin taking radiological measurements right away. The scientist and engineer are permitted to examine the craft as long as they stay out of everyone's way. Time is critical here, people. Let's get moving." [2]

Evens tells his men to set up a defensive perimeter and he has a squad of men to round up all of the civilians in the area and detain them behind his vehicle. Once the civilians have been rounded up, Evens tells them, "May I have your attention, please? The Army is in control here. This is a matter of national security. It is vitally important that each of you agree to remain silent about what you have seen here today. Failure to do so, will result in very stiff penalties. Is there anyone here who refuses to comply?" Seeing that they all shake their heads, no, he then says, "Good. We will now take down your names and addresses and allow you to leave the area, which you will do at once."

The medical team members don their protective suits and search for bodies without success.

The aeronautical engineer assesses the craft as not belonging to any aircraft, rocket, weapons, or balloon test that are normally conducted from the surrounding bases. The circular, disc-shaped "planform" does not resemble any design currently under development. There is a lack of any external propulsion system, power plant, intake, or exhaust for either propeller or jet propulsion. He notices the lack of any wiring, fuel systems, cables, motors, hydraulics, intakes, exhaust, or surface controls which strongly suggests that the craft was designed to travel outside of our atmosphere. [3] [4]

The engineer looks inside the craft and finds that there is a flight deck located inside the copula section. It is round and domed at the top. There is an absence of a canopy, observation windows, or any optical projection. However, there is a semicircular photo-tube array similar to television. The crew compartments seem to be hermetically sealed with no weld marks, rivets, or soldered joints. The craft components appear to be molded and pressed into a perfect fit. [5]

Evens is standing just outside of the craft and peers inside. He sees that the engineer is as giddy as a kid in a candy store. He watches as the engineer notices a hatch on the floor. He then sees the engineer opening the hatch, looking inside of it, and immediately vomiting on the floor of the craft. Evens rushes inside and asks the engineer, "What's wrong? Are you sick?"

The engineer leans back against a wall, wipes his mouth with his sleeve, and says, "No. But, I think you had better have a look inside that hatch".

Evens asks, "Are there more bodies? Is there radiation? What's in there?"

The engineer becomes annoyed at Evens and says, "Just look in the damned hatch, will you?"

Evens reluctantly moves over to the hatch and looks inside. There is a small chamber below the hatch that is filled with an amber colored fluid. Evens notices something bobbing around in this fluid and looks closer at it. *What is that?*, he asks himself. His eyes become wide opened as he recognizes the jaw, tongue, genitalia, anus, and eyeballs of the pilot. He also feels like throwing up, but overcomes the urge. Evens closes the hatch and helps the engineer to get outside for treatment by the medical team. [6]

Evens reports what has happened to the Colonel, who says "Well, I guess we now know what happened to the body parts that were taken from the pilot at the other crash site." Just then they see the radio-biological team leader run up to them and say, "Colonel, my team has detected high neutron levels in this entire area, with the highest levels found inside the craft. Although there is no immediate danger, long term exposure will begin to become harmful to the men here." [7]

The Colonel grabs the microphone of a secure radio unit and says, "Golf two, this is Delta three, over?"

They hear, "Delta three, this is Golf two. What is your status, over?"

Harbrough says, "Golf two, we have high radiation levels detected here. It is imperative that this operation be concluded as quickly as possible. Request heavy equipment and reinforcements so that everything can be transported as soon as possible, over?"

Static is heard from the speaker and then, "This is Golf two. Your request is approved. There will be a convoy arriving at your location by 0900 hours tomorrow. The craft is to be transported to Alamogordo Field, all biological materials are to be taken to the Army Medical Center at Wright Field, and any debris is to be transported across the White Sands Proving Grounds to the storage facilities of the Naval Research Laboratory. Those sites have already been alerted and will be ready when everything arrives."

The Colonel presses the microphone switch and says, "Golf two, this is Delta three. Roger, willco', out." He then turns to Evens and says, "It looks like we're spending the night here. Make sure that your men are able to maintain security until we leave and be ready for that convoy when it arrives."

Evens acknowledges his orders and runs off to insure that they are carried out.

The Colonel then tells Sergeant Murphy to assemble the team leaders for a briefing.

7/5/47 At the Home of Hollis Wilson in Corona, N.M.

Later that evening, Mr. Brazel drives into the town of Corona to visit with his uncle, Hollis Wilson. A mutual acquaintance from the town of Alamogordo is also there. After about an hour of pleasantries, the local politics, and the latest gossip, Mr. Brazel finally says, "Hollis, I found a bunch of strange stuff on my ranch yesterday."

"Strange stuff? What are you talking about, Mac?"

Mr. Brazel takes a deep breath, lets it out, and says, "This is going to sound really crazy. But, I swear Hollis, I'm not making this up. There is stuff there that I don't think anyone has every seen before. I took some of it over to my neighbor's place to see what he thought about it. But, he couldn't figure it out either. I mean, some of this stuff ain't no thicker than the tin-foil in a pack of cigarettes, it weighs nothing', and yet it can't be cut, bent, or burned. You can bend it back and forth. But, you can't put a dent in it that will stay. I took a sixteen-pound sledgehammer to one piece and couldn't even put a mark on it."

Hollis laughs, "Aw, you're putting me on, Mac. What have you been drinking?"

"I'm not making this stuff up. Really. I wish I were. There are other pieces, too, which have some sort of strange writing on them, like hieroglyphics, that cannot be read. It's just a bunch of numbers and symbols that look like they mean something to somebody."

Slowly, the grin on Hollis' face turns into a look of amazement as he realizes that Mac is serious. The place becomes deathly quiet.

Finally, the other man says, "Maybe it's from a flying saucer."

Hollis says, "Yeah, that's what I was thinking."

Mac asks, "What are you guys talking about?"

"Well lately, there have been a whole bunch of people around here saying that they have seen flying saucers in the skies."

Mac's eyes become wide open. He says, "What? This is the first that I have heard about that."

Hollis says, "Actually, I thought it was all a bunch of wacky people just wanting a little attention. But now, I'm beginning to think that there might be something to it all. Mac, that stuff on your ranch could be from one of the things that people have been seeing flying around in the area. You should tell somebody about this."

"Who am I going to tell?"

"How about the sheriff?"

Mac thinks about it a while and says, "Well, I got some things to do in Roswell tomorrow anyway. Maybe I'll stop in and talk to the sheriff about it."

7/6/47 The Plains of San Augustin, New Mexico

It is early in the morning when the military convoy arrives at the outer perimeter of the crash site.

Evens walks up to the lead truck, sees a Major in the front seat, and salutes him. Then, he says, "Good morning, Major. May I see your ID and orders?"

The Major hands them over and Evens checks everything carefully.

Satisfied, he hands them back, saying, "Welcome to the middle of nowhere, Major. We were expecting you to be bringing a lot of heavy equipment with you." The Major says, "Thanks, Captain. We had to leave them back on the dirt road, three miles from here. They couldn't make it over the desert. So, the Engineers are making their own roadway here. I have a detachment of Military Police with us, from Kirtland Field. So, I left a squad of them there to watch over the engineers until they get here. Who is in charge here?"

Evens tells him about Colonel Harbrough and shows him where the command post is located.

Evens takes charge of the reinforcements. He orders some of them to cordon off all access roads heading west near the crash site from Highway 285. He orders the others to collect all debris in a sweep of the surrounding area. As the debris is gathered, Evens takes inventory of every piece and has them put it into crates which are sealed and loaded onto trucks. He also has several armed Military Policemen guarding each truck and the crating process.

The Colonel is surprised to see civilians walking up to him with papers that identify them as scientists from the General Advisory Committee of the Atomic Energy Commission. Most notable of which is Dr. Robert Oppenheimer, along with Project Paperclip specialists Wernher von Braun from Fort Bliss, Dr. Ernst Steinhoff from the Army Medical Corps, and Dr. Hubertus Strughold from Aeromedical Labs at Randolph Field. They have orders to examine the craft and make recommendations. The Colonel gladly escorts them to the craft. [8]

At the craft, Dr. Oppenheimer meets Dr. von Karman, the scientist assigned to Alpha Team. Together, they go inside of the craft and examine the interior. They enter a compartment that appears to be the power room. A possible atomic engine is discovered there. It looks like a donut shaped tube, made of what appears to be a plastic material, surrounding a central core.

They notice that the tube is translucent and approximately one inch thick. It appears to be filled with a clear substance. A large rod, inside the tube, is wrapped in a coil of what appears to be a copper material. An electrical potential is believed to be the primary power of the reactor.

Underneath the power plant, a ball-turret is discovered, approximately ten feet in diameter. They believe that this turret is the main propulsion system, which functions like a bladeless turbine. On the deck of the power room, there is what resembles typewriter keys which possibly control the reactor power plant. There are no conventional electronics or wiring seen connecting the controls to the propulsion turret. [9]

Back at the command post, the scientists tell Colonel Harbrough their recommendations. They state that the power and propulsion systems have been damaged. It is suggested that, due to the radiation, the entire craft should be wrapped with lead lined blankets, which they brought with them. This would enable the craft to be shielded against radiation leakage and permit it to be transported with minimal danger to the civilian population in the area.

The Colonel concurs and orders the engineers, who have just arrived, to proceed as the scientists recommended.

The engineers have just completed leveling a dirt roadway so that their heavy equipment could be brought in place. First, a large crane is positioned near the craft and secured in place. Then, a tractor, pulling a long flatbed trailer, parks alongside the craft. The shielding material is unfolded onto the trailer.

Under the supervision of the scientists, the craft is attached to the crane and then hoisted into the air. Several men keep the craft steady by holding onto ropes attached to the craft. The crane moves the craft over the trailer and gently lowers it onto the shielding material. Then, the craft is covered with the shielding material and fastened securely to the trailer. Finally, wooden planks, plywood, and a large tarp are placed over the craft in order to disguise the overall shape.

7/6/47 Chaves County Sheriff's Office, Roswell, N.M.

Mr. Brazel drives into the town of Roswell to buy a new truck. While there, he stops by the Sheriff's office with a box full of some of the debris from his ranch. He shows Sheriff George Wilcox the strange metallic pieces and says, "Sheriff, I was at my sheep ranch, some forty miles from here, when I heard an explosion two nights ago and discovered a lot of this stuff scattered on my property the next morning."

The Sheriff looks at a few of the pieces and asks, "What kind of stuff is this?"

Mac takes a deep breath, lets it out, and says, "I have no idea. I was hoping that you could tell me. But, it looks like it might have come off an airplane or something."

The sheriff thinks about this and says, "This sounds like something that the Army would be interested in knowing about. Have a seat while I call the Roswell Army Base." Mr. Brazel does as he is told while the Sheriff calls the base.

Major Jesse A. Marcel, the ranking officer in charge of intelligence at Roswell Field, was notified of the Sheriff's call while eating lunch at the officer's club. He decides to meet with Brazel and hear what he has to say.

At the Sheriff's office, he is introduced to Mr. Brazel and says, "Hi. I'm Major Marcel. I'm told that you found some metal-like debris on your property. Can you tell me about it?"

Mr. Brazel shows the Major his box of debris and tells him about the explosion that he heard, the debris that he found, and about the strange qualities of the material that he discovered. He says that he thinks it may be from something that crashed out there.

The Major decides that this is a matter that had better be brought to the attention of Colonel William Blanchard, the commanding officer of Roswell AAF. He asks Brazel, "Would you accompany me back to the base and tell my commander what you've told me."

Brazel says, "I still have some things to do. But, I could meet with you here in about an hour or so."

The Major agrees to meet with him then and leaves for the Base. [10] [11]

7/6/47 At Base Commander's Office of Roswell A.A.F.

After requesting to speak with the Base Commander, Major Marcel is permitted to enter his office. The Major stands at attention before the commander's desk and says, "Major Marcel requesting permission to speak with the Colonel about an urgent matter, Sir".

Colonel William H. Blanchard says, "At ease, Major. Have a seat and tell me what the matter is. I'm very busy."

The Major sits down, swallows hard, and says, "Sir, I've just been speaking with a local rancher who says that he heard an explosion and discovered a lot of unusual material scattered on his property two days ago."

"And he's just telling us about it now? What kind of material did he find?"

Marcel swallows again and says, "Well, Sir. He showed me things that were out of this world, such as some very hard, light weight members with strange symbols on them which could not be read. He described other pieces that were very thin, like tinfoil, which could not be bent, cut, or burned."

The Colonel's eyes are wide open as he says, "Yes. You're right. That does sound awfully strange. Did this rancher say that these materials were from a craft of some kind?"

"It was his opinion, Sir, that they were from something that had crashed out there. I am due to meet with him again in half an hour."

The Colonel thinks to himself, *this could be one of the flying saucers that people have been talking about. It could be the biggest story of the century!* "Major, I want you to take whatever you need and investigate this matter throughly. Retrieve all of the materials that you can find and then report back here to me. Is that clear?"

Major Marcel stands and says, "Yes, Sir. I will obtain the assistance from someone in the Counter-Intelligence Corps and leave right away."

"Very good, Major. Dismissed." Once the Major has left the office, the Colonel then reaches for the telephone to call the office of General Spaats, who is the Army Air Force Chief of Staff. [12] [13]

7/6/47 At the Debris Field on Brazel's Ranch

It was quite late in the afternoon before Mr., Brazel returned to his ranch, followed by Major Marcel, in his '42 Buick, and the senior counter-intelligence officer by the name of Captain Sheridan Cavitt, driving a Jeep Carry-all. Mr. Brazel invited the men to come into his small ranch house. After lighting a kerosene lamp, he offered the men some cold pork and beans with crackers to eat for supper. [14]

7/6/47 At the Command Post of Site LZ-2

Later that evening, Evens conducts a briefing with the troops that are assigned to the convoy transporting the craft to Alamogordo Field. He tells them, "Although we will be traveling at night and on roads that are rarely traveled, you must be constantly alert for civilians in the area and the possibility of an ambush. Stay sharp. Drivers, maintain a safe distance from the vehicle in front of you. But, keep it close. Don't fall back unless you are experiencing mechanical difficulties. The convoy will be followed by two wreckers to take care of any vehicles that break down."

Evens continues, "The security detail remains with the package at all times. If it stops, you stop and maintain security. Traffic control, keep moving and keep the roadways clear. Scouts, be especially watchful of accidents, pedestrians, and possible ambush sites. I will be in the lead truck. Now, you all know your assignments, the radio call signs, and procedures. This convoy must get through. It is a matter of the highest importance for national security. Everyone here is expendable. If the package is lost, you had better be dead. Are there any questions? Good. Then, let's get going. Move out!" [15] [16]

7/7/47 At a Hangar of Alamogordo Army Air Field

The convoy arrives shortly before dawn. Evens exits his vehicle and watches as the truck, carrying the craft, drives into a hanger. He supervises closure of the hanger doors and the proper security for the package. Just then, a three star General enters the hangar and walks over to him. Evens salutes and states, "Sir, Captain Evens reporting the secure delivery of the package." [17]

The General returns his salute, sees Evens' wrinkled and filthy dress uniform, and says, "Very good, Captain. I am General Twining, Chief of Air Materiel Command. Did you have any problems with the transport?" [18]

"Negative, Sir."

The General smiles and says, "Very fine. You've done well, Captain. You are to be commended for all that you have accomplished. Accommodations have been provided for you and your men. I now assume responsibility for the package. I will make sure that the men are taken care of, once they finish cleaning and stowing their equipment. You look as if you could use a shower and bed. There is a jeep and driver waiting outside to take you to your quarters."

"Thank-you, Sir. I stand relieved." They salute and Evens walks outside, feeling pleased with the way that everything has turned out. At his quarters, Evens takes a long, hot shower and goes right to bed.

7/7/47 In an Office at Alamogordo Army Air Field

Later, that same day, Lt. General Twining meets with General Spaats, who has just arrived from Washington, D.C. The Chief of Staff says, "All right, let's have it. Just what exactly is it that has been recovered from the desert?"

Twining shakes his head and says, "I don't have the slightest clue, General. It appears to be an aircraft that is unlike anything that I have ever seen before. It is badly damaged and appears to have been split open when it impacted with the Earth. We have no idea where it came from, who made it, or even what it's made out of. Now, whether it came from Russia, the Moon, or anywhere else, I just cannot say."

General Spaats presses his lips tightly together and then says, "Well, what can you tell me?"

"I know that this disk shaped craft is not anything that we have ever seen before. Because it has no control surfaces or external components for propeller, jet, or rocket propulsion, this strongly suggests that this craft was developed for flight in outer space."

The General's mouth is wide open. He then regains his composure and asks, "Were there any problems with bringing it here?"

Twining says, "Yes, several of them. Four members of the recovery team's medical staff became ill while retrieving the dead bodies from inside an escape module. They died a short time later from unknown causes. Several Military Policemen, assigned to provide security, have suffered nervous breakdowns. One man has even committed suicide. And, everyone involved with the recovery operation has been subjected to high levels of radiation."

General Spaats shakes his head and says, "My God." He then asks Twining, "What security measures are in place regarding what was found?"

"Everyone involved with the recovery operation had security clearances and 'need to know' access. The actual transportation of the craft here was uneventful." [19]

Twining states, "There were civilians at the landing site when the recovery team arrived. However, their identities were ascertained and they have all been sworn to secrecy."

"What about the Rancher who reported finding debris on his property?" Twining thinks about this for a moment and then says, "I don't know. An Intelligence officer, from Roswell Field has been ordered to investigate and recover all materials. But, he has not been heard from since he departed. I think we had better get someone over there to take charge of that situation and I think I know just the person to send."

Ten minutes later, Evens is standing at attention before the Generals, saying, "Captain Evens reporting as ordered, Sir."

"At ease, Captain." Twining smiles, walks up to Evens, and says, "I'd like to shake your hand." Evens is stunned as he puts his hand out. Twining shakes it vigorously and says, "You did real well with the recovery of the downed craft, Captain. I am aware of the effort that you put forth to insure security. You are to be commended. I'd like to introduce you to General Spaats, Chief of staff."

The General shakes Evens' hand and says, "How do you do?"

Evens says, "It's a pleasure to meet you, Sir."

Twining invites Evens to sit down. When everyone is seated, he tells Evens, "Captain, we have a situation that we'd like you to handle for us. It seems that a civilian rancher reported that he found a lot of strange materials scattered on his property two days ago. An Intelligence officer from Roswell Field was dispatched to investigate and recover the materials. But, he has not been heard from since he left. We think that these materials could be from the craft that you recovered. We'd like you to go to the Roswell Base and insure the safe delivery of all materials to Andrews Army Air Field."

Evens jumps to his feet and says, "I understand, Sir. You can count on me to do whatever is necessary."

"Very good, Captain. You are dismissed."

7/7/47 At the Debris Field on Brazel's Ranch

Shortly after daybreak, Mr. Brazel showed the men where the debris was scattered on his property. Marcel was acquainted with most everything that was in the air at the time and he realizes that what he sees there is not part of any sort of plane, missile, weather balloon, or tracking device. He doesn't know what it is. But, they collect all of the debris that they can handle. When the Carryall is filled, they begin to fill the trunk and back seat of Marcel's Buick.

Marcel looks for anything that might resemble instruments or electronic equipment, but doesn't find anything. However, Cavitt does find a black, metallic-looking box, that is several inches square. But, since there is no apparent way to open it, they throw it in with the rest of the stuff. When they had collected all that they could carry, they thanked Mr. Brazel for his cooperation and drove back towards the base. But, since it was starting to become dark, the Major decides to drive home and report to the base commander in the morning.

When he arrives at his house, he takes some of the debris into his home with him. He knows that his wife will never believe him unless he shows her some proof. After greeting his wife at the front door, he shows her the materials and explains what had happened. He is very excited to be showing his wife what he has found. He wakes up his son and shows him the strange materials on the kitchen table. His son plays with the pieces, which were like nothing that he had ever seen before. [20]

Crisis Management

7/8/47 At the Public Relations Office of Roswell A.A.F.

Lieutenant Walter Haut is the Public Information Officer for the Roswell base. At the moment, his eyes are wide open, his mind is reeling with ideas, and he is breathing hard. He rushes into his office, sits down at his desk, and starts scribbling something on a sheet of paper. A Sergeant, assigned to his Public Relations staff, enters the office and asks, "Hey Lieutenant, what's up? What did the base commander want to talk to you about?"

Haut stops what he is doing, looks up and, with a big grin on his face, he says, "I get to tell the world about the biggest story of the century. Colonel Blanchard has just ordered me to write a news release about a crashed flying saucer that the army has recovered." [1]

The sergeant lets out a long breath of air and says, "Well, I'll be a monkey's uncle! Were there any survivors?"

"I don't know. But, I've got to hurry and get this written so that I can deliver it into the hands of the local news agencies right away." He rolls a clean sheet of paper into his typewriter and starts typing. After six different rewrites, he finally settles on the following news release for the press:

Roswell Army Air Base, Roswell, N.M.

8th July, 1947, A.M.

The many rumors regarding a flying disc became a reality yesterday when the intelligence office of the 509th Bomb Group of the Eighth Air Force, Roswell Army Air Field, was fortunate enough to gain possession of a disc through the cooperation of a local rancher and the sheriff's office of Chaves County.

The flying object landed on a ranch near Roswell sometime last week. Not having phone facilities, the rancher stored the disc until such time as he was able to contact the sheriff's office, who in turn notified Major Jesse A. Marcel of the 509th Bomb Group Intelligence Office.

Action was immediately taken and the disc was picked up at the rancher's home. It was inspected at the Roswell Army Air Field and subsequently loaned by Major Marcel to higher headquarters. [2]

7/8/47 At the Base Commander's Office of Roswell A.A.F.

Major Marcel arrives back on base later that same day and goes directly to the Base Commander's office. After conferring with the Sergeant at the front desk, the Major enters Colonel Blanchard's office with a box of recovered materials under his arm. "Major Marcel reporting as ordered, Sir."

The Colonel looks at the box, frowns, and says, "Be seated, Major, and give me your report."

Marcel sets the box on the floor and sits in the chair in front of the Colonel's desk. He reports how he and Cavitt met with Brazel, spent the night at his ranch house, and found the debris that was scattered on his property the next morning. Then, Marcel shows the Colonel some of the materials from the box and describes the unusual qualities that they exhibit.

The Colonel asks, "You only found debris? Not a whole craft?" Marcel says, "We only found debris, Sir. There are two vehicles full of the stuff parked right outside."

The Colonel thinks about this for a minute and then tells his orderly to have Captain Evens report to his office immediately. He then looks at Marcel with a troubled look on his face and says, "It seems that we have a problem. Our public relations officer has taken it upon himself to notify the press about a flying saucer that crashed and was recovered by you."

"What?"

The Colonel glares at Marcel and says, "You heard me. The press will undoubtedly try to contact you for confirmation about the press release. I want you to say nothing to reporters about this incident. Nothing. Is that clear?"

"Yes Sir."

Captain Evens enters the office and is introduced to Major Marcel. The Colonel tells Marcel, "Captain Evens is in charge of securing all materials that have been recovered. You, and the other man with you, are to transport everything you have to whatever location that the Captain specifies. Is that clear?"

Marcel acknowledges his orders, and the two men are dismissed. The Major reaches for the box, and Evans asks, "Is that some of the recovered items?" When Marcel says that it is, the Captain replies, "I'll take that." Marcel reluctantly hands it over to him, and the men leave the office together.

7/8/47 In the Control Tower at Muroc A.A.F.

Later that evening, the Base Commander of Muroc Army Air Field (later to be known as Edwards Air Force Base in California) rushes into the top level of the control tower, shouting, "Alright Andrew, what the hell is going on?"

"Colonel, radar is tracking multiple unidentified targets flying at incredible speeds over the base in our restricted air space. We have just received four separate reports of flying, disc-shaped objects that have been sighted over the Rogers Dry Lake Site."

"Have there been any threatening or provocative actions taken by these objects?"

"Not as yet, Sir."

The Colonel frowns, thinks about this for a moment, and says, "Get me the Army Air Force Chief of Staff on a secure line right away."

When the call is put through, the Colonel says, "General Vandenberg, this is Colonel Winston here. We are tracking multiple unidentified flying objects over the base, in restricted air space. Do you have any recommendations as to how we should proceed?"

"Yes I do, Colonel. You are to use every available means at your disposal to bring them down."

"But sir, they have made no threatening moves yet."

"You mean none that you know of, don't you. Colonel, they are violating restricted airspace over our most sensitive military installations. Now, I want you to defend our country and attack immediately. Is that clear?"

"Yes, sir!"

The Colonel hangs up the telephone and tells the Major, "Sound the alarm! I want this base on full alert status right now. The unidentified targets are hostile. I repeat, hostile. Launch the ready response interceptors immediately. Give me that microphone. Vanguard One, this is Muroc One, over?"

"Muroc One, this is Vanguard One. Read you loud and clear, over."

"Vanguard One, we have multiple hostile targets over the base. You are to launch immediately and attack the bogeys. We will vector you to the targets. This is not a drill, over."

"Roger, willco', Muroc One, Vanguard group is launching."

"This is Muroc One, out."

The Colonel sits down and watches the four F-51 fighter aircraft take off down the main runway. He listens as his men direct the aircraft toward the targets on radar. He hears them say, "Vanguard One, Target One is stationary, at two-four miles, North, Northwest of your position. Turn left to three, three, six degrees."

"This is Vanguard One, turning… I have a visual on Target One. It appears to be hovering at approximately one thousand feet above the ground. It is circular in shape and glowing very brightly. Missile away! What the hell? Base, Target One just flew off to the West at an incredible speed. The missile did not even come close to it."

"Vanguard One, be advised that Target Two is heading in your direction from the Southeast, collision course."

"This is Vanguard One, I have a visual on the bogey. It is directly above me, matching my speed, and glowing brightly. I am climbing to engage… Base, I have lost visual contact. Can you vector me to the target?"

"Negative, Vanguard One, we just lost radar contact. There are no other targets in the area."

"Roger, Base." [5]

7/9/47 In the White House, Washington D.C.

Lieutenant General Hoyt Vandenberg enters the Oval Office of the White House and greets President Harry S. Truman, who says, "Have a seat, General, and tell me what you wanted to see me about." Lt. General Vandenberg, after distinguishing himself in World War II, became the Director of the Central Intelligence Group, which was the predecessor of the CIA. Then, in April of 1947, he was named as the Army Air Force Chief of Staff.

The two men sit on couches across from one another. The General says, "Sir, a number of unidentified flying objects, similar to the one that we recovered, were detected by radar and visually sighted over Muroc Army Air Field in California last night. Under my orders, the objects were attacked. However, the UFOs were able to elude a missile attack and even flew just above one of the fighters before it vanished from sight and radar detection. There were no casualties and no damage to the aircraft involved."

"My God!"

The General takes a newspaper from his briefcase, hands it to Truman, and says, "I think you may want to have a look at this, Mr. President."

The President reads the headlines of a Roswell, NM newspaper, which state, "RAAF Captures Flying Saucer On Ranch in Roswell Region". President Truman looks up from the newspaper, obviously upset, and asks, "How could this have happened, General? I thought you said that this would be kept quiet."

The General clears his throat and says, "It appears that the alien craft initially impacted at a different location than where it was recovered. Debris, from this initial location, was recovered by personnel from the Roswell Base. They knew nothing about the other craft. It would appear that someone there took it upon themselves to tell the press."

"Damn it, General! This story could start a national panic. Just what do you intend to do about it?"

While keeping his back ramrod straight, Vandenberg squirms in his seat and says, "Well, Mr. President, with your approval, we will release a cover story that will discredit this story."

Truman asks, "What kind of cover story?"

"Well sir, we can say that what was recovered was a crashed airplane, rocket, or weather balloon."

"Very well, see to it, General. We have to nip this thing in the bud before it gets out of hand."

"Yes, Mr. President."

Then, General Vandenberg says, "Sir, there is another matter which I think you should be aware of. We are using a number of civilian scientists and engineers to examine the recovered craft, power plant, and other materials. These people all hold security clearances and have been authorized for "need to know". However, many of them have expressed a desire to have the recovered items made available for examination by some of the world's leading scientists. This, of course, would preempt the strict security measures which are currently in effect."

President Truman ponders this for a moment and says, "Obviously, that is not acceptable. We need to send someone down there to assess what we have and to meet with these people in order to determine their character, motives and reactions in the event that assistance is not permitted. Do you have any suggestions on who we could send, General?"

Vandenberg thinks for a moment and says, "Lt. General Nathan Twining is the chief of Air Materiel Command and is currently with the recovered craft at Alamogordo Field. He is fully briefed and quite capable of accomplishing this task."

"Very well", says the president, "I will have a Directive drafted and dispatched to him right away. Which facilities are involved?"

"The White Sands Proving Ground Command Center, the Sandia Atomic Energy Commission facility, and possibly Kirkland Army Air Field. General Eisenhower will have to be consulted about that, Sir." The President asks if there is anything else. When Vandenberg indicates that he has nothing further, President Truman says, "Alright General, you may go now. I have things to do here and so do you." [6]

7/9/47 At the Base Commander's Office of Roswell A.A.F.

Colonel Blanchard answers his telephone. Brigadier General Roger Ramey, commander of the Eighth Air Force District at Fort Worth, is calling. He shouts through the telephone, "What, in God's name, is wrong with you, Blanchard? How could you be so stupid as to allow the press to get a story like the one I've just read in the newspaper? Don't you think that

I should have been consulted about this first? You know, I'm not the only one who is upset about this. I've just received a tongue lashing from General Vandenberg and now it's your turn. What do you have to say for yourself?"

The Colonel clears his throat and says, "Well General, I briefed my Public Relations Officer about the information that I had, at the time, in order for him to be prepared for the possibility of public exposure on this matter. However, he took it upon himself to distribute releases about the incident to the press. I was not aware of what he was doing until I received a telephone call from a reporter asking for confirmation on the story."

"And, what did you tell him?"

"I said that I had no comment and I instructed everyone involved in this matter to also say the same thing, if asked."

The General says, at a lower volume, "That's the first smart thing that you've done so far. As of right now, there is a complete news blackout from the Roswell Base. I want all of the recovered wreckage to be loaded immediately aboard a B-29, under armed guard, and flown to my headquarters here at Carswell Field, in Fort Worth, Texas. I also want Major Marcel to accompany this material to my headquarters. And finally, I want you, Colonel, to go on an immediate leave of absence and leave Lt. Colonel Payne Jennings in command of the Roswell Base. Is that clear?"

The Colonel takes a deep breath and says, "Very well, Sir." [7]

7/9/47 In General Ramey's Office at Carswell A.A.F.

"Major Marcel reporting as ordered, Sir." General Ramey says, "You have caused us quite a problem, Major. There are several reporters and photographers waiting in the next room for a press conference. I am going to tell them that what you found was a weather balloon and you are going to confirm this story. You are going to tell them that you were mistaken in your initial identification of what you recovered. Is that understood?"

That son of a bitch, the Major thinks to himself, *He wants me to tell the world that I screwed up and that I was mistaken.* "Yes, Sir."

The General tells his adjutant, "Bring in the materials." The adjutant ushers Captain Evens into the room, with a box in his arms. He is ordered to place the box on a table. General Ramey examines the contents of the box and selects a few nondescript pieces. He has them placed on some brown paper that is spread out on the floor. Members of the press are allowed into the room to take pictures of the material. But, the newsmen are able to see very little of the recovered materials and none of the important things that have markings on them. The photographers are then ushered back out of the room.

The General walks up to Evens, sticks out his hand, and says, "You must be Captain Evens."

"Yes, Sir."

They shake hands and Ramey says, "I've heard a lot about you, Captain. And, all of it was good. You can take these materials back to the plane and continue your transport of them to Wright-Patterson Field."

Evens replies, "Yes, Sir". He gathers up all of the materials and leaves the room with them.

The adjutant has two soldiers bring in a deteriorated weather balloon and place it on the brown paper. They leave and a Warrant Officer enters the room. The Warrant Officer is briefed on what is expected of him. He starts to protest until he sees the stern look on the General's face. The General then permits the waiting members of the press to enter the room. He waits for the flashing lights and the noise to die down.

General Ramey clears his throat and says to the crowd, "Gentlemen of the press, may I have your attention, please? I am Brigadier General Roger Maxwell Ramey. I am the Commander of the Army's 8th Air Force District. I have an announcement concerning the press release regarding the reported capture, by the Army, of a crashed flying saucer. Upon further investigation, it has been discovered that what was actually recovered was simply a weather balloon."

Pointing toward Major Marcel, the General says, "This is Major Jesse Marcel, the man who made the initial discovery. Major, would you please inspect what we have lying on the floor here and tell us if this is what you found?"

The Major makes a big show of inspecting every piece of the weather balloon and declares, "Yes Sir, this is what I found yesterday on a sheep ranch, 30 miles Northwest of Corona, New Mexico."

"Thank-you, Major."

The General then points to the Warrant Officer and says, "This is Warrant Officer Irving Newton. He is in charge of the Base Weather Office and Flight Services here at the Carswell-Fort Worth Air Base. Warrant Officer Newton, would you please inspect what we have lying on the floor and attempt to identify what it is?"

Newton, who is very disgruntled about having to be called away from his duties in order to do this, walks over to the device, takes one look at it, and says, "Sir, this is a deteriorated Rawin sonde type of weather balloon."

"Are you sure?"

"I'm positive, Sir. I see at least one of these every day in the normal course of my duties."

"Very well. You are dismissed".

As Newton exits the room, the General says, "Well, there you have it, gentlemen. I'm afraid that the crashed flying saucer story has turned out to be nothing more than a weather balloon mistakenly identified."

Several reporters try to ask the General some questions until he says, "This concludes the press conference. No questions will be answered at this time. Thank you all for coming. Good-bye." The General hurriedly leaves the room, followed by his adjutant and Major Marcel, while the newsmen shout questions at them. [8]

7/10/47 In the Situation Room of the White House

President Truman is being briefed by the Chief of Staff of the Army Air Forces, Lt. General Hoyt Vandenberg. Also present for this meeting is Vice President Alben W. Barkley, Secretary of State George C. Marshall, and Secretary of Defense Admiral James V. Forrestal. They are all seated at a long table. There is a large map of the world along one wall which shows the deployment of all American forces. There are several Teletype machines in the rear of the room. A large projection screen, at the front of the room, shows a map of the South Western United States with markers in several places. General Vandenberg is standing behind a podium at the head of the table. Everyone in the room is in a somber mood.

The General states, "Between 25 June and 2 July, there were 15 sightings of unidentified flying objects. This map shows their locations. These sightings were confirmed by radar, in Arizona and New Mexico. As a result, a rapid deployment team was established to respond to any situation of direct contact with the UFOs. At 2332 hours, on 3 July, radar stations detected two UFOs while in preparation of a V-2 rocket launch near White Sands Proving Ground. There appeared to be a midair collision with a scout plane in the area and the response team was mobilized to investigate the incident."

The projection screen changes to a map of Southern New Mexico with the designations of LZ1, LZ2, and LZ3 marked on it. The General takes a drink from a glass of water and continues, "A damaged escape module and five dead alien bodies were discovered at the crash site labeled LZ1 along with the body of a pilot and the scout aircraft not far away. The pilot appeared to have been mutilated with several organs missing. The wreckage of a disc-shaped object was discovered at the crash site designated LZ2. A living, non-human being, was also discovered at this site by local law enforcement officers, who took the entity to Los Alamos National Laboratories, where it is being cared for now."

President Truman asks, "Excuse me, General. But, didn't you say that this was a midair collision with three objects? What happened to the other one?"

General Vandenberg clears his throat and says, "We don't know what happened to one of the craft, but we believe that the third object impacted at Site LZ3 at nearly a vertical angle, which makes it impossible for us to determine if it was of similar design as the other craft. We have reconnaissance aircraft searching the area now for the other object, but it has not been discovered yet." [9]

The President says, "Alright, continue General."

The General states, "When the Recovery Team arrived at Site LZ2, they discovered that there were several civilians in the area who witnessed the craft. They were debriefed, sworn to secrecy and then released. The team secured the site while the wreckage was recovered. Debris of a similar type was also recovered at another crash site, designated LZ3. It appears that the UFO initially impacted with the Earth at this site and became airborne again before coming to rest at crash site LZ2. The cover story of a recovered weather balloon appears to have curtailed interest resulting from the earlier press release of a crashed flying saucer that was recovered by the Army.[10]

"Inquiries, regarding the recovered items, have been restricted at the bases which are involved. All Teletype, telephone, and radio transmissions are monitored for any disclosures of the finds. Civilians who might have seen or handled some of the wreckage, or viewed bodies, were detained under the McNab law until all remaining evidence was recovered and stored at secure facilities. The witnesses were debriefed by Counter Intelligence and warned of the consequences for talking to anyone about this.

"All civilian and military personnel involved with the recovery operation had "need to know" access with proper security clearances. Although several military policemen suffered nervous breakdowns and one even committed suicide, the M.P. details from Alamogordo and Kirtland performed security functions properly. [11]

"The Secretary of Defense has been kept apprised of all information regarding this incident. The only cabinet member that may know of the details is the Secretary of State. Some information of the recovery operation has also been shared with Representative John F. Kennedy, who had limited duty as a naval officer assigned to Naval Intelligence during the World War II. General Eisenhower will see a showing of the recoveries next month." [12]

The projection screen changes to a photograph of a dead extraterrestrial being. The General clears his throat and resumes the briefing with, "None of the five bodies, which were recovered at Site LZ1, survived entry into our atmosphere due to unknown causes. The occupants appear, in most respects, to be human with some anatomical differences in the head, eyes, hands, and feet. They have a slight build at about four feet tall, with grayish-pink skin color. They have no hair on their bodies. They were clothed in a tight fitting flight suit that appears to be fire proof. Some of the bodies appeared to be burned on their head and hands. Their overall stature remains one of young children. Major Charles Rea and Dr. Detlev Bronk are scheduled to conduct an autopsy on one, well preserved cadaver later this week. [13]

"Several medical personnel became contaminated upon coming in contact with the body fluids of the alien bodies. One technician was overcome and collapsed when he attempted the removal of a body. Another medical technician went into a coma four hours after placing a body in a rubber body-bag. They were rushed to Los Alamos for observation. Four of the personnel later died of seizures and profuse bleeding. All four were wearing protective suits when they handled the alien bodies. It is believed that the four may have suffered from some form of toxin or a highly contagious disease. In the opinion of the senior AEC medical officer, current medical equipment and supplies are wholly inadequate in dealing with a large-scale outbreak of the alien virus.

"There was also great concern over the detection of airborne radiation over the state of New Mexico. Radiation readings from several airborne monitoring flights over the crash site indicated a high neutron count. The neutron count dropped off as the planes flew a considerable distance from the site." [14]

The projection screen changes to a photograph of the craft at the crash site. General Vandenberg states, "The recovered object has been assessed as not being any aircraft, rocket, weapons, or balloon test that is normally conducted from the surrounding bases. The lack of wiring, fuel systems, cables, motors, hydraulics, intakes, exhaust, and surface controls, strongly suggests that the craft was designed to travel outside of our atmosphere. Discovered inside the craft, were the body parts, believed to have come from the mutilated pilot found at Site LZ1. It is the assessment of the ULTRA investigation team that this is either an elaborate hoax or the U.S. has played host to beings from another planet." [15]

The projection screen changes to an aerial view of Muroc A.A.F., with four markings on it. The General says, "On 8 July, there were four separate sightings of unidentified disc-shaped objects flying over Muroc Army Air Field and Rogers Dry Lake secret testing site in California. One object passed over an F-51 aircraft at a time when no known aircraft were in the vicinity. All forms for defensive weaponry have proved to be ineffective against incursions, by these craft, over our most sensitive military installations."

President Truman asks, "Why would extraterrestrial beings be coming to the Earth at this time?"

The General says, "Mr. President, the aliens appear to be interested in our military installations where nuclear weapons are stored and where the V-2 rockets are being tested. I suggest that they may be coming to Earth in order to study our military potential as a prelude to invasion."

Secretary of State Marshall says, "That could be true, General. However, another possibility is that they may only be trying to determine what threat that humanity may pose to them, if we become able to venture out into space, ourselves."

President Truman asks, "General, why do you suppose the aliens mutilated the pilot?"

The General shrugs his shoulders and says, "Well Sir, they may simply want to examine life on this planet or they may want to use the body parts for biological, genetic, or nutritional purposes."

The President says, "I am concerned about the fact that we have no way of knowing if the alien's intentions are hostile or only academic. It is only a matter of time before additional sightings and contacts occur again."

The Secretary of State says, "Mr. President, it is vitally important that we should try to develop diplomatic relations with this extraterrestrial race. It is obvious that this is a highly intelligent species. There could be much to be gained by cultural and technological exchanges."

Admiral Forrestal says, "With all due respect, Mr. Secretary, I would like to remind everyone that these beings have violated the restricted airspace of our most sensitive military installations. I believe that we should consider the possibility that this may be a prelude to war with these beings."

The President says, "Well, we have to do something, and fast, before everything gets out of control and panic ensues. First, we must make absolutely certain that everything involved with the aliens is kept secret until we can find out what we are dealing with. General, I am holding you personally responsible for the secrecy of all alien related matters."

"Yes, Sir."

"We must be prepared to deal with other incidents that are certain to follow. Mr. Secretary, I want the State Department to be prepared for diplomatic relations, should open contact be established. Until then, we must continue to recover all downed craft within our borders and utilize our best scientists to find out, as much as we can, what we are dealing with. At the same time, however, we must be prepared to defend ourselves against a possible attack or even an invasion. Admiral, I want the Defense Department to prepare a contingency plan for the defense of the United States against any eventuality."

The Admiral says, "Yes, Mr. President."

"Meanwhile, the Vice President and I will draft new legislation for the security of this nation. That is all, gentlemen."

7/12/47 General Ramey's Office at Carswell A.A.F.

"Captain Evens reporting, as ordered, Sir." General Ramey comes around from behind his desk, shakes Evens' hand, and says, "It's good to see you again, Captain. Have a seat." The two men sit down and the General tells Evens, "The Chief of Staff, in Washington, is pleased with the excellent work that you did with the recovery operations, Captain. You are being promoted to the rank of Major, effective immediately."

Evens' eyes pop wide open with that piece of information and says, "Thank you very much, General".

"Don't thank me. You've earned it."

The General leans back in his chair, thinks for a minute, and then says, "I'd like to know what your feelings are with regard to the aliens."

The new Major says, "I don't like them very much, Sir. I saw what the aliens did to the pilot and, if it were up to me, I would like to be the one who leads the first attack against them."

Ramey tells Evens, "I'm afraid that, if there ever is a battle, you would probably be called on to go in afterward and pick up the pieces."

The General grabs a sheet of paper from off of his desk, hands it to Evens, and says, "I have a new assignment for you. I am putting you in charge of security at the Roswell Base. You are ordered to contact everyone involved in this matter and insure that they keep silent about what they know. Most people will cooperate for patriotic reasons. With some people, financial assistance may be sufficient. However, others may require intimidation or termination. You are authorized to do whatever is required to guarantee security on this matter, including the use of lethal force. This is a matter of ultimate importance to the United States of America. Now, I need to know if I can count on you to fulfill this mission, Major." [16]

Evens answers, "Yes sir, you can count on me."

"Very well. I will be at the base on the 16th and 17th of this month to check on how everything is progressing. You are dismissed, Major."

7/14/47 At Military Police Headquarters, Roswell Base

Major Evens enters a room where George A. Wilcox, the Chaves County Sheriff, and his wife, Inez, are seated at a table. Evens says, "Good morning Sheriff and Mrs. Wilcox. My name is Major Tom Evens. I am in charge of security regarding the Brazel matter. Are you two alright?"

Sheriff Wilcox is furious. He shouts at Evens, "Don't try to pretend to be concerned for our welfare, Major! You are unlawfully holding us against our will. You have usurped my authority, confiscated a carton of crash debris that Mr. Brazel entrusted to me, and have even barred my deputies from the crash site. What is the meaning of this miscarriage of justice?"

Evens says, "I'm sorry to have offended you, Sir. But, this is a matter of national security. I am asking both of you to cooperate and agree to never reveal anything about this incident to anyone."

The Sheriff asks, "And, what if we refuse?"

"Well sir", Evens replies, "In that case, you and your entire family will have to be terminated."

The Sheriff shouts, "You can't do that!"

Evens says calmly, "We can and we will. Can we rely on your cooperation in this matter?"

Mr. and Mrs. Wilcox look at each other in horror and then nod their heads in agreement.

"Very good. Thank you for your assistance in this matter. You are free to go." [17]

Evens enters a room where Mr. Brazel is being held.

Brazel yells at him, "How much longer are you going to keep me here? I've been here for almost a week now. I know my rights. This is damned illegal and it ain't right. You try to do a good deed and this is what you get for your trouble?"

Evens tells him, "I apologize for inconveniencing you like this. But, it is necessary for national security."

"I don't give a damn about that. I only want to go home."

"We just want to make sure that you will do your patriotic duty and remain quiet about the debris that was found on your farm."

"It was my patriotic duty to report what I found and look at what it has gotten me?"

Evens thinks for a moment and says, "I believe that you should be compensated for the damages that have been done to your land. You are in the market for a truck, aren't you?"

Mr. Brazel's head jerks up and he enthusiastically states that he is.

Evens says, "Well, if you were to obtain a new truck, you realize that you would be expected to keep quiet about the debris. There would be serious repercussions if you failed to comply."

"Okay. I understand. I agree to cooperate."

Evens says, "Very well. You will be allowed to leave after you have received a complete physical examination", and then he leaves the room. [18]

Evens enters another room where a twelve year old girl is being held under the watchful eye of a military policeman. Evens asks the M.P. for his baton and it is handed over to him. Evens looks at the girl while repeatedly slapping his hand with the baton. He tells the girl, "I understand that you have played with some unusual materials that were collected by your father, the town's fire marshal."

"That's right. I sure did."

"I also understand that you are refusing to keep silent about it."

The little girl takes a deep breath, lets it out, and says, "My mother has taught me to always tell the truth. I will not lie about it. I did see and play with the funny stuff."

While hitting the baton on his open hand, Evens raises his voice and tells her, "You did not touch anything. You did not see anything."

The girl defiantly says, "Yes, I did".

Evens slams the table with the baton and yells at her, "No, you haven't! If you cannot understand this, than you will be taken out into the desert where you will never be heard from again. No one will ever know what happened to you. I am going to ask you one last time. Will you cooperate?"

The girl is crying as she says that she will.

Evens smiles and says in a normal tone of voice, "Very good. You are permitted to leave. Your parents are waiting right outside the door."

The girl runs from the room, crying.

Evens hands the baton back to the M.P. who comments, sarcastically, "You're a real swell guy." Evens says, "I know. I just saved that little girl's life."

Discovery

7/16/47 In Gen. Vandenberg's Office at the Pentagon

Lt. General Nathan Twining is seated in front of General Vandenberg's large oak desk. He has just delivered his report, entitled "Air Accident Report on 'Flying Disc' Aircraft Stored at White Sands Proving Ground, New Mexico", directly into the hands of the General. It contains his findings resulting from a Presidential Directive to investigate the UFO incident. The data furnished in this report was provided by his Air Materiel Command engineering staff and scientific personnel from the Jet Propulsion Laboratory, CIT, and the Army Air Forces Scientific Advisory Group.

While Vandenberg is perusing the document, General Twining takes this chance to look around the room. It is truly an office befitting the Chief of Staff of the Army Air Forces. He has a wonderful view of the surrounding countryside through a huge, curtain draped window behind where the General sits at his desk. There is a U.S. flag at the right of the window and an Army pennant, with ribbons, on the left. There is a world globe in the right corner and a large map of the world on a long, wood paneled wall. There are doors that lead to his private restroom and to a small kitchen where a steward is preparing coffee and pastries. Large couches, chairs, and tables are behind Twining.

General Vandenberg looks up from the document and says, "This report has been well written. I shall approve it for distribution to the President. I know that you were simply acting on a directive from the President. But, I am concerned that a report like this could be very damaging, if it ever became public knowledge. For this reason, I am going to have this document classified as Top Secret, and for eyes only."

Twining asks, "Damaging? In what way, Sir?"

Vandenberg says, "For example, your report states 'It is the collective view of this investigative body, that the aircraft recovered... are not of U.S. manufacture for the following reasons: The circular, disc-shaped "planform" design does not resemble any design currently under development... The lack of any external propulsion system, power plant, intake, or exhaust, either for propeller or jet propulsion, warrants this view."

"The German scientists from Fort Bliss and WSPG have also been unable to make a positive identification of these discs as being a secret German V weapon. The lack of any markings, ID members, or instructions in Cyrillic, has caused serious doubt that it is of Russian manufacture either."

Twining raises his head confidently and says, "That is our conclusion, Sir."

Vandenberg looks straight at Twining and says, "Alright then, where did it come from?"

Without batting an eye, Twining says, "We do not know that information for certain, Sir. We are only confident in the fact that it is not from this world."

General Vandenberg says, "The analysis of the craft from scientists like Dr. Robert Oppenheimer, Dr. Wernher von Braun, and Dr. Theodore von Karman, carries a lot of weight. Their discovery of a possible atomic engine, that has no conventional electronics or wiring that connects the controls to the propulsion system, might give the impression that this technology is far in advance of our own."

General Vandenberg continues with, "And, their description of a flight deck with no canopy, observation windows, or any optical projection might give the impression that this is a craft from another world. Especially when it describes a crew compartment that is hermetically sealed via a solidification process with no weld marks, rivets, or soldered joints and that it appears to be molded and pressed into a perfect fit. A person might get the idea that this is something that we cannot technically do at the present time."

Twining says, "And they would be correct in that assumption, Sir." [1] [2]

7/18/47 The Army Medical Corps Facility of Wright Field

Major Charles Rea and Doctor Detlev Bronk, wearing contamination suits, enter a brightly lit operating room along with an Army photographer who is filming everything. A dead alien body is lying on a table with its head facing upwards. There is a tray of medical instruments located at the head of the table, on the left side. There is another table, with medical supplies, against the left wall. Someone, wearing a surgical mask and gown, watches from behind a viewing window in the far wall. The cadaver is extremely odorous which could be due to its deterioration.

The doctors examine the body and discover that it is humanoid in appearance with a slight build at approximately four and a half feet tall. It has a large, uniquely shaped head supported by a thin neck. The body is completely hairless. The skin is scaly with a grayish-white color. The scales are very tiny similar to a white snake. The head, by human standards, is over sized in relation to the torso and limbs. The eyes are large, opaque black, and positioned at a slightly slanted upward angle. The ears are positioned much lower on each side of the head and it has a uniquely shaped, turned-up nose. The mouth has no lips, but it has tiny sharp teeth, a tongue and an orifice that extends only about three inches deep.

The arms and legs are extremely thin, with the arms reaching nearly to the knees. The hands have only four fingers with a suction cup at the end of the fingers. There is a slit in the crotch area with a penis inside and a very small rectum. The feet are small and have four toes with claw-like nails similar to a dog's nails. The dark covering over the eyes is removed with tweezers to reveal cat-like eyes. There are also eyelids that can cover the eyes.

Major Rea grabs a scalpel and makes in incision down the center of the upper torso, from the collar bone to the crotch. A green viscous liquid becomes evident. Then, another incision is made along the collar bone and the skin covering each side of the chest area and abdomen is pulled apart, exposing a rib cage and large organ. The rest of the body consists of a homogeneous spongy tissue infused with circulatory systems, glands, and other amorphous structures. There is no digestive system, bladder, urinary tract, lungs, or heart, as would be found in a human body. The large organ is removed for later examination.

Next, Major Rea takes a hand saw and saws off the top of the skull to expose the brain matter in the cranium. It is discovered that there is a partition-type of ridge bone running directly through the center of the skull, from front to back, which completely divides the two brains. The brain capacity is larger than humans. It is estimated to be between 2500 and 3500 cubic centimeters, compared to 1300 cubic centimeters of humans. The neural matter is removed and found to be unlike any other type of brain matter, with many more lobes than human brains have. It is also found to contain a crystalline material.

The two doctors take the large organ, which they removed from the alien cadaver, into another operating room similar to the previous one. They place the organ on the center table and dissect it.

"Look at that!" says Doctor Bronk to Major Rea, "This organ has the combined function of a heart and a lung."

The Major says, "Well, that explains how the respiratory and circulatory systems function. However, we still don't know how the body consumes nourishment or excretes wastes. There is no digestive tract and the rectum is far too small. The mouth cannot even function as a means to ingest food."

Doctor Bronk asks, "Is it possible that the nutrients could be absorbed through the pores in the alien's mouth?" "Yes, that may be possible."

The men take samples from inside the alien's mouth and examined the cross sections of these samples through a microscope. They are astonished to find that the samples contain pores that can transfer nutrients to the homogeneous spongy tissue, which runs throughout the body. They also find that, although much smaller than for humans, the rectum is able to excrete waist products, which suggests that the alien bodies are much more efficient in converting food into energy.

Finally, the doctors decide to examine the mutilated body of the pilot found at the first crash site. The man had been emasculated and his rectum had been removed. An incision had been made just under the tip of the chin and extended all the way back to the esophagus and larynx. The tongue had been removed from the lower portion of the jaw and the eyeballs were removed from their sockets.

The body had been completely drained of blood with not a drop of blood to be found anywhere. When they examined body samples under a microscope, they found that there was no vascular collapse due to death by bleeding.

Even more startling was the discovery that the incisions had been made with something that produced intense heat. They both noticed the cored out incisions in the rectal and genital areas that was made with surgical precision. The anus was removed as though a plug had been extended all the way up to the colon.

Doctor Bronk stated, "The 'cookie cutter' type of incisions, are sharp and well defined. They all have smooth edges. We could never make such intricate incisions as these."

When they were finished, the two men rushed off to their offices to write their reports. [3] [4] [5]

8/25/47 In the Oval Office of the White House

President Truman greets Congressman John F. Kennedy and invites him to sit down. When the two men have settled into facing chairs, the President says, "I understand that you have been briefed about the recovery of a flying disc." Kennedy states that this is true. Truman says, "Due to the fact of that incident and because additional contacts with extraterrestrials are anticipated, I have had the National Security Act presented before Congress. I am sure that you agree with the need for security, regarding other-world visitation, in order to prevent mass hysteria." [6]

Kennedy states, "Yes Mr. President. I concur with the need for security in this matter. I also agree with the need for a National Security Council, comprised of the President, the Vice President, and the Secretaries of Defense and State, to make decisions regarding national security. I believe that the creation of the Air Force as an independent branch of our military is also a good idea. But, I must say that I am concerned about the creation of a Central Intelligence Agency." [7]

Congressman Kennedy says, "I am concerned that this agency will become too powerful and turn into a Big Brother that watches what everyone does."

President Truman states, "I assure you that the only purpose for the CIA is to keep the alien matter contained. It will be strictly limited in its scope and it will be answerable to congressional scrutiny."

"Well, in that case, Mr. President, I will be happy to give the bill my full support."

"Thank you for your support. I knew that I could count on you. I can tell that you will go far in public service."

9/19/47 In Gen. Vandenberg's Office at the Pentagon

Stan Edwards is the military liaison representative with the Central Intelligence Group, a predecessor of the CIA. He sits very quietly as General Vandenberg reads a report that Stan has just delivered. It is entitled, "Memorandum for the Military Assessment of the Joint Intelligence Committee". It is a preliminary report on the examination of Unidentified Disk-like Aircraft.

Stan can tell that the General is not pleased with what he is reading. He notices that the General's teeth are clenched, his facial muscles are tense, and his body is rigid. Stan hates his job. During the war, he joined the Army, completed Officer's Candidate School, and served with the Counter-Intelligence Corps in England. After the war, he became an administrator with the Central Intelligence Group and was eventually assigned as the military liaison officer.

If it were not for the fact that he was in the middle of a nasty divorce, and the father of two small children, he would have quit this job long ago. It was actually the long hours of the job that drove his wife and him apart from one another. And now, he rarely has any chance to be with his children and he hates having to deal with the intimidating, self-serving military brass. Stan is a good looking guy with a slim build, he is 5'7" tall, and has a light complexion. He is from Colorado and is only twenty-five years old. Although his job requires him to wear a suit and tie every day, he still thinks of himself as a cowboy underneath.

The report that General Vandenberg is reading states, "Pursuant to recent world events, domestic security problems within the Atomic Energy Commission, the intelligence reports of "Flying Saucers", and the intrusion of unknown aircraft over the most secret defense installations, a classified intelligence project was warranted.

"The National Security Act of 1947 established a Central Intelligence Agency under the National Security Council. When the Director of Central Intelligence assumes his official responsibilities, the National Intelligence Authority will be abolished. The files pertaining to unidentified aircraft sightings, intelligence personnel, and funds of the Central Intelligence Group will be transferred to the Agency.

"The recovery of an unidentified planform aircraft on 7/6/47, 10 miles N.W. of Oscura Peak, and a debris field 75 miles N.W. of the Army's 509th Atomic Bomb Group at Roswell AAF is confirmed. The capture of this craft has convinced the Army Air Forces S-2, the Army G-2, and Navy ONI, that the craft and wreckage are not of U.S. manufacture.

"Until a clear directive from the President is issued, there can be no coordinated scientific examination of the objects. Research scientists at the Air Forces Research and Development Center at Wright Field are using their test facilities and a new biological laboratory in an ongoing study program. The offices of JRQB, FBI, and the State Department are acquiring any intelligence from MI5 and MI6 on possible Soviet long-range reconnaissance aircraft/missile research and development tests." [8]

General Vandenberg is clearly upset by what he has just read. He shouts at Stan, "Are the people at the Central Intelligence Group out of their damn minds? It seems that they have asked everyone and their brother if the Soviets have a long-range reconnaissance craft like the type that we have recovered. Why don't they just tell everyone what we have and invite them to come see it?"

Stan does not say anything. He keeps his lips pressed tightly together and hopes that the General will not shoot the messenger. The General then says, "I want you to tell the people at the CI Group that I have assessed the Joint Intelligence Committee and that I am not pleased with their intelligence."

Stan stands up, says, "Yes, Sir. I will relay your message", and hurriedly leaves the office.

9/24/47 In the Oval Office of the White House

President Truman greets Dr. Vannover Bush and the Secretary of Defense, Admiral James Forrestal. The President says, "Thank you, gentlemen, for coming on such short notice. I called you here to obtain your advice on how best to deal with the alien situation. There are too many people involved and too much information for one man to deal with all of it. It is affecting my ability to run the country effectively. What do you think that I should do?"

Dr. Bush says, "Well Mr. President, I believe that a small group, composed of leading scientists, military, and intelligence personnel, should be established to process the information and advise you on matters concerning the extraterrestrials."

Secretary Forrestal states, "I concur with Dr. Bush, Sir. I believe that they could be of great help to you in this matter, Mr. President."

Truman asks, "How many people do you think should be in this group?"

"I believe that twelve would be sufficient," says Dr. Bush.

Truman says, "Very well. That seems like sound advice. Mr. Secretary, I would like you to begin making inquiries and compile a list of possible candidates, including yourself, Dr. Bush, and the Director of Central Intelligence.

The Secretary smiles, hands the President a piece of paper, and says, "It has already been done, Mr. President. This is my list of recommendations to the group. These men are now ready to devote their full attention and resources to the alien situation."

The President looks at the list and asks, "You propose naming the group 'Majestic Twelve'?"

"That's right, Sir."

"Very good. I will draft a special, classified executive order right away to authorize you to create such an advisory group and to have it responsible directly and only to the President." [9] [10]

9/26/47 The National Security Council, Washington D.C.

President Truman brings the first meeting of the National Security Council to order. The Council consists of the President, the Vice President, the Secretary of State, and the Secretary of Defense. The President states, "As you all know, the National Security Act, which was recently passed, calls for the creation of the National Security Council, the Air Force as a separate defense department, and the Central Intelligence Agency. Although the bill defines the CIA's legal mandate and places restrictions on it's activities, we must now establish what the relationship is of the CIA to the NSC."

The Council unanimously approves two new directives, NSC 4-1 and NSC 4-2, which give the CIA the power to conduct covert activities without reporting to anyone. Secretary Forrestal also recommends that the Navy be granted full operational control over all alien related projects and this is approved as well. [11]

11/30/47 In a Conference Room at the Pentagon

As the Chairman, Dr. Vannover Bush brings the meeting to order. He states, "Welcome, everyone. This is the first meeting of the study group, which will be hereafter known as Majestic-12. Let the record show that all twelve members of this group are present. The members are: Admiral Roscoe Hillenkoetter (the first director of the CIA), Dr. Vannover Bush (organized the Office of Scientific Research and Development which led to the production of the first atomic bomb), Admiral James Forrestal (Secretary of Defense), Lt. General Nathan Twining (Commander of Air Materiel Command), Lt. General Hoyt Vandenberg (Air Force Chief of Staff), Dr. Detlev Bronk (Physiologist and biophysicist who chaired the National Research Council), Dr. Jerome Hunsaker (Aircraft designer who chaired the Departments of Mechanical and Aeronautical Engineering), Mr. Sidney Souers (Executive Secretary to the NSC), Mr. Gordon Gray (Assistant Secretary of the Army), Dr. Donald Menzel (Director of the Harvard College Observatory), General Robert Montague (Base Commander at the Sandia AEC facility), and Dr. Lloyd Berkner (Executive Secretary of the Joint Research and Development Board).

"This group was established under a direct presidential directive that was signed on the 26th of September, 1947. We are tasked with the responsibility of providing answers regarding other-world visitation and what it portends for mankind. The studies, regarding other-world visitation, include technology exploitation, interplanetary travel, and cultural communications. The first order of business is a review of what is known at this time."

Dr. Berkner states, "It is my conclusion that no country on this Earth has the means and the security of its resources to produce such a long-range aircraft as that which has been recovered. It is the consensus of the Joint Research and Development Board that the recovered object is interplanetary in nature."

Dr. Menzel states, "I consider it likely that we are dealing with beings from another solar system entirely. There are millions of stars in our Milky Way galaxy which are large enough to support their own solar systems. If only one tenth of one percent of those solar systems have a planet with the right conditions to support life, then there are hundreds of life-supporting planets. Only man would be arrogant enough to consider himself as the most intelligent species in the universe."

Dr. Bronk states, "After completing an autopsy on one of the dead alien beings, it is my tentative conclusion that, although the creatures are human-like in appearance, they are not of any species that is known to have ever inhabited this planet. The biological and evolutionary processes responsible for their development have apparently been quite different from homo-sapiens. I suggest that the term "Extraterrestrial Biological Entities", or "EBEs", be adopted as the standard term of reference for these creatures. My complete report has already been made available to you. Our primary attention now has been paid to information of bio-medical intelligence interest, particularly in the biological warfare programs. Our efforts are also currently focused on psychological operations development for Cold War Central Intelligence activities."

Admiral Hillenkoetter says, "We have submitted the numerous examples of what appear to be a form of writing, which were found in the wreckage, to our staff of code-breakers, linguists, and analysts. So far, their efforts to decipher this writing remain largely unsuccessful. However, the live alien being, known as EBE-1, which was discovered at the second crash site may be of some assistance in helping us to establish communications with its race. Although the entity has no vocal cords, our doctors are conducting an operation that should enable it to speak. It is extremely intelligent and it should be able to learn English rather quickly."

Dr. Bush states, "Because of the unique nature of the materials under study, a multi-layered security structure is in effect. Most of the results have been given to private research and development labs for further study. However, the utilization of Project Paperclip specialists has yielded valuable results in new weapons research of flight dynamics, biological and chemical agents, mind control, and intelligence gathering techniques."

The group struggles with the issues concerning the potentials for using the alien technology, the capabilities of alien intellect, and the possibilities for both disaster and advancement with the alien beings. This group also deals with the possibilities of what may happen if the alien issue is revealed to the general public. Their final recommendations include keeping everything involved with the aliens classified, obtaining the resources to examine the alien technology without congressional scrutiny, and finding a way to communicate with the aliens.[12] [13] [14] [15]

12/30/47 In a Briefing Room at Wright-Patterson A.F.B.

Major General L.C. Craigie, the commanding General of the newly formed Air Force, calls a meeting together of the highest-ranking members on his staff. He says to them, "I have called this meeting in order to address the issues put forth in a document, dated 23 September 1947, by Lieutenant General Nathan Twining, the commander of the Air Materiel Command. I quote from that document, 'the phenomenon reported is something real and not visionary or fictitious.' This document recommends that, 'Headquarters, Army Air Forces, issue a directive assigning a priority, security classification and Code Name for a detailed study on the matter.' And that, gentlemen, is exactly what we are going to do." [16] [17]

The General says, "I am approving the recommendation for a 2A classified research project and designating it Project Sign. This project is tasked with the responsibility of investigating all incidents involving UFOs and extraterrestrial life in order to ascertain their validity, cause, and impact. Due to the fact that contact with the general public will be inevitable, during the investigation of these cases, I am specifying that the project will also be known to the public as Project Saucer. This project will be based out of Wright Field. Captain Robert Sneider has been assigned as the official project officer, under the supervision of Colonels Howard McCoy and William Clingerman. Also assigned to this project, are civilian technical intelligence engineers Alfred Loedding, Lawrence Truettner, and A.B. Deyarmond." [18] [19]

1/18/48 In Gen. Vandenberg's Office at the Pentagon

Major Evens reports as ordered to General Hoyt Vandenberg, the Air Force Chief of Staff. "Be seated, Major", the General says, "I have reviewed your report on the security at Roswell Air Base and I approve of the measures that were taken there. You are to be commended for the fine work that you have accomplished there. You are being reassigned to the Air Technical Intelligence Center at Wright Field as the liaison officer for a new project called Sign. This is an important mission and you will have the opportunity to make a favorable impression on some very important people."

The General tells Evens about the Majestic-12 group and the objectives of Project Sign. Then he says, "I am concerned about the direction that the project may take in exposing the fact that UFOs are extraterrestrial craft. Your official job is to act as liaison between Project Sign and Majestic-12. However, I also want you to keep me apprised of the unofficial activities of the project members."

Evens realizes that he has just been ordered to spy on the project and does not care for the job one bit. But, in true military fashion, he says, "Yes, Sir!"

The General says, "In order for you to be able to evaluate the information gathered by Project Sign, you will be given access to the case files from the Central Intelligence Agency. I would like to introduce you to Stan Edwards, the military liaison with the CIA. You will be working with him while on this assignment."

Evens looks to his right and sees Edwards standing next to him with his hand out, saying, "Nice to meet you."

The two men shake hands and Evens responds with, "Likewise, I'm sure." Evens tells the General, "Thank you, Sir, for this opportunity to serve. You can count on me."

"Very well. Dismissed." Evens and Edwards then leave the office together.

7/28/48 In Evens' Office at Wright Field, Dayton, Ohio

Major Evens and Stan Edwards are going over the CIA files on the cases currently being reviewed by Project Sign. There are several stacks of folders on Evens' gray metal desk. It is a small office with walls that are painted in two shades of green. Evens is seated behind his desk and Stan is seated in front of it. They are both sitting on uncomfortable metal chairs and are bent over the small desk, reading the file folders. There is a dirty window behind Evens that overlooks the parade grounds. There is nothing covering the window and the only other pieces of furniture are a filing cabinet, a coat rack, and trash can.

Evens shakes his head in amazement and says, "There are dozens of seemingly inexplicable cases that are being reported to the Air Technical Intelligence Center (ATIC) each week. How in the world are we ever going to keep up with them all?"

"I have no idea. Just take a look at these cases."

June 24, 1947: Mount Rainier, Washington at 3:00 PM. Kenneth Arnold witnessed nine crescent-shaped objects that flashed among the mountain peaks "like saucers skipping on a pond."

June 24,1947: Cascade Mountains, Washington at 3:00 PM. Fred Johnson saw a number of "disc-shaped" craft overhead and noticed that his compass was spinning wildly.

July 3, 1947: Harborside, Maine at 2:30 PM. Astronomer John Cole, of South Brooksville, Maine, watched for 10 to 15 seconds while ten very light objects, with two dark forms to their left, moved like a swarm of bees toward the northwest. A loud roar was also heard.

July 4, 1947: over Emmet, Idaho at 8:17 PM. United Airlines Captain E.J. Smith, First Officer Ralph Stevens, and Stewardess Mary Morrow watched for 10 to 15 minutes while 4 objects with flat bottoms and rough tops moved at varying speeds, with one high and to the right of the others.

July 6, 1947: Fairfield-Suisan Air Base, California. Captain and Mrs. James Burniston watched for one minute while one object, having no wings or tail, rolled from side to side three times and then flew away very fast to the southeast.

July 7, 1947: Phoenix, Arizona. William Rhodes watched a "heel-shaped" object that circled near his home. He took two photographs of the object, which disappeared a few minutes later.

July 8, 1947: Muroc Air Base, California at 9:30 AM. First Lieutenant Joseph McHenry, Technical Sergeant Ruvolo, Staff Sergeant Nauman, and Janette Scotte watched while two silver disc-shaped or spherical objects, apparently made of metal, flew a wide circular pattern. One of them later flew a tighter circle.

July 9, 1947: Meridian, Idaho at 12:17. Idaho Statesman, aviation editor, and former B-29 pilot Dave Johnson watched for more than ten seconds, from an Idaho Air National Guard AT-6, while a black disc, which stood out against the clouds, made a half-roll and then a stair-step climb.

July 10, 1947: Harmon Field, Newfoundland, Canada between 3:00 and 5:00 PM. Three ground crewmen, including Mr. Leidy, of Pan American Airways, watched briefly while one translucent disc or wheel shaped object flew very fast, leaving a dark blue trail. It then ascended and cut a path through the clouds.

July 29, 1947: Hamilton Air Base, California at 2:50 PM. Assistant Base Operations Officer, Captain William Rhyerd and ex-AAF B-29 pilot, Ward Stewart watched while two round, shiny, white objects estimated to be 15 to 25 feet in diameter, flew 3 or 4 times the apparent speed of a P-80, also in sight. One object flew straight and level. The other waved from side to side like an escort fighter.

September 3, 1947: Oswego, Oregon at 12:15 PM. Mrs. Raymond Dupui watched as twelve to fifteen round, silver objects flew an unstated pattern.

October 1947: Dodgeville, Wisconsin. An unidentified witness watched for one hour while an undescribed object flew circles.

October 14, 1947: Eleven miles N.N.E. of Cave Creek, Arizona at noon. Fighter pilot, J.L. Clark, a civilian pilot named Anderson, and an unidentified third man watched for 45 to 60 seconds while one 30 foot flying wing-shaped object flew straight, from the northwest to the southeast. It flew at an estimated speed of 380 miles per hour and at an altitude of between 8,000 to 10,000 feet. It looked black against the white clouds and red against the blue sky.

April 5, 1948: Holloman Air Force Base, New Mexico in the afternoon. Geophysics lab balloon observers Alsen, Johnson, and Chance saw two irregular, round, white or golden objects. One made three loops then rose and disappeared rapidly. The other flew in a fast arc to the west during the 30 second sighting.

July 24, 1948: Robins Air Force Base, Georgia at 1:50 AM. Maintenance ground crewman Walter Massey saw a cigar-shaped craft that flashed overhead. He thought that he saw a flame coming from the rear.

July 24, 1948: Near Montgomery, Alabama at 2:45 AM. Eastern Airlines pilots Clarence Chiles and John Whitted watched a bright light head for their airliner and pass on the right. The craft was cigar-shaped and had a double row of windows along it. A flame shot out of the back. [20] [21]

Evens sits back in his chair, smiles, and tells Stan, "Gee, isn't it strange that the Roswell crash was not included in the files?" They laugh. Then, Evens says with a serious look on his face, "Because of the last two sightings, the members of Project Sign are convinced that they now have proof that flying saucers are extraterrestrial in origin. They are planning to state as much in an 'Estimate of the Situation' Report, which they are preparing right now."

Stan says, "Boy, I sure am glad that I am not the one who must tell General Vandenberg about that." Evens replies,

"Yeah, I know. I'm not looking forward to that meeting either."

12/16/48 In a Conference Room at the Pentagon

General Vandenberg calls the meeting to order. He tells the officers and civilian technical intelligence engineers of Project Sign, "I have invited you gentlemen here to defend your 'Estimate of the Situation' Report, dated September 19, 1948. Please present your evidence."

Alfred Loedding, who considers himself as the civilian project leader, states, "Sir, our conclusion, that UFOs are interplanetary craft, was based on the analysis of many highly credible reports which could not be explained in any other way." He then quotes many unexplained sightings as proof. [22]

When the members of Project Sign have finished with their defense of the report, General Vandenberg tells them, "Well gentlemen, I am not impressed with the evidence that you have provided here today. I do not buy your assumption of interplanetary vehicles and dismiss your position altogether. That is all. You are dismissed."

The project members leave without a word. After they leave the room, General Vandenberg tells his staff, "I want every copy of that report destroyed immediately. Project Sign will now be re-designated as Project Grudge and I want everyone involved in the project, except for the lowest grade military and civilian personnel, to be reassigned. Is that clear?" [23]

His staff all say in unison, "Yes, Sir!"

Evens and Edwards are also in the room and have watched what has taken place. After General Vandenberg and his staff leave the room, Stan says, "Jeez! Now I know what the Spanish Inquisition must have been like."

Evens asks, "Do you think the remaining members of the project will get the idea that General Vandenberg is not a proponent of the extraterrestrial hypothesis?"

Stan says, "I believe that we might even see Project Grudge take on a whole new direction."

Disinformation

2/12/49 In a Majestic-12 Meeting at the Pentagon

Dr. Vannover Bush is saying, "The ability to examine and evaluate the recovered alien craft is being hindered by our inability to fund these secret projects without being held accountable to congressional scrutiny. Therefore, funding must be generated by covert means."

"It is our plan to contact gangster Lucky Luciano, who was released from prison and deported to Italy, in order to begin preparing for the cultivation and shipment of heroin into the United States. The drugs will be transported by ships to the offshore drilling platforms along the gulf coast and brought ashore without customs or contraband inspections. From there, the distribution of the merchandise and the collection of revenues will be handled by the Delta Forces and the Naval Reconnaissance Office." [1] [2]

Secretary of Defense, James Forrestal becomes outraged and says, "I object to the use of illegal drugs to fund the black projects."

Dr. Bush tells him, "We have given this matter a lot of thought and this is the only way that we have found to be able to generate the necessary funds in a covert manner."

The Admiral asks, "What will happen if the operation is discovered by the local authorities?"

Admiral Hillenkoetter, as Director of the CIA, says, "Steps have been taken to insure that the parties involved are never brought to justice and that the operation is never exposed or compromised."

"Just so that we all understand clearly," Secretary Forrestal states, "You intend to generate funds by destroying the lives of thousands of American citizens, through addiction, who rely on us for protection?"

Dr. Bush says, "It is inevitable for illegal drugs to be imported and sold in the United States. We might as well be the ones to benefit from it and control the market in this country.

I understand how you must feel. But, there does not seem to be any other way to generate the needed funds covertly. I believe that the benefits, resulting from the advances in technology, will outweigh the damage that is done to the American people. You must think of the greater good involved. Besides, people are not being forced to take the drugs. They do so on their own volition."

Admiral Forrestal is enraged by what he has just heard and shouts, "But this is wrong! We will be breaking the law. Once we cross that line, we will never be able to go back. Something this big is bound to become exposed. And, when that happens, we will all have to answer to the American people."

Dr. Bush says, "I see no sense in continuing this conversation any further. I can tell that you are under a lot of stress regarding this. I believe that you need to take some time off and get some rest."

5/22/49 Forrestal's Room at Bethesda Naval Hospital

Admiral Forrestal is depressed as he lies on a hospital bed. He becomes overjoyed to see his brother enter the room. They hug and the admiral says, "Boy, am I ever glad to see you!"

His brother says, "I came as soon as I could, James. What's wrong?"

"I have been forced to resign and my personal diary has been confiscated by the White House. They brought me here, they say, out of a concern for my health. I have been placed here under the care of a Doctor Raines. He says that I am suffering from severe depression, anxiety, and acute paranoia."

His brother says, "I can tell that you are under the influence of drugs."

"I fear for my life here. There are people who are out to get me."

"Now, take it easy, James. I am going to make certain that you are discharged from this hospital right away. I'll be right back."

"Okay. But, please hurry."

His brother says, "Don't worry. I will." And he rushes out of the room.

Two men, wearing hospital orderly uniforms, enter the room. They grab the Admiral, pull a sheet from his bed, and take him across the hall to a small kitchen. One man ties the Admiral's hands behind him with the sash of the Admiral's robe. The other man ties one end of the sheet around the Admiral's neck and the other end to a radiator heater. Then, they throw the Admiral out of the 16th story window. The sheet tears and the body falls to the ground. The two men quickly leave the hospital. [3] [4]

Soon afterward, the brother discovers what has happened and rushes to the Admiral's body that is lying on the ground outside. Doctor Raines tells the brother, "I was afraid that this might happen. I have been treating the Admiral for Involutional Melancholia Psychosis.

He believed that he was the victim of plots and conspiracies of unidentified people who were out to get him." [5]

The brother shouts, "He was the Secretary of Defense, for crying out loud! Why didn't you believe him and provide him with some protection?"

"This is a naval hospital, Sir. The Admiral was perfectly safe here."

"Is that so, Doctor? Then, perhaps you can tell me how my brother was able to hang himself with his arms tied behind his back." The doctor does not say anything and just walks away.

8/14/49 In Evens' Office at Wright Field, Dayton, Ohio

Stan Edwards enters Major Evens' office, closes his door, and places a CIA folder on his desk. Then he takes a seat and says "You may want to have a look at this."

Evens opens the file, begins reading the cover sheet, and asks, "What is this? Another sighting of a UFO by a couple of ranchers?"

Stan says, "That's what I thought until I read the part where the sheriff of Catron County, New Mexico, took several days to make his way to the remote crash site near Datil, New Mexico. Have a look at his photographs, Tom."

Evens has a look at the pictures and shouts, "Holly Smokes! This craft looks just like the one we recovered near Roswell. I always knew there was a second craft that crashed there, but we never found it until now."

Stan says, "Yep. After the sheriff reported what he saw, a recovery team from Sandia Army Base took custody of all evidence, including six bodies. Everything was identical to what you discovered back in 1947. However, the bodies were in an advanced state of decaying. They had been in the desert for the past two years. Animals and time got to those bodies. The remains were transported to Sandia Base and eventually onto Los Alamos." [6]

Evens says, "I'll bet this never makes it into the files of Project Grudge."

9/18/49 At White Sands Proving Ground, N.M.

Major Evens is present to witness the launch of a V-2 rocket. He is seated in the VIP section of the Launch Control Room. It is a reinforced concrete building with a large window facing the rocket on the launch pad. There are three rows of consoles, inside the room, which are manned by scientists and engineers. A large clock on the front wall shows that it is almost 3:00 PM. The countdown proceeds smoothly. At exactly 3:00 PM, smoke and flames billow out from the bottom of the rocket as it lifts off from the launch pad without any problems.

Just then, a technician shouts, "Launch Director, Emissions Monitoring here. I detect broadband emissions coming from the northeast. The rocket begins swerving wildly out of control and is detonated in mid air.

An Air Force Captain shouts, "There!" and points out of the window. Everyone looks to see a flying disc hover for a few seconds and then fly away at an incredible speed.

Evens asks the Launch Director, "What happened?"

"Come with me", the Director says. They walk into a briefing room and close the door. The Director says, "You have been asked to come here in order to investigate a number of V-2 rocket launches that have failed. It had been assumed that the rockets were interfered with in some way because UFOs have been seen in the area during the launches. So, special monitoring equipment was installed and it has just confirmed electromagnetic pulses emanating from the UFO that we all just saw after the launch. I had to detonate the rocket soon after the launch because it started maneuvering out of control. But, now we know what is effecting the rockets. So, we are going to begin shielding the navigation systems and circuitry in order to counteract the jamming."

"What was in the payload of the rockets?"

"These were high altitude rocket launches to study radiation effects on living organisms. Why?"

Evens thinks about this and says, "It has been reported that alien craft have often been seen hovering over sensitive nuclear installations, especially in New Mexico. They were referred to as "green fireballs" and they have been found to cause a reduction in the amount of nuclear radiation that was in our atmosphere. I believe that the UFO may have been there to prevent damage to our environment." [7]

The Director says, "Are you crazy? That's that dumbest thing that I have ever heard!"

12/27/49 In the Press Room of the Pentagon

At a press conference, General Vandenberg walks out on stage and stands behind a podium. He says, "Gentlemen of the press, I am Lieutenant General Hoyt Vandenberg, the Air Force Chief of Staff. I am here to announce that, due to a lack of interest by the public, Project Grudge, the official investigation into flying saucer sightings, is being closed. A final report will be made available to the press as soon as it has been completed."

A reporter asks, "Just what, exactly, is the report going to conclude regarding UFOs, General?"

"The report will contain the case studies of 237 incidents by a number of experts, including Dr. J. Allen Hynek. They have been able to explain all but 23% of the sightings and that the Air Force's Aeromedical Laboratory believes that there are plausible psychological explanations for the remaining cases." [8] [9]

Another reporter asks, "Is it the Air Force's official position that there is nothing of substance to the UFO sightings, General?"

Vandenberg says, "This press conference is over", and he walks out of the room.

In the next room, the General's aide tells General Vandenberg, "Sir, another disk has just crashed. There is one fatality and one living alien. It is being confined at the Los Alamos facility in New Mexico." [10]

The General says, "Hot damn! Another living EBE. Is it healthy?"

"I don't know, General. The report did not say."

Vandenberg says, "Get a call through to Los Alamos on a secure line. I want to speak with the man in charge, right away. If word of this gets out, there is going to be hell to pay."

"Yes, sir!"

1/12/50 Facility YY-II at Los Alamos National Laboratories

CIA Director Roscoe Hillenkoetter is escorting General Hoyt Vandenberg though the facility and tells him, "EBE-2 was treated for minor injuries sustained during the recent crash of its craft, but it is in good health in another area of the complex." The two men enter a guarded room after a code is entered on a keypad. They stand in front of a two-way mirror and look into another room where EBE-1 is sitting at a table with a man that is wearing a lab coat.

Hillenkoetter says, "This is EBE-1. It is a male entity. The man there with him is Dr. Mendoza. He has developed a good working relationship with the entity. We have learned a great deal from EBE-1 since an operation was performed that enabled it to talk. It is extremely intelligent and it has learned to speak English quickly, mainly by listening to the military personnel who are responsible for its safety and care. It helped us learn from all of the items found at the two crash sites and showed us how some of the items worked, such as a communications device.

"The alien civilization that the EBEs come from is what we call the Eben Society. That was not a name they gave us. It was a name we chose. Their life span is between 350 and 400 Earth years long. EBE-1 explained that they live in a star system known as Zeta Reticuli, which is about 40 light-years from Earth. The Eben planet is within that star system. It took the EBE spaceship nine of our months to travel the 40 light-years, which means that they can travel faster than the speed of light. Time is very different on the Eben Planet, which, by the way, we call SERPO. Their day is approximately 40 hours long. That is measured by the movement of their two suns." [11]

The Director presses a button on an intercom device and says, "Okay, you can bring her in now."

They then hear, "Acknowledged, Sir. We will bring her over now."

General Vandenberg asks, "Who are they bringing over?"

He is told, "They are bringing over EBE-2 to meet with EBE-1 for the first time. EBE-2 is a female." Just then, EBE-1 stands up and looks around.

The General asks, "Can he hear us? He seems to know that something is about to happen."

"No, he cannot hear us. There must be some sort of psychic connection made with EBE-2 when she was removed from her enclosure."

The two men watch as a door opens and the other EBE enters the room followed by two military policemen. The three people walk to one end of the room and watch as the two EBEs slowly walk towards one another and touch each other's head. There are no other emotions expressed as they just touch and look at each other. The General says, "I don't like it. They are probably conveying information between the two of them on how to deal with us humans. I want them kept separate except for visitations of only two hours a day. We need to have EBE-2 independently verify everything that EBE-1 has told us. I also don't like referring to them as EBE-1 and 2."

"Okay, considering their large heads like the Peanuts characters, let's call them Charlie and Lucy." [12]

The General says, "Fine. I've seen enough" and he storms out of the room.

4/18/50 Air Technical Intelligence Center, Wright Field

The chief of Air Force Intelligence, Major General C.P. Cabell, is being briefed by Lt. Colonel N.R. Rosengarten, who is the chief of ATIC's Aircraft and Missiles Branch, along with the only ATIC investigator, Lt. Jerry Cummings. They have recently returned from investigating a series of spectacular sightings at the Army's Signal Corps Center at Fort Monmouth, New Jersey. Lieutenant Colonel Rosengarten tells General Cabell, "Sir, it is just not possible to investigate the UFO incidents properly with the funding and manpower that we have been allotted. The military officers, and the representatives of Republic Aircraft, have all complained about the quality of the work being done by the investigators of Project Grudge." [13]

The General's face turns bright red with anger as he tells the two officers, "That is because you are not using the funds and manpower, that you have, effectively. You will reorganize the entire UFO project and get the job done with the resources that you already have. Is that clear?"

"Yes, sir!"

The General stomps out of the room and Lt. Colonel Rosengarten tells Lt. Cummings, "Well, so much for trying to reason with the man. I think that I will ask Ed Ruppelt, an intelligence officer at ATIC, to reorganize Project Grudge." [14]

Lt. Cummings says, "I think that is a wise decision, sir. Ruppelt is trained as an aeronautical engineer and would know how to file the reports."

11/14/51 In a Majestic-12 Meeting at the Pentagon

Dr. Vannover Bush tells the group, "Gentlemen, I am pleased to report that funds are now available for the construction of a base to begin testing the recovered alien technology."

Admiral Hillenkoetter says, "The naval weapons testing site at Groom Lake, Nevada has been selected for this purpose. Its code name is DREAMLAND, which stands for Data Repository, Examination, And Maintenance Land, under Project Redlight."

Dr. Bush says, "The next item of business is the condition of the first Extraterrestrial Biological Entity. It is showing signs of being in poor health and its condition is slowly deteriorating. The EBE is under the care of Dr. Mendoza, who is doing everything that he can in order to keep the entity alive. [15]

"The next item is the fact that there have been a number of recent security leaks, which must be dealt with. Information has leaked out that discs are stored at Wright-Patterson Air Force Base in Dayton, Ohio. Viking Press has published a version of the Forrestal diaries. And, General Douglas MacArthur has made a public statement that interplanetary war is inevitable. I think we all can agree that it is time for General MacArthur to resign from military service.

"Finally, we should give consideration to the fact that President Truman is currently proposing the creation of an agency to deal with national security matters. It was found that current efforts fell far short of requirements and that the U.S. was unable to exploit intelligence information to its fullest potential. This comes after the Armed Forces Security Agency had been increased to 8,500 people and given a budget of 60.9 billion dollars. But, unlike the CIA, the National Security Agency will be established under total secrecy and will be free of any statute that would restrict the permissible scope of its activities. We may want to consider that the NSA could be used to monitor and contain the secret of the alien presence, decipher alien communications, and eventually establish an ongoing dialogue with any alien species that it can communicate with." [16]

7/27/52 The Aerial Phenomena Group at Wright Field

Stan Edwards enters the office of Major Evens, lays a folder on the desk, and plops down in a chair. He says, "This should make for some very interesting reading. It's the intelligence report on the UFO incidents over Washington, D.C."

Evens opens the folder and begins reading. The report says that on July 19, 1952, more than eight UFOs were tracked on radar at Andrews Air Force Base and Washington National Airport. These objects flew over Washington's most restricted airspace, passing over both the Capitol Building and the White House. [17] [18]

The objects would cruise along at low speeds of 100 to 130 miles per hour and then accelerate at an estimated speed of over 7,300 MPH. They were observed by experienced pilots and air traffic controllers over a period of several hours. F-94 military jets were sent aloft to intercept the bogeys. But, every time that the jets would close in, the UFOs would accelerate and disappear. The UFOs continued to reappear, over restricted airspace, during the entire weekend.

When the sightings first began, news reporters pressed into the radar room at National Airport to watch the UFOs cavort. However, the media were quickly ordered out of the building in order to prevent them from learning the reality of UFOs, should one be brought down. The sightings became front-page news throughout the whole country with headlines that read "Fiery Objects Outrun Jets over Capital - Investigation Veiled in secrecy Following Vain Chase" and "Jets Alerted for Saucers - Interceptors Chase Lights in D.C. Skies".

Responding to the clamor, Major General John Samford called a news conference for the afternoon of July 29. It was speculated that the hubbub over Washington was caused by temperature inversions, a natural phenomenon, which reflects light and can be picked up on radar. The news media then reported, "Air Force Debunks Saucers as Just Natural Phenomena." [19]

Evens says, "Ever since March, when the UFO investigations project was upgraded with the new name of Aerial Phenomena Group and a new code name of Project Blue Book, they have been engrossed in an effort to reorganize. They were completely unprepared for the rash of sightings that ensued. They were getting about 20 reports a day when these incidents over Washington began. Ed Ruppelt investigated and found that UFOs had been seen frequently over Washington (fifty targets were tracked on May 23 alone) and that each night there was a sighting, the temperature inversions were never strong enough to affect radar. Ruppelt also found that, while inversions occurred almost every night during June, July, and August, the slow moving, solid radar targets appeared only during the times that the sightings occurred. For that reason, the Washington National Airport Sightings are still classified as unknown."

Stan says, "Well, that's not going to make General Vandenberg very happy."

Evens says, "Maybe not. But he should be pleased to know that in the years of 1950 and 1951 combined, there were 379 sightings reported to the UFO project. Of those, all but 49 were explained to the satisfaction of the project officers. The sightings from 1947 to 1949 have also been periodically reviewed, and new solutions have been attached to the old cases. And, the situation now is out of control for Ed Ruppelt, who has been trying to organize everything." [20]

"Yes. That should make General Vandenberg very happy, indeed."

1/12/50 Facility YY-II at Los Alamos National Laboratories

The CIA Director and Dr. Mendoza are discussing the deteriorating condition of Charlie while they look through a two-way mirror at him. Admiral Hillenkoetter asks, "Why is he in such poor health?"

Dr. Mendoza states, "I believe that he is dying from natural causes, but I don't know for sure. We don't have any standards to compare EBE's body conditions with."

"How much longer does he have to live?"

The doctor says, "I just don't know."

The Director thinks for a minute and says, "Listen doctor, the situation is becoming desperate with numerous UFO sightings all over the country and even UFOs flying over the Capital and White House in Washington DC. A scientist has just figured out how the Eben communication device worked when he connected it to an energy source found in the Eben craft. It is vitally important that Charlie helps us to operate the device in order to establish communications with his race and try to bring the situation under control." [21]

The doctor shakes his head and says, "I will do what I can."

11/18/52 In President-Elect Eisenhower's Office

A preliminary briefing is being presented for President-elect Dwight Eisenhower by Admiral Roscoe Hillenkoetter. He states, "Recently, an Extraterrestrial Biological Entity that was captured after the crash of a UFO near Roswell, New Mexico in 1947 has died. However, this entity was of great assistance to us, and before his death, he sent six messages to his home world and we received several signals back in early fall of this year.

"The first message that EBE-1 sent was just to let his planet know that he was alive. The second message explained the crash in 1947 and the death of his crew. The third message asked for a rescue craft for him. The fourth message suggested a formal meeting with leaders of Earth. The fifth message suggested an exchange program and the sixth message provided landing coordinates for any future rescue or visitation mission to Earth.

"The incoming messages gave a time and date according to the Eben date and time system, and confirmed a landing location. However, once the message was translated by EBE-1, it was determined the date was over 10 years away. Fearing that EBE-1, who was sick at that point, did not translate the message correctly, our scientists began to translate the message, based on the Eben language that was taught to us by EBE-1. The entity assisted us as long as he was alive. But once he died, then we were on our own. We were able to translate about 30% of the Eben language, but complex sentences and numbers could not be recognized. We are making every effort to improve communications, but the outcome remains uncertain.

"The implications for national security are of continuing importance in that the motives and ultimate intentions of these visitors remain completely unknown. In addition, a significant upsurge in the surveillance activity of these craft, beginning in May and continuing through the autumn of this year, has caused considerable concern that new developments may be imminent.

"It is for these reasons, as well as the obvious international and technological considerations and the ultimate need to avoid a public panic at all costs, that the Majestic-12 Group remains of the unanimous opinion that imposition of the strictest security precautions should continue without interruption into the new administration. At the same time, contingency plan MJ-1949-04P/78 (Top Secret - Eyes Only) should also be held in continued readiness should the need to make a public announcement present itself."

Eisenhower says, "Thank you, Admiral, for that fine briefing. Once I officially become President, I intend to sign two new Executive Orders: 10-1 and 10-2. These orders will make it official for the Council on Foreign Relations, through the advisory committees of Majestic-12 and the Jason Scholars to provide direct assistance to the President of the United States." [22] [23]

12/14/52 In a Briefing Room at Wright-Patterson A.F.B.

Major Evens and Stan Edwards are present along with H. Marshall Chadwell, the Assistant Director of Scientific Intelligence, and Dr. H.P. Robertson. General Vandenberg enters the room and says, "Thank you Mr. Chadwell, for coming. Your memo to General Walter Smith, the Director of Central Intelligence, has been well received. The Air Force and CIA agree with your recommendation that, and I quote, 'In order to minimize risk of panic, a national policy should be established as to what should be told to the public regarding the phenomena.'

"The Air Force has added more than 1,500 sightings to the files and, more importantly, over 300 of them are unidentified. The situation has become intolerable. Part of the solution, we believe, would be the creation of a scientific panel that would investigate the UFO evidence and submit a public report that would minimize the risk of panic."

Chadwell says, "I will be happy to announce the creation of a scientific advisory board, chaired by Dr. Robertson here, to investigate UFOs and submit a final report."

The General passes a document to Robertson and tells him, "You will find this document to be of value when the panel has concluded it's investigation and is ready to submit it's final report."

The report states that nothing has been found to suggest that UFOs are anything other than misidentifications, hoaxes, and weather and astronomical phenomena. However, it also states that UFOs do, after a fashion, pose a threat to national security. Too many reports about UFOs at the wrong time could mask a Soviet attack on the United States. The report recommends that more competent screening or filtering of reported sightings should be implemented. This screening process can be accomplished with an educational program. The document states that the educational program should have two major aims: training and debunking. The training aim would result in proper recognition of unusually illuminated objects such as balloons, aircraft, meteors, mirages, and noctilucent clouds. The debunking aim would result in reducing public interest in flying saucers by using the mass media to reduce the current gullibility of the public and consequently their susceptibility to clever hostile propaganda. [24] [25]

Dr. Robertson says, "I concur with the views expressed in this document, Sir. With your permission, I would like to get started on this right away."

Vandenberg says, "I am pleased with your enthusiasm for this project. I would like to introduce you to Major Evens and Stan Edwards. They will provide you with whatever you need from the Project Blue Book files. Mr. Edwards, will you show these gentlemen the way to the Aerial Phenomenon Group?"

Stan says, "Certainly, General" and asks the two men to follow him.

The General says, "Major Evens, will you please stay behind? I would like to have a word with you." Once the others have left the room, Vandenberg asks for a status report on Project Blue Book.

Evens tells the General, "Sir, the investigative emphasis of Project Blue Book is beginning to erode. Ed Ruppelt is planning to demand that more investigators be found."

The General says, "The project is becoming too visible to the public. I am going to have the investigative responsibility moved from Blue Book to the 4602nd Air Intelligence Service Squadron. There will soon be a new Air Force Regulation, 200-2, which will require ATIC to be notified about UFO investigations, but not necessarily Project Blue Book. Project Blue Book will then be effectively eliminated, although it will continue to exist." [26]

Evens tells the General, "Sir, I do not believe that Ruppelt is going to like that very much."

Vandenberg says, "I am not concerned about hurting Ed Ruppelt's feelings. You have done a fine job, Major. Effective immediately, I am promoting you to the rank of Lieutenant Colonel."

Lt. Colonel Evens thanks the General, but he feels as though he has betrayed a good cause in order to gain a promotion

Formal Contact

3/27/53 In the Situation Room of the White House

President Eisenhower enters the room, sits in his chair overlooking a video monitor, and says, "Alright General, what is the situation?"

General Vandenberg clears his throat and states, "Well, Mr. President, the large object, that was discovered by astronomers earlier this year, will soon be in a position where it will have to change course, if there is going to be any possibility of it coming close to Earth. Because of it's immense size, it is highly probable that it is nothing more than a wayward meteor and that it will pass harmlessly through our solar system. However, in any case, we should know soon enough if it is an intelligently guided spacecraft."

The General points at the viewing screen and explains, "This is the view of the object through a high powered telescope." He then points out the constantly changing digital displays and explains that they indicate the tracking information of the object. The General says, "Please note that the movement is constant."

Just then, President Eisenhower says, "Not any more."

Everyone looks at the monitor to see that the object is slowly veering away from its previous trajectory. The General says, "Now, let's not jump to any hasty conclusions. This may only be the result of the object reacting to the gravitational forces in our solar system."

The monitor shows the object in the center of the screen again and the digital displays indicate the new tracking information. A mathematician, sitting at the large table, is busy working on the new tracking information with his slide rule. He checks his figures, double checks, and is then heard to say, "Mr. President, my calculations indicate that the object is angling to intersect with the Earth."

The President states, "It would appear that the object is intelligently controlled. This is either a prelude to an invasion or it may just be a cultural visit. In either case, it would appear that direct contact with an alien race is imminent. General, I authorize our military to go to defensive condition 3 (DEFCON-3). I want our military forces ready for any eventuality. Is that clear?"

Charles Wilson, the Secretary of Defense, responds with, "Yes, Mr. President."

Eisenhower then tells the Secretary of State, "Mr. Dulles, I want you to begin notifying the major governments of the world with regard to the current situation. However, I must stress the necessity to keep this secret in order to prevent a worldwide panic.

Just then, a telephone rings and the Secretary of Defense answers it. He listens for a while and then says, "Mr. President, electromagnetic signals have just been detected emanating from space." [1]

The President asks, "Are the signals in English?"

"We do not know, Sir. We do not currently have any communications equipment for that range of frequencies."

The President tells him, "Well, create the equipment right away so that we can find out what the intentions are of these extraterrestrial visitors as soon as possible. At least, I hope that they are only visiting."

5/2/53 In General Vandenberg's Office at the Pentagon

Lt. Col. Evens reports, as ordered, before General Vandenberg. The General says, "Be seated, Colonel. I have a new assignment for you. You are being reassigned here to the Pentagon where you will take command of Project Sigma. Communications has been established with a group of gray-skinned aliens, which are commonly referred to as Greys. They say that they are part of a Federation. Beyond that, not much else is known about their society." [2]

Evens says, "Yes, Sir. What are my responsibilities?"

The General says, "You will be responsible for maintaining the secure communication links between the National Security Agency and all alien cultures that are willing to communicate with us. This is a very important assignment. A lot of very important people will be watching to see how well you perform this mission." The General hands Evens a file and says, "I wish you luck with your new assignment, Colonel. Dismissed."

Evens takes the file, says, "Thank you for this opportunity, General", and he leaves the office in true military fashion.

10/19/53 In the project Sigma Center at the Pentagon

Evens is in charge of a small group of civilian engineers and Air Force technicians which operate and maintain all alien communications equipment. His group has sent several messages to the Eben race in the last six months, but there have been no messages received. It has been very difficult for his group to function on its own ever since EBE-1 died. But, they will continue to fine-tune their efforts in the hope of re-establishing communications once again. [3]

Another group under Evens' command has been involved with monitoring the radio signals emanating from the large object in Earth orbit and deciphering what is being communicated. They are now ready to establish two-way communications. After insuring that everything is functioning properly, Evens monitors the following messages between an entity, by the name of Kirok, and the National Security Agency:

X: What is the purpose for the abductions and mutilations done by some alien species?

K: It is part of the natural process.

X: Explain this natural process.

K: All experience is chosen by participants.

X: Would you care to comment on what is happening now with the aliens, the different governments on Earth? How do you see this from your viewpoint?

K: There are many paths of probabilities. All scenarios will happen that people conceive of.

X: Are you saying that we will continue to create reality out of existing situations?

K: Yes.

X: Does Kirok perform a function in your society?

K: He is the one who stretches reality.

X: Is the Earth scheduled for geological upheaval?

K: That is possible. The upheaval would be severe for some and not for others. Most will perceive changes.

X: What is the ultimate cause of this?

K: Agreements are made with the Whole with Itself...regarding its own evolution.

X: Are you aware of a group called the Network?

K: Yes. This is a group formed in a military manner.

X: From what origin does this group come?

K: From different origins.

X: Are they for the Many or for the Individual?

K: Ultimately they are for the Law of One.

X: There is another group allegedly called the Confederation.

K: This group is much larger than the first.

X: What is their orientation?

K: They exercise what they perceive to be control over others.

X: Are they for the individual or for the group?

K: They work both together and against each other.

X: There is another group which is allegedly called the Inter dimensional Association of Free Worlds. Would you comment on that?

K: This has to do with influence that is somewhat removed from our levels.

X: Tell us more.

K: I cannot determine the reason for the influence of the third group.

X: There are several groups called Greys. Where do they come from, Zeta Reticuli?

K: They come from within the whole Orion system.

X: Preceding the Essessani?

K: Yes.

X: The Essessani are our children, in essence?

K: -

X: There is a situation where within a two or three cycles of our sun, it has been said that there is a great grouping of beings coming this way. What is the purpose of this group?

K: Its purpose is survival.

X: Their survival?

K: Yes.

X: What of us?

K: You will be easy for them to deal with.

X: Is their origin Alpha Draconis?

K: We do not know.

X: Do you know about the Draco?

K: Yes. Their intentions are survival.

X: Are they a negative group?

K: They are different from you.

X: Are humans meant to assist them?

K: Probably not at this level...you are too different.

X: There have been comments amongst some that would indicate that this planet is hollow. Is this true?

K: There is more to it than the surface, yes.

X: Are you aware of the interactions between the Federation and the United States Government?

K: No, not beyond...the government has...all the major governments have information...contact with...non-resident beings. [4]

Evens gets the impression, from Kirok's answers, that the Federation is not being totally forthcoming with information that was requested from them. He is certain that the answers appear to be elusive and noncommittal. However, he feels that there is a lot of information that can be gleaned from the answers that were provided.

It appears to Evens that there are many groups of alien races which were referred to as the Network, Confederation, Federation, Draco, and Inter-dimensional Association of Free Worlds. There were references to beings originating from Alpha Draconis, the Greys being from the Orion Constellation, entities inside the Earth, and the Essessani as being related to humans. If Kirok was speaking the truth, then the Network is a military group, from different origins, which function according to the Law of One. The Confederation is a larger group of manipulative tyrants. And, the Federation is at a different level than the Inter-dimensional Association of Free Worlds. But, Evens wants to know what these beings look like, where they come from, and what their intentions are with regard to humanity and this planet. He wishes he could talk to Stan and find out what the CIA may know about these other beings.

12/7/53 At the Project Sigma Center in the Pentagon

Evens also monitors the communications received from people with psychic abilities who channel information while in a meditative state. Once in this receptive state, other entities are able to communicate through the meditator's body functions. This can result in "automatic writing" or "charging". Automatic writing is the process whereby an entity controls the fingers of hands placed over a keyboard to type out information. Charging is where the mediator's mouth is used to issue forth another's voice in order to communicate verbally. [5]

Evens watches as a psychic woman enters the meditative state and begins to channel information from her mouth with a man's voice. What follows is a dialogue between the channeled entity and a representative of the National Security Agency: "Greetings. My name is Patier. I am from a small cluster of stars called the Pleiades. The Pleiadians are a race of humans, not unlike yourselves, who have advanced thousands of years beyond your technology and spiritual understanding."

Question: "Where, exactly, in the Pleiades, do you come from?"

Answer: "Of the seven stars, which make up the Pleiades cluster in the Taurus Constellation, we come from the star known as Taygeta. There are nine planets that revolve around Taygeta. Four of these planets are inhabited by the Pleiadians. The home world is the planet Erra, with manufacturing processes confined to the other planets."

Question: "What is it like on your home planet of Erra?"

Answer: "It is just 10% smaller than Earth. The atmosphere there is similar to Earth's except that it has a much higher oxygen content. Nature there is also very similar, especially since samples of plants, minerals, and animals have been taken to the Pleiades and developed there. The surface gravity is slightly less than on Earth. A day on Erra is six tenths of a second less than on Earth. We have 13 months there, with a compensation every 23 years. Our year lasts a quarter of a day longer than on Earth."

Question: "What are the people like who live there?"

Answer: "The Pleiadians are humans, just like you, with few physical differences. Our skin is whiter than yours as a result of higher evolution. We are several million years older than you are as spirit forms. The Pleiadians live a more spiritual life style. This means that they are experiencing and learning more with their spiritual senses than with their material senses. There are no medical problems. They are able to control their health through psychic balance. The life span for a Pleiadian is more than 700 years.

"It is common for the Pleiadians to marry and have families, but the population is strictly controlled. Our society has eliminated all emotional problems such as envy and jealousy. Over thousands of years of development, our thought processes are tuned into one another at very high levels. If visitors to Erra project negative thoughts, they are asked to leave the planet so as to not disturb the wonderful balance of thought energy. The ability to project thoughts to another place on the planet is very common and it is the socially accepted method of visiting."

Question: "What is the society like?"

Answer: "Only 400 million humans live on Erra. Population control has come about in a desire to keep our society spread out and able to share the resources of the planet equally. Pleiadians on Erra live in a utopian world free of pollution, war, hunger, and disease thanks to advanced technology and spiritual awareness. Because the population communicates by telepathy, there is no dishonesty. All basic necessities are provided freely, and anything beyond that is acquired through individual barter. There is no money and, hence, no irrational grasping for wealth and power. The Pleiadians have no economics as you know of, but do have a system of sharing the resources of their world. Material possessions are all provided, based on individual contributions to the community."

"There are no large cities with towering buildings as on Earth. But instead, the small population of Erra is spread out into smaller communities that span the planet, connected by a series of sentient tubeways that not only transport the population, but educate and inform them along the way. The people live in more rural settings and keep a distance from each other. Nearly all of the manufacturing and production of products for living is done on other planets in our solar system so as to not upset the ecology on Erra. We have long since developed a balance with nature that is well protected. The planet has a green atmosphere, which is controlled, and it contributes to our health and stress-free way of life."

Question: "What is the government like?"

Answer: "What government is necessary is provided by a 'High Council' composed of the wisest and most evolved Pleiadians. Any changes to our social order must be approved by a vote of the highest percentage of the population. The Pleiadians are part of a federation of civilized worlds that live by the words of an advanced race in the Andromeda Galaxy. This race is so spiritually evolved that they no longer require a physical body. They are almost beings of light energy."

Question: "What is it that you want with humanity?"

Answer: "It is our desire to stimulate the human consciousness through the dissemination of information so that you can make the necessary changes to create a new world based on Saalome, which is a Pleiadian word meaning 'peace in wisdom'." [6]

Question: "How do you propose to accomplish this?"

Answer: "We desire to meet with your President and discuss this with him."

Response: "I will relay your request and provide you with an answer at this same time tomorrow."

Answer: "This is acceptable. Farewell until then."

12/8/53 At the Project Sigma Center in the Pentagon

Evens is very excited as he watches the psychic woman enter the meditative state. After a long time has passed, the woman begins to speak in a man's voice and says, "Hello. This is Patier calling Earth. Are you there?" Answer: "Yes, we are here. I am happy to report that the President is looking forward to meeting with you on February 20th, 1954 at noon, local time, on the runway of Muroc Air Force Base in California."

Response: "This is acceptable. We will be there. Please thank the President for meeting with us. Farewell until then."

2/20/54 On the Runway of Muroc Air Force Base

On the 15th of February, Evens was ordered to join the President's entourage, along with the psychic woman, as they traveled to Palm Springs, California. His orders were to insure that the psychic woman was present at the meeting and prepared to assist in communications with the Pleiadians. The public was told that the President was going on vacation, at the ranch of a friend, Paul Helms.

On the morning of the 20th, Evens, and the psychic woman, join the President, along with a small group of people, as they secretly leave the ranch for the trip to Muroc Air Force Base. They drive to the side of the runway and wait. Evens is ordered to have the woman attempt to make contact with the Pleiadians. However, when she tries to do so, nothing happens. Evens becomes nervous as everyone looks to him for results.

Just then, someone points and shouts "Look there!"

Everyone looks toward the runway. There is a disk-shaped craft hovering about ten feet from the ground, at a distance of about a hundred yards before them. Then suddenly, two more disks appear on each side of the first. Landing gear is extracted and the three craft land. Hatches, on the underside of the craft, are lowered and several human-looking beings exit their craft. They are very handsome and beautiful beings with a lighter complexion on their skin. They are wearing beautiful, long flowing robes. Evens and the psychic woman join the President, along with a small group of other people, as they walk toward the Pleiadians. Evens hopes that everything goes smoothly. [7]

Just then, one of the male Pleiadians says, in perfect English, "Hello. Thank you for meeting with us. I am Patier."

The President says, "It is nice to meet you. My name is Dwight Eisenhower. I am the leader of the United States of America. What would you like to discuss?"

Patier says, "We have come to warn you about the intentions of the Greys and to offer you our help."

The President asks, "What do you mean about the Greys?"

Patier states, "A race of beings from the Orion Constellation have a large craft in orbit around this planet and your government has been in communications with this group. These beings were once human as you and I, but after surviving long wars with nuclear weapons, they have become stunted and misshapen. We have come to warn you of their evil strategy to take the Earth for themselves. They are using humanity as raw materials for their effective re-birth as a thriving race. They claim to be from a dying planet and need your help. But, their actual intentions are to subjugate and control humanity covertly, or otherwise overtly if ne-cessary."

The President asks, "What are your intentions toward humanity?"

Patier says, "We are here to observe, assist certain especially suited and compliant Earth people to become prophets, support the independent free-will-based spiritual evolution of hu-manity, execute the evacuation of Earth peoples in certain circumstances, and help to prevent planetary and possible subsequent interplanetary disaster."

Eisenhower asks, "Why don't you appeal to the people of Earth directly?"

Patier says, "The Pleiadians are not able, by virtue of adherence to certain 'Galactic Laws' of 'restraint and non-interference' in developing planetary cultures, to effect mass contact un-less the populace of that planet clearly requests and is ready for it. Thus, only through proph-ets, and contact with world leaders, are we able to effect any change to the damage being per-petrated by malevolent entities from other worlds."

The President asks, "Would the Pleiadians be willing to provide us with advanced tech-nology so that we can combat the malevolent aliens on a more even field of battle?"

Patier says, "Earthkind is not ready to cope with our technology yet. Your people need more spiritual development in order to be able to deal with it. All Earth governments are going to have to destroy all of their nuclear weapons and missiles and teach their people unconditional love and acceptance. You must have a one consciousness and invite us, as a unit. If you do that, we will come and help you. If you do not, then we cannot help you." [8]

Eisenhower says, "What you ask would be difficult to accomplish. But, it would certainly make this planet a much nicer place to live. I will take your requests to my advisers and we shall consider this matter very carefully. I would like to thank you for this opportunity to meet with you. We will contact you again through psychic channels." The President looks at Evens, who nods his head in compliance.

Patier says, "Very well. It has been good meeting with you. We will be ready for your response. Fare well."

Eisenhower says, "Good-bye."

The Pleiadians walk back to their craft, enter them, and fly away.

2/24/54/ In a Majestic-12 Meeting at the Pentagon

Eisenhower tells his advisers what the Pleiadians had told him. He says, "I cannot see how it is possible to get all of the people of the Earth to unite as one and request help from the Pleiadians. But, I'm quite certain that it would make the planet a more peaceful and happier place to live."

Dr. Bush says, "They also stated that we would have to destroy all of our atomic weapons and missiles. I don't think that would be a wise move. What if their intentions are actually malevolent and they want us to destroy the only weapons that we may have to defend ourselves against them?"

The President says, "I don't think they are here to harm us. Besides, do you think we would stand a chance against them?"

Admiral Hillenkoetter says, "Perhaps not, Mr. President. But, the other nations of the world could not possibly be trusted to comply. Think about what you are risking by giving up our nuclear weapons. Before responding to the Pleiadians, I suggest that we initiate diplomatic relations with the Greys. They have offered to share their advanced technology with us. The Greys have said that their abductions of people and mutilations of cattle have only been for medical examination purposes. Who can blame them for that? They would have a great deal to offer us."

President Eisenhower agrees and Project Plato is implemented in order to establish diplomatic relations with the Greys.

3/13/54 At the Project Sigma Center in the Pentagon

Evens has prepared the psychic woman to be ready for the response to the Pleiadians. He is surprised to discover that communications are commencing between the NSA and the Greys. Evens monitors the communications and is astonished to find that diplomatic relations are being established between the U.S. Government and the Greys from the Marcob Empire. He watches as a formal agreement is negotiated. It contains the following provisions:

1. The United States will not reveal the alien presence and will not interfere with alien operations.

2. The United States will allow the aliens to maintain underground bases on United States soil.

3. The United States will allow the aliens to abduct its citizens on a periodic and limited basis for medical examinations with the provision that the people are returned unharmed and without memory of the interaction.

4. The aliens will furnish a periodic list of abductees. This list will be reviewed by the National Security Council.

5. The aliens will provide the United States with technology in beam weaponry, gravitational propulsion, mind control, and implant technology. [9]

In order to formalize this agreement, a meeting, between representatives of the U.S. Government and the Greys, is agreed upon. As a symbol of trust and cultural exchange, it is further agreed that a member from each race will be exchanged at that meeting. The meeting is arranged to take place on April 25th, 1954, at 6pm at Holloman Air Force Base. [10]

4/25/54 On the Runway of Holloman Air Force Base

Evens monitors the Project Sigma equipment and personnel to insure that communications will flow smoothly when the Greys arrive. Each member of the U.S. delegation is wearing a headset with a cable that is linked to Sigma personnel. Whenever any member speaks, their words are typed into a computer, which translates their meaning into signals that are transmitted to the Greys. Communication signals from the Greys are fed through a computer for translation and displayed on a video monitor. A person then pronounces the translation into a microphone for communication to all of the delegates.

Evens is surprised to see Stan here and walking toward him. Evens smiles and says, "Hey Stan, it's good to see you. How are you doing?"

"Fine, Tom. Just fine."

They shake hands and Evens asks, "What are you doing here?"

"I am here, as CIA liaison, to provide you with any information which may be helpful in this operation."

"Great! I am glad to be having your help with this."

Just then, the intercom erupts with, "Attention, attention, radar is tracking three objects coming from the East. One of the objects is much larger than the other two." Everyone watches as the two smaller disks hover over the runway, while a larger disk lands. A hatch opens and several small Greys emerge and walk around the ship. Evens notices that they are different from the dead aliens that he saw near Roswell, N.M. [11]

A U.S. delegate says, "Welcome to Earth". There is no response.

Evens tells Stan, "I have never seen those beings before."

Stan says, "They are referred to as the Belletrax species from the Betelgeuse System in the Orion Constellation. They are a cloned, slave race of beings. They exist as an electronically based space society, with a common social memory complex, which functions in essentially a hive mind. Their brains contain a crystalline network for telepathic communication and group control."

Evens notices that the approximate height of these Greys is between 3.5 to 4.5 feet tall, and they appear to have an average weight of about 40 pounds. Their heads are large in relation to their slender bodies with large black eyes and no hair. Their skin tone has a light gray color to it and they all appear to be wearing a one-piece, tight-fitting, silver-colored diver's type of suit with no pockets, buttons or zippers. Their movement is deliberate, slow, and precise. [12]

Just then, the small Greys part away from the hatch and three tall aliens emerge from the craft.

Evens asks Stan, "Who are the tall beings?"

Stan says, "The two Greys are from the Rigel System, which is also in the Orion Constellation. They are a part of a 'Markabian Empire'. These aliens have technology that is superior to ours. But, they appear to be lacking in the spiritual and social sciences. This is evident in their obvious lack of warmth, emotionality, and respect relative to humans."

Stan says, "These entities maintain a group mindset. The main operative in their social structure is obedience and duty. There are definite hierarchies within their social structures, which provide for each entity to have specific duties to perform. They originally started out as tall blond-haired humanoids from the Lyrae system. But, they were subjected to heavy radiation, due to a nuclear war over a long period of time, which changed their DNA to the point where they became stunted and misshapen. Their glandular structures were also affected, including their reproductive and digestive organs." [13]

Evens notices that the tall Greys appear to be from different species. One type is about eight feet tall and appears more human looking, except for its gray colored skin, a pronounced nose, and slanted black eyes. The other type of tall Grey appears to be about six and a half feet tall and is a taller form of the short Gray species, with similar large heads and large black eyes. [14]

Stan says, "The third tall being is a giant insect creature, about two meters tall that resembles a Praying Mantis. It is an Insectoid species that is no mere insect, but rather an intelligent, but somewhat hyper and jerky-moving, human-like life form that appears to be in control of the Greys. It has a long, narrow face, with long, narrow, large eyes, sharply slanted upward and outward in an almost narrow-V position, giving it an insect-like appearance. It has an extremely thin, long torsos, long, extremely-thin arms which are crooked into a sharp bend at the mid-joint, with the hand and fingers sloping almost vertically downward from the wrist, and legs that are also bent at sharp angles at the mid-joint, creating a crouched pose. The overall effect is the characteristic Praying Mantis look." [15]

Evens and Stan watch as the U.S. delegation and the three tall beings move closer to each other.

One of the delegates says, "Welcome to Earth".

The tall aliens respond with, "We are pleased that you have invited us to meet with you here."

"We are honored that you have come. We are pleased that diplomatic relations have been established and that a formal agreement has been reached between our two peoples."

"We are also pleased."

A U.S. delegate says, "As a sign of good will, we present you with this human as a representative of mankind."

A man steps forward.

The response is, "We accept your representative and present you with a member of our species."

The tall Grey, that appears similar to the short Greys, also steps forward.

Evens and Stan watch as the Grey being is ushered into a large truck that is parked nearby. Then, they see the human representative walk into the craft, followed by the small Greys.

The delegate says, "We would like to thank you for meeting with us and we look forward to a long and mutually beneficial relationship between our peoples."

"We are pleased to have come. We also seek a long and peaceful relationship. Farewell." The delegate says, "Good bye" and the delegation retreats as the two tall entities walk back into their craft. Everyone watches as the three craft ascend quickly out of sight.

Aftermath

5/12/54 The Hotel de Bilderberg, Oostebeek, Holland

The wealthiest and most powerful men in the world are here in this hotel. Among these men, is David Rockefeller, chairman of the board of the Council on Foreign Relations. His economic base is the Chase Manhattan Bank and Standard Oil. Also here is Baron Edmund de Rothschild of the House of Rothschild, C. Douglas Dillon of Dillon Read & Co., Robert McNamara of the World Bank, Sir Eric Roll of S.G. Warburg & Co. Ltd., Pierce Paul Schweitzer of the International Monetary Fund, and George Ball of Lehman Brothers.

These men are socializing with one another in a large meeting room. It is a brightly lit room with a long table in the center and chairs all around it. A podium stands at one end of the table. The room is handsomely decorated with rare paintings on the walls, and a huge crystal chandelier is hanging from the ceiling. Servants walk through the crowd, serving drinks. Someone taps on a glass in order to signal the start of the meeting. The men take their seats, and the servants leave the room, closing the doors behind them.

His Royal Highness, Prince Bernhard of the Netherlands, walks to the podium at the head of the table. The Prince is an important figure in Royal Dutch Petroleum (Shell Oil) and the Societe General de Belgique, a huge conglomerate cartel. He says, "May I have your attention, please. I am Prince Bernhard and I would like to welcome all of you here tonight. It has been 178 years since our forefathers began the great society known as the Illuminati. The leader of the Illuminati was a Jesuit priest by the name of Adam Weishaupt. This society was founded in secrecy and its members branched out to every major nation on this Earth. Today, many generations later, we hold the true power behind the seats of government in all of those countries. We have accomplished a great deal through the secret organizations which we have established in those nations."

"However", he says, "The time has come for us to reunite once again as a single entity in order to guide world affairs toward our ultimate goal of creating a one-world government. This new organization will be known as the 'Bilderbergers', after the site of our first meeting here at the Hotel de Bilderberg. The Bilderbergers will meet once, or sometimes twice, a year to confer on how best to respond to world events and dictate international affairs. The Bilderbergers will be the supreme ruling body that controls our secret organizations, such as the Council on Foreign Relations in America and the Royal Institute for Foreign Affairs in England. There shall be an executive committee that meets all year round to prepare for the meetings and implement our new directives. These meetings will be guarded and held in total secrecy at different sites around the world." [1]

4/1/55 At a Meeting of the Majestic-12 Members

Dr. Vannover Bush is reading a report to the members of this group. Dr. Bush states, "Although the aliens assured the United States Government that the abductions (usually lasting about 2 hours) were merely the ongoing monitoring of developing civilizations, in fact, the purposes for the abductions have turned out to be:

1. Insertion of a 3mm spherical device through the nasal cavity of the abductee into the brain. The device is used for the biological monitoring, tracking and control of the abductee.

2. Implementation of post hypnotic suggestions to carry out a specific activity during a specific time period, the actuation of which would occur within the next 2 to 5 years.

3. Termination of some people so that they could function as living sources for biological material and substances.

4. Termination of some individuals who represent a threat to the continuation of their activity.

5. Effect genetic engineering experiments.

6. Impregnation of human females and early removal of fetuses in order to create cross-bred infants."

Charles Wilson, the Secretary of Defense, says, "Well, I guess that it should be obvious to everyone that the Greys have broken their agreement with us. They are abducting far more people than have reported to the National Security Council, including large numbers of children!"

Dr. Bush says, "It would appear that we have made an error in trusting the Greys."

Secretary Wilson asks, "Well, what are we going to do now?"

Admiral Hillenkoetter says, "There is very little that we can do except try to keep the information classified in order to prevent a panic. It is becoming increasingly obvious that things are not going as planned." [2]

Dr. Bush says, "I am glad that I no longer have to deal with all of this. Under edict number 5411, from the National Security Council, Dr. Henry Kissinger has been assigned as the new chairman of MJ-12. Doctor Kissinger, I stand relieved."

Kissinger walks over to Dr. Bush, shakes his hand, and says, "Thank you very much, Doctor". [3]

Dr. Bush says good-bye to everyone and leaves the room.

Kissinger sits in the chair vacated by the Doctor and states, "Gentlemen, I intend to maintain secrecy regarding everything to do with the aliens. I have learned that the Greys are currently engaged in an active war with a reptilian humanoid species from the Sirius System. I suggest that we attempt to contact the Sirians and ask for their help with regard to the Greys."

Secretary Wilson says, "What if this causes active fighting to break out here on Earth? It could cause great damage and loss of life. I am also concerned about what may happen if the Greys were to find out about what we are attempting to do and retaliate against us. We don't know anything about this other species. What assurances do we have that the Sirians would not be worse for humanity than the Greys?"

Kissinger says, "Well, I think we should communicate with the Sirians and find out just what their intentions are with regard to mankind."

The members of MJ-12 all agree that communications with the Sirians should be attempted. [4]

7/1/55 In the Office of Lt. Col. Evens at the Pentagon

Stan enters Evens' office, takes a seat, and asks, "So Tom, how is everything going?"

Evens smiles and says, "It's going rather well, actually. As you know, we have been having a difficult time trying to communicate with the Eben race. After about 18 months of fine-tuning our efforts, we were able to send two messages and we actually received a reply. With the help of several linguist specialists from several U.S. universities and even several from foreign universities, they have finally been able to translate most of the messages.

"We decided to reply in English and see if the Eben's could translate our language easier than we could theirs. Approximately four months later, we received a reply in broken English with sentences that contained nouns and adjectives, but no verbs. It took us several months to translate the messages. We then sent the Ebens our typed English lessons. Six months later, we received another English message. This time it was clearer, but not clear enough. The Ebens were confusing several different English words and they still failed to complete a proper sentence, but they had attained the basic skill level for them to communicate in English. In one message, they provided us with a form of the Eben alphabet, with the equivalent English letter. The written Eben language consisted of simple characters and symbols, but our linguist specialist had an extremely difficult time comparing the two written languages. Anyway, we are making great progress."

Stan asks, "So, what can I do for you today?"

Evens says, "I asked you to come over because I have been monitoring some communications with a species known as the Sirians and I was curious about them. Does the CIA have any information about this species?"

Stan replies, "Yes. We know quite a bit about them. Hold onto your seat. You're in for quite an education, my friend."

Stan begins with, "Sirius is known as the Dog Star, in the constellation of Canis Major. It is the brightest star in the firmament, and is more than twenty times as luminous as our own sun. The Sirians are a hybrid race with traits that are similar to both human and the Reptilian species. They are similar in appearance to humans except for the eyes, which have vertical slit pupils, and an elongated nose. They have short blond body hair under the tight fitting body suit uniforms that they wear. The Sirians are actively involved in a war with the Greys from the Orion constellation. They have formed an alliance with a tall Blond species against the Greys. They are working in underground bases on Earth for the purposes of abducting humans and programming them to function as biological war machines. They are also performing genetic work there with humanoid forms. [5] [6]

"We have an account from an abductee, who is a twenty year old woman from Las Vegas. She has brought out many interesting factors regarding the Sirians. All of her abductions have featured interactions on board a craft with three specific Sirian males. A Sirian female would also be there on occasion. One Sirian Male wore a red uniform, was 5'4" tall, and had dominance over the other two. He was very aggressive to the point of being mean. Another Sirian Male wore a black uniform, was 5'7" tall, and was generally even-tempered, except when he became upset. He appeared to have worked almost exclusively with genetics. The third Sirian Male wore a black uniform, was 5'0" tall, and he worked mainly with brainwashing equipment. He did not show any emotions at all during the experiences. [7]

"The Sirian Female had long hair, feminine features, and breasts. She wore a blue two-piece uniform with a pendant on her forehead. The males wore tight fitting hoods with round shaped receivers and a short antenna over their left ears. They wore insignias over their left breasts that were triangular in shape with either three parallel lines across it or a winged serpent inside of it. [8]

Evens says, "I'm curious about something, Stan. What did you mean about the Sirians being a hybrid race of both human and a Reptilian species? What Reptilian species are you referring to?"

Stan tells him, "The Reptilians are scaly, rough skinned humanoids that come from the Draco Constellation and the Capella System. These beings have elongated heads and they have dark colored skin. But, there are Reptilians with various colored skins.

"Their leader elite are the "Draco". They have special "wings", which are flaps of skin, supported by long ribs. These can be folded back against the body. They are also known as the "Dragon Race". The Draco are about 8 feet tall and have glowing red eyes. They have the ability to fly and usually operate at night. These entities were the source for some of the legends of the past relating to Gargoyles and Valkyries. It is also apparent that some of the qualities ascribed to vampires have also been taken from these creatures.

"There are elements of their species which do not have wings - the 'soldier class' and 'scientists' have none. They are all 'cold blooded' and must have a balanced environment to maintain body temperature. The 'soldier class' of the species can bury themselves in the ground and wait long periods of time in order to ambush their enemy. If need be they can survive on one very large meal every few weeks or even once a year. As a species, they are well suited for space travel due to their ability to hibernate. These reptoids have scales that protect them from moisture loss and they have no sweat glands.

"The scales, known as scutes, are much larger on their backs, making their skin waterproof. The scales elsewhere on the body are more flexible. They have three fingers with an opposing thumb. The eyes are catlike and large. They have twin nostrils at the end of a short stubby muzzle. They are mostly meat eaters. The mouth is more like a slit, but they do have teeth that are differentiated into incisors, canines, and molars. They average from 6 to 7 feet in height. [9]

"The Reptilians (amphibian) humanoids have been interacting with Earth for ages. Many contactees and abductees repeatedly describe an insignia of a Flying Serpent on the shoulder patch, badge, medallion, or on the helmet. The Serpent Race lives under the ground. The Draconian Empire is made up of Reptilian Humanoids, the Sirians, and various crossbreeds. They have set up bases inside of Venus, the Earth, and other locations. Earth is on their ancient space trade routes.

"Some Reptilians are known to eat humans in the same manner that we eat chicken. Children are preferred because they are generally unpoisoned by substances like caffeine, nicotine, alcohol and other things that adults are saturated with, as a group. The Reptilians don't seem to be dependent on humans as a food source, although part of their experimental work with us is toward the end of future food supplies and production. When they become involved with crossbreeding (humans and Reptilians), they are not doing it for racial survival but for the purpose of creating a subclass (slave race) within their own culture. These halfbreeds are used as biological war machines, slave laborers, etc. They are to be used as someone else's property.

"The Reptilians seem to have little regard for us as living beings. They think we are as ugly and repulsive to them as we ever portrayed them to be, and that we, the human race, are 'as valuable as weeds'. However, they do seem to consider some of us valuable property. One gets the feeling that they will continue to use us as they see fit, and, should we ever become a real problem to them, they would sooner wipe us out than deal with us at all.

"They do not fear us and consider themselves far superior to us in all comparisons. They supposedly consider the surface of this planet to be a poisonous, inhospitable environment and 'allow' us to live here, since they live below the surface and in space. We and our surface environment function as a physical buffer, or living shield, around their home underground." [10]

5/12/56 At White Sands Proving Ground, N.M.

At approximately 3:00 AM, local time, Major William Cunningham and Sergeant. E-6 Jonathon P. Lovette, of the United States Air Force Missile Test Command near Holloman Air Force Base, are out in a field downrange from the launch sites. They are looking for debris from a missile test. Sgt. Lovette walks over the ridge of a small sand dune. Major Cunningham hears Sgt. Lovette scream in terror and agony. The Major, thinking that the Sergeant had been bitten by a snake or something else, runs over the crest of the dune and sees what appears to be a silver disk like object, that is hovering approximately twenty feet off the ground.

Sgt. Lovette is screaming as he is being dragged into the craft by a long snake-like object that is wrapped around his legs. Major Cunningham freezes in terror. He watches as a hatch closes behind the sergeant and the disc ascends very quickly straight up into the sky. He then realizes that he is alone in the desert. When he finally regains his senses, he reports the incident to Missile Control, over his jeep's radio. Missile control reports back that the craft was sighted by radar. The Major is admitted to the White Sands Base Dispensary for observation. Search parties go out into the field looking for Sgt. Lovette.

5/15/56 At White Sands Proving Ground, N.M.

After three days of searching, the nude body of Sgt. Lovette is found approximately 10 miles downrange. The body has been mutilated; the tongue had been removed from the lower portion of the jaw. An incision had been made just under the tip of the chin and extended all the way back to the esophagus and larynx. He had been emasculated. His eyes and genitalia had been removed. The anus had been removed as though a plug was extended all the way up to the colon. There was no sign of blood within the body or anywhere on the ground. [11]

8/12/57 At a Meeting of the Majestic-12 Members

Henry Kissinger is addressing the members of MJ-12. He reports, "Through our channels of communication, the Greys have stated that they are not responsible for what happened to Sergeant Lovette and they do not know who is."

"Yeah, right", says Defense Secretary Wilson. No one in the room believes that the Greys are telling the truth.

Dr. Kissinger also states, "The Sirians have communicated that they are unable to do anything to help us with regard to the Greys because of a truce which is in place on Earth."

Secretary Wilson sarcastically asks, "Okay, Doctor Kissinger, where does that leave us?"

Kissinger says, "I believe that it is time for us to begin considering the possibility that life, as we know it, may not be possible on Earth in the future. We have all seen the report, which states that the course of human evolution will make the planet uninhabitable by the year 2000. So, I believe that it is only prudent for us to discuss various alternatives. Alternative 1 is to allow things to continue the way that they are going and hope that things can be repaired. Alternative 2 is to arrange for underground cities and facilities to be built in order to insure the survival of select groups of people and Alternative 3 is the migration to other planets. Alternatives 2 and 3 are considered to be the most viable. However, in order to implement Alternative 3, alien technology will be needed. In order to enhance the work currently being conducted under Project Redlight, the construction of a facility to test recovered technology, should be given top priority. Are there any objections?" The room becomes silent. [12]

11/25/57 In General Twining's Office at the Pentagon

Lt. Colonel Evens reports, as ordered, to General Twining, who is now the Chairman of the Joint Chiefs of Staff. The General tells Evens, "At ease, Colonel. I would like to commend you for the fine work that you have accomplished with Project Sigma. Effective immediately, you have been promoted to the rank of full Colonel. I wanted to be the one to tell you, myself. Congratulations."

"Thank you, General."

"You deserve it. I recall that you have served your country well throughout the years. Well, your services are needed once again, I'm afraid. You are being transferred to a new facility at Groom Lake, Nevada, where you will be in charge of security there."

The General tells Evens, "This facility is code named DREAMLAND, which stands for Data Repository Evaluation and Maintenance Land. It has been constructed in the proximity of an alien underground base known as S-4. This is where the process of obtaining alien technology has begun. In addition to your responsibilities for the security of DREAMLAND, you are also ordered to report on the progress being made there and the morale of the people working there. Can I rely on your cooperation for this assignment, Colonel?" [13]

Evens smiles and says, "Yes, Sir. Thank you for this assignment, General. You can be sure that I will give it my very best effort." However inside, Evens is not looking forward to returning to the deserts of Nevada once again.

3/9/58 At Dreamland in Nevada

Colonel Evens watches as buses, with blacked out windows, arrive at the facility. He sees the civilian scientists, engineers, and technicians disembark and get herded into lines by military policemen, who treat them like raw recruits. He looks around and sees signs with a Grey alien peeking up over the words, "You are being watched".

After the civilians have had their credentials checked, Evens watches as they are made to pass through a narrow corridor with flashing lights and audio messages, which are played repeatedly. He notices that the civilians appear to be dazed and confused as they exit the corridor. Evens asks his Executive Officer, Major Connors, what is happening to them. He is told that the Orion process is used to make the civilians forget their work when they leave the facility and remember it again when they return. Evens becomes concerned about how mind control techniques are being used on innocent American citizens. He then notices that video cameras and Military Policemen are always watching the civilians.

Evens determines that none of this is doing anything for the morale of the people who work there. In order for him to find out what the civilians are thinking, he dresses into civilian clothes and poses as a scientist. He befriends another scientist there by the name of Bob. Evens asks him, "Where do you think all of this stuff comes from?"

Bob says, "I am convinced that the technology that we see being tested here is of alien origin. I determined this hypothesis after seeing the furniture inside a craft. It had really small chairs inside. That was just extremely shocking. I asked myself, 'why does it have little furniture inside?' I realized that this stuff was just a little too advanced for a group of scientists to have created and, you know, keep it secret. Things began to click together just all too fast."

Bob says, "I have given names to each of the craft, such as 'Top Hat', 'Jell-O Mold', and 'Sports Model'. They all operate without any hitches at all and they look brand new. A few of the disks have been completely dismantled in order to find out how they work. But, others are fully operational. During one test flight that I witnessed, I saw the bottom of a craft begin to glow blue and to hiss like high voltage does on a round sphere. It lifted off the ground quietly, except for that little hiss in the background, and even that stopped as soon as it reached about 20 or 30 feet. This test of the Sports Model was a short one. It made only a few moves before settling back down to the ground. I didn't see who was actually flying the craft, but I was very impressed, nonetheless."

Evens asks, "What do you think about all of the security precautions that they have in place here?" Bob says, "The excessive caution and intense secrecy contributes to the plodding pace of the program and is the main source of my disenchantment with this whole project. It's just outright unfair not to put this in the hands of the overall scientific community. There are people much more capable of dealing with this information, and by this time would have gotten a lot further along than this small select group of people working out here in the middle of the desert. We don't even have the facilities, really, to completely analyze what we're dealing with here."

Evens asks, "Who do you think is behind all of this?"

Bob says, "The group that runs this project, whether it really is the Navy or they just say that, apparently has executive power. They don't report to anyone. It's not an overall government project. It's not something that Congress appropriates money for. I don't believe that Congress even has any knowledge of it at all."

Evens asks, "How do the spacecraft work?"

Bob says, "Well, there's no action/reaction system to it. There's no, like in a jet engine, exhaust gas being thrown out, no propeller or noise. It's just, for all intents and purposes, magic. An antimatter reactor allows the spaceships to produce their own gravitational fields, which is how they are able to travel the vast distances between worlds in such a short period of time."

Bob continues, "Gravity distorts time and space. Just like if you had a water bed and put a bowling ball in the middle. It warps it down like that. That's exactly what happens in space. Imagine that you were in a spacecraft that could exert a tremendous gravitational field to actually warp space and time, and fold it. By shutting that off, you'd be a tremendous distance from where you were but time would not have even moved because you essentially shut it off."

Evens asks, "How can you control gravity?"

Bob replies, "Well, the thing is, when you harness gravity, you harness everything. It's the missing piece in physics right now. We really know very little about gravity. At least that's the way it used to be. But now, the technology to harness gravity not only exists, but it is being tested right here. And, if such technology is beyond human capabilities, then it must have come from someplace else."

Evens asks, "How do the spacecraft use gravity?"

Bob says, "There are two modes of travel. There is a low speed mode and a high-speed mode. In the low speed mode, the craft is actually very vulnerable. It sort of bobs around as it sits on a weak gravitational field. It's essentially sitting on three gravity waves. It can focus the waves behind it and essentially keep falling forward. In the second mode, they increase the amplitude and the craft begins to lift. It performs a roll maneuver and turns over. As it begins to leave Earth's gravitational field, they point the bottom of the craft at the destination. They converge and focus the three gravity amplifiers on a point that they want to go to, then they bring them up to full power, and this is where the tremendous time-space distortion takes place. It whips them right to that point."

Evens asks, "How are these craft powered?"

Bob says, "You may not believe me. But, I have seen an element that cannot be found on the periodic chart of elements. This element, called 115, can be stored in lead casings. It is impossible to synthesize an element that heavy here on Earth. But, the government has 500 pounds of it. Element 115 is the fuel for the antimatter reactors on board the spacecraft. Antimatter is produced when you bombard 115 with electrons.

"Element 115 could also make one heck of a bomb. A kilo of antimatter can produce the energy equivalent of 45 10-megaton hydrogen bombs. We're talking about hundreds and hundreds of megatons off a small piece of this stuff. It sounds incredible, but total conversion of matter into energy isn't that difficult. So, it's not something you'd ever want to have fall into just anyone's hands."

Evens asks, "How do you suppose that it could possibly be produced?"

Bob says, "It would take an infinite amount of power and an infinite amount of time. The substance has to come from a place where super-heavy elements could have been produced naturally, such as next to a much larger sun where there would be greater mass. Maybe a binary star system, a super-nova, or somewhere where there is just a bigger release of energy to synthesize these things naturally. It has to be a naturally occurring element." [14]

Evens thanks Bob for talking with him and returns to his office where he changes back into uniform. He reaches for the telephone, dials a number, and asks to meet with the Director of Research.

An appointment is made and, at the appointed time, Colonel Evens enters Dr. Teller's office. The two men meet, shake hands, and Dr. Teller asks, "Well, Colonel, how may I help you?"

Evens says, "I have been speaking with one of your scientists and he has told me of some very disturbing things which I would like to ask you about."

Teller says, "Certainly. Go ahead and ask."

"Well, it seems that, due to the tight security restrictions that we have in place here, there is not enough manpower, equipment, or facilities available to adequately evaluate the technology that has been made available to us. Is this true?"

Dr. Teller's face has turned bright red with anger. He stares at Evens with contempt and says, "Absolutely not. We have the best facilities and the brightest minds available working on this project. I am personally responsible for insuring that everything is made available for our task here. Are you asking me if I am doing my job properly?"

Evens responds with, "No, Sir. I was asking if the security restrictions prevented you from obtaining the best equipment and scientists in the world."

Teller calms down a little and says, "Well, we are not able to use anyone who does not have a security clearance and we cannot use the equipment in any non-secure facilities. But, I assure you, Sir. We have everything that we need to accomplish our mission."

"I see. Do you feel that the security procedures here negatively impact the effectiveness or the morale of the personnel who work here?"

"No."

Evens thinks to himself, *This guy is lying through his teeth!*

With his best poker face, Evens says, "Very well, Sir. I have just one more question to ask. Do you feel that the aliens have been forthright in providing us with technology which we can use for our own purposes?"

Dr. Teller has a troubled look on his face as he squirms in his seat. He says, "The Greys have fulfilled their obligation by providing their advanced technology to us. It is not their concern whether we are able to make use of it or not."

Evens says, "Oh, I believe that it is their concern. Good day to you, Sir."

Evens hurries to his office in order to begin his report on the situation. But once there, he notices a newspaper story which reports that Edward Ruppelt, the disgruntled man that had been in charge of Project Blue Book, has mysteriously died of a heart attack. Evens wonders if it could be possible that Ruppelt was murdered in order to keep him quiet.

Insiders

11/29/60 The Office of the Secretary of Defense

Colonel Evens enters the office of the Secretary of Defense, Thomas Gates, Jr. The Secretary holds out his hand and says, "Welcome, Colonel Evens. Thank you for coming. Please, be seated."

The two men sit down in large, plush chairs, facing one another. Secretary Gates says, "I have been reviewing your background, Colonel. It is most impressive. You have served your country well. I have asked you to come here today because your country needs your special services once again. You are being reassigned back to the Pentagon."

Evens cracks a smile. He is delighted to be leaving the desert once again.

Then, the Secretary says, "You are being assigned back on Project Grudge," and Evens' spirits sink again. The Secretary sees the frown on Evens' face and says, "Don't worry, Colonel. It will not be the same as before."

He tells Evens, "When John Kennedy was elected President, he asked to be briefed about the extraterrestrials. Kennedy was shown the Project Blue Book reports, and he was not impressed, due to the fact that he had been briefed about the Roswell incident. Kennedy was then shown Eisenhower's briefing report when he became President back in 1952. Well, now Kennedy wants a complete report regarding extraterrestrials, from 1953 until the present."

The Secretary tells Evens, "You are being assigned the task of preparing Project Grudge/Blue Book Report Number 13. However, this time, you are to hold nothing back and include all of the gory details. I want the report to cause the President to piss in his pants."

Evens says, "To do as you say, Mr. Secretary, I am going to need access to all of the material from Majestic-12 and the CIA. I would like to request that Stan Edwards, from the CIA, be assigned to this project again as liaison with the CIA."

The Secretary says, "You will have this man's full support and you will have full access on all of the material available."

Evens says, "Thank you, Mr. Secretary, for this assignment. You can count on me."

He then begins to leave when the Secretary says, "Oh, Colonel, just one more thing. You have been invited to attend the next meeting of the Council on Foreign Relations. Congratulations. This is quite an honor."

Evens is handed the invitation. He has no idea what he has just been invited to or why he should feel so honored.

12/12/60 In Colonel Evens' Office at the Pentagon

Colonel Evens looks around at his new office in the Pentagon. He thinks back to his past when his office consisted of a metal desk, two wooden chairs, a locking filing cabinet, and a coat rack on a hard tiled floor. Now, he has a nice wooden desk, comfortable chairs, a coffee table and couch. There is even a small kitchenette in one corner of the room with a sink, cupboards, and a coffee machine. The walls are covered with wood paneling and the floor is covered with thick carpeting. He now has two locking filing cabinets, a world map hanging on one wall, and lots of lighting. And, for the first time, he has his own secretary who has a small office just outside of his office door. Yes, Evens is quite pleased with his new surroundings.

Evens can hear Stan Edwards yelling at his secretary, just outside his office. Stan is asking, "What jerk decided that I should be reassigned back to Project Grudge? I've already served my time in Purgatory and I have no desire to return." Then, he sees Evens standing in the doorway to his office and asks, "Are you the one who is responsible for this?"

Evens grins and says, "Yep. I'm afraid so." He holds out his hand and the two men shake hands. Evens invites him into his office.

After sitting down, Stan says, "Damn it, Tom. I had a nice cushy job at the agency. This had better not be another gigantic waste of time."

Evens assures him that it is not and tells him what the Secretary of Defense wants them to do.

Stan smiles and says, "Now, that's more like it. I would be delighted to help you write that kind of report."

"Good! That's great."

Then, Evens gets a serious look on his face and says, "Stan? I've been invited to attend a meeting of the Council on Foreign Relations. I've never heard of this council. The Secretary of Defense congratulated me for it. What did he mean?"

"It means that you are being groomed to become a General. The Council on Foreign Relations is the most influential, semi-secret organization in America. Their membership includes the wealthiest people of this nation along with the owners and directors of the top corporations that control the economy of this country."

Stan explains, "The Council on Foreign Relations was created during a meeting that was held on May 19, 1919, in the Majestic Hotel of Paris, France. The formal membership in the C.F.R. is composed of close to 1500 of the most elite names in the areas of government, labor, business, finance, communications, the foundations, and the academy. It has staffed almost every key position of every administration since those of F.D.R. All of the heads of the CIA since 1947 have been members. Almost every Secretary of State and Secretary of Defense have been members. Almost every senior member of the government and most of the long-time members of Congress either are members or have been members of the C.F.R. Those are the people who rule this nation."

Evens asks, "But, why have I never heard of this group before?"

Stan says, "I doubt that one American in a thousand so much as recognizes the Council's name, or that one in ten thousand can relate anything at all about its structure or purpose."

"Okay. You've got me curious now. What is their purpose?"

"Well, it is their goal to have a New World Order under a One-World Government."

"Are you saying that it is the goal of these Americans to have the United States Government give up its sovereignty to this one world government?"

"Yep."

Evens is astonished by this and asks, "How can our military leaders be a part of such a treasonous act?"

Stan says, "Well, only those people who agree with their objectives ever get to become admirals or generals. That would tend to provide a rather strong incentive to obtaining their cooperation. You have been invited to attend one of their meetings in order for them to determine if you have the right stuff to become a general."

Evens is confused and asks, "But, what does the Council on Foreign Relations have to do with extraterrestrials?"

"The members of Majestic-12 are the people who control all of the alien related projects. You will find that they are all members of the Council on Foreign Relations and that they came from the study department of the Council on Foreign Relations because the Council offered to help Truman when the UFO crashed near Roswell, New Mexico, back in 1947. The Council has been secretly advising every president since it's inception in 1919. At no time in our history, has there ever been an executive policy, from the executive branch of our government, which has ever disagreed with recommendations from the Council on Foreign Relations. That should tell you just how powerful they are." [1] [2]

Just then, Evens starts to feel trapped.

2/15/61 In the Oval Office of the White House

Robert McNamara, the new Secretary of Defense, is greeted by President Kennedy and is asked to have a seat in the chair in front of his desk. Kennedy sits down behind his desk and asks, "Mr. Secretary, I would like to know why I have not received the Project Grudge Report yet regarding extraterrestrial visitation?"

McNamara says, "It is currently being prepared, Mr. President. But, more time is required in order to provide you with a thorough report."

"Very well. But, I want to see it just as soon as it is available. I would like to make it clear that I will not tolerate any delays."

"I understand you clearly, Sir. There will be no delays."

Next, the President states, "I would also like for you to arrange for me to visit the facilities where the extraterrestrials and their craft are being kept."

The Secretary shifts his weight in his seat, clears his throat, and says, "I'm sorry, Mr. President. I am unable to comply with your request. The site is not under military control and you do not have the authority to enter that facility."

President Kennedy becomes angry and asks, "You have been there. Have you not?"

"Yes, Mr. President."

"It is on United States soil. Is it not?"

"It is, Sir."

Kennedy shouts, "Well, I am the President of this country and the Commander and Chief of all military forces. I will order the Army to invade it, if necessary, in order for me to gain access."

"But Sir, that area is protected under the provisions of a treaty with extraterrestrial beings and they have the technology to prevent that from happening. However, I will look into obtaining the necessary authorization for you to gain access, Mr. President."

"Very well. You may go now."

3/21/61 The Council on Foreign Relations Building

Evens walks into the banquet room wearing a suit and tie, as called for in the invitation. He sees several men, dressed in business suits, talking with each other in small groups. There are waiters passing through the crowd, carrying drinks. Everyone seems to have a drink in their hand, so Evens accepts one from a waiter. The people seem to be in a pleasant mood while they socialize with one another. Evens feels very much out of place.

Just then, Evens hears someone say, "He's here!" Everyone in the room becomes excited and very anxious.

Evens asks a gentleman, that is standing next to him, "Who has arrived?"

He is told, "It's the Chairman of the Board, David Rockefeller, of course."

Evens watches as the sea of people part so that Rockefeller, and his entourage, can pass into the meeting room. Everyone applauds as he passes through the room. Then, everyone walks into the meeting room and sits down. All doors are closed behind them.

The Board of Directors sit behind a long table, at the far end of the room. At the podium, a speaker brings the meeting to order. He welcomes everyone to the meeting and introduces David Rockefeller.

Rockefeller says to the members, "Good evening, Ladies and Gentlemen. I am very pleased with your participation and accomplishments. But, there are many challenges that we must face together." He then starts to describe the economic situation. Evens has no understanding of economics and is growing bored very rapidly. But then, Rockefeller starts talking about things that do concern him and he wonders how Rockefeller knows about them. [3]

Rockefeller says, "President Kennedy intends to compel the steel manufacturers to roll back their price increases. He also intends to reduce the oil depletion allowances and close corporate tax loopholes with a new tax reform bill." The crowd responds with horror upon hearing each of these issues.

Then, Rockefeller states, "The President has asked Secretary of Defense, Robert Mc-Namara, to reappraise the entire defense strategy, capacity, commitments, and needs with a tendency toward down sizing the military and reducing defense spending." This is received by the crowd in a most unfavorable way. "It will be necessary for all of us to bring pressure to bear upon the President in order to reverse these disturbing trends." [4]

After the meeting, a man walks up to Evens and says, "Good evening, Colonel Evens. You have been invited to attend a private meeting in the back room. Would you follow me, please."

Evens agrees and follows the man to another room where a few men are sitting at a small table. Evens is asked to join them. So, he sits down. He recognizes one of the men as the new Secretary of Defense, Robert McNamara. McNamara tells Evens, "We have been watching your career accomplishments for a long time. We are very pleased in the way that you have dealt with the alien situations."

Evens thanks the Secretary and wonders how they are able to discuss something as sensitive as his top secret dealings with extraterrestrials.

David Rockefeller asks, "What did you think of the meeting tonight?"

Evens says, "I was very impressed with the Council's organization and ability to respond effectively to current events." This was something that he felt that he could say truthfully.

Then, Rockefeller asks, "Where do your loyalties lay, Colonel?"

Evens clears his throat and says, "Although I am obligated to obey the orders of the Commander-in-Chief, I also understand the need for a united One-World Government." This pleases everyone at the table.

Rockefeller asks, "Would you be interested in becoming a member? You would benefit greatly from an association with the council."

Evens smiles and says, "I would be honored, Sir."

11/6/61 In Colonel Evens' Office at the Pentagon

Evens and Stan are reviewing recent UFO activities. Stan says, "Look at this. Radar stations, at Cape Canaveral, locked onto an object that followed a Polaris missile over the Atlantic Ocean."

Evens says, "Damn! That's fast. Now, I have one for you. Vice President Johnson's private aircraft crash landed recently. Radar tracked UFOs in the area."

"Do you suppose that this was a deliberate act against the Vice President?"

"I don't know. Johnson doesn't have any real power. I don't know what value that the Vice President would be to the aliens." [5]

Stan and Evens then read a report which indicated that 221 U.S. Army personnel were abducted by UFOs from Fort Ord, California, and had small devices implanted into their brains. All were sedated through the efforts of 600 other soldiers who were recruited for this purpose and debriefed. Many suffered severe physical and psychological trauma. They, and their families, were sequestered. Stan says, "221 soldiers? That's a lot of human beings for just some sort of experiment." [6]

Evens replies, "Yeah, I guess that someone must have thought that they were expendable."

The two men then read about another report of an abduction that took place on September 20th, 1961. A couple, by the names of Betty and Barney Hill, were abducted while driving along a deserted road, at 2:00 in the morning, on their way to their Hew Hampshire home from Montreal. The Hills reported their sighting of a UFO to nearby Pedes Air Force Base, who's radar station tracked a UFO at the same time and location as was reported by the Hills. [7]

The final report that the men look at, states that, on September 21st, two Boeing 707 commercial airliners encountered a large donut shaped UFO over the Pacific Ocean. Evens sets the report on a stack with the others and says, "Damn! There's a lot going on now, and it sure don't look good."

12/7/61 In the Oval Office of the White House

President John F. Kennedy and his brother, the Attorney General, Robert Kennedy, are discussing current affairs. Robert says, "You know, when you stated, last month, that 'The United States is neither omnipotent nor omniscient', you really upset those people who have so much to gain from a strong military-industrial complex."

The President says, "I don't care. I am more concerned that the federal deficit is at three billion dollars at a time when the military-industrial complex budget is at $47 billion." [8]

The President says, "The board of inquiry into the Bay of Pigs disaster has shown me just how powerful the military-industrial complex and its intelligence-security force has become. I have discovered that the CIA and the Pentagon has misled me terribly in regard to that fiasco and I can tell you that I will be highly skeptical of any information from those sources in the future. However, I have attempted to correct that situation with National Security Action Memoranda 55 and 57, which holds the chairman of the Joint Chiefs of Staff personally responsible for all military activities and limits the CIA to only small covert operations."

Robert's eyes grow large and he tells the President, "The CIA and military leaders are not going to appreciate having their power base divided like that."

The President says, "Well, it was necessary in order to bring the nation's paramilitary and undercover operations under some semblance of control." [9]

The President asks how his brother's war is going against organized crime.

Robert says, "It could be going better. J. Edgar Hoover still maintains that the F.B.I. is still unable to find any evidence that organized crime syndicates exist in this country. This is in spite of the fact that the Kefauver Senate Select Committee provided ample evidence that it does. And, even though I was able to have the INS deport Carlos Marcello, the head of a New Orleans based crime syndicate, I have just found out that he has returned."

"However", he says, "I have uncovered a close relationship between organized crime and a military intelligence organization. It seems that the Navy, during World War II, began an association with the Mafia in order to help the war effort. After the war, this Mafia-Navy partnership moved to the Office of Strategic Services, which became the forerunner of the CIA. In 1946, a convicted gangster, known as Lucky Luciano, was granted an executive clemency and deported. In Italy, he organized an international narcotics syndicate that supplies most of the heroin that is shipped to this country, where it is received, processed, and distributed by the Delta Forces, under the supervision of the Naval Reconnaissance Office. The revenues received from the illegal sale of these drugs are used to fund the Black Projects." [10] [11]

The President says, "Well, I intend to take care of that situation right now." Robert McNamara has been kept waiting outside of the Oval Office all of this time.

The President tells his personal secretary to ask McNamara to come into his office. The two Kennedy brothers greet him upon his entry and ask him to sit down. They sit on couches, with McNamara across a coffee table from the Kennedys. The President says, "Mr. Secretary, I have asked you to come over here today in order to respond to some troubling accusations which I have just learned about. As a member of the Executive Committee for the Bilderbergers, a Director of the Council on Foreign Relations, a member of Majestic-12, and the Secretary of Defense, I thought you might have some knowledge about such things. [12]

McNamara says, "I will be happy to respond, if I can, Mr. President."

The President states, "It has been brought to my attention that the NRO and Delta Forces are importing and distributing illegal drugs in this country in order to pay for MJ-12's Black Projects. Is this true?"

McNamara gives an icy stare to Robert Kennedy and then tells the President, "I flatly deny any knowledge of this activity, what-so-ever."

The President nods his head and says, "Very well. Would you have any information regarding several American citizens that have been abducted by an alien race, with assistance provided by people working for MJ-12?"

McNamara sits back and says, "Yes, Mr. President. It is my understanding that these activities are occurring for purely scientific research purposes with the abductees being returned unharmed and with no conscious memory of the incident."

The Attorney General asks, "Mr. Secretary, is it your understanding that this sort of thing is legal?"

McNamara replies, "This is one of the provisions in an agreement that the United States Government has with an extraterrestrial race." [13]

The President asks, "Mr. Secretary, when am I going to be briefed on the alien related activities and be permitted to visit DREAMLAND?"

McNamara clears his throat and says, "A full report should be available for you soon, Mr. President. You will then be able to visit the test site after being briefed on the matter."

The President pounds his fist on the coffee table and shouts, "Damn it! You guys better get your stuff together because I'm going to tell the public everything. I will appeal directly to the American people on national television. I will tell them all about the aliens, what's going on, and allow the people to decide for themselves what should be done about it."

McNamara stands and says, "I will make your position known to the people concerned with these issues, Mr. President." [14]

"Very well, Mr. Secretary. You may leave now."

After he has left, Robert says, "You know, of course, what people he was referring to."

3/3/62 At a Board of Directors' Meeting for the C.F.R.

The Board of Directors is in a somber mood in the headquarters building for the Council on Foreign Relations on 68th Street in New York City. Robert McNamara is telling the directors about his visit with the Kennedys and relays the President's ultimatum. He says, "Well, there you have it, gentlemen. I believe that the President is serious about his intentions to tell the American people about the aliens. I have discussed this matter with the Executive Committee of the Bilderbergers over a secure telephone line. It is their unanimous opinion that we must prevent that from happening, at all costs. Prince Bernhard, in particular, is very upset over this." [15]

David Rockefeller says, "Clearly, we must find a way to prevent the President from carrying out his threat. But, it will take quite some time to make the necessary preparations."

"I can postpone the release of the Grudge report to the President for only a few more months. But, that is all."

"Very well, that should give us sufficient time. When everything is ready, you will release the report to the President and we will decide on whether to proceed with drastic measures, based upon the President's response to the report."

Coup d'Etat

3/16/62 At the Office of the National Security Adviser

Colonel Evens is shown into the office of McGeorge Bundy, the National Security adviser. In proper military fashion, he marches in front of the adviser's desk and says, "Colonel Evens reporting as ordered, Sir."

Mr. Bundy leans back in his chair behind his desk and says, "Be at ease Colonel, have a seat and tell me what you wanted to see me about. McNamara said that you have something very important to report."

Evens assumes a more relaxed posture as he sits in the chair before the desk. He is very nervous since he has never met the National Security adviser before.

The colonel clears his throat and says, "Thank you for seeing me on such short notice, sir. But I consider this to be an urgent matter of extreme importance."

"Well, what is it?"

"Sir, during my duties of preparing the next Grudge report, I discovered that we recently received a message from the Eben race and our linguists have just translated the message. It says that the Ebens will be returning to Earth on 24 April, 1964 at the southern sector of White Sands Missile Range, New Mexico just as we had suggested for a cultural exchange." [1]

Mr. Bundy's eyes grow wide open and he says, "Yes, that is important news. That means that we only have about 25 months to plan for the event. I'll put the Air Force in charge of selecting and training an exchange team to go to their planet. This is a great opportunity for us to get first hand knowledge about another species on their home world. I will notify the president and get his approval for the exchange once the final team members have been selected. You need not include this information in your Grudge 13 report, Colonel."

"Yes sir."

Mr. Bundy reaches for his telephone and tells Evens, "Thank you. That will be all. You may go now. I have a lot of work to do here."

8/14/63 In the Oval Office of the White House

The President and the Attorney General, Robert Kennedy, are discussing current events. The President is really angry. He says to his brother, "Can you believe the gall of McGeorge Bundy? He is supposed to be my adviser on national security matters and now I learn that he has made policy decisions without even consulting me. He actually had the nerve to tell me that he has had the Air Force select a team of 16 volunteers to live on another world for a year in a cultural exchange with an alien being from their planet. Then, he asked me if it would be okay to allow the exchange to take place next year."

Robert asks, "What did you tell him?"

"I was so angry that I just left the room without saying anything. But actually, I think it's a good idea and I think I'll approve the project. I just don't care for Bundy doing this behind my back."

The President also tells his brother, "I am going to drop Lyndon Johnson from the 1964 Democratic ticket. That man has fought every move that I have made and I don't trust him. I also don't trust anything that the Pentagon tells me anymore. They told me that the Soviets had 500 to 1,000 ballistic missiles, when they actually have more like 50. That is the reason why I approved McNamara's announcement, on March 30th, for a reorganization of our entire military forces. This reorganization will close 52 military installations in 25 states and 21 overseas bases within three years. [2] [3] [4]

"I have also re-evaluated the U.S. Military's commitment to Vietnam and I am planning a complete withdrawal of all military forces from Vietnam by 1965. I am concerned that an escalating conflict could increase the federal deficit. The Federal Reserve has refused to support my plans for a balanced budget. So, I ordered the Treasury to print four billion dollars in bank notes." [5] [6]

Robert says, "Bypassing the Federal Reserve will really upset the international bankers."

"I don't care, Bobby. I only care about what is good for the country."

The President says, "The Cuban Missile Crisis of last October has made me more aware of the need for détente. That is why I had the hot line installed and that is why the Limited Nuclear Test Ban Treaty was negotiated and signed on August 5th of this year."

His brother says, "You know, that treaty has hurt your popularity by making you look like you are soft on communism."

"You should know that I do not make decisions based on whether it is the popular thing to do, or not. But, I am concerned about re-election. That is why I am planning a trip to Texas, where I am not the most popular person."

"I think that is a bad idea. I am concerned that this trip could affect you adversely."

The President asks how his brother's war on organized crime is going. Robert says, "Our situation improved when you distanced yourself from Judith Exner, after J. Edgar Hoover told you about her connections with organized crime."

"Hoover must have had us followed for months and watched everything we did together. But, he is going to learn a lesson for playing games with me. Hoover is reaching that age, in civil service, where retirement is mandatory. He has created a dynasty for himself at the FBI and I intend to see to it that he retires as mandated."

Robert says, "In any case, the activities of the CIA interfered with my efforts to stop organized crime. The Justice Department had initiated proceedings against a CIA agent, by the name of Robert Maheu, for placing an illegal wire tap on behalf of the gangster, Sam Giancana. Then, in May of 1962, the CIA's General Counsel asked me not to prosecute Maheu because the CIA had contacted Giancana and John Roselli to murder Fidel Castro and they were concerned about that coming to light. For that reason, I was forced to drop the charges. The drug problem is getting worse and an ever increasing number of citizens are being reported as either abducted or missing." [7]

The President says, "Well, don't worry. I will be briefed on the Grudge report soon and we will then know what is going on."

8/27/63 In the Intelligence Complex at Camp Perry, VA.

There are sixteen military personnel sitting in individual classroom tables and chairs. A door opens and a General enters the room with his aide. The aide shouts, "Atten-tion!" and everyone stands at attention.

The General says, "At ease. Take your seats. I am General Nathan Brown. I have come here to brief you on the purpose behind all of the testing that you have had to endure up until now and to ask you if you are still interested in pursuing this project."

The General sits on the corner of a desk in the front of the room and says, "You sixteen people here were selected from a list of about 56,000 selectees, which met our stringent requirements. Out of these military personnel, an initial group of 158 people were selected to undergo a battery of psychological tests, medical screenings and Positive Attitude Tests to demonstrate their abilities to endure hardship. You sixteen people are the best of the best that this country has to offer." [8]

The General stands and says, "Up until now, you have only been told that you have been selected for a special mission. I can now tell you what that mission is. It is a Top Secret mission known as Project Crystal Knight. It is based upon an incident that occurred in 1947 when two craft from another world crashed in the New Mexico desert." The eyes become wide open for all sixteen people and they are listening very intently now.

The General continues with, "There were a total of eleven dead alien bodies recovered from the crash sites and one living entity, which provided us with a lot of information and assisted us in establishing communications with his home world. A delegation of these beings will be arriving in April of next year, and they have agreed to a cultural exchange program. You people have been chosen to be representatives of mankind from planet Earth in a ten-year tour of duty on another world. Are there any questions?" [9]

A Navy Ensign raises his hand and asks, "Sir, I was curious about what planet we would be going to and what the beings are like that live there."

The General says, "I thought you might want to know about that. We refer to the planet as "Serpo". That is short for "Serponia", which is the closest sounding name that we can determine. Serpo is the third planet in orbit around a binary solar system with suns known as Zeta 1 and Zeta 2 Reticuli in the Reticulum Constellation, which are about 40 light-years from Earth. It takes nine months for the Eben, which is what we call their species, to travel between here and there. That means that they are able to travel faster than the speed of light." All 16 people let out a long breath upon hearing that news.

The General nods at his aide and says, "The Captain is passing out photographs of the living alien being captured after the crashes in 1947. We referred to it as Extraterrestrial Biological Entity One, or EBE-1, until it died of natural causes in 1953. Fortunately, another crash occurred in 1949 and a female entity, EBE-2, was captured and is still alive today. They have male and female genders. But the amazing thing is that all of them look exactly alike, which would tend to indicate that they are a cloned race of beings. However, they are very intelligent, but with few emotions." [10]

The General sits back down on the desk and says, "Now, let me tell you what you will have to look forward to in your preparations for this trip, should you agree to take part in this mission. You will all be taught space exploration by NASA personnel, Astronomy and general astrophysics, along with the Eben anthropology and their history. The non-medical personnel of this team will receive the U.S. Army Field Medical Training. All of you will undergo high altitude training while parachuting and in weightless conditions in zero oxygen environments.

"In addition, you will receive survival, escape and evasion training, basic weapons and explosive training, psychological training and anti-interrogation preparation, small unit tactical training taught by the U.S. Army Rangers, an Intelligence Gathering Course, Physical Stress Training, and you will be taught methods to cope with confinement and isolation. Now, if you survive all of that, then you will go through the Nutrition course and receive equipment use training along with Individual specialty training. Finally, you will learn Space Geology, basic Biology, and other highly classified training, which must all be completed within roughly six months of time. [11]

"While all of this is going on, every single record on each Team Member will be purged, including your Social Security records, Internal Revenue tax returns, medical records, military records, and any other identification records, which will either be destroyed or collected and placed in a special storage location. Each Team Member will be listed as "missing" on their official records and discharged on their unofficial records. Fortunately, all of you are career military personnel with no spouses or close family ties. When you return, you will be issued all of your back pay at the hazardous duty pay rate and tax free. You will then be free to live your life as you desire after the debriefing. Naturally, you will be closely watched for the rest of your lives to insure that you do not reveal any information about this mission. [12]

"Well there you have it, ladies and gentlemen. Naturally, you will need some time to think about this before coming to a decision as important as this. You will be given 24 hours. There will be no unfavorable repercussions and you will simply be reassigned if you choose not to accept this mission. Only twelve of you will go. The other four are alternates in the event that any of the original twelve are not able to complete their training in good health."

A Navy Captain says, "Excuse me, General. Would it be possible to have a vote now in order to find out how many of us have already decided to take this mission?"

"Yes, we can do that now, but the decisions will not be final until 24 hours from now. All of those who have decided to undertake this mission please raise your right hand."

Everyone raises their hand.

The General smiles and says, "Very good! You have all volunteered for this very important mission and I commend all of you. Alright, from this moment onward, you will no longer be known by your names, but by a three-digit number for security reasons and you are never to reveal your true identities until your return to Earth. Is that clear?"

They all shout, "Yes Sir!"

"Very well. Colonel, you will be the Team Commander and your designation is 102. Captain, you will be the alternate Team Commander and your designation is 105. Major, you will be the Assistant Team Commander with the designation of 203.

"We have three female members on this team. Captain, as one of two doctors, you will be designated 754 and Lieutenant, you will be an alternate doctor with the designation of 725. We also have two linguists and an alternate. Ensign, as one of the linguists, your designation is 475, and Sergeant, you will be the alternate with the designation of 452. As for you men, the Lieutenant Colonel here is the other doctor, designated 700, and the Lieutenant here will be the other Linguist with the designation of 420. We also have two pilots. Major, your designation is 225 and Captain, your designation is 308. [13]

"There are two Biologists. Ensign, you will be the Team Biologist with the designation of 518 and Captain, you will be the alternate with the designation of 572. There are also two scientists. Major, your designation is 633 and Lieutenant, your designation is 661. Finally Sergeant, that leaves you as the security specialist with the designation of 899. Ladies and gentlemen, think carefully about the mission that you have decided to undertake. We meet back here in 24 hours for your final decision. That is all. Dismissed."

9/9/63 In Defense Secretary McNamara's Office

Colonel Evens reports, as ordered, to Robert McNamara. McNamara welcomes him into his office and invites him to sit down. After the two men make themselves comfortable in large, plush chairs, the Secretary says, "I have invited you here, Colonel, because I have just reviewed the Grudge 13 report, which you wrote. I wanted you to know that I am very pleased with the content of that report. I am going to approve it for the President."

Evens says, "Thank you, Mr. Secretary. That means a lot coming from you, Sir."

Then, McNamara tells Evens, "I have decided that you will be the one to provide the briefing of the report to the President."

The Secretary says, "I want to make certain that you understand that there is a lot of significance resting on how President Kennedy responds to this report. It is imperative that the President should come to understand that it is in the best interest of the country for the Majestic-12 group to continue handling the alien situation. He must come to understand that he should stay out of the whole business altogether. I want you to scare the hell out of him. I have the greatest of confidence in your abilities."

Evens thanks the Secretary of Defense for this opportunity to serve his country, but feels nervous about what is being expected of him.

"Oh, by the way," says the Secretary, "We cannot be having a lowly Colonel brief the President of the United States. So, effective immediately, you are hereby promoted to the rank of Brigadier General. Congratulations! Actually, I received word of the Senate's confirmation of your promotion just this morning and I wanted to be the first to let you know the good news. You are expected to attend a promotion ceremony, this afternoon, in your honor. After all, it is not every day that you become a General."

Evens smiles and says, "Thank you very much, Mr. Secretary. You can rely on me, Sir." He leaves the office overwhelmed at all that has been laid on his shoulders.

9/15/63 In the Oval Office of the White House

Brigadier General Evens is briefing the President and Robert Kennedy on the Grudge 13 Report. Defense Secretary Robert McNamara is also present. Evens begins by saying, "Project Grudge/Blue Book Report Number 13 consists of three chapters and an extensive appendix including analysis, diagrams, and photographs. Chapter 1 describes recovered flying disk technology, chapter 2 contains the case studies of close encounters with civilians, and chapter 3 describes military encounters with UFOs.

"The sections within chapter 1 describe flying disk construction, power plants, and propulsion systems. The UFO construction section includes photographs and reports concerning captive sites and various recovered UFOs from the United States, Mexico, Canada, and Sweden by the Alpha Recovery Team. The Power plant section describes the design of generators which accomplish strain free molecular translation and includes design criteria for a simple generator and control system. The propulsion section describes the generation of space-time discontinuums and the generation of temporary pseudo acceleration locas. Included in this section is the final conclusion of Einstein's Theory of Relativity and possible applications of those conclusions.

"The case studies of UFO encounters in chapter 2 are divided into three types of categories: first, are subtle sightings; second, are sightings witnessed within close proximity; and third, are personal encounters with extraterrestrial life forms. Also included with the case histories of the third category, are descriptions of the people involved being moved, in the middle of the night, by the 'Men in Black' and relocated to various sites in the United States.

"One case of the third kind of close encounter, occurred at the Darlington Farm of Ohio in October of 1953. The farmer and his wife watched as little men carried away their 13 year old son into a huge fiery looking object. As it took off, the father fired several shotgun rounds at the object, to no avail. They found their dog with its head crushed in, but no sign of the boy. Within 48 hours, the Air Force had moved the father and mother, along with all of their possessions, to a Northwestern relocation zone; Z21-14. The mother was in shock and had to undergo a great deal of psychotherapy and deprogramming, as did the father.

"In Chapter 3, which deals with military encounters with UFOs, there are numerous reports of sightings, combat encounters, and damage assessments. There have been numerous occasions in which UFOs have been tracked alongside of fired missiles and, on one occasion, the missile was taken aboard a UFO while in flight. The speeds indicated were absolutely phenomenal. Personnel associated with the North American X-15 rocket plane project have reported experiencing missing time. Personnel at sensitive military and industrial areas have also experienced missing time. There have been two UFO incidents at Fort Riley, Kansas.

"There are also reports of various human mutilations. One of these mutilations occurred in March of 1956. A Major Cunningham witnessed Sergeant Lovette being abducted at the White Sands Missile Test Range in New Mexico. Major Cunningham saw a long snake-like object drag the Sergeant into a silvery disk, which hovered about 20 feet in the air and then ascended very quickly. Three days later, a search party discovered the nude body of Sgt. Lovette about three miles away. He had been mutilated with his tongue, eyes, genitalia, and anus removed. The initial autopsy report confirmed that his system had been completely drained of blood and that there was no vascular collapse due to death by bleeding. As you can see from the black and white photographs, the body had been exposed to the elements for a day or two, under the hot New Mexico sun."

"The report describes a number of recovery teams that were activated specifically for the purpose of recovering any and all evidence of UFOs. Most notably recorded in the publication is Recovery Team Alpha, based out of Wright-Patterson Air Force Base. Alpha Team has been extremely active in a number of areas and, on certain occasions, has traveled outside of the continental United States. Another detachment of the team is based at Randolph Air Force Base.

"The report includes an analysis of recovered UFOs and alien bodies by J. Allen Hynek and Lt. Col. Friend. This analysis contains autopsy reports with high quality photographs.

Photo 1 shows an alien being, which appears to be a little short of 4 feet, on an autopsy table. The nude body has no genitalia and is completely heterous. The head is slightly enlarged with a rounded cranium and a receding chin line. The eyes are almond shaped. There are slits where the nose would be. The mouth is extremely small, and there are holes where the ears would be. The hands are slightly longer than normal and reach down to about two inches above the knees. The wrists are very slender with no thumb and three fingers, which are direct extensions from the wrists. The palm is almost nonexistent. The color of the skin is a dark bluish gray.

"Other pictures show the alien body at various stages of an autopsy. The body was slit from the crotch to just under the chin. A green viscous liquid is in evidence. There is an internal organ that appears as a small cluster of multi-valve hearts or at least two hearts. There is no stomach or digestive tract. An analysis found that the body fluids were a chlorophyll based liquid which apparently dealt with photosynthesis or a similar process. Because the cadaver was extremely odorous, it is theorized that waste products are excreted through the pores of the skin.

"Other photos deal with a number of bodies which were vivisected in various ways. An autopsy was performed on a head to expose the brain matter within the cranium. A photograph shows a ridge bone or dividing partition-type bone running directly through the center of the skull, from front to back, dividing the two brains. There is another photo of a skull that was cut directly in half which shows an under developed esophagus and nasal cavities. There are also numerous photos of the flesh under extreme magnification. At the time of the report, 11 alien cadavers were being kept at Wright-Patterson Air Force Base. Additional alien cadavers were also being stored at 4 or 5 other medical institutions.

"Another photo shows three live aliens standing against a white tile wall. The beings are looking in different directions and appear to be confused. The report states that there are 17 different extraterrestrial species accounted for at the time of the report. The extraterrestrials are referred to, in the report, as A.L.F.s, for Alien Life Forms. The report describes how aliens contacted a U.S. Intelligence Agency for two initial meetings, one at Holloman and one at Homestead Air Force Base.

"The report also describes recovered UFOs which are being tested at a secret installation in the middle of the Atomic Energy Commission testing ground in Nevada, under a program known as Project Redlight. One UFO, that was being test flown by two Air Force Pilots, blew up as it attempted to leave the atmosphere in the mid 1950's. Two UFOs have been tested in a wind tunnel at Langley, Virginia. One UFO is stored at McDill Air Force Base and a damaged disc is stored at Elgin Air Force Base in Florida. This report also discusses civilian and military personnel who have been terminated in order to eliminate potentially dangerous elements to national security." [14]

President Kennedy says, "Thank you, General Evens, for a very thorough report. Could you tell me about the meetings that took place with the aliens? I'd like to know what U.S. Intelligence Agency met with them and what was discussed."

Evens quickly looks at Secretary McNamara, who has a stern look on his face, and then tells the President, "I'm sorry, Mr. President. I do not have that information."

The President whispers something in his brother's ear and Robert Kennedy leaves the office.

The President says, "Thank you Secretary McNamara and General Evens for coming and for providing such a fine report." McNamara and Evens stand, say their farewells and leave the office.

In the next room, a secretary hands a note to McNamara. He reads the note and tells Evens that he has an urgent matter to attend to and that he will meet with him tomorrow.

Evens acknowledges this and they walk in different directions. However, before exiting the building, Evens runs into Robert Kennedy, who tells Evens, "Would you follow me, General?" To Evens' surprise, he finds that they are walking back into the Oval Office, where the President is waiting.

President Kennedy says, "Thank you for meeting with me again, General. I wanted to meet with you privately and ask you some more questions about the report."

Evens realizes that he could get into serious trouble for this and says, "Sir, everything that I know is already in the report."

Robert tells him, "Don't worry, General. Anything that is said here will be kept confidential between us, and you have nothing to fear from anything that you say to us."

The President says, "I must know everything in order to deal with the situation effectively."

Evens thinks about this for a moment and says, "To tell you the truth, Mr. President, I am surprised that you do not already know everything since the Majestic-12 group was created to be responsible only to the President and to advise him on all matters concerning extraterrestrial life."

The President says, "Well, it seems that MJ-12 has been running things on their own for a long time and that the Grudge 13 Report was intended to persuade me to allow things to continue that way without interference."

"Yes, Mr. President. That is exactly what was intended."

President Kennedy tells Evens, "I need for you to tell me everything that you know, which is not in the report or which differs from the report."

Evens begins by telling them about being a part of the team that recovered the first crashed disc in 1947 and about the concerns which they had regarding the alien virus, radiation, and the body parts aboard the craft.

The President says, "But, none of that was presented in the Eisenhower briefing documents."

Evens states, "That is correct, Sir. Those briefing documents also neglected to report on a living alien being that was captured at the crash site. Those documents also state that projects Sign, Grudge, and Blue Book were established to gather information regarding alien activity. Although this was true of Project Sign, once they determined that UFOs were not of this world, the Air Force changed the project name, gutted the investigative staff, and did everything they could to disprove any notion that UFOs exist and are continuing to do so to this very day."

Next, Evens tells them about the communications which he monitored between the NSA and the Ebens, Greys and Pleiadians. Then, he tells them about the meetings at White Sands, Muroc and Holloman Air Force Bases and the formal agreement that the government entered into with the Greys. Then, he tells them about MJ-12's attempt to enter into an alliance with the Sirians. Finally, he tells them about what he discovered while at DREAMLAND. The Kennedys are stunned.

Robert asks Evens, "Have you ever heard about a plan to import and distribute illegal drugs in order to generate funding for the black projects?"

Evens says, "I have no idea, Sir, where the enormous amount of money is coming from to construct the secret facilities which I have personally seen, myself."

The President says, "Thank you, General, for your honesty. I assure you that everything you have said will be kept confidential."

After Evens leaves, the President requests the presence of Robert McNamara.

Later that same day, McNamara enters the Oval Office once again. The President tells him, "I have decided to take a more active role in dealing with extraterrestrials. First, I will visit DREAMLAND and then I will attend every meeting of the Majestic-12. How soon can a visit to the facilities be arranged?"

McNamara is stunned. His mouth is wide open. After a few moments, McNamara composes himself and tries to speak, "Aw, well, I, aw, I don't exactly know. I will do the best that I can, but this sort of thing takes time."

Kennedy becomes furious and says, "I believe that you are stalling, Mr. Secretary. You had better get started right away or I will call a press conference and tell the world about what has been going on here."

McNamara tells the President, "I will see what I can do", and he leaves the room.

11/21/63 In the President's Quarters of the White House

The President is sitting at a small desk in his bedroom. He realizes that it has been over two months since he demanded to see DREAMLAND and be present at all Majestic-12 meetings. Still, this has not yet come to pass. So, he has made up his mind to address the world in a televised address with news about alien contacts. He reaches for a pen and begins to write the following speech on index cards:

"My fellow Americans and people of the world, today we set forth on a journey into a new era. One age, the childhood of mankind is ending and another age is about to begin. The journey of which I speak is full of unknowable challenges, but I believe that all of our yesterdays, all of the struggles of the past, uniquely prepare our generation to prevail.

Citizens of this Earth, we are not alone. God, in his infinite wisdom, has seen fit to populate his universe with other beings, intelligent creatures, such as ourselves. How can I state this with such authority? In the year 1947, our military forces recovered from the dry New Mexico desert, the remains of an aircraft of unknown origin. Science soon determined that this vehicle came from the far reaches of space. Since that time, our government has made contact with the creators of that spacecraft.

Although this news may sound fantastic and indeed terrifying, I ask you not to greet it with undue fear or pessimism. I assure you, as your President, that these beings mean us no harm. Rather, they promise to help our nation to overcome the common enemies of all mankind; tyranny, poverty, disease, and war. We have determined that they are not foes, but friends. Together with them, we can create a better world.

I cannot tell you that there will not be any stumbling or missteps along the road ahead, but I believe that we have found the destiny of this great land: to lead the world into a glorious future. In the coming days, weeks, and months, you will learn more about these visitors, why they are here, and why your leaders have kept this a secret from you for so long. I ask you to look to the future, not with timidity, but with courage because we can achieve in our time, the ancient vision of peace on Earth and prosperity for all human kind. God bless you."

The President reviews what he has just written and is satisfied with the content. However, he needs someone to provide him with some honest feedback about it. He decides to give the cards with his speech to his old friend, Governor Connally, when he sees him tomorrow before they ride together in the motorcade through Dallas, Texas. He trusts Connally and is certain that he will provide the feedback that is needed. [15]

11/22/63 At Daley Plaza in Dallas, Texas

Two men enter a tall building known as the Texas School Book Depository. They casually walk up the stairs to the sixth floor and enter an abandoned room with windows that face Daley Plaza. From this vantage point, they can see Commerce, Main, and Elm Streets converge at the other end of the plaza and enter a railway bridge, known as the Triple Underpass. They can also see a grassy knoll and wooden picket fence to the right of Elm Street before them. They move several cardboard boxes around and assemble a rifle that they had concealed under their clothes. They know that the presidential motorcade will be traveling right past them on Houston Street and then turn left onto Elm Street where it will enter the Triple Underpass at the other end of the plaza. [16]

Three men, dressed as tramps, walk along the other side of the wooden picket fence. One of these men is a professional assassin known as Charles V. Harrelson. He is supported by E. Howard Hunt and Frank Sturgis. At a bushy area near the corner of the fence, there is a

Secret Service agent and a man who is dressed as a Dallas police Officer. This man is actually a French Corsican, known as Jean Soutre. He is also known as QJ/WIN with the CIA's ZR/RIFLE assassination team.

It is a hot, sunny day in Dallas as President Kennedy and First Lady Jackie Kennedy, along with Governor and Mrs. Connally, are riding in the back of a limousine with the top down. The Kennedys are waving to the pleasant crowds on each side of the vehicle when a loud explosion is heard and smoke rises from the fence on the grassy knoll. The President reacts to being hit in the throat. Mrs. Kennedy places her hand on the President's arm and looks at him in horror. Another shot is heard coming from the sixth floor of the Depository building. Governor Connally's hair flies up and his mouth opens as he is hit from behind.

Another shot is fired from the grassy knoll, but the bullet hits a freeway sign. There is another shot fired from the Depository building. But, that bullet also misses and hits the street just behind the limousine. Finally, as the wives are attending to their stricken husbands, the President's skull explodes in a halo of blood and brain matter. He is slammed violently backward to the left rear where he rebounds off of the back seat and falls to the floor. [17]

The hit teams behind the fence quickly disassemble their rifles and hide them in the tool bag of a railroad worker in the area. The sniper, posing as a police officer, and the Secret Service agent appear to be looking for the assassin and escape without notice. The three people, posing as tramps, appear to be drunk and oblivious to the situation. The police arrest them and take them to the police station. The men in the Depository building run from the rear of the building and enter a station wagon that departs so rapidly that a door is left open.

A man, by the name of Lee Harvey Oswald, is working at the Texas School Book Depository. He calmly leaves the building and is seen sneaking into a movie theater. The police are summoned and Oswald is arrested for the murder of President Kennedy. [18]

12/24/63 At a Bar in Washington, D.C.

Evens and Stan Edwards are celebrating Christmas Eve together in a local bar. After consuming a few drinks, Evens asks Stan, "Do you think Oswald acted alone to kill President Kennedy?"

Stan bursts into laughter and then turns very somber as he says, "Oswald didn't kill anyone. He was only used as a patsy for the crime."

Evens' jaw drops and his eyes become wide open for a few seconds. Then, he asks, "How do you know that?"

Stan gulps down a shot of tequila before saying, "I can't tell you that. But, you might find the motion picture film that Abraham Zapruder took of the assassination to be very revealing."

Evens asks, "What do you mean?"

Stan says, "Assassinations do not occur because an attacker gets in a lucky shot. They happen because the normal security measures for protecting the target are removed. The only Secret Service agents anywhere near the President when he was killed, were the two sitting in the front seat of the limousine. The driver slowed the car down during the shots instead of speeding up and the one in the passenger seat only looked back and watched rather than protecting the President after the first shot was fired. There should have been men standing on the side running boards and the back bumper as there were for the Vice President's car."

Evens shakes his head and says, "My God! What could have caused those agents to be involved in the assassination of someone that they are sworn to protect?"

"Well, didn't you find it odd that the CIA prepared a 350 page report on their RHIC-EDOM mind control projects so soon after the Kennedy assassination?"

"Are you saying that someone used mind control on those people?"

"I don't know. But, it is a possibility. The report describes a way of turning men into electronically controlled robots that can be programmed to kill on demand."

"How is that possible?"

"In the RHIC phase, which stands for Radio-Hypnotic Intra-cerebral Control, the individual is put into a trance and given suggestions that are activated by key words or tones. In the EDOM phase, which is an acronym for, Electronic Dissolution Of Memory, the memory of an individual is affected to either eliminate or alter the memory of events by electronically jamming the brain." [19]

Evens lets out a deep breath and asks, "Career officers are not ever debriefed by mind control, are they?"

Stan says, "You want to bet? The debriefing is done in such a way, that in many cases, it actually causes memory damage. They use several different things. I've seen guys coming back with blanks only in certain places of their memory. They use hypnosis and drugs. They also use electronic manipulation of the brain. When they use hypnosis, they'll use a set of earphones at the same time that repeat 'You do not know this or that' over and over. They turn on the sonics and the electrical patterns, which give you memory, are scrambled. You can't hear the ultra-sonics and you can't feel it, unless they leave it on too long and then it boils your gray matter."

Evens says, "I thought the research had stopped on ultrasonics?"

"Yeah, the research HAS stopped. They've gone operational. It ain't research any more. They know how to do it."

"Do the police use mind control?"

"At the highest levels, yes. The FBI uses it, and they give a lot of help to the local police. Our Constitution doesn't permit us to do much that is legal. But, let me tell you something. The cheapest commodities in the world are human beings."

Evens says, "Okay. That explains how it could be done. But, it still does not explain who is behind it. Who has all of the resources needed to accomplish this and then cover it up?"

"Well, the answer to that question can be found by asking, 'Who had the most to gain by the President's death and who had the means to assassinate him as well as cover it up?' Kennedy had planned to drop Lyndon Johnson as his running mate in the next election and now he is the President of the United States. Three days after Oswald was conveniently killed by Jack Ruby, while being transferred in police custody, President Johnson authorized the FBI to handle the investigation. It just so happens that Kennedy was also planning to force the retirement of the head of the FBI, J. Edgar Hoover. Two days later, Johnson appointed a 'Blue Ribbon' commission, headed by Judge Earl Warren, to examine the evidence and make a determination on the assassination. With evidence coming only from the FBI, the commission is certain to make the determination that Oswald was the lone assassin and that Jack Ruby only acted out of a desire for justice.

"Several people, who were involved in the assassination, were arrested shortly after the incident. But, with the cooperation of Sheriff Decker, all suspects were turned over to the FBI along with all evidence of the arrests. In addition, all stray bullets and other evidence, including a freeway sign that was struck by a bullet, have been removed. The FBI has been very effective at intimidating and coercing uncooperative witnesses.

"However, they still have some major problems to cover up. Several people saw two men, with a rifle, on the 6th floor of the Depository building beforehand. Still others heard shots and saw smoke coming from the fence-line on the grassy knoll. The Depository employees heard shots being fired on the floor above them. None of them saw Oswald on that floor, or saw him come down the stairs and exit the building. They did say that he looked calm, holding a can of Coke, afterward. Jack Ruby was seen running from the scene and was chased by a police officer as he drove away in a black car. Richard Carr saw two men run from behind the Depository and get into a Nash Rambler station wagon. Oswald was also seen leaving the scene in the same type of car.

Evens says, "Okay, Johnson and Hoover have the means to cover up what really happened. But, they do not have the resources to prepare an assassination."

"That's correct. There were at least two separate sniper teams involved, in addition to the two Secret Service agents in the limousine. Then, you have Oswald and Jack Ruby, who are known to be associated with organized crime. You can be sure that the FBI and the CIA have large files on these men. So does the Army intelligence service, which was suspiciously ordered to stand down on the day of the assassination. As you know, the President's brother, the Attorney General, has been waging war against organized crime. What better way to put an end to that war, than to remove his biggest supporter?" [20]

Evens asks, "So, who could possibly have access to the FBI, CIA, Secret Service, and the military, not to mention organized crime?"

"Well, it might interest you to know that there are high ranking members from all of those groups who belong to the same organization. That same organization also stands to benefit greatly with a strong military industrial complex as a result of the United States being drawn heavily into the Vietnam War. It just so happens that, two days before he was killed, the President approved an Accelerated Withdrawal Program to have our forces out of Vietnam by 1965. Two days after the President's death, Johnson rescinded that program with National Security Action Memorandum 273. Of course, the organization that I am referring to is the Council on Foreign Relations."

Evens asks, "What do you know about how the government works?"

"Don't kid yourself. This country is controlled by the Pentagon. All major decisions are made by the military. The CIA is just the whipping boy. The people in the National Security Agency are the ones who have the hit teams. Look into their records. You won't find a thing. Look into their budget. You can't. The CIA is just a figurehead. But as far as intelligence goes, the NSA is far superior to them and far in advance of the 'black arts'. The CIA gets blamed for what the NSA does. The NSA is far more vicious and far more accomplished in its operations. The American people are kept in ignorance about this. And, they should be, too."

Evens says, "What you're saying is that the military is more dangerous than the CIA or other intelligence groups?"

"The CIA gathers the information. But, the military heads the show."

"What you are suggesting, I guess, is that there is an invisible coup d'etat which has occurred in the United States?"

"Yep. There is a group of about eighteen or twenty people running this country. They have not been elected. The elected people are only figureheads for these guys who have a lot more power than even the President."

Evens asks, "You mean the President is powerless?"

"Not exactly powerless. He has the power to make decisions on what is presented to him. The intelligence agencies tell him only what they want to tell him. What people don't know is that the global corporations have their own version of the CIA. Where they don't interface with the CIA, they have their organizations that are all CIA trained. They have double agents inside the CIA that are loyal to those corporations. We've got a military dictatorship right now. But, it ain't overt. It's subtle."

Evens asks, "You mean those twenty men you were talking about?"

"Yeah. If the people of this country actually knew that, they would say 'no' the next time they were asked to go to war. They need the people behind them to fight the wars. And, if they knew the true facts of who's running things, there wouldn't be the following they'd need to defend the country. That fact alone keeps the sham of politics and 'free elections' going. The American people, like most people, have to feel that they have some say in what they do and that they're the 'good guys'. You've got to maintain the sham of freedom, no matter what. It doesn't make any difference what party is in charge. From an operational sense, the government would operate as it presently does." [21]

Evens says, "Well, I can tell that you are filled with the Christmas spirit."

Stan says, "Bah, humbug. What is there to be Christmasy about? There is no peace on Earth or any goodwill toward man."

"It doesn't sound like you hold out much hope for mankind."

"That's because I don't."

The Exchange

4/24/64 At White Sands Missile Range, New Mexico

After briefing President Kennedy about the Grudge 13 Report, Brigadier General Evens has been placed in charge of the Exchange Team that will be going to planet Serpo.

While the team members were undergoing their training at Camp Perry, there was little for Evens to do because the complex was isolated from the rest of the Intelligence Training Facility. But, the members also underwent specialized training at Sheppard Air Force Base, Wichita Falls Texas; Ellsworth AFB, South Dakota; Dow AFB, Maine; and even at isolated locations in Mexico and Chile. Since this required the members to come in contact with other people while on and off duty, they each had to be kept under close surveillance. It was especially difficult for them when they were asked for their names. They usually made up names in those situations, which worked as long as they remembered the names they had given.

Four of the Team Members were pilots and they had a wonderful time while they learned to fly the Eben craft that was captured in 1949. The plan called for these selected few to fly the craft back to Earth in case of an emergency. They spent many weeks at the Nevada complex learning to fly the recovered Eben craft. It wasn't hard to fly, once they understood the operation of the controls. Unfortunately, many of the UFO sightings back in 1964 and 1965 could be attributed to the test flights by our Team Members.

The General went with the team wherever they went and monitored the training that they had to endure. The worst thing he felt that they all had to go through was being locked inside a 5' x 7' box that was buried seven feet underground for five days, with just food and water and no contact with anyone else and in total darkness. But, they all performed admirably and all of the original team members completed the training in good shape and in high spirits. The Team was allowed about 15 days off duty, but they were closely guarded.

Just prior to their trip, the team members were transported to the United States Disciplinary Barracks at Ft. Leavenworth, KS and confined in locked cells. This prevented them from communicating with anyone from the outside world and kept each under close watch. Evens hated this treatment of people that were giving so much of themselves for humanity, but he did everything he could to ensure that they had every convenience and were treated properly by the guards.

Unfortunately, there was a change in plans. We received a message from the Ebens stating that they did not wish to make the exchange during their initial visit to Earth. They wanted to meet with our official representatives first and then plan the exchange in person. This created many problems since our Team was ready for the exchange. We sent a return message, but we did not receive a reply.

In December of 1963, the Ebens sent a message confirming the time, date and location of their landing. The message stated that two craft were en route to Earth and would make the appropriate landing at the pre-arranged location. However, our government was suffering from the loss of President Kennedy during this time period. Some on the project wanted to cancel the exchange because of his death. But President Johnson was briefed and decided to continue with the event, although Johnson didn't really believe that it would happen.

Two locations were prepared. One "cover" location was on Holloman Air Force Base near Alamogordo, New Mexico and the other, which would be the actual landing location, was west of Holloman near the southern entrance to White Sands Proving Grounds. General Evens was on site for the event along with the Team Members. The first Eben craft entered our atmosphere during the afternoon of April 24, 1964. The Eben craft landed at the wrong location, near Socorro, New Mexico. We were able to communicate a message to the Eben craft that they landed at the wrong location. The second Eben craft picked up the message and landed at the correct location.

The Eben craft landed exactly at the location we sent. There were 16 senior U.S. Government officials on the ground. Some were political and some were senior officials, including military officers. The Ebens exited their craft and walked under a pre-fabricated canopy. The Ebens gave gifts of their technology. They also used a crude translation device, which appeared to have some sort of microphone with a read-out screen.

The senior U.S. official was given one of the devices and the Eben kept the other one. The officials spoke into the device and the screen showed a printed form of the voice message, both in Eben and English. It was crude and hard to understand everything that was said, but it worked well enough for the two species to communicate with one another.

EBE-2, known as Lucy, exited from the back of a Van parked nearby and walked up the ramp into the Eben craft. A cylinder with the remains of Charlie (EBE-1) was carted toward the craft by four men until an EBE levitated the cylinder into the craft. Another EBE exited the alien craft and walked over to the van. The side door was opened, the EBE sat down inside, the door was closed, and the van drove away.

The Ebens stated that they were willing to receive the twelve humans and 90,500 pounds of their supplies, but not until the following year. July of 1965 was set as the date of the exchange and the location decided upon was the Nevada Test Site at Area 51. When all business was concluded, the Ebens said farewell and expressed wishes of peace and friendship.

Our officials expressed their gratitude for the meeting and wished them a safe journey home. With that, the Ebens re-entered their craft and flew away. [1]

7/11/65 At the Nevada Test Site of Area 51

After the meeting at White Sands, the Team Members were transferred back to their cells at Ft. Leavenworth where they were kept until May of 1964. Then they were transported back to Camp Perry where they were kept isolated for the next six months, going over the same training that they received previously. Naturally, General Evens remained with them and in-sured security as well as assisting them whenever he could. He actually became close friends with the Team Commander.

In April of 1965, the team was transported back to Ft. Leavenworth where they were con-fined there until July of 1965. Evens made sure that all of their needs were met and that they were treated well by the guards. The team's spirits remained remarkably high and they be-came even higher as the date of their departure approached. Three days before the scheduled transfer, they were transported to the Nevada Test Site. When they arrived, they verified the inventory of all their supplies, which included the following:

MUSIC – The Team Members took the following types of music: Elvis Presley, Buddy Holly, Ricky Nelson, The Kingston Trio, Brenda Lee, The Beach Boys, Bob Dylan, Peter Paul & Mary, The Beatles, Loretta Lynn, Simon & Garfunkel, The Hollies, Chubby Checker, Bing Crosby, Dinah Shore, Vera Lynn, Tommy Dorsey, Ted Lewis, Ethel Merman, the Everly Brothers, Lesley Gore, Marline Dietrich, The Platters, Doris Day, Connie Francis, the Shirelles, Frank Sinatra, Dean Martin, Perry Como, Guy Lombardo, Glenn Miller, Rosemary Clooney, Al Jolson, Christmas Music, and U.S. Patriotic Music. The Classical music in-cluded: Mozart, Handel, Bach, Schubert, Mendelssohn, Rossini, Strauss, Beethoven, Brahms, Chopin, Tchaikovsky, and Vivaldi. Also included were Indian Chanting Music, Tibetan Chants, and African Chants for the intended benefit of the Eben hosts.

CLOTHING – The Team Members took the following clothing: 24 pairs of specialized flight suits, 112 pairs of underwear, 220 pairs of socks, 18 hats including jungle style and regular ball caps, 50 different types of footwear, military clothing, load bearing belts and har-nesses, military backpacks, 30 pairs of civilian casual pants, shorts, sleeveless shirts, 15 pairs of athletic shoes, 100 pairs of athletic socks, 8 athletic supports, 24 pairs of thermal under-wear, 24 pairs of thermal socks, 6 pairs of cold weather boots, military-style hot weather clothing, 60 pairs of gloves military work-style, 10 containers of military-style sanitary gloves, 6 pairs of cold weather gloves, 10 laundry bags, disposal surgical gloves, military-style warm weather jackets, military-style cold weather jackets, civilian-style warm and cold weather jackets, 10 pairs of warm weather sandals, 24 military safety helmets, 24 military-style flight helmets, and 1,000 yards of fabric for the repair and making of clothes.

MEDICAL EQUIPMENT – The Team Members took the following medical equip-ment: Portable X-ray machine, 100 pre-packed medical kits for advanced trauma care, exam-ination scopes for the stomach bladder and rectum, eye examination equipment 120 pre-packed surgical kits, 120 pre-packed military field medicine kits, 30 military-style field medical sanitation kits, 75 water testing kits, 50 water analysis kits, 75 FAST kits, 1,200 food testing kits, 500 pieces of miscellaneous surgical tools, 5,000 packages of insect repellent, 250 medical intravenous kits/with fluids, 16 pre-packed detailed medical testing kits, 50 pre-packed field medical testing kits, 5 military Medical Portable Hospital Tents with base, 2 Military Medical Portable Deployment Kits, 18 Military Medical Blood testing kits, 3 portable military chemistry testing stations, 2 Advanced Biological Testing Kits, 15 Military Radiation Treatment Kits, and 1,000 pounds of miscellaneous medical equipment.

TESTING EQUIPMENT – The Team Members took the following testing equipment: 100 pieces of geological testing items, 2 military soil testing stations, 2 chemistry testing stations, 6 radiation testing meters, 2 military radiation testing stations, 2 biological testing stations, 2 100cc tractors, 4 100cc digging tool tractors, 10 pre-packed military Soil Testing Kits, 16 astronomical telescopes, 2 Military Star Stations, 4 military power generators (1-10,000 watts), 4 civilian power generators, experimental solar collecting equipment, 50 portable two-way radios with FM frequencies, 6 military combat radio platform kits, 50 pre-packed military radio repair kits, 1,000 different frequency tubes, 30 pre-packed military electrical testing and repair kits, 3 solar testing stations, 1 experimental solar testing station, 10 solar collection panels with collector containers, 15 air sample collection kits, 6 diamond drills, 10 military special access kits, 1,000 pounds of C-4 explosives with 500 blasting caps, detonating cord, time fuse, Military shape charges, and a Nuclear Detonating Kit.

MISCELLANEOUS EQUIPMENT and ITEMS – The Team Members took the following miscellaneous equipment/items: 100 military blankets, 100 military sheets, 24 pre-packed military combat deployment kits, 80 pre-packed military combat tent kits, 4 military mobile kitchen deployable kits, 6 military survival stations for warm weather, 6 military survival stations for cold weather, 2 military weather stations – combat style, 50 military weather balloons, 24 military handguns, 24 military rifles (M-16s), 6 M-66 weapons, 2 M-40 grenade launchers, 2 military 60mm motor tube with 30 rounds, 100 military air burst flares, 5,000 rounds of .223 ammunition for the M-16 assault rifles, 500 rounds of .45 ammunition, 60 M-40 rounds, 15 Freon dispersal containers, 15 compressed air dispersal containers, 20 tanks of oxygen gas, 20 tanks of nitrogen gas, 20 tanks of miscellaneous gases for cutting equipment and testing, 75 military-style sleeping bags, 60 military-style pillows, 55 military-style sleeping platforms, 6 pre-packed military deployment combat field living platforms, 250 different style padlocks, 6,000 feet of different types of rope, 24 repelling kits, 10 seismic deep hole drills, 1,000 gallons of fuel, 4 military-style phonographs, 10 Military cassette players, 10 reel-to-reel tape players, 60 belts, 10 military sound collection equipment kits, 25 military Intelligence Collection Kits, and 1,000 other miscellaneous items.

VEHICLES – The Team Members took the following vehicles: 10 military-style combat motorcycles, 3 military M-151 Jeeps, 3 military trailers, 10 Military repair kits for jeeps, 10 Military repair kits for the motorcycles, 1 Military lawn mower, and 1,500 gallons of fuel for all of the above items.

FOOD – The Team Members took the following food items: 10 years of C-Rations, 25 pre-packed containers, 100 pre-packed containers of freeze-dried food items, 100 cases of various canned food items, 7 years worth of vitamins, 100 containers of energy bars/snack items, 1,000 gallons of water, 150 military survival food kits, 16 boxes of various alcoholic wines, 150 cases of drinking fluids, chewing gum, lifesaver candy and various other miscellaneous food items.

MISCELLANEOUS ITEMS – The Team Members took 2,000 pounds of various other items. In addition to these supplies, each Team Member also took a "pill" with them. The pill was standard issue for intelligence agents operating behind enemy lines. The pill could end their life if, for some reason, the Ebens turned out to be hostile. Selected Team Members also carried small containers of liquid Nitrogen. Ebens were vulnerable to extreme cold. In case the Eben's turned hostile, the liquid nitrogen could be used to neutralize Ebens during an escape attempt. The Team Members were instructed to spray the substance directly into the face of an Eben. [2]

Evens is nervous as he watches the twelve Team Members march to their designated position in preparation for boarding the alien craft when it arrives. He can tell that some of them are showing signs of being worried and anxious. But, most of the team is in high spirits with smirks on their faces. At exactly ten hundred hours, a huge disk-shaped craft descends from above. It is much larger than the previous craft they have seen and it makes no sound at all. Batteries of photographic and video cameras are all pointing at the craft as it hovers about a foot off the ground.

A doorway opens, a ramp lowers to the ground, and an Eben representative disembarks. Only a selected few officials are present this time to meet with the EBE. After a few introductory comments are made on the communication devices, an official points at the pallets of supplies for the team. Other EBEs disembark to measure the size and weight of the pallets. When all is found to be acceptable, the 90,500 pounds of supplies are loaded on board the craft.

While all of this is taking place, Evens watches as two EBEs walk over to the team and he wonders if he will ever see them again. He is feeling sad to see them leave, especially the Team Commander, who he considers to be a good friend. The Team Commander is speaking into a microphone for a journal to be recorded on a small magnetic tape cassette recorder. He uses three-letter code names for the Eben control personnel and three-digit numbers for each Team Member. [3]

The Team Commander says into a microphone, "We are ready. Hard to think we finally made it. Team is motivated and calm. Final briefing by MTC and MTB. Cargo packed in EBE craft. Might have some problems with guns. Will be talking to the MVC. 899 (Security) and 203 (Asst. Commander) will have overall charge of weapons. No sync system or we don't know about them. Everything moving smoothly. 700 (Doctor 1) and 754 (Doctor 2) will give each member final check before boarding.

"OK, the supplies have been loaded on the craft and it fits. But we have to transfer all of it to the bigger ship once we get to rendezvous point. Really excited about this. No reservations by anyone. MTC asked all members to make final decision. The team all said go. We go."

7/11/65 On Board the Alien Craft

The Team Commander says into his microphone, "Interior of EBE craft is big. There are three levels. This is different than the one we trained on. I think that was a scout craft, this one is a shuttle craft. We stored the cargo in lower level. We will sit in the center level and the crew will sit in the upper level. Strange looking walls. They seem to be dimensional. There are three stations, four of us will sit in each station. No seats just benches. We wouldn't fit in those small crew seats.

The MVC says we don't need anything special, no O2 or helmets. Don't know what to do with them. OK, final checks. MTC gave us final words. One prayer was said. 475 (Linguist 2) really nervous. 700 (Doctor 1) will watch him. The hatch is closed. No windows. We can't see out. Everyone is seated in their respective seats on the bench. No retention harnesses. OK, well, bar across us.

The craft is starting its engine, or what they call energy thrusters. Seems like we are moving but nothing happening inside. Still able to report this. Really dizzy now. 203 (Asst. Commander) sitting next to me and he is faint. Something feels really funny. I can't think straight.

DAY 1 – Entry 2

We made it to the rendezvous craft. We don't know where we are, but it seemed like we all fainted or was really confused during this trip. According to my wrist watch, it took about six hours or maybe more. We left at 1325 and it is 1939. But not sure of the day. We flew into the big ship. We are standing in a bay or something.

There are many EBEs helping us. They seem to understand we are confused. The cargo was off loaded in one big move. The platform containing the cargo was moved without unloading the individual cargo. This ship looks like the inside of a real big building. The ceiling is about 100 feet high in this area of the ship.

OK, we are being moved into another part of the ship. OK, we moved to another room or area. What a big ship. I just can't describe how big this is. It took us about 15 minutes to walk to our area. Seems like it is something special for us. The chairs are bigger. But there are only 10 of them. OK, I guess 203 (Asst. Commander) and myself will sit in different location above these seats.

We are moved by some sort of elevator, but I can't understand how it works. Everyone is hungry. We have our backpacks containing some C-rats and I guess we eat now, but must ask the MVC. I can't find him and we can't communicate with the two EBEs here.

They seem to be real nice. 420 (Linguist 1) will try to use his language skills. Almost funny. Sounds like a screaming match. We just used sign language indicating we want to eat.

One of the EBE brought us a container with something in it. Doesn't look good but I think it is their food. Looks like mush or oatmeal. 899 (Security) will taste it. Well, 899 said it tastes like paper. I Think we will all stick to C-rats.

OK, MVC finally showed up. Told us we will begin trip soon in two mils. I think he means minutes but don't really know. Maybe it wasn't such a good idea to eat before leaving. We don't feel any weightlessness and we don't feel dizzy. But we don't know what to expect from this point on. They are indicating we must sit in the chairs.

Entry

I'm not sure just how long we were in the containers. We sat in the chairs and a clear container was placed over us and the chair. We were isolated in this bubble or sphere. We could breath OK and could see out, but we really felt dizzy and confused. I think I fell asleep or fainted. I think this is another day, but my watch says one hour since we sat, but I think it is the next day.

Our time instruments are located in our backpacks which are stored in another area of this room. We are still in these spheres but it seems OK. Well, 899 (Security) figured out how to get out because he is standing up. He opened my sphere. Not sure if we should be out of this thing. 899 (Security) said an EBE came in and looked at us and left. Other team members sleeping. 899 (Security) and myself walking around this room.

I retrieved the time instruments. Seems like we have been traveling about 24 hours or so. No windows to see. Originally we were told it would take about 270 of our days. OK, EBE came in and pointed to the chairs, I guess we need to go back and get into them.

Entry

Since I am not sure of which day it is I won't state a day as to my entry, so I'll just say entry. We are all sick. Dizzy, upset stomachs. 700 (Doctor 1) and 754 (Doctor 2) gave us medicine to settle our stomachs. But we really feel bad. We seem to be unable to focus our eyes and seem to not know which way to turn up or down and don't know the way to sit down. Really bad feeling.

Medicine helps a little. We are able to eat a little. 700 and 754 (Doctors) tells us to eat and drink the water we brought along. We are doing that and feel a little better. I can't concentrate on anything so I can't report anymore right now.

Entry

Feel a lot better. EBEs came in and did something to the room. It all seems clearer and we are not so confused and dizzy. We ate again and drank more water. Feeling a lot better. We are out of the spheres, but must stay in them at certain times.

EBE showed us a series of lights above the entry panel. Green, Red and White lights. If the light is red, we must sit in the spheres. If the light is white, we are OK. EBE never explained the Green light. Maybe that isn't good.

We have no idea what day it is, only that it is 2319. Our date recorder isn't working very well, according to 633 (Scientist 1). He thinks we have been going for 10 days but not really sure. We have been confined to this room for the entire time. I think this room was made for us and we are safe in this room.

Maybe it wouldn't be wise to leave it. No weightlessness. Don't know how they do it. But we do feel a little lightheaded when we walk. Seems room is pressurized. Ears are popping a lot. If we have to sit in this room for 270 days we will really be bored. We can't really do much. All our equipment is packed away.

We have our backpacks but they only contain a few items. We want to clean up, but can't find a bathroom except the containers we are using to relieve ourselves. They are small metal containers that are emptied by the EBE every now and then. EBE brings us food, their food. We tried it and it tastes like paper really no taste but maybe it is something special for space travel. 700 (Doctor 1) is eating it. He seems OK but it is upsetting his bowels. Their water is milky looking but tastes like apples. Strange.

Entry

It has been a long time since I have made an entry. We are guessing that we have been on the ship for 25 days. But we might be off by about five days. We were locked into our spheres for a long period of time. We had to leave in order to relieve ourselves and finally were able to open the spheres.

But when we did, we all got sick, really sick. Dizzy, confused and some couldn't walk. We had trouble urinating and moving our bowels. 700 and 754 (Doctors), who ate the EBE food didn't seem to be as sick as us. They treated us with medicine. EBE came in and pointed a blueish light on our heads. We felt better, much better after this.

But he pointed to the chairs and we figure we must get back into them. We showed him our waste containers and pointed to the chairs in a confused manner. He understood and then left the room. EBE came back with small containers we could place inside the spheres.

He also brought in small jugs of the milky liquid and made a motion for us to drink it. So we went back into the spheres and just sat there with the waste containers and the jug of the milky stuff. We drink that and seem to be better, except 518 (Biologist), who seems to be sick. But we were cautioned to stay inside the spheres.

Entry

I don't have any idea how long we stayed in that spheres this time. But EBE came in and made a motion for us to come out. We were able to move around without being dizzy or sick. EBE even allowed us to leave the room. We walked along a very narrow hallway for a long period of time, maybe 20 minutes. We then got into some sort of elevator, which moved fast because we could feel the motion.

We came out into a very large room that contained many Ebens sitting in seats. Maybe this is the control center. Our escort made a motion to go into the room. We could see control panels which contained many lights. There were four different stations containing six Ebens each. They were in levels.

The top level inside this room contained just one seat. One Eben was seated in that chair. We figure he must be the pilot or commander. He seemed busy with an instrument panel. There were many television screens, but they all showed Eben language and series of lines, both vertical and horizontal. Maybe some sort of graph.

We were able to wander around without any Eben bothering us. 633 and 661 (Scientists) were really interested in this. 633 (Scientist 1) seemed better. There was one window. But we could not see anything. It was dark but we could make out wavy lines. Maybe some sort of distortion in time. We must be moving faster than light speed, but we can't see anything out the window.

OK, MVC finally arrived. He explains in broken English, that we are halfway to home planet. Everything is functioning properly and we all will feel better once the craft gets out of this time wave, as he calls it. MVC says we can walk around any part of the ship, but we must stay together.

We must be shown how to operate the movement centers. We are thinking he is referring to the elevators. It seems simple, just placing your hand over one of the operating lights, white and red. White moves it and red stops it. We hear some type of ringing sound, but MVC says it is only space sounds, whatever he means by that. We were able to walk around the ship, but it is so large it is difficult to understand how such a large ship can move so fast.

633 (Scientist 1) wants to see the engines. MVC takes four of us to the engine room or whatever they wish to call the room. It contains large, very large metal containers. They are in a circle, with the ends of each pointing into the center. Many pipes or some type of large tubes connects them.

In the center of these containers is a copper colored coil or something looking like a coil. There is a bright light being shined from a point above into the center of the coil. We hear a very dull hum, but no major loud sounds. 661 (Scientist 2) thinks it is a negative matter versus positive matter system. [4]

Entry

I dreamed of Earth. I really had some vivid dreams of Colorado, the mountains, the snow and my family. It was as if I was really there. I had no worries and never thought of my situation inside the foreign spaceship. Then I awoke. I was confused and disoriented. I was in a bowl, well, it looked like a bowl to me. I don't remember how I got here. My first thought was to my crew. I pushed open the top of this glass bowl and it opened. I heard a hissing sound coming from the seams or seals. I looked around and saw that I was inside a room. Not a room I remember. But all of us were inside these glass bowls. All the other crew members were asleep.

I climbed out and realized my legs were really sore. But I climbed out and went to each glass bowl and checked on the crew. I found only eleven of us. Somebody is missing. But who? I am so confused. I'm also very thirsty. I can't find any of those water bottles. We had some but I can't find any. My eyes are really having a problem focusing. But, I have to record everything. I found number..... He is alive. Who is missing? I have to look at each bowl.

This room is large. The ceiling looks like a bed mattress. The walls of this room are soft. Not very much in this room except for the bowls and some tubes running from the bowls to the floor. I see lights flashing on the bottom of each bowl. There are bright lights in the ceiling. Inside the mattress or something. I can't open these bowls. I've tried everything. I must get some help from the Ebens. I found a door but it won't open. I can't remember how we opened the other doors.

How long have we been in these bowls? I can't seem to remember much. Maybe the traveling in space causes problems with a person's mind. They told us this during training but we never had anyone travel this far in space before. We are the specimens. Maybe I should go back into the bowl. Maybe I awoke too early. My wristwatch says it is 1800 hours. But what day, what month, what year? How long have I been asleep?

The floor seems to be soft with wires running in a criss cross pattern. I see some type of television screen in the corner of the room. I think it might monitor the other bowls. I can't read anything on the screen because it is in Eben language. I do make out lines, maybe health monitoring lines on the screen. I hope that means everyone is breathing and is alive.

But we are missing one man. Did I forget something? Did someone die? I can't remember. I have some type of rash on my hands. Real burning sensation. Maybe it is radiation burns from something. But where are the radiation monitors we had in our packs? Where are our survival packs? I can't find anything. I am returning to the bowl. I am lying down. I will stop making entries in this diary.

I am awake again. Ebens are in the room. My bowl is open. Some of my crew are walking around. The Ebens are helping them. I climbed out of my bowl. The English speaking Eben sees me and I asked him if everyone of my crew was alright. He doesn't understand, "alright". I point to the crew. I say eleven. Where is number twelve? EBE-1 then points to a bowl that is empty and says, Earth man is not living. OK, someone died. But who?

My crew is walking around in a state of confusion. I can't get anyone's attention. They look like the living dead. What is wrong with them? I asked EBE-1, what is wrong with them. EBE-1 replied, space sick, but will not be sick soon. OK, that makes sense. I have no idea how long. We are still flying but don't know how long. EBE-1 brings some fluids and something looking like a biscuit. Fluid tastes like chalk and the biscuit doesn't have any taste. We all eat it and drink the fluid. Almost instantly we feel better.

OK, get organized. I told 203 (Asst. Commander) to round up all of the crew. Found 308 (Pilot 2) missing. Must be the dead crew member. EBE-1 came back and led me to 308 (Pilot 2). He was in a bowl, something like a coffin. 700 and 754 (Doctors) will examine 308. EBE-1 cautioned us not to take 308 out. I don't understand the caution. 700 and 754 (Doctors) are here. I try to tell EBE-1 that these guys are our doctors and must examine 308. EBE-1 said no, because of infection. I guess 308 (Pilot 2) must have had some sort of infection and it could be contagious. But is 308 dead? Don't know. We will take EBE-1 advice. 700 and 754 (Doctors) just looked into the bowl and said it looks like 308 is dead.

Everyone else looks OK. The fluids and biscuit must have contained some type of energy food. We can focus our eyes and can actually think. No one can remember how we got into this room. All our equipment is here. Everyone is concerned about our status. EBEs are friendly but won't tell us much. 899 (Security) is concerned with being locked into a room.

633 and 661 (Scientists) think we should be keeping busy. I agree. I order everyone to get their packs and ration belts, inventory everything inside and see if something is missing. That will occupy the team for some time. My wristwatch says it is 0400. But what day? Date? Don't know. Very strange not being able to gauge time. We have no reference inside this room or this spaceship. The year clock that we brought will be unpacked once we can get to the stowed gear. We don't know where that is.

All crew inventoried packs and ration belts. Everything is accounted for. 899 (Security) wants to arm himself with a handgun. I said no. We don't need guns. No EBEs have been hostile towards us. We got out a compass. It doesn't work. We got out our radios. We will keep them on our belts. Don't know if they work away from the room. But we turned them on and they work. We can hear each other. Good, we have communication. But we must be careful. The battery life is only about two days.

I suggest everyone start writing down their thoughts. Keep some sort of a diary, like I am doing. I was ordered to do this and will continue to do it as long as I can. But I won't keep it day by day, since I can't tell when a day ends. 661 (Scientist 2) suggests we make up a calendar and a time system as long as we are here. Good idea, he will do that. The calendar will run on a seven day system. We will use our wristwatches to gauge a 24 hour period and then consider that one day. We will start at 0600, which is in about 45 minutes.

518 (Biologist) set up the air monitor. Seems we are breathing regular air. The team is joking about 518's nomenclature use for regular air. Good that we have some humor. OK, this is the beginning of day 1, it is 0600 hours. 661 (Scientist 2) will keep the calendar. We should have done this before. We have no idea how long we have been inside this spaceship or how long we have been traveling. Didn't we get into the command station? Maybe I dreamed it. I can't find the first part of my diary.

EBE-1 came in. Told us journey almost over. Led us to hallway. We got into moving room and moved to another part of the ship. We came out into a large room with many items, I can't identify them but they look like clothing chests or bedroom chests. We are also led to a large table with food.

EBE-1 tells us to eat. He said, "Good food, eat."

Well, we all look at each other. 700 and 754 (Doctors) say "Let's eat."

OK, we find plates. Seems like ceramic plates real heavy. I chose something that looks like a stew. I then got a biscuit, same as we ate earlier. The drinks were in metal containers. Same fluid we drank earlier. We all ate. Very little taste in the stew. Something like potatoes, maybe cucumbers, some type of stems. Not really bad. The biscuits taste the same. Everyone sat and ate. We found something like apples but didn't taste like apples. They were sweet and soft. I ate one. Leaves an after taste in my mouth. Team looks happy. Some are joking about not having any ice cream.

OK, the MVC is in the room. First time we saw him. He speaks through EBE-1. The language really bothers my ears. The high pitch sounds and then the vocal tones sound very strange. EBE-1 tells us MVC wants us to prepare for landing.

OK, how do we do that?

We must get into bowl room and get in bowls. No one wants to do that but if we have to we will do that. We are led back to the moving room and travel back to the bowl room. We climb into the bowls. Some use the pot for relief of our bowels and bladders. Then we climb into the bowls. The lids close but we are awake. We just lie there. I fall asleep.

First Day on Planet Serpo

Entry

The bowl lids have opened. My wristwatch says 1100. I guess it is still day 1. We climb out.

EBE-1 is at our side. He tells us "Landing home".

OK, I guess we are there. We gather our gear. 700 (Doctor 1) reminds us to wear our sunglasses once we exit. We pack up and walk down a long hallway and then into another moving room. We travel for one minute. Then a door opens. We are in a large room. We see our stowed gear. Large room, many smaller spaceships stored here.

A large door opens. Bright light. We see the planet for the first time. We walk down the ramp. There is a large number of Ebens waiting for us.

We see a large Eben, the largest one we have seen yet. He comes forward and starts speaking to us. EBE-1 translates a welcome message from the Leader. I guess this guy is the leader. About one foot taller than the others. The leader tells us we are welcome to the planet. He called it something we do not understand.

EBE-1 isn't doing a good job translating. But we are led to an open arena. Looks like a parade field. The ground is dirt. Looking up, I see blue skies. The sky is very clear. We see two suns. One brighter than the other. The landscape looks like a desert, Arizona or New

Mexico. No vegetation that we can see. There are rolling hills but nothing but dirt. This must be the central village or town.

We landed in an open area with large structures like electrical towers. Something is sitting on top of these towers. On the center of the village is a large tower. Looks like a concrete structure. Very large, maybe 300 feet. Looks like a mirror is placed on top of this tower. All the buildings look like adobe or mud huts. Some are larger than others. Looking in one direction, can't tell any actual compass readings but there is a very large structure.

All the Ebens are dressed in the same clothing, except for some of the Ebens who were on the spaceship. Now I see others dressed in a dark blue outfit, different from the others. Each Eben is wearing some type of box on their belts. All have belts. Can't see any children, but maybe they are the same size too. Our boots leave an imprint into the soil. The brightness is almost too much for our eyes without sunglasses.

Looking around 360 degrees, I see buildings and barren land. Can't see any vegetation. I wonder where they grow their food. What a planet. Hard to believe we will have to live 10 years here. But a journey of 1000 miles begins with one step. Can't remember who said that but that just came to mind. But large numbers of Ebens are welcoming us. They seem friendly.

Then, almost shocking us, someone speaks English. We all look around and see an Eben. This Eben speaks very good English. This Eben, we call EBE-2, speaks almost fluent English, with exception of not really pronouncing the letter w. But EBE-2 does a good job speaking English. EBE-2 says we are welcome to the planet Serpo. OK, that is the name of their planet. EBE-2 shows us a device and tells us everyone of us must wear it. It looks like a small transistor radio. We put it on our belts.

The weather is extremely hot.

Asked 633 (Scientist 1) to take temperature.

633 says it is 107 degrees. Very warm.

We take off top jacket and that leaves us with a one piece flight suit.

The Ebens look at us but seem very friendly. Some are wearing some type of shawls. I asked EBE-2 about that,

EBE-2 says they are females.

OK, I see. They all look alike. Really hard to tell one apart except for uniform. Some have different colored uniforms. I asked EBE-2 about that, EBE-2 says military uniform. OK, that makes sense.

EBE-2 led us to a series of huts, looking like adobe style houses. There are four. Behind them is an underground room, or storage area. It is built into the ground, underground.

We have to walk down a ramp. The doors look like military igloos that store our atomic bombs on Earth. All our gear that was taken off the spaceship is stored there. We walked down into this area. Very large room. Very cool, a lot cooler. We might have to sleep here. All our gear is there. Sixteen palates of gear.

This igloo is made up of something like concrete but not the same texture. Feels like soft rubber but still hard. The floor is made of the same stuff. There are lights in the ceiling. Looks like spot lights. They have electricity.

We must inventory all our gear sometime.

We go back to the huts. The huts are cooler than outside. But still very warm.

We must get organized. I tell EBE-2, we will need to be alone and get organized. Then I realize EBE-2 is female.

She says OK. We will be left alone.

I asked for the body of 308 (Pilot 2).

EBE-2 seems to be confused and doesn't know about any body.

I explained to EBE-2 who held her hands across her body and bowed her head. It was really an emotional sight because she was almost crying.

EBE-2 told us that the body would be brought to us but she must check with her trainer.

The word trainer kind of shocked me. Is EBE-2 in training and someone is teaching her? Or is the word trainer in Eben something different in English. Maybe that means leader or commander. Don't know. But EBE-2 left.

I told 203 (Asst. Commander) to gather everyone in the lower storage area. We will have a team meeting.

633 (Scientist 1) suggested we start the calendar as of today. It is 1300 on our Day 1 on planet Serpo. [5]

Entry

We had a serious problem. How do we explain our science to an alien entity, who doesn't know Einstein, Kepler or any of the other scientists of our time. Simple mathematics seems so foreign to them. EBE-2 is the smart one. She seems to understand our language more than EBE-1. She even seems to understand our basic math. We started with the basic math. 2 plus 2. Then progressed on. She understood and even caught on so quickly that she continued on without our help. We realize she has a great IQ when she repeated 1000 times 1000 and came up with an answer.

We showed her our slide rule. It took her a couple of minutes to figure it out, although I don't think she fully understood all the symbols on the slide rule. She is really something. We found a personality in her. Maybe because we have more contact with her than the others.

She is very warmhearted, one can just sense that in her. She really cares about us and she even worries about us. During our first night, she seemed to make sure everything was just right for us. She warned us of the heat and the light. She mentioned that SERPO does not get dark, like Earth. I wonder how she knew that. Has she visited Earth? Maybe she is just educated on Earth's properties. Maybe they have books about Earth.

Anyway, on the first night, she told us about the winds, what winds. Gusty winds start just when the one sun sets. The other sun does not but stays in the lower horizon. The winds blow dust, free dust into our huts. We had a very difficult first night. We call it night but it seems that the Ebens just call it a period of their day. EBE-2 knew the word day but didn't compare it to Earth's day. Maybe she hasn't been to Earth. We didn't sleep well during our night. The Eben's don't sleep, like we do. They seem to rest for periods of time and then wake and go about their business, whatever that might be.

Day 2 on Planet Serpo

Entry

When we awoke, EBE-2 was there, outside our hut. I opened the door and she was waiting. Why? How did she know we were awake? Maybe the huts are being monitored by some sensor. EBE-2 told us to follow her to the eating place. She didn't use the word dining hall or chow hall or facility. She used the word place. Once I gathered the team, we walked across the village. I'll call it a village for the sake of wording.

We entered a large building. It seemed to be large, based on the small stature of the Ebens. There was food on tables. I guess we'd call this place a chow hall. Ebens looked at us but carried on eating. Do they not cook inside their huts? Maybe everyone eats here. We walked to the food tables. Same food we saw and ate on the spaceship except some items were different.

They had large bowls of something like fruits. Strange looking things. They also had something like cottage cheese, it tasted like sour milk but after the initial taste, alright. I encouraged each team member to eat and drink. We might as well get used to the food. But 700 (Doctor 1) tells us to eat just one of their meals a day and stick to our C-rations for the other meals. That way, our system will adjust to the Eben food. We sat at a table, small compared to our standards and ate.

The Ebens numbering, probably about 100, just ate and didn't really bother us. Every now and then, we would catch Ebens staring at us. But we were the freaks, not them. We are the visitors. We are the aliens. We must really look strange to them. We all look different, they all look the same. How can they compare us to them? They can't. We stare at them, they stare at us.

We then see a different looking Eben. Very strange looking creature, large, long arms, almost floats along with long legs. Can't be an Eben. We all stare. This creature just floats by us and didn't even look at us. I find EBE-2.

She is eating with three others. Once I approach her, she stands and almost bows her head towards me. Maybe just a greeting, have to remember that.

I ask her about the creature we saw, I ask if that was some other type of Eben. EBE-2 seems confused.

She asked me what creature.

I used the word creature. Maybe that was an insult or maybe she didn't know the word. I pointed to the thing at the other end of the building.

She then saw what I meant. EBE-2 said, no Eben, just visitor. Like you, pointing to me.

OK, I see, they have other alien visitors here. I guess we are not the only ones. I then asked EBE-2 what planet did that visitor come from?

EBE-2 said, something like CORTA, not sure of the exact word although I asked her to repeat it twice.

OK, where is CORTA?

She walks me to a television, at least it looks like one. It is positioned in the corner of the building. It is set up like some type of command station.

She places her finger on the glass and something appears. The universe? Star systems. I don't recognize any of them. She points to a spot and says CORTA.

OK, where is Earth?

She points to another spot and says Earth. Based on this television glass space map, CORTA and Earth are very close. But I don't know the scale of this map. Maybe they are a trillion miles apart or maybe 10 light years. But they seem close. I'll have to have one of the scientists look at this and see.

OK, I thank EBE-2.

She seems pleased. She almost looks like an angel. She seems so very nice. She touched my hand and pointed to my table and said, eat. Good eat?

I laughed and said, yes, good chow hall food.

She looked puzzled. I guess she doesn't know what a chow hall is.

I pointed to the building and said, chow hall, Earth eating place.

She repeated what I said, chow hall, Earth eating place.

I laughed and walked away. Now she will think all Earth restaurants are called chow halls.

We returned to our huts. We must get better organized. We have a meeting. Everyone seems OK. We wonder about latrines. Where do we relieve ourselves?

EBE-1 comes by, almost as if he was reading our minds, maybe they can even do that. He shows us pot in hut.

We all wondered what that was. OK, that is our latrine. Realized that won't work very well but we'll do what we can. Then we realize the pot has some sort of chemical inside. Our wastes are dissolved or something like that. Can't really tell. Each of the four huts has one. That will work for the time being.

EBE-2 tells us to walk on ground. Not sure what she means by that but 420 (Linguist 1) says that might be to just walk around. OK, that we will do.

I organize the teams. I will remain with 225 (Pilot 1). I want 633 and 661 (Scientists) to look at the television glass map and see if they can tell which star system is CORTA. I ask 518 (Biologist) to take temperature readings and general weather observations. I know it is hot. Very hot. Must be over 140 degrees.

754 (Doctor 2) warns us to keep covered from sun radiation. She says radiation levels are high. Doesn't sound very good to me.

This reminds me of Nevada, 1956, during one of the atomic bomb testing. We had hot weather and we had to worry about the radiation from the atomic blasts. Now we are on a strange planet 40 light years from Earth and we have radiation and heat. But we have to explore. That is why we were sent.

We start walking around. 475 (Linguist 2) will take photographs with our military cameras. I hope the film is not affected by the radiation. How do we develop it? Maybe we didn't think of everything.

I team up with 225 (Pilot 1). We walk to a large open door building. We walk in and it looks like a classroom but no Ebens are here. There is a large television tube. It takes up the entire wall. There are some lights flashing on this television tube. We examine the tube. It is very thin. I wonder how it works. Where are the tubes or the electronics. But maybe they are more advanced in this area than us. They must be. We don't find much else in this building.

We move on. Wow, it is so very hot. I hope 1 get use to it. We find a large tower. Looks like an antenna tower but it has a large mirror. We saw this when we first arrived yesterday. We find an Eben standing near the door but he moves to one side. We ask him if he understands English. He just stares at us but seems friendly. I guess he doesn't speak English. We move on into the building, Can't find any stairs. But we see some type of round glass room. Maybe it is an elevator.

Then we hear English. We turn around and find EBE-2 standing there. Where did she come from?

I ask her if we may explore this building.

She said yes, of course, She points to the glass room and says go up.

OK, we enter the glass room. The glass door closes and it goes up real fast.

In no time we are at the top. But what is this? We ask EBE-2, what is this?

She points to the sun and then points to the top of the room, where the mirror is located. She then points to the ground.

OK, we see it. The tower is in the middle of a circle. The circle is situated on the ground. In each quadrant of the circle is a symbol. I see that the sun is directed through the mirror maybe this isn't a mirror as we know it since the sunlight travels through it, but once the sunlight travels through it, the light is directed on a symbol within the circle.

EBE-2 says that when light contacts symbol then Ebens make change. Not sure what that means. Maybe she means it tells the Ebens what to do.

225 (Pilot 1) seems to think it is a sun dial. When the sun strikes a symbol, the Ebens change what they are doing and do something else.

Maybe the Eben day is structured. Or maybe this is their clock. Strange. But we are on an alien planet.

I'm glad I still have my sense of humor.

This is only our first day, first day of school. We have a lot to learn. We have to keep an open mind. We can't keep comparing things to Earth. We have to open our minds to new ideas and new science. All these things are foreign to us but we must learn. I pointed to my wristwatch and then pointed to the ground and in a gesture to show EBE-2 that the two items are time pieces. Not sure if she understood. But I said time and she then understood. Yes, she said, Eben time, pointing to the ground.

I pointed again to the wristwatch and said, Earth time. EBE-2 then almost smiled and said, no, no Earth time on SERPO.

OK, that makes sense.

225 (Pilot 1) said, she just told us that Earth time doesn't work on SERPO.

Yes, I guess she did.

What good are our watches or time device here? They don't work. We have to start using Eben time. But we must also maintain our time because we must know when to leave. Ten years seem like a million. Maybe based on Eben time that it might just be a million years. Let's hope not. No time to think about home, we have a mission and duties to perform. We are a military team and we must maintain that idea.

225 (Pilot 1) and myself go back into the glass bowl and go down to the ground.

We walk into another building, large again. Inside we find rows and rows of plants. This must be some sort of greenhouse. They are growing food. Many Ebens are inside. They look at us with some glares. But we just walk in and around.

One Eben comes up to us and speaks but in Eben. He seems to be telling us something. He points to the ceiling and then to our heads. Maybe he is telling us to cover our heads.

We must find EBE-2. We go back outside and then find EBE-2. She always seems to be near. Now we understand why, she is monitoring us by the devices we are wearing on our belts. I ask EBE-2 what is that building. She says food making place. OK, maybe we contaminated the place. We told her that another Eben spoke to us and then pointed to our heads. EBE-2 seemed confused and walked back into the building with us. The same Eben exchanged words with EBE-2.

EBE-2 then told us that we must wear a cover on our heads in order to enter. Why? But we don't argue.

This other Eben produces some sort of cloth hat and we wear it. We walk about. The Eben seem happy. We look at their plants. They are growing food in soil. They have a watering system. They also have some sort of transparent cloth over each plant. I point to the watering system and ask EBE-2, if that is water, drinking water.

EBE-2 said yes. Then she senses we are thirsty. EBE-2 leads us to a place near another entrance and offers us water, at least we think it is water. Tastes like chemicals but it is water. Actually tastes good. [6]

Subsequent Days on Serpo

The leader of the Ebens is a larger creature than the others. He seems to be more aggressive than the other Ebens. When I say aggressive, I don't mean in a hostile way. He seems to be the boss, similar to me, as the team commander. His voice, although after all this time, I still can't understand any words, is harsh and with a tone that is different from the rest. 203 (Asst. Commander) claims the leader has an attitude. I agree. He is extremely friendly to us and has accommodated all our requests. The leader has requested many things from us. Most of which, we have provided.

One strange thing is our blood. He wanted all of us to supply blood samples. EBE-2 explained that the blood, or health fluid as EBE-2 explained it, was necessary for them to supply any medicine to us if we should ever need it. 700 and 754 (Doctors) feels that a blood sample might just be used for other purposes. We have not allowed the Ebens to utilize 308's (Pilot 2) body for experiments. They took all 308's blood without my approval. I reported about that in log 3888. We had a very tense situation with the Ebens about that.

When we traveled to the building housing 308's body, we were confronted by several Ebens. EBE-1 showed up and I explained that we wanted the body of 308. EBE-1 told us the body was in storage and we could not take it. We told EBE-1 that we will take it. The eleven of us walked by the Ebens, numbering six, and walked into the building. They did not attempt to stop us. While inside, we could not open any of the containers. There was some type of system, maybe crypto style that was being used to lock the containers.

We did find the container housing 308's (Pilot 2) body. We decided to send 899 (Security) to our storage area and get some explosives to open the container.

EBE-2 showed up with the leader. EBE-2 was extremely polite and asked us to wait. She used the word please several times. In fact, she actually used the English word beg. We backed off and I told EBE-2 that we wanted our friend's body and we wanted to examine it. EBE-2 translated that to the leader. There was a long exchange of words between the two.

Finally, EBE-2, who seemed very frustrated, told us that the leader would like us to go to another location and speak with another Eben, a doctor, about the body of 308 (Pilot 2). EBE-2 explained that everything we wanted to know about 308's body would be explained to us by the Eben doctor, who EBE-2 said spoke English.

I told EBE-2 that I would leave 899 (Security) and 754 (Doctor 2) here to guard the body and I would take the others to the location containing the doctor. EBE-2 translated that to the leader. Again, there was a long drawn out exchange of words between the two. It lasted for several minutes.

Finally, EBE-2 stated that the leader would like all of us to leave this building and go to visit with the doctor. I told EBE-2, no, I would not leave the body of 308 (Pilot 2) alone. I felt that this was going to be a confrontation. I told 518 (Biologist) and 420 (Linguist 1) to go back, obtain our handguns and come back ASAP. I was not going to allow the Ebens to countermand my decisions. When EBE-2 heard this, she told me to wait and placed her hand against my chest. I told her to translate that to the leader. Again, there were several minutes of word exchanges between the two.

EBE-2 then stated that the leader would bring the doctor here to discuss the situation with us. EBE-2 asked me to please don't send your men for guns. Guns are not needed. We can settle this without guns. Please don't.

I told EBE-2 that we would not get the guns but we would not leave until we saw 308's (Pilot 2) body. The leader did something with the communication device on his belt.

About 20 minutes later, three Ebens showed up inside this building. One of the Ebens, who identified himself as a doctor, spoke very good English. This doctor had a strange sounding voice, almost like a human's voice. This doctor did not have a high pitch accent, like EBE-1 and EBE-2. I was very impressed with this doctor. I just wonder where he has been for these past 18 months. We never saw him before.

This doctor told us that 308's (Pilot 2) body was not inside the container. The Ebens have done experiments with 308s body because they considered it an honor to have such a specimen to work with. The doctor told us they have used 308's body to create a type of cloned human being. I stopped the doctor at this point. I told the doctor that the body of my teammate was the property of the United States of America, planet Earth. The body did not belong to the Ebens. I did not authorize any experiments on the body of 308 (Pilot 2). I explained that humans consider a body to be religious. Only I could have authorized the use of 308's body for experiments.

I demanded to see the body. This doctor explained the body was gone. This doctor said all the blood, body organs were taken out and used to clone other beings. The use of the word beings really scared me and the others. 899 (Security) became extremely angry. He called the doctor curse names. I ordered 899 to be quiet. I then told 203 (Asst. Commander) to take 899 (Security) out of the building. I realized this matter could really blossom into a major incident. I could not allow that to happen.

There were just eleven of us and we realized that if the Ebens wanted to imprison us or kill us, they could do it very easily. But I didn't think the Ebens would resort to such behavior. I was not going to allow this incident to advance into something worse. I realized there wasn't much we could do about what the Ebens have done with 308s (Pilot 2) body. EBE-2 looked very upset. EBE-2 told me that everyone should be nice. She repeated the word nice many times. EBE-2 did not want this matter to escalate.

I kind of felt sorry for EBE-2. She was trying to mediate the matter. 203 (Asst. Commander) suggested we return to our living quarters and have a team meeting. I told the leader that I did not want any further interference between whatever is left of 308s body and experiments. I pointed my finger towards the leader's face. EBE-2 translated, along with the doctor. The doctor, who was extremely straightforward, told me that nothing further would happen with the body, but advised me very little was left of the body. EBE-2 then told me the leader was concerned that we were upset. That we were their guests. That the leader was upset that we were offended. The leader did not wish to upset us and promised that nothing further would happen to the body.

I thanked EBE-2 and had her relay that to the leader. We returned to our huts. Everyone was upset, especially 899 (Security). I told each member to calm down. I explained our situation, as if each team member didn't already realize it, that we were only eleven military personnel. We had no way of fighting the Ebens. We did not come 40 light years to start a war with the Ebens. A war we could not win. We could not even win a simple fist fight with the Ebens. Yes, maybe we could beat them up but what then? We have to realize our situation and act accordingly. I ordered each member to reconsider the situation and to except the facts about 308's body. I told 633 (Scientist 1) and 700 (Doctor 1) to investigate this cloning procedure with the English speaking Eben doctor. Let's get all the facts about what they did with the body and what we can find out about the body and the Eben's experiments with the body.

EBE-2 came to the hut. I told EBE-2 that 633 and 700 were going to examine what was left of 308's body. They would also conduct research into the Ebens experiments done on 308's body. EBE-2 looked very concerned. It is sometimes difficult for us, even after the time we have been on this planet, to determine the meaning of facial expressions on Ebens faces. EBE-2 replied that she must first obtain approval.

Approval was a new word for EBE-2. She must be reading or learning our language. Maybe she is just picking up our words. I told EBE-2 that she can go get permission but that we were told when we arrived that we did not have any restrictions on where we went. EBE-2 said she would speak with the leader. 633 (Scientist 1) and 700 (Doctor 1) gathered test equipment and prepared themselves for the examination of the Eben laboratory.

According to our time devices, EBE-2 came back about 80 minutes later. EBE-2 said it was alright for my men to visit their laboratory.

I decided that I would also visit it. I, 633 and 700 were escorted by EBE-2 to the laboratory facility. We had to be taken by the heli-transport device, as we call their helicopters. It took us sometime before arriving at this location. According to our compass readings, which are not really compass readings but we made points of references and according to them, we traveled north.

The facility was large, by Eben standards. The building looked like a large single story windowless school. We landed on the roof, or maybe just a landing zone on the roof. We were escorted down a walkway or ramp. They don't have ladders on this planet. They have ramps. We arrived in a room with white walls. We then walked through a hallway into another larger room. We met our English speaking doctor. We saw many other Ebens, all dressed in a bluish colored one piece suit. Different from their ordinary suits I spoke of in past entries.

The doctor told us that all the experiments done inside this building, he didn't call it a laboratory, just a building, are done to create cloned beings. We were lead into another room, where there were rows of containers, looking like glass bathtubs. Inside each bathtub were bodies. I was shocked, as were 700 and 754 (Doctors). Bodies. Strange looking bodies. Not human bodies, at least not all of them. We started walking down the space between the tubs. We looked into the tubs. These were hideous looking creatures.

I asked the doctor what type of creatures were inside these tubs. The doctor told us that these creatures came from other planets. 700 (Doctor 1) asked the doctor were these creatures dead when they arrived? Or did the Ebens bring them here dead. The doctor said all the creatures were brought to the planet alive. 700 asked if the creatures were kidnapped or brought here against their wishes. The doctor was not sure of the word kidnapped. The doctor seemed puzzled. The doctor asked about the question. 700 said that these creatures were taken from another planet and brought to Serpo without permission from them or their leaders of their planet. The doctor said that these beings were brought here for experiments. These creatures are not intelligent beings. EBE-2 then used the word animals.

OK, now I understand. All these creatures are animals from other planets. The doctor didn't seem to understand the word animal. EBE-2 and the doctor exchanged words in Eben and the doctor then said, yes, they are animals. I then asked if there were any intelligent creatures in this building. The doctor said, yes, but that all of them were dead when they arrived on Serpo. 700 (Doctor 1) asked to see these creatures. The doctor corrected 700 by saying beings. OK, I guess creatures are animals and beings are like humans.

Let me first provide a description of these creatures inside these tubs. They are not all alike. The first creature I see inside the tub looks like a porcupine. It appears to have a tube placed inside of it. The tube leads to a box underneath the tub. The second creature I see looks like a monster. It has a large head, big deep set eyes, no ears, a mouth, but no teeth. It is about five feet long and has two lower legs but no feet. It has two arms but it doesn't appear to have any elbows. It has hands but no fingers. This creature also has a tube going through it.

The next creature looked like nothing I can compare it to. It had blood red skin, two spots in the middle, maybe eyes. No arms or legs. It had a very strange odor. The skin appeared to be blotchy with scales. Maybe like a fish. Maybe it is a fish. The next creature was human like. But the skin was white, not skin white, the color white. The skin was wrinkled. The head was large, with two eyes, two ears and a mouth. The neck was very small. The head almost looked as if it sat on the lower torso. The chest was thin, with large bone like protrusions. The arms were curled, with hands but no thumbs. The legs were also curled with feet but only three toes. I couldn't look at any more creatures.

We walked down another hallway, through a room, down a ramp, into another room. We came into a room that looked like a hospital room. There were many beds, or at least some type of bed, Eben style bed. I described them before. In each bed was a living being, as the doctor called it. The doctor told us that each being was alive and well cared for. 700 (Doctor 1) asked the doctor if these beings were ill or sick. EBE-2 had to translate that but the doctor said, no, they are being lived. The three of us seemed really stunned by that word lived. I asked EBE-2 what the doctor meant. EBE-2 exchanged words with the doctor. EBE-2 then used the word grown.

700 Doctor 1) asked the doctor if these were the cloned beings that he mentioned before. The doctor said yes that each being was being grown, using the same word as EBE-2 just used. 754 (Doctor 2) asked the doctor if these beings were being grown like a plant. The doc-tor said yes that is a good comparison. 700 (Doctor 1) asked the doctor how are they grown. The doctor said that certain parts of other beings were used to grow these beings. The doctor said he could not explain the process in English because he didn't know the words. 700 then asked EBE-2 if she could explain the growing process. EBE-2 said she did not know the Eng-lish words. EBE-2 said that parts of the blood and other organs are used to mix a substance that is placed inside the bodies of these beings. That was all EBE-2 could explain in English.

I told 700 (Doctor 1) to go back and get 420 (Linguist 1) and bring him back. While we waited for 420, we looked at these beings. They were breathing. They looked like humans, most of them. Two of the beings on the end looked like humans with dog heads. These be-ings were not awake. They were either sleeping or drugged. 420 (Linguist 1) returned. I told 420 to see if he could translate the method used to grow these beings. 420 then spoke with EBE-2. 420 is really good. However long we have been here, some guess about 18 months Earth time, 420 learned the language well. 420 then said that the growing process involved cells taken from other beings, grown and mixed with chemicals and then inserted into the bodies of other beings. That was about all 420 could explain. 420 did not know the words EBE-2 used. But the word cells was used.

EBE-2 then told me that some things were taken from inside the cells. 700 and 754 (Doc-tors) then asked if the items taken from inside the cells were cell membranes or identification markers for the cells. EBE-2 translated that to the doctor. Both seemed confused and said they could not explain the process because they did not know the English words for it. 700 (Doctor 1) used the word advance biological extraction of the cell membranes. But neither EBE-2 nor the doctor knew anything about that process.

I asked 754 (Doctor 2) if he might understand what they were doing. 754 said that human cells contain smaller substances that can identify the structure with the membranes of the cell. This isn't something that Earth technology has advanced but 754 has read about it prior to leaving. But 754 doesn't think that Earth technology can be used to grow living cells into what the Ebens have done. The Ebens must have found a way to grow cells and to make them into living beings. 700 and 754 (Doctors) said nothing like this is known on Earth.

I then asked the doctor if 308's (Pilot 2) body was used to create a being. The doctor said yes, and showed us the being. I was shocked, as was 700 and 754 (Doctors). This being, with our teammate's blood and cells, looked like a large Eben. But the hands and legs were similar to humans. How could they have grown this being so quickly? Obviously, this is well above our intelligence. I saw all I wanted to see. I told the doctor that we would like to leave.

EBE-2 saw that I was upset and touched my hand. Instantly, I felt concern. EBE-2 was really concerned about what I saw. EBE-2 said we leave. We traveled outside this building, a building that I did not wish to see again. I saw the dark side of this civilization. The Ebens are not the humane civilization we thought they were. But I must say they didn't hide anything. The doctor spoke straight to us. Just like the Ebens. They don't know how to lie. Seeing what we saw will change our impression of the Ebens as long as we stay on this planet. [7]

The Planet

It took our team, in an Eben craft, nine months to travel the distance to planet Serpo. During the trip, all of our team members were frequently dizzy, disoriented and suffered headaches. The Team Members did not experience any weightlessness during the trip. The craft was very large and allowed the team to exercise. Once the team arrived on the Eben planet, it took us several months to adjust to the atmosphere. During the adjustment period, we suffered headaches, dizziness and disorientation.

The Eben planet is located within a solar system of the Zeta Reticulum Star System. The planet has two suns but their angles are small and allowed some darkness on the planet depending on one's location. There is a period of darkness, but not total darkness.

The planet is tilted which allows the northern part of the planet to be cooler. The planet is a little less than Earth's size. The atmosphere is similar to Earth's and contains the elements of Carbon, Hydrogen, Oxygen, and Nitrogen. Zeta Reticulum is approximately 37 light years from Earth.

The bright suns of the Eben planet also presented other problems. Although the Team has sunglasses, they still suffer from the bright sunlight and the danger of sun exposure. The radiation levels of the planet are a little higher than that of Earth. We are careful to cover our bodies at all times.

The Ebens have no forms of refrigeration, except in industry. The temperature of the planet, at the center portion, stays between 94° and 115°. There are clouds and rain, but not frequently. At the northern hemisphere of the planet, the temperature drops to between 55 and 80 degrees. This is too cool for the Ebens, or at least most of them. Our team did find Ebens living in the north, but in very small villages.

Our team eventually relocated to the north in order to stay cool. The ground transportation used by our team is similar to a helicopter. The power system is a sealed energy device that provides electrical power and lift for the craft. It is very easy to fly and our pilots learned the system within days. The Ebens do have vehicles, which float above the ground and do not have any tires or wheels.

There are leaders, but no real form of government. There is virtually no crime that has been seen by the team. They have an army, which also acts as the police force. But no guns or weapons of any type have ever been seen by our team. There are regular meetings within each small community. There is one large community, which acts as the central point of the civilization. All the industry is at this one large community. There is no money.

Every Eben is issued what they need. No stores, malls or shopping locations. There are central distribution centers where Ebens go to obtain items of needs. All Ebens work in some capacity. Children are kept very isolated. The only trouble our team members got into was when we attempted to photograph Eben children. The Army politely escorted us away and cautioned us not to do it again. [8]

Statistics on the Eben planet were collected by our team. Serpo moves around one sun only. The other sun is within the two orbits. The planet's diameter is 7,218 miles. Its mass is 5.06 times ten to the power of 24. The distance from Sun 1 is 96.5 million miles and the distance from Sun 2 is 91.4 million miles. The planet has two moons. Its surface gravity is 9.60m/s 2. Its rotation period is 43 hours and it orbits Sun 1 every 865 days. It has a tilt of 43 degrees. The temperature varies from 43 to 126 degrees. The planet's distance from Earth is 38.43 light years away. The nearest planet to Serpo is named Otto at a distance of 88 million miles. It is colonized by Ebens with research bases, but there are no natural inhabitants there. There is a total of six planets in the Eben solar system. The nearest inhabited planet to Serpo is named Silus with creatures of various types, but no intelligent life forms. The Ebens use the planet to mine minerals. It is 434 million miles from Serpo. [9]

Our Team includes two geologists (they are also cross-trained as biologists). The first thing our geologists did was to map the entire planet. The first step was to divide the planet in half, thus creating an Equator. Then they established a Northern Hemisphere and Southern Hemisphere. Within each hemisphere, they created four quadrants.

Finally, they established the "North and South" Poles. This was the easiest method to study the planet. Most of the Eben communities are placed along the Equator. However, there are some communities established north of the equator in each of the four quadrants in the Northern Hemisphere. There are no communities located at either pole. The southern pole is desert. It is barren land with virtually no precipitation where absolutely nothing grows in this area.

There are volcanic rock formations and part of the extreme south contains a rock desert. Temperatures in the south pole were measured at between 90° and 135°F. Going further north from the south pole in Quadrant 1, the Team found extrusive rocks. This indicated some volcanic activity in the area. Our team found numerous volcanoes in this area.

The Team found several fissure eruptions in this region, with standing water. The water was tested and contained high levels of sulfur, zinc, copper and other unknown chemicals. Moving from east to Quadrant 2, the Team found basically the same volcanic fields of rocks.

However, in one particular location near the north end of Quadrant 2, the Team found an Alkali Flat. On Earth, these were formed by streams flowing into a desert or arid location. Our team found hard mud covered by alkaline salts. Some vegetation was growing in this area.

Moving to Quadrant 3, the Team found a form of Badlands: An arid region that is lined with deep gullies with sparse vegetation. The gullies or valleys were extremely deep, some going down 3,000 feet.

The team found the first Serpo animal in this region. It looked like an armadillo. This creature was extremely hostile and tried to attack the Team several times. The Eben guide used some type of sound device (sonic-directed sound beam) to scare away the creature.

Moving to the Equatorial region, our team found desert-style landscapes, which contained patches of vegetation. The team found numerous pockets of water fed to the ground by Artesian Wells. This water was the freshest, containing only the unknown chemicals. It tasted good and the Ebens drank and used it. Our team still boiled it because during culture tests, unknown types of bacteria were detected.

Moving to the Northern Hemisphere, the Team found a major change in climate and landscape. One Team Member, who had coined it Quadrant 1, in the northern hemisphere, named it "Little Montana." The Team found trees, similar to the Evergreen style of Earth trees. These trees were milked by the Ebens. A white fluid was extracted and drank.

Numerous other types of vegetation were found in this region. Standing water, possibly fed by either Artesian Wells or fissure eruptions was found. In one area, marsh lands were seen. Large plants were observed growing in the marshy area. The Ebens used these plants for food. The bulb of the plant was very large. The bulb tasted something like a melon.

Our Team eventually moved to an area in Quadrant 1 in the northern hemisphere. This area contained moderate temperatures [50° - 80°] and ample amounts of shade. The Ebens built a little community for the team. Most of the remaining exploration of the planet was done from this point. The Team only explored the southern hemisphere once, obtaining geological information.

Because of the intense heat, the Team decided not to venture back. The Team continued to explore the northern hemisphere, where, as the Team traveled towards the north pole, the temperature cooled considerably. The Team found mountains rising to an elevation of 15,000 feet and valleys that sank below the basic mark the team established for "sea level." Lush green fields were found containing a form of grass, but contained bulbs. The Team coined these fields, "Clover Fields," even though the bulbs were not clover.

The radiation levels were lower in the northern hemisphere than at the Equator and southern hemisphere. The north pole contained cold weather and the team saw the first sign of snow. Blankets of snow littered the landscape around the north pole. The snow measured about 20 feet, at its deepest.

The temperature was a constant 33°. Our Team never found the temperature to vary in this region. The Ebens could not stand to be in this region for long. They suffered extreme hypothermia. The Team's guide wore a suit, similar to a space suit with built in heaters.

Our Team found evidence of past Earthquakes. Fault lines were found along the northern tip of the southern hemisphere. Exfoliation was observed along with extrusive rocks, which indicated magma flows in the past.

Our Team collected hundreds of samples of Serpo soil, vegetation, water and other items for testing on Earth. During our Team's exploration, we discovered numerous types of animals. The strangest was the "Beast" which looked like a large Ox. The animal was timid and never seen to be hostile. Another animal looked like a Mountain Lion, but had long fur around the neck. This animal was curious, but was not considered hostile by the Ebens.

During the exploration of Quadrant 4 of the southern hemisphere, the team found a very long and large creature that appeared to be a snake. This creature was "deadly," as explained by the Ebens. The head of the creature was large and contained almost human-like eyes. This was the only time our Team used their weapons and killed the creature.

There was a lengthy discussion about weapons. At the end, the Ebens didn't really care. So our Team Members decided to take some just in case. Not for a fight, God knows, as our Team is vastly outnumbered, but for the safety aspects of it as the weapons make the members *feel* safe.

The Ebens didn't appear to be upset that the Team killed the creature, but were upset they used a weapon. The team brought four .45 caliber Colt (standard military issue) handguns and four M2 carbine rifles. After killing the creature, the team dissected it. The internal organs were strange and nothing similar to an Earth-style snake. The creature measured 15 feet long and 1.5 feet in diameter. The team was curious about the eyes.

Examination of the eyes revealed cones, similar to human eyes. The eye contained an iris and the back contained a large nerve, similar to the optic nerve feeding into the creature's brain. The brain was large, much larger than any Earth-based snake. The Team wanted to eat the meat from the creature, but the Eben guides politely told them "No." [10]

The bodies of water on Serpo do not contain fish, as we know. Some bodies, near the equator, do contain strange-looking creatures, similar to eels (small and about 8–10" long) and are probably a cousin of the land-based "Snake." There is something like a jungle, near the marshlands, but not the jungles that we're familiar with. [11]

Here is some information about the animals on Serpo. — The Armadillo-like creature was not aggressive. It just scared the Team Members. The Eben guide directed some type of sound (very high pitch) at the Armadillo creature and that scared it away. These creatures were seen at several locations around the planet. Some were larger than others, but they were not aggressive.

Only the snake-like creature was aggressive, which forced the Team to kill one. The snake-like creatures were located in just one location and the Team never saw another one.

As for birds, there were two types of flying creatures. One resembled a hawk and the other looked like a large flying squirrel. Neither were aggressive and the Team could never catch one for examination.

As for insects, they had small bugs, similar to cockroaches, but smaller. They were harmless, but did get into the Team's equipment. They had a hardened shell, with a soft interior body. The Team never observed any flying insects, such as flies, wasps, etc. Several other small bugs were found and identified. [12]

The Ebens

The Eben civilization was estimated to be about 10,000 years old. They evolved from another planet, not on Serpo. The original home planet of the Ebens was threatened with extreme volcanic activity. The Ebens had to relocate to Serpo in order to protect their civilization. This occurred some 5,000 years ago.

The Ebens fought a battle with an enemy for a period of time. Our Team Members estimated the war lasted about 100 years, but, again, that is our time. The war was fought using particle beam weapons, developed by both civilizations. The Ebens eventually were able to destroy the enemy planet, killing the remaining enemy forces. The Ebens warned us that several other alien races within our galaxy are hostile. The Ebens stay away from those races.

The interplanetary battle, which the Ebens fought with another race, occurred about 3,000 years ago. The Ebens lost many thousands in their battle. The Ebens completely eliminated all of their enemies. The Ebens have never fought another war since. The Ebens have been space travelers for the past 2,000 years. The Ebens first visited Earth about 2,000 years ago. [13]

The Ebens have a very stable, structured civilization. Each male has a mate. They are allowed to reproduce (in somewhat the same sexual way we do), but are limited to only a specific number of children. Our team never saw a family with more than two children.

The Eben civilization is so structured that they planned the birth of each and every child, spacing them apart to allow the proper social grouping of the civilization. Eben children mature at a super rate, compared to Earth children. Our team watched live births, attended to by an Eben doctor, and then watched the development of the child over a period of time. They matured at an alarming rate.

The Ebens have scientists, doctors and technicians. There is one educational facility on the planet. If one is chosen, you attend the facility and learned the job one was best qualified and suited for. Although it is extremely difficult to judge or measure, the team estimated each Eben's IQ to be 165.

The Ebens have no single ruler. There is a "Council of Governors," which the team named. This group controls every single action on the planet. The members of the council seem to have been around for a long time. Since Ebens don't age – or at least our team couldn't detect aging – it is difficult to judge the age of each member.

There are about 100 different villages or living locations for the Ebens. The Ebens only use a small portion of their planet. They do mine minerals in remote areas of the planet and they have a large industrial plant in the southern portion of the planet near a body of water. Our team determined this plant had some sort of hydro-electrical operation.

The Ebens developed a different type of electrical and propulsion system, which is unknown to the team. They are able to tap into a vacuum and bring back an enormous amount of energy from that vacuum.

Our team's living quarters, which consist of several small buildings, contain electricity powered by a small box. This small box supplies all the power our team needs. Ironically, the electrical equipment our team brought on the trip works using our power source only.

Ebens do die. The team members saw deaths, some from accidents and some from natural causes. The Ebens bury the bodies, similar to our method. Our team saw two air accidents involving their intra-planet flying vehicle.

The Ebens worship a Supreme Being. It appears to be some sort of deity relating to the Universe. They conduct daily services, normally at the end of the first work period. They have a building or church they enter to worship.

Our team found limited supplies of commodities on the planet. Large buildings are used to harvest food products. The soil is not rich in a lot of minerals. Ebens use a form of organic agriculture to harvest food items. [14]

As to the Eben culture: They have a form of musical entertainment. The music sounds like tonal rhythms. They also listen to a type of chanting. The Ebens are dancers. They celebrate certain work periods with a ritual dance. The Ebens form a circle and dance around, listening to the chanting type of music. The music is played on bells and drums, or something similar to them.

There are no televisions, radio stations or anything like that. The Ebens play a game, something like soccer, but with a larger ball. The object is to kick the ball down a field into a goal. The game has very strange rules and is played for long periods of time. They also have another game, mostly played by the children that consist of making formations with groups of Ebens. They seem to really enjoy the game, but our team cannot understand the game.

Although the Eben civilization have no televisions, radios, etc., each Eben has a small device belted to their waists. This device gives orders to perform a particular task, provides news of pending events, etc. The device displays a screen, similar to a television screen but in a 3-D style format.

The Ebens live in a very simple society. The individual Eben family contains a male, female and at least one child. Our team did find some families with as many as four children.

We later learned those families were caring for children of Ebens who were either on Traveling Missions (exploring the universe) or dead Ebens.

The individual Eben families live a simple life. Their homes are constructed of clay, some type of material similar to wood, and some metal. The houses all look the same. They appear to be something from the Southwest, looking like adobe. The interior of the house consists of four rooms. One room was the sleeping room where all Ebens slept in the same room on mats, a food preparation room (kitchen), a family room (the largest in the house) and a small waste room.

The Ebens do not have a physiological need to release body wastes as we do, but the Ebens do have small collection locations in the residence for their body wastes. The Eben's body is extremely efficient in processing all food taken in. Their body wastes consist of a small amount of fecal matter, similar to a small cat dropping.

Our Team Members never saw any urine excretion from an Eben. On the other hand, our Team Members' wastes consisted of a large amount of both fecal matter and urine. The Ebens accommodated our team by digging large waste reception sites for our Team Members' waste.

Although our Team Members honored the privacy of the Ebens, our Team was allowed to witness births. Our team, snooping around, was also able to capture the sexual activity of the Ebens. The males and females have similar sexual organs and perform intercourse as humans do. The frequency of sexual activity does not appear to be as often as our society performs it. It is believed that they perform the act for pleasure and reproduction.

Food is a problem for our Team Members. Our Team consumes mostly military-style C-Rations, but eventually we had to switch to Eben food. The Ebens have a variety of food items. They grow vegetables similar to potatoes, but they tasted different. They also have some type of lettuce, turnips, and tomatoes. They were the only items similar to ours.

The Eben's also grow other vegetables. These are strange looking round items with long vines. The Ebens cook the vines and eat the large portion of the plant raw. The Ebens have some type of white liquid, which we first thought was a form of milk. But after tasting it, our Team realized it was different, both in taste and content. The liquid comes from a small tree located in the northern portion of the planet. The Eben's literally milk the tree for the liquid. It appears to provide some sort of pleasure to drink the stuff. But, our Team Members never got a real "taste" for the liquid.

The Ebens do cook food. They make pots of stew, which is extremely tasteless to our team. We used a lot of salt and pepper with it. They also bake a form of bread. It is non-yeast bread and tastes fairly good, but causes extreme constipation to our Team Members. We have to drink large quantities of water in order to digest the bread.

The one common food that Ebens and our Team Members liked was the fruit. The Ebens eat a great quantity of fruit. The fruit, although different from anything we know about, is sweet. Some of the fruit tastes something like melons, while others taste like apples.

Another problem was the water. The water on Serpo contains a number of unknown chemicals found by our team. Our Team eventually had to boil the water before drinking it. Seeing this, the Ebens built a large plant that processed water for our Team.

Our Team witnessed an aircraft accident that killed four Ebens. The Ebens performed a form of ritual at the crash site. The Ebens transported the bodies to a medical facility and examined the bodies. Our Team Members were always allowed to accompany the Ebens, except during rest periods, when the Ebens close their doors for privacy.

Our Team Members saw the sorrow in the eyes of the Ebens during the death of their own. Later, after the last work period of the day, the Eben's had a "funeral," at least that is what our Team concluded it was. The Eben bodies were wrapped in a white cloth. Several types of liquids were poured over the bodies. Large numbers of Ebens would stand in a circle, chanting.

The sounds became almost nauseating to our Team Members. The ceremony lasted for a long time. Finally, the bodies were placed in metal containers and buried in a remote location away from the communities. After the burial, the Ebens had a feast. Large tables of food were brought out and everyone ate, danced and played games. This occurred at every Eben death witnessed by our team. [15]

The Team

It is difficult to speak science to the Ebens. How do we explain Einstein? How do they explain their Einstein? We have a difficult time relating our science to them. However, they seem to understand our physics and chemistry quicker than we can. We managed to observe some strange things about their technology.

First, we took apart one of the devices, they placed on our belts. It wasn't easy. There were no screws or bolts holding it together. We had to break the thing. The electronics inside were nothing we have ever observed. There were no transistors, tubes, rectifiers, coils or other electronic components like our technology. This thing had just wires and some bulges in the wires at certain points. There were two components, which none of us have ever seen.

We could not use our frequency counter to determine the frequency it transmitted and received. It was out of our range. 633 and 661 (Scientists) used some other equipment to analyze the thing but couldn't understand it. We asked the Eben Scientist, whom we called EBE-4. The problem was the translation. EBE-2 had to translate because EBE-4 didn't speak English. A lot is lost in translation even though EBE-2 does a pretty good job with English.

We showed EBE-4 one of our portable radios. The Motorola FM radio was pretty complex to us. It was new and contained four channels. 661 (Scientist 2) took apart the radio in front of EBE-4, explained the parts and the different crystals we use for frequency. EBE-4 couldn't understand it. He seemed as lost with our radio as we did with theirs. EBE-2 told us that EBE-4 couldn't understand the radio or how it worked. So that was our dilemma. How do we exchange science?

Each of our civilizations must learn from the other. So, we decided to begin a school. Our first days were pretty tough. We started with simple things, which we thought would be similar to what they would know. We chose light. 661 (Scientist 2), who did some teaching before, started with wavelengths. 661 started with non-visible light and the different angstroms. Then 661 showed them the spectrum of light. 661 showed them cosmic rays and how we measured them. Then he went to gamma rays, x-rays and ultraviolet light. 661 explained that light was what we called electromagnetic waves. Over a period of Eben days, 661 explained everything he knew about light, frequencies and a description of the frequency bands.

During this time, several other Ebens came in and listened. EBE-2 was extremely tasked with translating this. EBE-2 had a difficult time explaining everything 661 said because she didn't know the Eben words for everything. But she did an outstanding job of describing what 661 was saying. I don't think EBE-4 got everything 661 said but it didn't take long for EBE-4 to realize what 661 was describing. 661 then showed EBE-4 a repair manual for one of our test equipment. Since everything, or almost everything, we brought was military, it was a military manual. The manual contained schematics of the circuits. EBE-4 was completely lost. But eventually figured out what 661 was showing him was the inside of the test equipment.

661 then started showing the basics of electricity. Ohms laws: different formulas to figure voltage and amperes. EBE-4 was confused, to say the least. But one of the other Ebens, who had come in to listen, grasped the idea quickly. We called this Eben, EBE-5 or the Einstein. This Eben was smart, exceptionally smart. After three years, we finally met an Eben who could grasp our science. The only problem is he couldn't speak English. But he asked questions, which EBE-4 didn't really do. Although it took several lessons to teach EBE-5 what each letter meant in a formula, EBE-5 finally realized what we were saying.

This Eben must have had an IQ of 300. EBE-5 actually solved some simple problems set up by 661 in basic electricity like solving for the amount of resistance in a circuit and simple things like that. It was a remarkable scene. EBE-5 became our ace student. We couldn't get rid of the guy. He followed us around and asked questions through EBE-2. When EBE-2 wasn't available, he would simply point and shrug his shoulders. We'd speak to him in English or have 420 or 475 (Linguists) translate to him. But only 420 (Linguist 1) could understand most of what EBE-5 was saying.

This came to another interesting point. EBE-5 looked a little different than the rest of the Ebens. During the last several years, we have noticed some of the Ebens, especially the ones who live up north, look different. There heads seem to be bigger. They have a more weathered looking face. EBE-5 is from the north. He lives in the second village to our north. The distance is approximately 5 kilometers. I drew the map in entry 4432, showing all the villages in the north. I'm sure they have more villages farther away but we haven't visited them yet. EBE-5 also does not have a mate. This is strange but not totally uncommon. We have found several Ebens without mates. We haven't delved into the personal life of EBE-5 but 518 (Biologist) wants to.

I explained in one entry about the Eben technology when it comes to screws, bolts, etc. They don't have any. Everything they make is sealed with some sort of solder or melting method. When we visited their manufacturing plant, we were amazed at how efficient they were with manufacturing furniture, their helicopters or flying devices. We still haven't seen their main spacecraft manufacturing plant. It must be in the far west and south. I'm sure we will visit the place someday.

We still have seven years, or at least seven Earth years left. As I mentioned before, we have totally lost track of Earth time. We gave that up many of our years ago. We have gauged our time on Eben time, which is extremely complex, as I mentioned before. We had a feast today. What a feast. We used our last C-Rations but the Ebens didn't really care for our food. We did kill a beast. As I mentioned before, the Ebens allowed us to kill the beasts for meat. The meat isn't really bad, 899 (Security) says it tastes like Bear, which I never ate. But Ebens look at us very strange when we eat meat.

Strange, they can clone creatures and other species of humans but they can't eat meat. How strange they are. But they allow us to do just about anything we want and eating meat is something we need for the protein. We used the last of our salt and pepper, which does make eating their food more of a challenge. The Ebens don't have anything similar to salt and pepper. They do have an herb, as we call it, something like Oregano, which they use. It has a tart taste but we have developed a taste for it. The feast was great.

We participated in the dances, which the Ebens really like. They get great pleasure dancing and playing their strange games. I described the games before but during this feast, we saw something different. The game was played like chess but with Ebens standing on a large square area of the compound. The squares were divided into 24 sets. Each set had another 2 spots. Just how or why the Ebens moved was a mystery to us. One of the Ebens would say a word and then another Eben would move. It appeared that it was a team game with six Ebens on each side. We couldn't figure it out but at the end, the Ebens danced with each other, signifying a victory, we think. It was a fun day.

Our Team brought along softball equipment for sporting activity. The Ebens watched the game and laughed out loud. The Eben laugh sounds like a high-pitched yell. Eventually, the Ebens started playing the game, but they never got used to catching the ball before it hit the ground.

Our Team also played touch football. Again, the Ebens watched the game intensely and then played it themselves. But again, like softball, the Ebens never figured out they had to catch the football before it hit the ground!

My team played softball, with some hard-nosed Ebens, who have learned the game. Well for the most part. They still haven't figured out they have to catch the ball before it hits the ground. But they had fun. We have found some extremely gifted athletes among the Ebens. Then again, we found some who had no athletic ability. Just like humans. Our softball game ended when the rains came. We ended up inside the community building. We finished our meals and separated to our living area.

As we do each day, we have our end of day briefing. We check each other for psychological condition and medical health. Our day ends and we start our eight hours of rest. Ebens have a different period of time, as I mentioned before. They rest about four hours, for every 10 hours working time. But we must consider their hour is longer and that their days are longer. So we stopped using our time and used the Eben time.

It is difficult to understand but this is only a diary. Once I return to Earth, I can explain the time difference and how we had to use their time instead of ours. I keep writing about the time in every diary entry but it is important to note that even though we have been here for about three years, Earth time, we have given up Earth time and utilized the Eben time. We tried to use their two suns as a counting system but that didn't work. We then tried to use our own watches but that didn't work. So we gave up our time pieces and just used the Eben's time tower. Each village has one and it is easy to understand the symbols. Each symbol means a certain time and certain work period.

EBE-2 came by after the feast. EBE-2 was concerned with 754 (Doctor 2). As I mentioned in one past entry, 754 became sick. But he has recovered. We don't know what he suffered but 700 (Doctor 1) treated him with penicillin, which worked. We all have had some sort of sickness since we've been here except 899 (Security), that guy is a solid rock. He hasn't been sick, not even a cold. 706 and 754 (Doctors) are keeping detailed records of each team member and their medical and physical condition.

We have tried to keep a steady physical fitness program since we arrived. Some time we follow it and sometime we don't. But everyone is in pretty good shape, at least physically. Mentally, that might be another story. Some team members miss Earth, as I do. But no team member has broken down or has needed some type of psychological help from 700 or 754 (Doctors). Our screening process was great. Keeping busy is our medicine. We keep extremely busy, exploring and doing our mission goals.

At one of our team meetings recently, 203 (Asst. Commander) and myself decided to give up the military greetings, saluting that each member did the first time they saw us. I decided we maintain our military bearing and manners but we will give up the saluting. Each team member agreed. I have no problem with that. The Ebens just stared at us when we did that. But they also have their greetings. Ebens exchange greetings depending on the time of day. They hug on certain times, touch fingers on other times and bow at other times. We still haven't figured out why they do that. EBE-2 just explained it was a formal greeting method.

Ebens live a very strict life. They keep a regimented life style. We have seen some variances but only a few. The military keeps everyone in line. The military acts as a police force, as I mentioned before. They do not carry any weapons but they do have different uniforms and every Eben respects that uniform. The military are patrolling all the time. They walk in pairs and seem to be extremely friendly but can be very strict. We saw two Ebens walking across a field. Two military members quickly approached the two Ebens and pointed to a building. The two Ebens walked to that building with the military members. The military members were yelling something at them. At the time, neither 420 nor 475 (Linguists) were available for translation but I figured those two Ebens violated some custom or law.

We have been warned by the military when we approach something we are not supposed to approach. The military are very respectful when they deal with us but they don't allow us to violate any of their customs or laws without warning us. When we first killed one of the sand snakes, we had six military members at the scene in no time. It took a great deal of diplomacy to deal with that situation. But the military never touched us nor threatened us. The Ebens have adjusted to us just as we have adjusted to them.

We carry on our mission and they allow us to do just about anything. The one forbidden act is not to enter a private living house. We did that once and was politely escorted out by the military. There seems to be more military than actually needed. They do have weapons, as I mentioned before. We rarely see any military member with those weapons. But we have seen them during the alert that occurred some time ago.

EBE-2 came into our living compound, just after one of our rest periods. EBE-2 was excited and told us to stay inside and not to exit our living quarters. We asked why and EBE-2 said that an unknown spacecraft had entered their planet's orbit. But EBE-2 assured us that the military would take care of the problem. We naturally went into our own alert. We issued our weapons and stood by to guard our living area.

We violated her instructions and went outside. We watched the skies and saw a lot of air traffic. We then saw all the military members with weapons and something that looked like field packs. They were in full fighting gear, as 899 (Security) called it. The alert didn't last very long and EBE-2 came back, looked at us a little curious and then told us everything was alright and the alert was over. We asked her if the unknown spacecraft was identified. She said it wasn't a spacecraft but just a natural piece of space debris and left it at that. We didn't believe her but we had no way of knowing any difference. We returned to our normal routines. [16]

The Team is able to communicate with the Ebens about 50% of the time, but there are some things that we were never able to communicate. Although each Team Member was taught the Eben tonal sounds/language, it is difficult for the Team Members to remember each tone and the use of other sounds with the tones. The two linguists on the Team practiced and learned enough to basically communicate. Humans could make the Eben tonal sounds, but one had to practice and practice and practice. It took a long time for anyone studying the Eben language to make the sounds. Some of the sounds were similar to high pitch singing sounds. The bottom line is that it could be done. Our Team had the Eben communication device with us, but it contained only about 500 English words. This was not enough to fully communicate.

The Ebens learned English, but had difficulty pronouncing words exactly correct. For example, Ebens could not say the letter "L." So, if the Eben's were trying to say the word "look," it came out "ook." There was one Eben, who was a space traveler, who could speak English better than the other Ebens who had learned it. This Eben was codenamed "Noah" by the Team. Every time the team had to communicate important information, they turned to Noah.

A group of Ebens learned to understand English and a few other Earth languages. This group contained the "Travelers," as our team called them. Our Team Members connected themselves with the Travelers. Although the Team couldn't always understand their responses, the Eben travelers understood our Team, most of the time. During this time period, the only exchange of information was simple. [17]

The Ebens, not being able to completely explain something to our team, used a form of sign language by pointing to the object or item they wished to explain and made hand movements. Two members of our team eventually grasped that method of communication.

Although we did establish some form of communication, it was crude and not always helpful for our Team when something complicated happened. For example, when our first Team Member died in an accident, it was hard to communicate with the Ebens. The member died instantly, therefore, no medical care was provided. Our two doctors examined the Member's body and determined the injuries were consistent with an accidental fall. Initially, the Ebens never interfered with our care or offered to provide any of their medical care.

However, once the Ebens – a very benevolent and caring people – saw our team members crying, the Ebens stepped in and offered to attempt some sort of medical care. Although our doctors felt the Team Member was medically dead, they allowed the Ebens to try their own medical care. Most of this was either through sign language or speaking to the Travelers who could understand some English.

The Ebens transported the Team Member's body to a remote area of the largest community. They took the body into a large building, apparently their hospital or medical center. The Ebens used a large examination table to view the body. The Ebens ran a large bluish-green light beam over the body. The Ebens watched a display that appeared on a large screen that looked like a television screen. The readouts were in the Eben written language and thus our team could not understand it.

However, there was a graphic display, similar to a heart beat graph. The solid line was not wavering. Our doctors understood that meant the same thing that their equipment measured: the heart was not beating. The Ebens administered some liquid through a needle. This was done several times. Eventually, the heart started beating.

But our doctors knew the internal organs of the body were damaged, but couldn't fully explain that to the Ebens. The Ebens finally made a sign, placing both their hands to the chest and bowing their heads. Our team members knew that meant the body was dead and nothing could be done.

The Ebens showed affection to our Team. During the last work period, the Ebens had a ceremony for the dead Team Member, the same ceremony used when an Eben died. Our team held their own service, attended by the Ebens. The Ebens were extremely curious about our religious service. One Team Member, who was acting as a minister, performed a death service. Our Team was eternally grateful for the Eben's caring attitude for our dead friend. [18]

National Security

8/19/65 At the National Security Facility

Brigadier General Tom Evens has been summoned to report to the National Security Agency at Fort Meade, half way between Washington and Baltimore, in Maryland. A Captain is driving the General North on the Baltimore-Washington Parkway, past miles of rolling, tree covered Maryland countryside. They exit the parkway and turn right onto Savage Road.

A huge, three story building, shaped like a large, boxy, squared off 'A', appears before them. The entire complex is surrounded by a ten foot Cyclone fence and multiple rows of barbed wire. There is another tall Cyclone fence inside that one and an electrified high-voltage fence between them.

They park in the VIP parking area, Evens gets out of the car and walks toward the Main Building. As he gets closer, he notices that the building is a glass and concrete structure with a pea green stone-chip exterior. There are several different types of antennas mounted on the roof.

Evens walks up the twelve steps and enters through a set of glass doors. He encounters two armed Marines who ask him what his purpose is for being there. The General tells them and is directed to enter another set of glass doors on the right.

Evens walks through the doors and enters a modern, brightly appointed reception room. He walks up to one of the receptionists, tells her who he is and that he has an appointment with a Mr. Jack Steele.

She telephones that person and informs him that his visitor is here. After hanging up the telephone, she asks Evens to sign in and issues him a red and white striped badge, with the words, 'ONE DAY' marked in large, bold letters on the front.

A short time later, a tall, thin man, with a permanent stern look on his face, enters the room, signs a log sheet, and then walks over to where Evens is standing. He says, "General Evens, my name is Jack Steele. Would you follow me, please?"

The two men walk in silence through a set of controlled access doors and down a long corridor. There is a huge shimmering mosaic of the agency's seal at the end of the passageway. They turn to the left, walk through the lobby, and enter one of the six elevators that are there. On the third floor, they walk down a hallway, past a secretary, and enter an office. It is a very nice office with wood paneled walls, plush carpet, and a wall sized window behind a large oak desk. [1]

"Won't you please be seated?"

Evens sits in front of the desk and Jack Steele sits behind it.

Outwardly, Evens is very cool. But inside, his stomach is churning. He cannot keep from wondering if what he told the President has gotten him killed. Ever since Kennedy was assassinated, he has been worried that Kennedy may have told someone about the things that he said. And if he did, he worries that the powers that be may have figured out who told him. He fears that he is walking into an investigation where mind control techniques are going to be used on him. And finally, he considers the possibility that he is about to be terminated.

Mr. Steele says, "I am in charge of counter-intelligence on affairs dealing with UFOs and extraterrestrials."

Evens' stomach winds even tighter.

Mr. Steele says, "I will be transferring to another department soon and you, Sir, are being asked to take over this section."

Without flinching a muscle, Evens' internal organs begin to relax.

Mr. Steele says, "Let me assure you, General, that, although you will be wearing civilian clothes here, you will not have to resign your commission in the Army and you will continue to receive your full military benefits. You have been recommended for this position, due to your familiarity with the subject matter involved and because of the fine service that you have provided in the past."

Evens says, "Thank you, Mr. Steele. What, exactly, would my responsibilities include in this position?"

Mr. Steele has a wicked smile on his face for a moment and then returns to his permanent frown. He says, "Well, unlike all of your previous jobs where you only assisted other people to make the hard decisions, this job will enable you to be the final authority on how national security threats are dealt with regarding UFOs and extraterrestrials. Although a certain amount of visibility goes along with this job, as long as you deal effectively with the possible exposure of information regarding UFOs and ETs, you will have a free hand to deal with things as you see fit. Of course, this also includes the use of lethal force."

Evens decides, right then and there, that he is going to do exactly as he is expected to do. He has learned a lesson with his dealings with the Kennedys. He decides to do this job the best that he can and never go astray ever again. He asks, "What are the guidelines?"

"You are authorized to use whatever means that are necessary in order to covertly prevent public exposure of alien related material. The entire resources of the NSA, CIA, FBI, and the local authorities are at your disposal. There is a tremendous amount of power that is associated with this job, to influence domestic and foreign affairs. Have you ever played God, General?"

"Yes I have and I didn't care for it very much."

Mr. Steele says, "Well, if you decide to take this job, you will be required to deal with the following threats to national security:

1. The isolated reporting of true sightings and contacts.

2. Outsiders that penetrate security or obtain classified information via any means.

3. Insiders who knowingly breach security and reveal classified information.

4. Anyone who unknowingly compromises security.

5. Outsiders who obtain physical or photographic evidence.

6. Outsiders who maintain independent ongoing alien contact.

7. Outsiders who act as contactee confidants and relay evidence or information to the public.

8. Exposure of classified information through the media - print, radio, or TV. [2]

Mr. Steele states, "You will maintain responsibility for keeping the alien presence contained so long as there are only limited and isolated contact events. However, a widely verified mass contact event will cause your efforts here to become terminated. Other departments are assigned the responsibility of dealing with those issues."

Evens thinks about all of this for a moment and then says, "Thank you, Mr. Steele, for this opportunity to serve my country."

4/23/66 At the Office of Congressman Gerald Ford

As Evens enters the office, he is greeted by Congressman Gerald Ford who says, "Good morning, General. Please, make yourself comfortable and tell me how I may help you."

Evens sits on a couch across from the Congressman and says, "Sir, I have come in regards to the declaration that you have made before Congress, urging them to look into the subject of UFOs. I am here in an attempt to persuade you to halt these proceedings."

Congressman Ford considers this for a moment and says, "I was not aware that the Army considered UFOs to be a subject that they took seriously."

Evans says, "I am not here on behalf of the military, Congressman."

"Well, just who are you representing, then?"

"I am not at liberty to say, Sir. However, I would like to assure you that the military confidentially considers the subject of UFOs to be a very serious matter and it is believed that it is not in the public's best interest to be made aware of some deeply troubling aspects regarding this subject."

Congressman Ford says, "I see. I don't suppose that you could share with me what these deeply troubling issues are."

"No Sir. I'm afraid that I cannot do that."

Ford thinks about this for a few seconds and then says, "Very well, General. You may go back to where ever you came from and tell whoever you work for that I have decided not to pursue the matter in Congress any further." [3]

"Thank you, Congressman. I will."

8/30/66 At the National Security Agency Facility

Stan Edwards has just entered the building and has been directed to the reception area. He walks up to the receptionist and says, "Hi. I've been told to meet someone here from the Office of Security, M5. My name is Stan Edwards."

The receptionist politely asks him to sign in and she telephones someone from M5. Stan signs the log form and clips on the red and white striped, 'ONE DAY' badge and feels very foolish wearing it.

A few minutes later, a door opens and Stan sees Evens enter the room. Evens holds out his hand and says, "Hello Stan. It's good to see you again."

They shake hands and Stan says, "I might have known that it would be you having me come all of this way to bring these files from the agency. How are you doing?"

"Come with me and find out", Evens says after signing the log sheet.

The two men enter the controlled access doors and walk down a long corridor together. Stan notices the badge that Evens has dangling from a cord around his neck. It is colored green with his picture, some computer punched holes, and is laminated in plastic. Stan asks, "Gee how do I get a badge like that?"

Evens smiles and says, "Believe me, Stan. You do not want to know what you'd have to go through to work here."

The two men enter Evens' office. Stan stops, looks around at the spacious office, and says, "Wow! Nice place you got here, Tom.

Evens says, "Yeah. I guess I've come a long way since we first worked together at Wright Field. Have a seat and let's take a look at the current UFO files that you brought over from the CIA."

Stan opens his briefcase and hands two folders over to Evens. While Evens looks at the files, Stan sits down in a large, comfortable chair. He asks, "Just what exactly do you do here in order to rate such a nice office?"

Evens looks up from the folders and says, with a serious look on his face, "I am in charge of counter-intelligence, dealing with all aspects of keeping the UFO and extraterrestrial matters secret."

Stan lets out another whistle and says, "That's quite a responsibility. Why would you accept a dirty job like that?"

"After what happened to President Kennedy, I've decided to do just exactly as I have been told to do and I suggest that you do the same."

Stan doesn't say anything and just stares at his old friend in disgust.

Evens looks down at a folder and reads about a massive wave of sightings occurring in the Soviet Union. He is pleased that the KGB has been successful at preventing reports of these sightings from reaching public attention. Next, Evens looks at the other folder and finds out that in June, flying disks interrupted important tests at the NSA's Pine Gap facility near Alice Springs, Australia. Evens is certain that no information about this incident will ever be revealed by the people who work at that facility. He is pleased that there are no major foreign incidents that he must deal with. [4]

12/12/67 In Evens' Office at the N.S.A.

Evens is reviewing his files on what has occurred in 1967.

Astronomer James E. MacDonald saw a classified version of the 1953 Robertson Report and became a critic of the Air Force and the CIA. He made a public statement that UFOs may be visitors spying on this planet.

Evens is pleased that the threatening telephone calls appear to have been effective in preventing him from making any further public statements on the matter. [5] [6]

In October of 1967, Britain was hit by a wave of disk sightings. Evens recalls that it took a major effort to keep the media from reporting anything about it.

In December, a man by the name of Schirmer, related details of having been abducted, brought to an underground base, and then released.

Evens believes that his efforts to discredit Schirmer were effective in preventing anyone from believing his story. However, Evens realizes that the story of weird looking creatures, described as Mothmen, that were seen in West Virginia, was just too strange to be kept from being reported in the press there. He realizes that there is a limit on how far he can go to prevent information from escaping to the public. [7]

5/30/68 In Evens' Office at the N.S.A.

Evens is a very busy man these days. He has been having a difficult time getting the local press to not report on the many flying disk sightings in the area around China Lake, California. This is most troublesome, especially since the disks, with spheres on the bottom, are known to be flown by U.S. Navy personnel. However, he was successful at killing the press story of a horse in Nevada that was hit by a beam from a disk, in front of witnesses. The beam had caused all of the spinal fluids and blood to be drained from the horse's body.

Stan Edwards is in Evens' office with more files from the CIA. They indicate that flying disks have been frequently seen in the demilitarized zone of Vietnam. This has required the use of special teams to debrief and assert secrecy compliance on the military personnel who witnessed the craft.

A Special Forces investigative team was also dispatched to the area to retrieve a B-52 Bomber that had been forced down by a UFO. Communications received from the crew, during the incident, stated that they were "...under attack by a UFO..." which appeared as a "...large light...".

The plane was found intact, sitting in the jungle, with no swath indicative of a crash landing. Only the bottom of the fuselage showed any damage. There was no damage to the underside of the engine pods and the entire crew was found dead inside of the aircraft. Their bodies had been mutilated. [8]

However, Evens is concerned about another serious domestic problem to national security. He asks Stan, "Do you remember Dr. J. Allen Hynek?"

Stan says, "Yeah. He was the guy who submitted the analysis of all UFO and ET data for the Grudge/Blue Book Report number 13 that we worked on together."

"That's right. Well, it seems that he is publicly criticizing scientists for not investigating UFO reports. He is stirring up a lot of trouble."

"What are you going to do about it?"

"I have decided to initiate a series of threatening anonymous phone calls and staged close-call accidents to remind Dr. Hynek that he should keep quiet. I hope that it will be sufficient." [9]

12/14/68 In the Oval Office at the White House

Evens is conducting a briefing for President-elect Richard Nixon, regarding UFOs and extraterrestrials. He concludes by saying, "Implications for national security are of continuing importance in that the motives and ultimate intentions of these visitors remain completely unknown. In addition, a significant upsurge in the surveillance activity of these craft, beginning in May and continuing through the autumn of this year, has caused considerable concern that new developments may be imminent.

"It is for these reasons, as well as the obvious international and technological considerations and the ultimate need to avoid a public panic at all costs, that the Majestic-12 Group remains of the unanimous opinion that imposition of the strictest security precautions should continue without interruption into the new administration. At the same time, contingency plan MJ-1949-04P/78 (Top Secret - Eyes Only) should be held in continued readiness should the need to make a public announcement present itself." Evens notices that the Eisenhower briefing document has had the desired effect of intimidating the new President.

12/19/69 In Evens' Office at the N.S.A.

Evens looks back on 1969 and acknowledges two important events that occurred, which helped his efforts to contain the UFO secret.

The first event was the release of Edward Condon's book, entitled "Scientific Study of UFOS". It was very successful in attempting to further obscure the subject to the public. The other event occurred when the Air Force publicly declared that UFOs had no basis in reality and that Project Blue Book was being abandoned "out of a lack of interest". However, this was met with a great deal of skepticism by the general public. The Air Force continued Project Blue Book on a classified basis. [10] [11]

Evens remembers that a great deal of damage was done when, on July 20th and 21st, radio hams picked up the chatter of Neil Armstrong and Buzz Aldrin as they were treated to views of huge alien spacecraft surrounding their landing site on the moon. Because the conversations were taped and heard by a wide range of people, it took a major effort by several agencies to reduce the damage that had been caused.

In October of 1969, Governor Jimmy Carter reported that he had witnessed a UFO. Evens considers this to be of little significance. [12]

Also in 1969, The American Association for the Advancement of Science held a Symposium on UFOs in Boston. Dr. James MacDonald faulted the scientific community for not adequately studying the data regarding UFOs. He is a highly respected astronomer who is drawing too much public attention on this matter.

Evens realizes that their previous warnings to him have gone unheeded. He decides to have MacDonald watched closely. Evens realizes that extreme measures may have to be used in order to keep him quiet. [13] [14] [15]

6/15/71 In Evens' Office at the N.S.A.

Three days ago, Evens found out that Dr. James E. MacDonald was about to go public with sensitive information regarding extraterrestrials. He knew that he had no other choice in this matter, except to make a telephone call. And now, Evens is reading a report which states that Dr. James E. MacDonald mysteriously drove out into the desert and shot himself in the head. Evens knew that he would not sleep well tonight. [16] [17]

9/19/72 At a Meeting of the Majestic-12

Dr. James C. Fletcher, the NASA Administrator, is briefing the Majestic-12 members on current events regarding the Apollo Program of landing men on the moon. He says, "Based upon the information gained from the Apollo Program, it is the opinion of all NASA scientists that the moon is inhabited by extraterrestrials. The following is a summary of the evidence that proves this hypothesis.

"First, in November of 1966, Lunar Orbiter II took photographs of the moon, from a distance of twenty-nine miles. These photos revealed several slender pyramids, or obelisks, and a series of transparent domes that appear to contain cities or large stations. Results of the Lunar Orbiter's gravitational experiments indicated that the interior of the moon is less dense than the outer parts. This suggested that the moon could be hollow. [20]

"On July 20th, 1969, Neil Armstrong and Buzz Aldrin landed on the moon with Apollo 11 and were treated to views of huge alien spacecraft surrounding their landing site. They brought back lunar rocks that contained processed metals of brass, mica, amphibole, and large amounts of near-pure titanium. Apollo 12 brought back soil samples from the Sea of Crisis that contained rustproof iron particles. "On November 20th, 1969, after the Apollo 12 crew returned from the moon to their command ship, they sent the lunar module crashing back onto the moon. It struck the surface about forty miles from the Apollo 12 landing site, where ultra-sensitive seismic equipment picked up vibration waves that took 8 minutes to reach a peak and then lasted for almost an hour in decreasing intensity. [21]

"Although Apollo 13's landing was canceled, due to mechanical problems, it was still able to send its third stage crashing onto the moon with an equivalent force of 11 tons of TNT. Although the seismic equipment was more than 108 miles from the crash site, recordings showed reverberations that lasted for 3 hours and 20 minutes and traveled to a depth of 25 miles. [22]

"Recently, on May 13th, 1972, a large meteor struck the moon with the equivalent force of 200 tons of TNT. This sent shock waves deep into the interior of the moon, but none came back. This confirmed that the moon is either hollow or contains large cavities. In addition, three large cigar-shaped objects were sighted on the floor of the crater Archimedes in November of 1970." [23]

Dr. Kissinger says, "Thank you, Dr. Fletcher, for that fine briefing. Gentlemen, we have just received a message from the Greys, through our diplomatic channels. This message is a warning for us to get off of the moon and to stay off. It is my recommendation that all further missions of the Apollo program should be canceled."

Dr. Fletcher shouts, "You can't do that! We have another launch scheduled for the 7th of December. What are you going to tell the American people? What are you going to tell all of the people who have worked so hard on this program?"

Kissinger says, "The American people have lost interest in the space program. Most people feel that funding could be better spent for domestic programs to help the needy. I think that will provide justification for cutting funds and canceling any further missions. We'll allow the next launch to continue. But, that will be the last one."

12/11/73 In Evens' Office at the N.S.A.

Evens is reviewing what has taken place in 1973. He realizes that, from late 1972, there have been numerous sightings of disks occurring in South Africa, Latin America, Eastern Europe, Canada, and in Australia. Evens recalls that it took a major effort to prevent the press from reporting it in the United States. On October 25, 1973, a disk buzzed the National Security Agency High-frequency transmitter facility at NW Cape in Western Australia. [24]

12/22/74 In Evens' Office at the N.S.A.

Evens looks back on 1974 as being a very strange year. He recalls that this is when large numbers of animal mutilations began to occur in Texas. Evens had to come up with the cover story for the local police to tell the press, which was that a cult is suspected. When police officials objected to this story, he had to have pressure brought to bear in order to have them cooperate. [25]

9/23/75 In Evens' Office at the N.S.A.

Evens has been watching the strange political events happening in the United States recently. First, he watched as Spiro Agnew resigned as Vice President, after being sentenced for tax evasion. Gerald Ford was then put in his place. Next, when President Nixon resigned, as a result of the Watergate incident, he watched as Gerald Ford became the first unelected President and Nelson Rockefeller was appointed to be his Vice President. Finally, he noticed that no other president has ever had so many attempts made to assassinate him. He realizes that Nelson Rockefeller could finally become President of the United States after repeatedly failing to be elected to the office.

11/23/75 At an Executive Meeting of the N.S.A.

Evens is standing behind a podium, in front of the executive officers of the National Security Agency. He states, "Gentlemen, I stand before you to bring to your attention a very serious incident which could expose the alien abductions to the American public. This incident took place in the Sitgraves National Forest of Arizona. It was in this location that a young woodcutter by the name of Travis Walton was abducted by extraterrestrial beings in a UFO. The UFO was witnessed by six of his fellow workers. They were riding down a dirt road in a pickup truck when they saw an object hovering off to the side of the road. They saw a glowing, disk shaped object about ninety feet away from them.

"Travis Walton reportedly got out of the truck to get a closer look at it. But, when he got closer to it, his friends reported that the disk blasted him with some sort of ray or bolt of light. The witnesses saw Travis flying back through the air and hit the ground about 10 feet or so from where he had been standing. At that point, the men panicked and quickly drove away in their truck. Later that evening, Mike Rogers and the other five witnesses returned, only to find Travis Walton missing.

"They told this story to police and came under suspicion of murder. An intense search for Travis Walton proceeded for three days, using a large posse, dogs, and a helicopter. They were unable to find him or any signs of where he was. Finally, it was suggested that the six witnesses take a polygraph test to prove the truth or fallacy of their story. The examiner wrote in his report that they had told the truth. That apparently, there had been a UFO.

"The Sheriff, Martin Gillespie, has been quoted as stating that he is sure that they saw a UFO. The witnesses have been examined by psychologist Dr. Jean Rosenbaum and found to have no psychological abnormalities. This story has been widely publicized and has the potential of causing a national uproar." [26]

Lt. General Lew Allen, Jr., the Director of the NSA, says, "Thank you, General Evens, for bringing this matter to our attention. How do you suggest that this matter be handled?"

Evens responds with, "Sir, it is my recommendation that the Greys should be contacted, told of the threat of mass exposure to their abduction activities, and request that Travis Walton be returned unharmed, as soon as possible."

The Director says, "I concur with your recommendation, General. This matter will be passed along to the interested parties right away. Thank you for the briefing. That will be all."

11/29/75 In Evens' Office at the N.S.A.

Evens is reading the report on Travis Walton.

Five days after he was abducted, Travis was returned and he told authorities what happened after he had been hit by a blinding beam of light and fell unconscious. He stated, "When I regained consciousness, I was laying on my back. I came to, slowly. I was in a lot of pain in my head and chest area. At first, I thought I was in a hospital. But, when I could finally see, I saw these beings standing over me. And, I just became hysterical. They were about five feet tall. They had no hair, no eyelashes or eyebrows. They had very large heads, very large eyes. The rest of their features; nose, mouth, and ears were small. They were very white looking.

"I knocked them away from me and jumped off the table there. And, they started to come toward me. I grabbed an object off of the bench there and threatened them. They stopped and turned around and left the room. I was afraid that they'd come back, so I left there. And, looking for a way out, I went into another room where there was a chair. There was some kind of projection or viewing thing in this room where you could see a map of the stars.

"A man came in, while I was trying to find a way out there. This was a human looking person. They'd pass in a crowd, this individual on Earth. He was bigger than me, taller, and more muscular. He was a very large individual. I went up and tried to talk with this guy and he didn't answer me. He led me outside of this craft, that I was in, which was apparently parked inside of a large room or building or larger craft. And, led me out of this room into another room where some other beings like himself, put me unconscious.

"When I regained consciousness, I found myself lying on the roadway. I saw a craft hovering there that sat there for a moment and just shot straight up. That was the last that I've seen of them. I ran down into the town there and called my family. They came and got me. One of the biggest shocks that I had to deal with when I returned was finding out that this brief period of time had somehow taken over five days. When I found out that I had been gone for that long, it just blew me away. My brother told me about it. I was stunned. He asked me to feel my face and I had a week's growth. My mind just reeled at that because, as far as I knew, it was the same night.

"The thing that bothered me most about the whole experience where those eyes. When they looked at me, it seemed like they were looking straight through me. You just can't understand how it would be if you were right there."

After his return, Travis Walton also passed a polygraph test, verifying the truth of his UFO experience. Evens had instituted a campaign to discredit Travis Walton, with some success. But, he also felt glad that he had something to do with his return. [26]

11/26/77 In the Communications Center at the N.S.A.

Evens rushes into the VIP room of the communications center after being ordered to report there as quickly as possible. He is out of breath and realizes that he is not as fit as he once was. He looks through the large window into the communications center and notices that everyone is rushing around and extremely busy at their consoles.

James Francis, the Deputy Director of the National Security Agency, notices Evens standing there and he waves for him to come over.

Mr. Francis tells the General, "I am glad that you could get here so fast. We have an urgent matter occurring in England right now that you should be aware of. Since 5:12 PM GMT, a BBC television station in Southern England has been overpowered, which interrupted a news bulletin being read by Ivory Mills. In his place, a message is being delivered over that channel by someone claiming to be Gramaha, the representative of the Asta Galactic Command. We have no idea how the television transmitter is being inhibited or where the audio signal is coming from. Have you ever heard of anyone by that name or title?"

"No sir, I have not."

The Deputy Director looks at a monitor and says, "Okay, I see that the broadcast has just ended and that normal operations have resumed at the television station. I am having a transcript of the message prepared now. Do you have any suggestions on how we will be able to mitigate the affect that this may have caused?"

Evens thinks for a moment and says, "It should be easy enough to issue a cover story that this was just a college prank."

The Deputy Director looks at Evens with a disgusted look on his face and says, "The amount of expensive equipment needed to overpower a powerful television transmitter certainly takes the incident out of the realm of a college prank. Don't you think so?"

"You're right, sir. I think the best thing to do is to have the press ignore the situation as though it never happened."

Just then, an Air Force Captain says "Excuse me, Sir. Here is the transcript you requested of the message just broadcast" and hands Mr. Francis a piece of paper.

He reads it aloud: At 1712 hours, Greenwich Mean Time on 26 November, 1977, an audio signal overpowered a local television station in Southern England for five and a half minutes. A male voice was heard to say in a slow, deliberate, and calm authoritative tone, "This is the voice of Gramaha, the representative of the Asta Galactic Command speaking to you. For many years now you have seen us as lights in the skies. We speak to you now in peace and wisdom as we have done to your brothers and sisters all over this, your planet earth.

We come to warn you of the destiny of your race and your world so that you may communicate to your fellow beings the course you must take to avoid the disasters which threaten your world and the beings on our worlds around you. This is in order that you may share in the great awakening, as the planet passes into the New Age of Aquarius. The new age can be a time of great peace and evolution for your race, but only if your rulers are made aware of the evil forces that can overshadow their judgments.

Be still now and listen, for your chance may not come again. For many years your scientists, governments and generals have not heeded our warnings; they have continued to experiment with the evil forces of what you call nuclear energy. Atomic bombs can destroy the earth and the beings of your sister worlds, in a moment. The wastes from atomic power systems will poison your planet for many thousands of your years to come. We, who have followed the path of evolution for far longer than you, have long since realized this - that atomic energy is always directed against life. It has no peaceful application. Its use, and research into its use, must be ceased at once, or you all risk destruction. All weapons of evil must be removed.

The time of conflict is now past and the race of which you are a part may proceed to the highest planes of evolution if you show yourselves worthy to do this. You have but a short time to learn to live together in peace and goodwill. Small groups all over the planet are learning this, and exist to pass on the light of the dawning new age to you all. You are free to accept or reject their teachings, but only those who learn to live in peace will pass to the higher realms of spiritual evolution.

Hear now the voice of Gramaha, the representative of the Asta Galactic Command speaking to you. Be aware also that there are many false prophets and guides operating on your world. They will suck your energy from you - the energy you all know as money and will put it to evil ends giving you worthless dross in return. Your inner divine self will protect you from this. You must learn to be sensitive to the voice within, that can tell you what is truth, and what is confusion, chaos and untruth. Learn to listen to the voice of truth which is within you, and you will lead yourselves on to the path of evolution.

This is our message to you our dear friends. We have watched you growing for many years as you too have watched our lights in your skies. You know that we are here, and that there are more beings on and around your earth than your scientists admit. We are deeply concerned about you and your path towards the light, and will do all we can to help you. Have no fears, seek only to know yourselves and live in harmony with the ways of your planet earth.

We of the Asta Galactic Command thank you for your attention. We are now leaving the planes of your existence. May you be blessed by the supreme love and truth of the Cosmos." [27]

The Deputy Director looks up from the paper in horror.

He tells Evens, "Well General. Do whatever you have to do to curtail exposure of what has just happened. I have to get this to the Director right away."

Evens smiles and says confidently, "Don't worry, sir. After the initial responses, this event will be forgotten in no time at all and people will just go about their daily business."

"I certainly hope that you are right."

12/15/77 At the Dreamland Facility in Nevada

Jimmy Carter has just been elected President. He made a campaign promise to make every piece of information about UFOs available to the public. So, Evens has arranged to give Carter a tour of DREAMLAND. First, they enter a hanger and walk inside a disk.

Carter is surprised to discover that the craft appears to be much larger inside than outside.

Evens explains that the effect is due to the fact that they have passed into another dimension.

Next, Carter watches as the craft takes off into outer space with no sensation of movement. They see the Earth from outer space. When they return, Carter changes his mind about exposing information about UFOs. [28]

6/19/78 In Evens' Office at the N.S.A.

Evens escorts Stan Edwards into his office with more files from the CIA. They sit down, without saying a word to each other. Their friendship has been strained beyond the breaking point.

Stan hands Evens the files and he reads about the latest reports on UFO related incidents. He reads about a massive wave of sightings that is still occurring in England.

On March 18, 1978, William Herman was abducted by aliens who told him of the existence of a "network" of civilizations.

Sixty-two professional astronomers report seeing UFOs.

Evens realizes that Dr. James MacDonald's mysterious suicide death in 1971 has not had the desired effect of being a deterrent to others, as he had hoped.

Evens also reads about a vivid, prolonged close encounter that occurred at Baker's Creek Falls, near Armidale, Australia. There were multiple witnesses and a shoot-out occurred with the disk, near Fort George. Evens knows that this is something that should not have been reported on by the press in the United States. But, he discovers that the story was leaked to the press by someone who identified himself as "The Observer". Evens thinks that this person could become a threat to national security and a real problem for him to deal with.

Stan says, "Well, this is the last time that you will be seeing me here. I am retiring from the agency next week. I am going back to live in my cabin in Colorado, where I was raised."

"Well, I'm sorry to see you go."

"Oh, that's bull shit! We haven't been talking to each other for years now. I don't much care for the sort of work that you do here, and you know it. I think you have sold yourself cheap to the government. Well, good luck to you. But, before I go, I'd like you to take a look at Executive Order 11051, which President Carter has just issued."

Stan hands the order to Evens, who reads it and discovers that it authorizes the creation of the Federal Emergency Management Agency. He also finds that it gives the Office of Emergency Planning and FEMA the authority to put emergency measures into effect under any pretext of increased international tensions or economic or financial crises. Evens realizes that this Executive Order has the potential for placing the United States under Martial Law under any pretext. [29]

Evens knows that the previous Presidential Executive Orders of 10995 through 11005, were emergency measures that enabled the government to take control over all essential goods and services. This includes the communications media; all electric power, fuels and minerals; all food resources and farms; all means of transportation including; highways, seaports, railroads, inland waterways; all airports and aircraft; all health, welfare, and educational functions; all housing and finance authorities and all public funds. They also authorized the relocation of whole communities, as well as drafting all citizens into work forces. [30]

Evens is stunned by what could possibly happen to the United States of America.

He looks up at his old friend, who says, "Good-bye, Tom. Try to remember who you really work for and think about what you are doing to the people of the country that you have sworn an oath to protect and defend against all enemies, foreign and domestic."

And with that, Stan walks out of the office for the last time.

7/14/78 At White Sands Proving Grounds, New Mexico

Today is the day that the Exchange Team is returning from Planet Serpo. They were only supposed to be gone for ten years, but it has turned out to be a total of thirteen years.

Since Evens was in charge of preparing this team for their mission, he feels the need to be here when they return. Radar stations have locked onto an unidentified craft, which just entered our atmosphere. The General is getting very excited now. He looks up in the night-time sky and watches as a glowing craft descends closer and finally lands on the ground. Evens feels like it is taking forever for the hatch to open and the ramp to extend, but it eventually does.

Evens' heart is pounding now as he sees one person and then seven more of the Exchange Team walk down the ramp. He is smiling from ear to ear as he walks up to his old fiend, the Team Commander, puts his hand out, and says, "Welcome back."

The Commander smiles broadly, gives Evens a big hug, and says, "Thanks Tom. It's good to be back."

This catches the General by surprise. He knows the cameras are capturing everything they do, but he eventually gives in to the urge and hugs him back. He is also surprised to see all of the other team members hugging and shaking his hand. He wonders why they have not saluted him. [31]

Evens says, "I count only eight of you. Where are the others?" The Commander says, "Unfortunately, one of the team died while en route to Serpo of an apparent heart attack and another died as a result of an accident during our stay there. Two other members of the team chose to remain on the planet voluntarily. They fell in love with the culture of the Ebens and the planet and they were not ordered to return. The remains of the two who died on Serpo have been placed in coffins, which are on board the craft along with our things."

Evens says, "It looks like you folks have kept in good shape. Do you have any health problems?"

The Commander says, "Well, we have all received a large dose of radiation during our stay on Serpo. But other than that, we are doing okay and we are very glad to be back on Planet Earth." [32]

Evens then watches as the team members are taken away in vans for their de-briefing. Confrontation

10/12/79 In Evens' Office at the N.S.A.

It is 5:00 PM and Evens is ready for a relaxing weekend. He puts his files back into the file cabinet, closes the drawer, spins the combination dial, and grabs his coat. On his way out of his office, he says, "Good night" to his secretary. She says, "Oh General, you have an urgent call on the secure line with authorization Samson." Evens freezes in his tracks, turns, and asks, "What authorization did they give?" "Samson, sir." "Very well, I will take the call."

Evens reenters his office, throws his coat down, unlocks the drawer to the secure telephone. He says into the receiver, "Evens authorization 1 2 Mike 7." He then hears a recorded voice say, "Authorization accepted. Connecting." Next he hears, "General Evens, this is Captain Avery, commanding the 423rd Military Police detachment for the Dulce Base. Sir, a civilian scientist from the underground facility here is missing along with many classified documents. We suspect that this individual has taken them and intends to release them to the public."

Evens angrily asks, "How is it possible that this man could escape from there undetected, Captain?" "Well sir, we believe that he may have hid among trash that was brought up from below and then concealed himself under the trash truck when it departed to dump the trash. We instituted a complete search of the facility and we have no idea where he may be now." Evens clinches his teeth and says, "I assume that steps have been taken to prevent this from happening again." "Yes sir!" Evens grabs a pen and says, "Very well. What is this man's name and social security number?" "It is Benjamin Lawrence Davis 547-34-9041, sir." Evens writes this down and says, "This matter is not over for you, Captain. You have a lot to answer for. Good bye!"

10/15/79 At a Surveillance Detail in Baltimore, MD.

It is 7:42 PM and Evens has been supervising the surveillance team involved with monitoring the activities of the escaped scientist's wife, Linda Davis. It has been three days since the scientist escaped and Evens worries that he may never be captured. He knows that the best chance to catch him is when he attempts to see his wife again after being stationed at the Dulce base for the last six months. But so far, there has been no sign of him.

Evens is using NSA agents for this detail in order to minimize the risk of being revealed, but he will use every resource from the CIA, FBI, and local authorities to catch this man who could expose everything about the government's involvement with ETs.

Evens hears over the radio, "Echo 1, Mobile 4 here. The wife has exited her journalism class at the college and is walking toward her vehicle. She is alone. No sign of the target."

"This is Echo 1. Roger."

10/15/79 Inside Linda's Vehicle

Linda Davis is driving from the parking lot at the college when she hears, "Linda, it's Ben." She yells, "Ben?" "Don't turn around. Keep going. I escaped from the government facility where I was working and they're looking for me. It was horrible there. They wanted me to keep working there for another six months. I couldn't take it anymore. I had to see you again." Ben reaches from behind the front seat and touches her hand.

Tears are falling from Linda's eyes as she says, "Oh Ben, I've missed you so much. Let's run away together." Ben says, "We can't. They're watching you. I've seen them. I need you to do something for me. I have placed copies of evidence about the place I was working at under your seat. You need to find a way for people to see it. It has pictures and documents that show horrible things that the U.S. Government is involved in with beings from other worlds. But, you must be careful."

Linda says, "I can't do that. I wouldn't know where to start or who to go to with this." Ben insists, "You have to, or no one is going to be able to do anything about the atrocities being committed in underground facilities all across our country. You're studying to be a journalist, aren't you? Well, this is the biggest story of the century, and you've got to tell it."

10/15/79 With the Surveillance Detail

"Echo 1, this is Air Mobile 2. I have an infrared fix on an adult individual lying behind the front seat of the wife's vehicle." Evens reaches for the handset and says, "All units, this is Echo 1. Move in now. Apprehend the man in the wife's car. Do it now!"

Suddenly, a van pulls in front of Linda's car, which forces her to stop. Other cars drive up, armed men get out and drag Ben from Linda's car. He is holding a large manila packet tightly to his chest with both arms. Another van pulls up and Evens jumps out. He recognizes Ben from a picture he has of him and calmly says, "Good evening Doctor Davis. It is nice to make your acquaintance. I'll take that, if you please." Ben reluctantly gives the packet to Evens, who takes it and motions for the agents to take him away.

While they force him into a van, Linda yells at Evens, "You bastard! That's my husband! You better not hurt him." Evens turns to her and says, "I assure you, madam, he will be as safe as in your arms." Evens and the other men get back into their vehicles and drive away. Linda is crying as she gets back into her car, but then she remembers about what Ben said of having put something under her seat. She reaches down and discovers a packet, similar to the one that Ben was holding, under her seat. She drives away vowing to do as her husband asked her to do.

10/16/79 At a Meeting in the National Security Agency

Evens is standing before the executive committee of the NSA once again. He says, "Gentlemen, I am here to brief you about a serious incident which could have far reaching implications regarding the joint US/Alien underground bases. A disgruntled scientist from the Dulce Bio-Genetics Facility fled with videos, pictures, and documents, intending to expose the atrocities that he found there. This man was captured three days later. However, while in the process of being debriefed, he killed himself by causing an overdose of the drugs that we were giving to him. I recovered a packet of items that he took from the base, but there is no way of knowing if he made copies of this material and distributed it to anyone else."

Evens describes what was contained in the recovered packet, saying, "There were lots of technical documents that discussed copper, molybdenum, magnesium, and potassium. There were papers with charts and strange diagrams. The papers discussed ultra violet light, gamma rays, and how to avoid detection through the use of certain colors. The papers tell what the aliens are after and how the blood and body parts taken from mutilated animals and humans are used. They state that the aliens absorb the nutrients from a biological slurry mixture for nourishment."

Evens takes a drink from a glass of water and then continues with, "The papers also state that the DNA from cattle and humans are being altered in order to create artificial human beings. They further state that countless women are being used for breeding and experience 3 month pregnancies. There were about 25 black-and-white photographs and a video tape, with no dialogue, all taken inside of the Dulce Facility. They show the facilities for mass producing hybrid fetus entities." [1]

The new Director of the NSA, Vice Admiral Bobby Ray Inman, tells Evens, "I am concerned about further incidents by other personnel fleeing our underground bases with sensitive information. General, I want you to go to the Dulce underground base to assess security procedures there, determine what the concerns are of the personnel who work there, and make recommendations to correct any potential problems. You will have full access to the facility. It is very important that the facility continues to function without any further interruptions."

Evens says, "I understand, Sir. You can count on me", and he leaves the room.

10/18/79 On the Top Level of Dulce Base

Evens arrives at the base by riding in a silent shuttle car through a high speed underground tube system. It took only half an hour to travel from Washington, D.C. to Dulce, New Mexico. Evens is met by a pretty female guide by the name of Mary.

Mary helps him to pass through the initial security screening process. Once inside, she takes him on a tour of the first level complex. He is shown a huge park setting, a shopping mall, and the in-processing facilities. She shows him where he is to report, at 0800 hours, tomorrow morning.

Next, Mary shows him the cafeteria and his temporary living quarters, complete with living room, bedroom, and bathroom.

Evens says, "This is very nice. Could I buy you something to eat for supper?"

She laughs and says, "Everything here is free, General. But, if you'd like, we could have supper together."

"Yes, I would like that, Mary."

As they walk toward the cafeteria, Evens thinks that this is a pretty nice place to be stationed. He asks, "What are the other levels of the facility like?"

Mary says, "I don't know. I have never been down there. I really don't know anything about them."

The next morning, at exactly 0800 hours, Evens enters a small auditorium where several people are seated. He takes a seat and browses through the documentation provided there.

A man walks up to the podium, and says, "Good morning. My name is Captain Adams. I am the In-processing Administrator for this level. I would like to welcome all of you here to the Dulce facility. I will brief you on the in-processing procedures that you will all be going through in preparation for descending to the lower levels.

"But first, I would like to provide you with a general description of the Dulce facility. This is a joint facility, used by both humans and extraterrestrial entities. This base lies under a kilometer of rock, south of the town of Dulce, New Mexico.

"The initial base was covertly built, in the late 1940s, under the cover of a lumbering project. The base has been built in stages using alien technology. Most everything in the base is controlled magnetically, including the lighting.

"The upper three levels were built on top of a pre-existing alien base. The base consists of a many-leveled cylinder with tunnels radiating out in several directions.

"The first level contains the administrative offices and facilities for processing personnel in and out of the base.

"The second level contains the housing and services for the humans who work in the lower levels.

"The third level contains the laboratory complexes and offices for all independent human related projects.

"Level 4 is a joint research facility dealing with the human aura, telepathy, dreams, and hypnosis.

"Level 5 is the alien quarters.

"Level 6 is a genetics laboratory using alien technology and Level 7 contains biological storage and production facilities.

"In-processing will take a total of three days. The medical personnel will be poking and prodding you in every way possible to eliminate any chance of you taking any contagious diseases to the lower levels. Then, you will be inoculated and briefed on the rules and operating instructions that must be followed exactly. Any deviation will summon security personnel immediately.

"Finally, you will be weighed in the nude and issued uniforms and an identification badge that will enable you to gain access into the areas of the facility which you have been authorized to go into. Then, you will be taken to the second level, assigned quarters, and shown where to find everything that you may need there. Someone, from the department where you will be working, will then show you around to your work areas and introduce you to your fellow workers. Now, we have a few forms for you to fill out." [2]

10/21/79 On the Second Level of Dulce Base

It has been three days, and Evens has survived the in-processing procedures. He has just arrived on the second level and has been assigned his new quarters. It is a small room that he shares with three other men. There is a small table and chairs in the center of the room and two sets of bunk beds along the walls. He is pleased that he has been assigned a lower bed. There is a lavatory in the next room with a small shower, toilet and sink. He discovers that he will be eating in a military style dinning hall and that only the basic necessities have been provided for. He finds the conditions to be crowded with no privacy at all.

The next morning, there is a knock at the door of Evens' quarters.

"Come in", Evens shouts.

The door opens and a tall, physically fit man in a guard's uniform enters the room and stands at attention. He says, "General Evens? Sir, my name is Lieutenant Briggs. I have been instructed to provide you with a tour of the security division."

"Very well", Evens says and follows the officer out of the room. While walking along a corridor, Evens notices a strange looking device in the officer's holster and asks him about it.

He says, "It's called a flash tube weapon. It is effective against both humans and aliens alike."

After using the officer's badge in the doorway, they enter the central monitoring station. It is a dimly lit room with several video monitors installed along the far wall with several people viewing them. Other people are operating control panels. It is a busy place with people running about and talking into headsets.

The Lieutenant instructs Evens on the security measures being undertaken there. Then, the Lieutenant offers to give Evens a tour of the facility.

But Evens declines and returns to his quarters. He then borrows an outfit that the scientists wear there from one of his roommates. Evens puts it on and goes out on his own.

10/22/79 On the Lower Levels of Dulce Base

Evens poses as a medical doctor, specializing in gynecology. In the dining area, he meets one of the civilian scientists there, by the name of Gary Henderson. He introduces himself and says, "I just got here yesterday. What in the world is going on here?"

Gary says, "What's going on here, is out of this world. And, believe me. You don't want to know."

"Oh, I do", Evens says enthusiastically, "I really do! Could you show me?"

Gary says, "Okay. But remember, you asked for it."

First, Gary takes Evens to Level 4, where he states, "The research here is all geared toward the control and manipulation of Human beings. The technology is at a state where they can manipulate the bioplasmic body of humans and program them through the introduction of programmed reactions and images which will induce the desired result of having complete control over them. In addition, they can remove an individual's consciousness and replace it with another consciousness, either synthetic or alien." [3]

Gary shows Evens what the aliens are doing to the people that they abduct. The first device that Evens is shown is called an Inculcation Bar. It is a rectangular metal box that is used to impress humans with information by forceful means. It has multi-colored lights displaying a sequence of blue-green-red-green-blue and the numerical sequence of 1-2-3-4-5-4-3-2-1. The subjects lie on their back on a metal table directly beneath the bar. At the foot of the table, level with the surface, is a metal console box with cables connecting to the table. The attendants are dressed in red jump suits, and the room itself is bathed in red light, except when inculcation therapy is in progress.

Gary says, "Catecholine Beta-Lipotropin 4753 is the technical name for a substance often given to abductees. It has the effect of removing certain body blocks and, at the same time, gives a boost to the awareness/intelligence level of the abductee. It is a mixture that acts like a cerebral cortex 'roto-rooter'. With another method, the subject dons a helmet bearing wires and needles. A crystal cube is put into a niche on top and a strobe light flashes in resonance with the brainwaves of the subject. The abductee's head becomes filled with pictures that gradually form a pattern of response. The abductee is given a learned motion-picture-response system to become trained to do a complicated task in a brief amount of time.

"Sometimes the abductee is hypnotized or made to sleep and a high frequency microwave emission is used as a carrier wave with which to send encoded data into the nerve/ridge-response system. This data can be triggered later by a prearranged stimulus-response signal that will be present in the environment of the subject. Sometimes the bio-energetic field itself is used as a carrier wave and the data is encoded in sound-code-symbols or symbols in facsimile form." [4]

Gary shows Evens something called the Reichian Based Programming Device. He says, "It is used by the Greys to manipulate human abductees. It applies energy fields that keep the human in a pre-orgasmic state in order to allow mind control and programming to take place.

It is often used during sperm and ovum extraction processes, as well as for between-lives programming and memory washing."

Evens watches as a man is placed on a table and connected to pads placed at eight points on his body, including the genitals. Long black wires extend from the pads, which are suspended from a silver colored oblate spheroid. Gradually, the man's body begins to quiver with excitement. He is kept at a state of sexual arousal without being able to reach a climax. Gary says, "The Reichian State is induced electronically to remove buried information in the subconscious and reprogram the person. When the programming is over, the subject is restored to "normal" with either blocks on memory of the whole thing happening or given a total implant of "what went on that day" as a substitute to memory. [5]

Gary shows Evens some tiny devices and says, "Many of the individuals who are abducted, are implanted with small devices used for monitoring and control. These devices are as small as 3mm in size and can be spherical, egg-shaped, or flat. Inside the small spherical devices, there is a crystalline matrix embedded with micro-electronic circuits. Engineering estimates have brought the interaction of the device to within quantum ranges, which ties in the function of consciousness modification." [6]

Gary tells Evens, "The aliens possess technology whereby the literal soul " I " of a human being is subjugated for the purpose of using human bodies and souls for hosting alien souls and 'subtle' bodies. This process is used to enable an alien soul to migrate from its source residence and use a human body and soul to anchor their presence to this time-space dimensionality. This process of migration may take a substantial time period of setting up linkage, anchoring, partial migration, and eventually total migration where the alien now has a body in this dimension. The alien may either effect a complete fusion with the human soul, coexist with the human soul, depose the human soul from the human body and fully take over the human body control functions, or effect subjugation of the human soul into automatic only body functions." [7]

Gary says. "The replication of humans is an ongoing process that has a part to play in the manipulation of events on this planet. During this process, the individual's responses, memories, and habit patterns are copied from the human to be duplicated. The original can then be preserved or processed into basic biological components. The clone will then function as the original, except that the entity is under alien control. There is also an apparent minority of cases where the synthetic duplicate's consciousness is directly replaced by an alien consciousness. There have also been cases where a soul has been removed from their body and placed in another body and, by removing conscious memory of the first life, the transplanted personality is then convinced that they are the person of the second body." [8]

Next, Gary takes Evens to Level 6. He tells Evens, "This is a bio-genetics laboratory, using alien technology. It has been referred to as "nightmare hall" by the employees who work here. They are attempting to breed slave beings here, which are suited for specific tasks."

Evens is amazed to see multi-legged humans who look like half human and half octopus. There are also furry creatures that have hands like a human, cry like a baby, and mimic human words. There are huge mixtures of lizard humans in cages. There are birds, fish, seals, and mice that can barely be considered those species. And, there are several cages of winged humanoids that are bat like creatures. They are between three and a half and seven feet tall. [9]

Evens sees that Level 7 is worse. There is row after row of thousands of human children and adults in cold storage. Here too are embryo storage vats of humanoids in various stages of development. Also on level 7 are the production areas for humanoids and vats containing animal and humanoid body parts. Evens notices that there are several human beings that are stored in clear cylindrical containers over 6 feet in height, suspended in a yellow or amber fluid. They are alive and conscious but unable to scream or to say a single word.

Gary says, "I frequently encountered humans in cages, usually dazed or drugged, but sometimes they cried and begged for help. We were told that they were hopelessly insane, and were involved in high-risk drug tests to cure insanity. We were told to never attempt to speak to them at all. At the beginning, we believed that story. Then, we discovered the truth about what was really going on here. There are many of us here who are fed up with everything and are just waiting until our time is up so that we can go home and never have to think about this again. As you know, our memories will be chemically erased before we leave here." [10]

Just then, Evens watches as a Grey entity takes a small child into the next room. She has fair skin, blond hair, and is about five years old. She is crying and saying, "I want to go home. I want my Mommy and Daddy. Please, let me go home. I want my Mommy." The Grey being shows no emotion at all as he takes her away. Evens is burning with rage inside. He wants to help that little girl. He wants to help all of them. But, he knows that there is nothing that he can do for them.

Evens turns to Gary and says, "Thank you, Gary, for showing me what is really going on down here. I have to leave now. But, I'll see you again soon." He shakes Gary's hand and returns to Level 3.

Evens walks into the security division and tells Lt. Briggs, "I need access to a secure communications link, right now." The Lieutenant shows Evens into an office, points to a telephone, and leaves. Evens dials the number for the Director of the NSA.

"Hello. This is Admiral Inman."

"Admiral, this is General Evens calling. Sir, I have discovered that there is wide spread discontent among the employees who work here. I believe that a confrontation is imminent and I cannot see any way to avoid it, other than to shut this place down."

The Director says, "That is not an option. You are ordered to do whatever you can to defuse the situation and prevent any interruption to the operation of that facility. Is that understood?"

Evens says, "Yes, Sir" and hears the line go dead.

10/22/79 On Level 7 of Dulce Base

A small group of scientists is talking to Gary about Evens.

One of them asks, "Who is he?"

"He told me that he was a Gynecologist that had just recently arrived."

"Do you believe him?"

"I don't know. He seems sincere enough. But, sometimes he looked as though he recognized things down here that he says he has never seen before."

"What if he was sent here to spy on us? What do we do if he suspects the existence of the resistance unit that we have formed here?"

Gary says, "I don't know. But, to be on the safe side, I think that we had better attempt our escape right now."

"But, it's too soon. We're not ready yet."

"I don't think we have a choice. Okay, you all know the plan. Contact the others. Alice, you take your group and collect all of the documents and evidence about what is going on down here that you can get a hold of. Jim, you take your group and free as many people as you can. My group will obtain weapons and access cards. We all meet at the central elevator doors in fifteen minutes from now. GO!"

Everyone, except Gary's group, scatters in different directions. Gary passes out the knives to the others and says, "Okay, this is it. We must get the weapons and access cards from the guards without setting off the alarm. Split up into your three-man teams and neutralize your targets. Good luck."

They all leave for their assigned positions. Gary holds his knife with the blade under his forearm, hidden by the sleeve of his lab coat. He casually walks into the hallway, toward the guard there. He sees that the other two members of his team are on each side of the guard. As Gary walks up close to him, he asks, "Hey, what's up?" Just then, both of the other men grab each arm of the guard and hold him in place. Gary sees the frightened look on the guard's face as his fist brushes along the guard's neck. The knife in Gary's hand slices into the man's neck, from ear to ear. They hear that horrible gargling sound as the guard's body goes limp. Gary grabs his flash tube weapon and access card. The other men let the body fall to the floor and look at Gary in shock. Gary puts the incident out of his mind and tells the other men to follow him.

Alice and her group of people are madly rushing about, picking up everything that they can find that will show the world what is going on there. Jim, along with his group, have just run up to the control console in front of three cylinders where people are kept in suspended animation. He says, "God, I hope this works" and starts throwing switches and pushing buttons. They watch as the cylinders start to drain the amber fluid that they were filled with. When the fluid drops below the head level of the person inside each one, they watch as the heads fall forward. Then, they see each person emptying their lungs of the fluid, take a deep breath of air, and then start coughing. Eventually, they regain normal breathing again and look at the men before them, who are crying with joy. Some of them stay to help the people out of the cylinders while others leave to free the people trapped in other cylinders and cages.

Fifteen minutes later, the central elevator area is filled with the people who have gathered to escape together. Gary is pleased to see that the little girl who wanted to go home is with them. He presses the intercom button and says, "Control, this is Level 7 leader, requesting central elevator for routine garbage dump to the surface."

"You're a little early, aren't you?"

"Yeah, but they want to get rid of this stuff now. It's stinking up the place."

"Okay. Request approved. The elevator is coming down to you now."

"Roger. Thanks." Everyone is extremely nervous as they wait for the elevator to arrive. Gary thinks to himself, *just ten more minutes, and we will be free once again.*

Just then, two of the tall Grey species walk into the area and see what is going on. One of them raises a communicator to his mouth. But, before he can speak, Gary points his weapon at the alien and fires. There is a bright flash, and the alien falls to the floor. Gary then points his weapon at the other alien who does not move.

Alarm bells go off, and lights are flashing.

Gary presses the intercom button again and says, "Control, this is Level 7 leader. There is a false alarm here. One of my men set off his weapon by mistake. There is no damage done."

"What is your authorization code?" Gary doesn't know the code, but says, "I can't give it to you right now. I'm busy. I'll get back to you."

"Who is this?"

A bright flash fills the room and the man standing beside Gary falls to the floor. Gary looks around the room and sees another alien reaching around a doorway and firing a flash tube weapon towards him. He misses.

Gary takes aim and fires his weapon toward him. The alien disappears behind the wall and Gary shouts, "Everybody listen! Stay down and move into the next room quickly. We'll cover you. Don and Steve, you cover the other entryway. Allen and I will cover this one."

The others move into the next room.

Evens was in Security Headquarters when the alarm went off. He looks at one monitor and sees a group of frightened people huddling together. He looks at another monitor and sees four men with weapons pointed in various directions. He recognizes one of them as Gary, the one who gave him a tour of the facility. Evens finds Lt. Briggs and asks for a status report. The Lieutenant says, "Sir, there appears to be a revolt by a group of scientists who have obtained weapons and are attempting to escape through the central elevator shaft. They shot and killed one, or more, of the aliens and are holding another one hostage. I do not know what happened to the guards that those men took the weapons from. I presume that they are dead. But, I am sending every available man."

Just then, they see a flash of light and one of the men falling to the floor in the monitor.

Evens asks, "Is that your men firing?"

"No, Sir. My men are not anywhere near there yet. That shot must have come from one of the aliens who also have access to weapons."

"Is there any way for me to talk to those men down there?"

"Yes, Sir. They have an intercom near them. All you have to do is just press this button and talk into the microphone."

Evens says into the microphone, "Gary, it's Tom. I'm the guy you gave the tour to earlier."

They see Gary press the intercom button and hear him say, "Hello Tom. What can I do for you? I'm a little busy right now."

"Yeah, I can see that. Listen Gary. You folks appear to be in a little bit of trouble there. So, I'm going to have the elevator sent down to you. You get everyone inside the car and I'll have you taken out of harm's way. What do you say?"

"Will you take us to the surface?"

"No, Gary. I can't do that. You'll be brought right here to me where I'll take care of you."

Gary says, "No thank you, Tom. I have hostages here and we are either leaving this place or we will not leave at all."

There is a bright flash of light seen in the monitor, followed by another and then another. It is obvious that the men are in the middle of a major fire fight. Evens looks at another monitor and sees several short Grey aliens firing their weapons from a hallway. He looks at another monitor and sees several more aliens running along another hallway, carrying weapons.

Evens yells into the microphone, "Gary, you are being surrounded by several aliens with weapons. You haven't got a chance there. Let me get you out."

Gary shouts, "You either take us to the surface or you can go to Hell!"

Evens tells the Lieutenant, "Lower the elevator to level 7 and have your men standing by to receive those people on this level."

The Lieutenant says, "Yes, Sir" and then issues the appropriate orders.

Evens says into the microphone, "Okay Gary, you've got a deal. I'm having the elevator sent down to you now. Hang in there a little while longer and we'll let you go home."

Gary shouts, "Well, you'd better hurry. I don't think we're going to last here much longer."

Evens tells Lt. Briggs, "Take whatever forces you need, Lieutenant, and get those people out of there."

The Lieutenant says, "Yes, Sir. But, if I may remind the General, those people are probably the ones who started the confrontation with the Greys in the first place and they probably killed some of my men as well. They brought all of this on themselves and they deserve whatever they get."

Evens becomes enraged by what was said and says, "I am in command here, Lieutenant. Those people are valuable assets to this program. Now, get them out of there!"

The Lieutenant says, "Yes, Sir" and hurriedly leaves the room. Evens says into the microphone, "Hang on, Gary. Help is on the way."

Gary is surprised to see the Greys walking right through the walls in the next room. They are killing the people there with blasts from their weapons. Gary and the other men with weapons run into the room and start firing their weapons at the aliens who retreat back through the walls.

The elevator finally arrives.

Gary, and the other people, start heading for it. But, before they are able to leave the room that they are in, more aliens appear through the doorway and begin firing at them. The men shoot back. But, while their attention is toward the waiting elevator car, the aliens come through the walls and start shooting the people. The men with weapons respond as best that they can.

Evens is monitoring all of this from Security Headquarters. He tells Gary, over the intercom, "Stop shooting, Gary. Stop shooting! I have sent a message to the aliens to also stop shooting."

But, nobody is listening as the weapon exchanges continue. Nearly all of the people are dead by the time that the Delta Forces arrive. They lay down suppressing fire and begin to evacuate those still alive and wounded. But, the large numbers of Grey beings and their ability to appear, fire, and disappear rapidly prove to be no match for the humans. Eventually, they are all killed.

Evens uses the translation equipment to talk with the aliens and assure them that there will be no further violence from the humans. He is able to convince them that they only want to return to normal operations as soon as possible. He tells them that he is going to come down there alone and unarmed in order to show his good intentions. Evens takes the elevator down to the seventh level. The elevator doors open and Evens sees the room full of dead bodies. He shows the aliens that he is unarmed and is amazed to see the dead alien bodies being beamed away. The living aliens leave him alone in the room with all of the dead human bodies. Evens will find out later that there were a total of 44 scientists and 66 military servicemen that were lying dead before him, including Gary, the Lieutenant, and the little girl that he wanted to save. As he walks through the carnage of the aftermath, Evens remembers how

General Ramey once told him that, if there was ever to be a battle, he would have to go in afterward and pick up the pieces. [11]

Personal Contacts

5/18/80 In the Green Mountains of Vermont

Evens has been very depressed ever since he returned to work from his Dulce base assignment.

The Director of the NSA was very pleased with how Evens dealt with the crisis and with his ability to get the base back in operation so quickly. He was promoted to the rank of Major General and awarded another medal.

But lately, Evens has felt the need to get away from it all. So, he took a leave of absence from his duties, put together enough supplies to last him for three days in a backpack, and traveled to the Green Mountains of Vermont. He is determined to hike to a remote spot in the woods and get away from it all.

On his second day of hiking, Evens encounters another man, sitting alone beside a stream.

The other man appears to be in his mid-twenties with straight, collar-length blond hair. He is rather slender and appears to be slightly over six feet tall. He looks up as Evens approaches and says, "Good day".

Evens smiles and says, "Good day to you, stranger. It surprised me to find someone else out here. We must be thirty miles from the nearest town. Do you have a campsite nearby?"

The man said that he did not and Evens noticed that the man had no backpack or provisions.

Evens asked, "How long have you been in the area?"

The man replied, "Three days".

Evens wonders, *What has this guy been eating for the past three days, pine cones?*

Thinking that this guy was a little too strange, Evens starts walking back to the trail.

The man calls out to Evens and asks if he could walk with him for a while.

Reluctantly, Evens agrees and the two men set out on the trail together.

After walking for several miles, Evens is sweating and out of breath. But, he notices that the other man is completely unaffected by their long and arduous hike. Since dusk was approaching, Evens decides to pitch his tent and make a campfire for cooking supper.

The other man merely squats on the ground nearby.

Evens cooks a meal for himself and then brings out a bottle of wine. He pours out some wine for the both of them into paper cups and says, "My name is Tom. What's yours?"

"My name is Khyla."

Evens is surprised by this and says, "I've never heard that name before. Where are you from?"

"Would you believe me if I were to tell you that I am from another planet?"

Evens decides to humor him and asks, "Oh yeah? Which one?"

"I am from a solar system that revolves around Procyon, a binary yellow-white and yellow star system that rises before Sirius in Canis Minor, about 11.4 light years from Earth. I am from the fourth planet in orbit around the Procyon double star system. We are generally referred to as Blonds because of our blond hair and blue eyes." [1]

Evens stops smiling as he notices that the other man is serious. He takes a closer look at Khyla, who appears to be a tall handsome human, slender but muscular, masculine yet ethereal.

Khyla appears to have black around his eyes, almost like coal. His face is close to exquisite, but definitely masculine. He has a gaunt face with high cheekbones and piercing cobalt-blue eyes. He has fine blond hair that is almost shoulder-length. His skin is a pale flesh color, with a whitish overtone. [2]

Khyla says, "Some Blonds have high intellectual and verbal abilities, while others are mute and telepathic. The ones with speech abilities will respond violently if attacked or threatened. But, the telepathic type will not. Both types are careful to avoid exposure, and usually encounter humans in quiet isolated places. They contact females more frequently. They may just stare and observe humans, then retreat. Blonds were sometimes mistaken for angels in earlier centuries. The Blonds do not seem to age, and consistently appear to be from 27 to 35 human years old, no matter what their real age may be."

Khyla tells Evens, "My people originally came from a star system known as Rigel. Then, a Great War took place. Before the Great War, Rigel was a vast empire, which had been the source of most galactic seeding. All Rigelians were tall Blonds. A colony had already been established on Procyon. The Great War was a civil war of Rigelians versus Rigelians, and lasted the equivalent of three Earth centuries. The bodies of the Rigelians became deformed and mutated into what has become known as the Greys. Behold the bitter fruit of victory. The Greys are a genetically damaged species. If terrestrial humans were to survive a nuclear winter, they might well look like that, several generations later.

"A group of Rigelians who realized that the Great War was about to break out took off for the Procyon colony in crude, clandestinely built ships. At that time, all the sophisticated equipment was owned by the state. They were the only Rigelians to escape the cataclysmic devastation. All those who had remained on Rigel were transformed into the Greys.

"After the Great War, and the Rigelians had become the Greys, it took them thousands of years to reconstruct their society. They were damaged, not only genetically and in their glandular systems, but also mentally and psychologically. As soon as the Greys had reconstituted a power base, they launched an attack on the Blonds who had escaped to the Procyon colony.

"Although the Blonds of Procyon had been spared the extreme chromosome and glandular damage sustained by those who had stayed behind on Rigel, they did suffer some radiation damage during their warfare with the Greys, which was minor in comparison. However, it is this that has rendered our females vulnerable to a disease that is decimating our numbers. The mute, telepathic Blonds, who do not have speech abilities, suffered more extensive radiation damage than those who retained their speech ability. Just as in terrestrial warfare there are sometimes traitors, defectors, deserters and prisoners of war, so there are in warfare between extraterrestrials. And just as in terrestrial warfare there are periods of truce, during which teams from opposing armies may cooperate temporarily on certain projects, so there are periods of truce in warfare between extraterrestrials.

"Having come in war, but having been unable to obtain any decisive victory, the Greys expressed the desire to make peace. We had not wanted to fight with the survivors of the Rigelian Great War to begin with, and gladly accepted their offer. As time went by, they said that they wished to normalize relations and be our friends. We were in doubt as to whether it would be safe to trust them, and debated the issue for a long time. Then finally, we decided that we should trust them, as they were the only surviving remnant of our original ancestral stock, though horribly deformed by what they had endured.

"The Greys began to visit us, first a few as ambassadors, then as specialists in various domains where their expertise could be useful to us, as participants in different programs, which involved mutual collaboration, and finally as tourists. What had begun as a trickle became a flood, as they came in ever-increasing numbers, slowly but surely infiltrating our society at all levels, penetrating even the most secret of our elite power groups.

"The one secret that remained beyond their grasp, because the part of their intelligence that was capable of understanding its subtle complexities had atrophied during the nuclear winter that had caused the mutation of their species, was our ability to travel through time. How then did we fail to foresee our own future, and the fatal mistake we were making when we first let them in? They began by unobtrusively gaining control over key members of our society through techniques unknown to us, such as telepathic hypnosis that manipulates the reptilian levels of the brain. They established a kind of telepathic hypnotic control over our leaders. Over our leaders and over almost all of us, because it was as if we were under a spell that was leading us to our doom, as if we were being programmed by a type of ritual black magic that we did not realize existed.

"Just as a few of the original tall Blonds clandestinely left Rigel when the Great War was about to break out, so did a few of the original tall Blonds clandestinely leave Procyon. They escaped into the corridors of time just before the Greys completed the slow undermining that culminated in their sudden takeover of Procyon. Those who stayed behind came under the total domination of the Greys.

"After what happened to Procyon, no true Blond would collaborate voluntarily with the Greys. The Greys have taken some prisoners of war, who have no choice in the matter, and are forced to work with them in order to survive, with the hope of escaping. There are also a few Blonds who have become degenerate renegades, space pirates and mercenaries who sell their services to the highest bidder. But many of us remain free, and continue the fight to the finish with the life form that has become our hereditary enemy. We choose to remain in exile in the corridors of time, where they cannot reach us, rather than to live under the domination of the insidious Greys. It is dangerous for us to venture forth from the corridors of time, but occasionally we do so for hit-and-run strikes, similar in nature to a cosmic version of terrestrial guerrilla warfare.

"The Greys have the ability to camouflage themselves as Blonds through mental energy projection. Blonds do not ever project themselves as Greys. Sometimes Blonds are physically real, but are prisoners of the Greys. The Greys must paralyze or destroy their ability to teleport through time and other dimensions in order to take them prisoner. The Blonds that you see on the same ships as the Greys, working with them, are hybrids or they are clones. One way to distinguish the clone is that they all look alike. The real Blonds have distinct facial feature differences, and do not look alike. The clones have thick necks and coarsely muscular bodies. They do not have the ability to teleport or to travel inter-dimensionally. They can be contacted by telepathy, but are unable to send. They can be given orders telepathically. They are zombie-like flesh robots. You can tell that they are of low intelligence by looking into their eyes.

"The real Blonds are also muscular, but have slender necks and agile bodies. Their eyes are alert and of high intelligence. Physically they are almost identical to humans. The main difference being, that by human standards, their blood circulatory system is underdeveloped, while their lymphatic system is overdeveloped. This gives them stronger immune systems than terrestrial humans. The hybrids are in an intermediate state between the real Blonds and the clones. We must periodically enter a substantial physical form for a period of repose, or to breed progeny, in order to continue to survive, but otherwise we constantly travel the vast corridors of time. That is why we may appear to fade in and out like holographic images to human perception.

"What I have come here to communicate, if only to one or two people or to a small group, is that what happened to our culture, is also in the process of happening to yours. It is the same fate that our own culture suffered. And the Blonds that you see with the Greys are either hybrids, clones, or prisoners of war because no true Blond who got out untouched, unscathed, uncrossed with those Greys would ever be with them. He or she would prefer to be in a state of nonexistence.

"Humanity is not about to be invaded. Humanity is not in the middle of an invasion. Humanity has been invaded! The invasion has taken place, and is nearly in its final stages. Great invasions do not happen with thundering smoke and nuclear weaponry. That is the mark of an immature society. Great invasions happen in secrecy.

"If you were a highly advanced culture about to invade a relatively primitive culture, you would not do it with a flourish of ships showing up in the heavens, and take the risk of being fired upon. That's the type of warfare less evolved mortals would get into. You would begin by creating intense confusion, with only inferences of your presence, inferences which cause controversial disagreement.

"You would go to the most secret and powerful organizations within the society. In the case of the United States, you would infiltrate the CIA, and through the use of techniques unknown to them, you would take over some of the key people in their innermost core group. You would proceed in the same fashion to take over key members of the KGB. You would also create great dissension among the public at large, some individuals and groups insisting that they have seen UFOs, others insisting with equal vehemence that such a thing is not possible, and that they are either liars or deluded.

"You would make yourselves known to various elite in-groups, who would offer you protection out of greed, expecting to acquire more perfect knowledge than anyone else on the planet of this ultimate secret to end all secrets. They would covet you, and you would trust their covetousness.

"You would occasionally let your ships be seen by some of the ordinary citizens, so that the elite governmental groups would become involved in attempts to keep them quiet, clumsily squelching attempts to make information about UFO activity public. This would result in the mass population losing confidence in the veracity of their elected officials. There would be constant arguments about whether the persistently reported phenomena genuinely existed, thereby setting the population and the government at each other's throats. You would also set the two major superpowers at each other's throats. By subtly causing economic turmoil, you would set the "Haves" and the "Have-Nots" at each other's throats. In all possible ways, you would plant the seeds of massive discontent.

"After you had manipulated the population to the point where your covert control was complete, you might decide to go overt, and let a few ships land in public. But you would not go from covert to overt until you were sure of the totality of your control. You would start doing crossbreeding, escalating the process to the maximum from generation to generation, in order to create hybrids between the Greys and humans. Perhaps in a century or two, some of the Greys would begin to physically intermingle with Earthlings.

"There will be series after series of "natural" disasters, some genuinely natural, some human-induced through aberrant scientific activities such as underground nuclear testing. Others deliberately induced by the Greys through the technology that they are in possession of. When approximately three-quarters of the planet's population has been eliminated in this fashion, the Greys can then make an overt appearance as saviors from the skies, distributing food and medicine to the survivors. As the survivors line up to receive their quotas of food and medicine, implants will be inserted, supposedly to aid in further food distribution, actually to guarantee complete Grey control with no possibility of rebellion. From the point of view of the Greys, terrestrial humanity will have been reduced to manageable numbers and to eternal submission.

"The reason the awful little Greys mutilate animals is the stuff that they eat. They eat pulverized harmonic secretions, what you would call subtle essences. They live on the stuff of life. There is something deathlike about their species. They always bring about the death of animation and the death of individuality. How do I know? I am a Blond from Procyon. We were a culture that could travel through time, but also lived on a planetary sphere. And the little Greys, our insidious little friends, did to us exactly what they are doing to you now.

"There are other extraterrestrial groups that you would be able to work with and travel in the vehicles of. But, the track record that the Greys have left behind them leaves no room for doubt as to their malignancy. The only reason that the Greys have such a degree of dominance over you is because your elected officials stupidly made clandestine agreements with them. These agreements bind you to them in an exclusive alliance that is respected by other space races, allowing them to install themselves in underground bases that are impregnable to your weaponry. This is a situation that you must now find a way to extricate yourselves from."

Evens asks Khyla, "What do the Blonds think about humanity?"

"The Blonds from Procyon have a benign attitude toward humanity, except for their strong disapproval of your inhumanity to each other. The Procyonian basic purpose is The Law of One, which is service to others. Their motivation for breeding with humans is to tune up the frequency of your species, in order to help you to help yourselves. Their concern is for the well being of all forms of life, not just humanity. The entire biosphere will benefit if you fulfill your positive potential, instead of self-destructing and destroying your planet's biosphere in the process.

"The Blonds have a deep moral repugnance for the activities of the Greys on this planet at this time, and are willing to help humanity, if humanity will take effective steps to stop its pollution of the planetary environment. The Greys have become a criminal species, and will be treated as such. However, any species that pollutes its own environment to the point of endangering the survival of its planetary biosphere is also guilty of a cosmic crime.

"Humanity as a collective entity may create whatever destiny it chooses for itself. These paths include enslavement, nuclear destruction, and peaceful flourishing growth. Whatever path humanity selects is right for it. What a traveler through time learns is that nothing in this cosmos can ever be forced. Everything happens and unfolds as it should, even when you are confronted with the idiocy that has brought about the potential end of your species as you know it. The Rigelians and the CIA have put in motion the potential for a rather drastic mode of learning. This can be altered at any time. Whatever it may be, the outcome is always as it should be. However, this does not mean that you should sit back and take no action."

Evens asks, "What should humanity do?"

Khyla says, "At this stage, one thing you can do is to provide the public with as much information as possible. This will make it more difficult for the collaborators and Greys in disguise within the government to continue to work against humanity in favor of the Greys.

"At some point, help may come from outside, from my own and/or some of the other space races. There is no reason why one should not send out telepathic appeals for help, in the form of prayer or meditation or whatever way is appropriate to the individual, to the higher forces in the cosmos. They do exist and are sensitive to such signals. There are extraterrestrial and other-dimensional cultures, which are capable of harnessing the innate power of entire galaxies, which could be of immeasurable help in liberating your planet from domination by the Greys, if you could persuade them to help.

"Besides the Blonds and the Greys, ships from many other space cultures are watching planet Earth at this time with extreme interest. Scientists from other space cultures are studying what is going on here during this decisive period of your history. If your elected representatives had not so stupidly made a deal with the only aliens that were willing to provide them with weapon systems, with the short sighted goal of overpowering the Russians, the Greys would not have achieved their present dominance. You would now be exchanging ambassadors with a wide variety of space cultures." [3]

Evens falls asleep and when he wakes up, Khyla is gone. He thinks about what Khyla told him last night and realizes that what he has been doing is helping the Greys to take over the planet by keeping their presence here secret. He is stunned by this fact, but he does not know what to do about it. If he were to quit his job, someone else would simply do the job in his place. If he tries to tell anyone what he knows, he would surely be terminated. Suddenly, he feels trapped and helpless. He packs up his belongings and returns home.

5/20/80At Evens' House in Baltimore, Maryland

That night, Evens thinks some more about his current situation as he lies in his bed before going to sleep. Suddenly, he has an intuitive sense of foreboding. He notices a change in the air and is surprised to realize that the normal sounds of his environment have become silent. He becomes frightened and tries to reach for his pistol, but discovers that he cannot move. He becomes dizzy. He has trouble breathing and feels constricting pressure in his chest. He worries that he may be having a heart attack, but realizes that he is completely paralyzed except for being able to move his eyes. [4]

Just then, he sees a short Grey being on each side of his bed, looking down at him with their big black eyes. Evens becomes filled with terror at being completely helpless under their control until he feels an unnatural calmness come over him.

He can tell that these beings are about four feet tall with large heads and slender bodies. Their skin tone is a light gray color and they have no hair. Their large heads have large black eyes and pointed chins. The rest of their features of nose, mouth and ears are very small. They are wearing one-piece, tight-fitting, silver-colored diver's type suits. These beings take

Evens by his arms and levitate his body toward a closed sliding glass door in his bedroom, which they pass right through. Once he is floating outside, Evens becomes engulfed in a bright white light from above and rapidly ascends upwards. [5]

5/20/80 Inside an Alien Spacecraft

The next thing Evens knows is that he is seated on a bench along a curved wall. He feels dizzy and disoriented, but slowly becomes fully conscious again. He sees other people being directed past him by the short Greys along a hallway. They all appear to have a dazed expression on their faces except for a little girl, who looks at him with a sad look on her face.

Just then, a short Grey being takes Evens by his arm. He feels the need to be compliant and cooperative as he is directed to stand and walk into the next room, which appears similar to a rounded doctor's office with a table in the center. He finds himself lying on the table facing upwards. Then, he notices a tall Grey being standing over him. It is about seven feet tall with a pronounced nose, slanted black eyes and has a stern look on its face. Its whole body, except for the face, is covered by a black, close-fitting diver's type of suit.

Evens watches as this entity positions its head and eyes directly over his face, only about three inches away. Evens feels the need to look into the being's eyes while it is staring into his eyes. He actually sees something moving inside of the entity's eyes. Then he senses danger and immediately looks away from the being toward the right. The creature turns Evens' head toward his left so that it can see into his eyes, but then Evens shifts his eyes to the left. His head is then turned to his right.

Evens decides that he will not let this being look into his eyes, no matter what may come. He keeps shifting his eyes back and forth to the melody of an old campfire song he remembers from his childhood. He sings to himself, "100 bottles of beer on the wall. 100 bottles of beer. You take one down and pass it around. 99 bottles of beer on the wall..."

The Tall Grey becomes frustrated at not being able to make eye contact with him. Evens senses the being talking to him telepathically, saying "Stop what you are doing and stare straight ahead."

"98 bottles of beer on the wall. 98 bottles of beer ..."

Next, Evens telepathically hears, "If you do not stop what you are doing, I am going to have to hurt you."

97bottles of beer on the wall. 97 bottles of beer ..."

"I am going to cause you to have pain. You will not like it."

"96 bottles of beer on the wall. 96 bottles of beer ..."

After other tall Greys also fail to make eye contact with Evens, he senses them saying that they will have to process him at another time. [6]

A short Grey makes Evens get off of the table and sit on the bench outside the room once again. Then, the being walks away.

Even though Evens is still paralyzed, he decides to attempt to move only his little finger. He concentrates hard on moving his finger. Slowly, but surely, he becomes able to move his finger, then another finger, then his hand, his whole arm, and finally his whole body. He is elated at being free once again. He decides to have a look around this craft. [7]

Evens walks down the hallway and looks through the doorway of another operating room. He sees a woman on the table with her legs in stirrups like those found in a gynecologist's examination room.

There is a Tall Grey entity sitting on a short stool holding an instrument in the woman's vagina.

Evens is surprised to also see an Insectoid and Reptilian being intently watching the procedure inside the room. He wonders what they are doing there and then realizes that those races must also be accomplices to everything that the Greys are doing to mankind. [8]

Just then, Evens watches as the Tall Grey removes some sort of biological sac from the woman's womb. The sac is opened and a small human/Grey hybrid fetus is removed. It has a human body with a large head and large black eyes.

The Tall Grey takes the newborn baby to the mother for her to suckle, but she shouts, "No! Take that ugly thing away from me!"

The fetus is then handed to a short Grey, who places it in a tank filled with liquid nutrients and takes it into another room.

The Tall Grey returns to its short stool and prepares to insert another biological sac into the woman.

Evens feels that he has seen enough here and moves on down the hall. [9]

Evens peeks into another room where some hybrid toddlers are playing with human toys like trucks, teddy bears, dolls, planes, and balls. Others are playing with alien toys like a ball with swirling colors, which dances about in mid air. Evens is amazed to see one child cause objects to float across the room to him by simply staring at them. This group consists of mixed-stage hybrids. Some of them look mostly like the Greys with very little hair and big black eyes while others look almost human with different colored hair and eyes. They all seem to know when another is going to move and they all move in unison. [10]

Evens has seen enough of this, so he moves on to a large room where several people are seated and are watching a screen with images of mass destruction. They see atomic bombs exploding and the aftermath of devastated cities lying in rubble with dead people everywhere. These people are then told that this is going to happen, that it need not happen, and that humans will cause it. The aliens then tell the people that they are working for them to avoid this unhappy scenario. They also say that their breeding program is the hope for the future that will lead to peace and contentment. They say they can bring about a happy ending to the horror. [11]

Evens is amazed that everyone believes this without question. He then moves on and looks into another room where there is row after row of human adults and children in hundreds of glass cylinders. They all appear to be sleeping in their street clothes or pajamas. He wonders why the aliens would want to keep these people in suspended animation. The aliens are obviously taking these people somewhere. But, is it for experimentation, to populate other worlds, or for nutritional purposes? Evens thinks to himself, *That's enough! I can't take any more of this* and he returns to the bench where he had been sitting. [12]

A short Grey entity walks up to him and Evens senses him asking where he had gone. He says, "I was looking for the restroom." The Grey takes him by the wrist into another room where there is a bright white light.

5/21/80 At Evens' House in Baltimore, Maryland

Evens wakes up from a deep sleep. He sits up and realizes that he has been lying on top of his bed and not under the covers. He feels groggy and light headed. When he is fully conscious, he remembers all that had happened and realizes that it was not a dream. He looks at the clock on his night table and sees that it is time for him to get ready for work.

Acclimation

12/22/80 Evens' Office at the National Security Agency

Since his vacation, Evens has returned to his job at the NSA and unenthusiastically resumed his duties there. He has told no one about his contacts with Khyla or the Greys, but has thought about little else. He is now forcing himself to concentrate on recent events that have occurred, regarding UFOs.

In 1979, Charles Tucker, the director of the International UFO Investigative Bureau, said that UFO activity had increased by more than 300% in the past six years. A poll of 8,000 members of astronomy organizations revealed that 23.9% had seen UFOs.

J. Allen Hynek stated that he had received over 1,500 reports from policemen, regarding UFOs, over the past year. And, in a national poll, 68% said they had seen UFOs. [1]

In 1980, a book entitled, "The Roswell Incident" was published by William Moore. It provided evidence and witness testimony to expose what really happened back in 1947.

The Mutual UFO Network Journal published an article on Project Redlight.

Evens wonders how they obtained that information.

In May of 1980, Judy Doraty and her son witnessed a calf being abducted by a UFO near Cimarron, New Mexico. They were also abducted, taken to an underground base, and implanted with small devices.

Evens notices that someone, known as "The Observer", was responsible for having this story reported by the press. He remembers that this person has interfered once before.

In August of 1980, disks intruded into the Manzano Weapons Storage Area in New Mexico.

On August 8th, a Sandia guard discovered a disk next to a building that contained nuclear materials.

In December of 1980, the Cash-Landrum case occurred where both women received severe radiation poisoning during an encounter with a U.S. disk that was escorted away, in full view of the two women, by 23 military helicopters. The disk that harmed the two women with hard radiation was a Project Redlight asset. [2]

Evens discovers that this story was leaked to the press by the person who identifies himself as "The Observer" once again. This guy is really beginning to upset Evens now. He decides to begin an investigation in order to find out who "The Observer" really is.

3/7/81 The Presidential Retreat at Camp David, MD

The newly elected president of the United States, Ronald Reagan, is meeting with his advisers, the Director of Central Intelligence, William Casey, and a contract employee of the CIA known as the CARETAKER, who is the custodian of information relating to UFOs and ETs. There were many meetings held between March 6 and 8, 1981 to brief the president about extraterrestrial contacts. The following is a transcript of what was discussed at one such meeting:

PRESIDENT: I have listened intently to this briefing. I have many questions, which I realize traverses several different layers of secrecy. I don't want to mix up the different layers. But I can see how government bureaucracy exists. That is one thing I can probably change as President! Bill, let's go to the next layer.

WM CASEY: Mr. President, do you want the same people involved?

PRESIDENT: Yes, let's just continue.

WM CASEY: OK, CARETAKER, take over.

The CARETAKER: Thank you. When EBE was alive, he showed us two devices. One was a communication system and one was an energy device. The communication system did not work without the energy device. Eventually, a scientist from Los Alamos figured out the two systems and connected them. After EBE died, we were able to send transmissions, as I said earlier. EBE built up a strong friendship with a U.S. Army Major, who was his guardian.

The two of them decided that one of Eben's first messages (of the five sent) was a request for an exchange program between the Ebens and our military personnel. Remember I mentioned six messages. The sixth consisted of landing coordinates for Earth. That information wasn't clearly documented back then. We are not sure of the exact chain of events between EBE and the Major. As I said earlier, we were able to eventually communicate with the Ebens.

Over a period of a few years, we could send and receive information. We finally received a startling message from the Ebens. They wanted to visit Earth, retrieve their spacemen bodies and meet with Earthlings. They provided a time, date and location. We figure that the Ebens were continually visiting Earth and had probably mapped it. However, the date was about eight years in the future. Our military figured something was wrong and that maybe the

Ebens were confusing Earth time with Eben time. After a long series of messages, it was determined the Ebens would land on Earth on Friday, April 24, 1964.

PRESIDENT: Just how did we figure the date?

The CARETAKER: Mr. President, these messages occurred over a period of several years. By this time, we both had a working knowledge of the other's seasons, which also figured into our time periods. We had a working knowledge of their 40-hour days. They were a little smarter than us, being able to comprehend our language and our time periods.

PRESIDENT: OK, that makes sense. But... (not understood)... about... (not understood)... the aliens?

The CARETAKER: Mr. President, we did have a basic understanding of their language. We could understand basic words and symbols. They understood more of our language than we did theirs.

PRESIDENT: OK, then what happened?

The CARETAKER: Well.... WM CASEY: Mr. President, this is where things get very interesting.

PRESIDENT: OK, I'm waiting.... (not understood)

The CARETAKER: Our government, specifically, MJ-12 met in secret to plan the event. Decisions were made, then changed many times. We had just about 25 months from the time we finally received their message of the date to prepare for their arrival. Several months into the planning, President Kennedy decided to approve a plan to exchange a special military team. The USAF was tasked as the lead agency.

The USAF officials picked special civilian scientists to assist in the planning and crew selection. The team members' selection process was the hardest to accomplish. Several plans were suggested and then changed. It took months for the planners to decide on the selection criteria for each team member. They decided that each member must be military, single, no children and a career member. They had to be trained in different skills.

WM CASEY: CARETAKER, let's just go into the general stuff here, I don't think the President wants to know every single minute detail.

PRESIDENT: Well, if I had the time, I would. (not understood)... but, I understand that.

The CARETAKER: Mr. President, a team of 12 men were selected. However, during this time period, President Kennedy died. The nation was shocked, as you know....

PRESIDENT: Yes, everyone was shocked. I can understand what must have happened during the project when John died.

The CARETAKER: President Johnson continued the program. When it came time for the meeting, we were ready. The landing occurred in New Mexico. We had everything prepared. We had a hoax landing location just in case it was leaked. The landing occurred and we greeted the Ebens. However, a mix up happened. They were not prepared to accept our exchange personnel. Everything was placed on hold. Finally in 1965, the Ebens landed in Nevada and we exchanged 12 of our men for one of theirs.

PRESIDENT: One? Why just one?

WM CASEY: Mr. President, this wasn't clearly documented in the reports that we read.

PRESIDENT: One... was this their ambassador?

WM CASEY: Well, something like that. We just called it EBE 2. We'll discuss that later.

The CARETAKER: Mr. President. Our team of 12 went to the Eben planet for 13 years. The original mission called for a 10-year stay, however, because of the strange time periods on their planet, the team stayed three additional years. Eight returned in 1978. Two died on the planet and two decided to stay.

PRESIDENT: OK, this is just AMAZING! I can see, about that movie. The movie was based on a real event. I saw that movie. 12 men left, along with Richard Dreyfuss.

WM CASEY: Mr. President, yes, the movie was similar to the real event, at least the last part of the movie.

PRESIDENT: OK, a lot to digest. I want to hear about the hostile ones.

ADVISER #1: Mr. President, may I step in here?

PRESIDENT: By all means, ADVISER #1, do.

ADVISER #1: Well, Mr. President, the hostile alien species is responsible for abducting some humans. We can clearly prove some 80 Americans were abducted from about 1955 until the present, the last known one in July of last year. We have a special military intelligence unit keeping track of these abductions. We have FBI agents attached, to assist us when needed. We have NSA and in some instances, CIA personnel helping.

Unfortunately, we don't have the technology to know when these hostiles will abduct. We get the information afterward. We interview the victim and place them under hypnotic trances. Some of the victims remember the entire event without hypnosis, while others need hypnosis to relate what happened. We haven't found one single death directly related to the hostile aliens. We have had deaths that were attributed to the abductions... suicides. We recorded five of them.

But, Mr. President, these are the abductions we know about. We have no idea how many other abductions are occurring in this country or around the world. These hostile aliens are pretty sneaky. They seem to appear and disappear, which is beyond our technical understanding. They also seem to float or defy gravity. We have actual photographs of them doing this. We have a classic abduction incident that was recorded by military intelligence personnel. It happened in 1979 near a military base.

PRESIDENT: Where?

ADVISER #1: In New Mexico.

PRESIDENT: What's with New Mexico? The aliens seem to like that state. Do we know why?

The CARETAKER: Excuse me, may I speak?

PRESIDENT: Yes, CARETAKER, step in.

The CARETAKER: New Mexico is similar to the home planet of the Ebens. Since we do not know which planet the Trantaloids come from...

WM CASEY: Wait... ADVISER #4?

ADVISER #4: I think we do. I think the Ebens gave us that information. We know the star group. It is close to our solar system, well, I mean in astronomical terms. Maybe 20-25 light-years away. They are actually closer to us than the Ebens are.

PRESIDENT: So that means they can travel like the Ebens travel? I mean using those black holes or whatever you call them?

ADVISER #4: Yes, Mr. President, they can travel in the same fashion as the Ebens. However, according to the Ebens, the Trantaloids use a different form of propulsion. Something like matter versus antimatter.

PRESIDENT: And that means?

ADVISER #4: Mr. President, basic physics...

WM CASEY: Mr. President, do you want to go into the physics of this?

PRESIDENT: Oh, no, no, I don't think I'd understand it.

ADVISER #4: I was just going to say that we know that when matter is placed next to antimatter, there is a great deal of energy released. If one could harness that into a propulsion system, that would be great. But we don't have the capability to do that.

PRESIDENT: Do we have one of their spaceships?

The CARETAKER: Yes, well, partially. A crashed one.

PRESIDENT: OK, can we or do we have the technical knowledge to understand it?

WM CASEY: No, Mr. President, we don't.

PRESIDENT: We can make atomic bombs, go to Mars and we can't understand their science?

WM CASEY: Adviser #4?

ADVISER #4: Mr. President, their technology is probably 1,000 years more advanced than ours ... maybe even more. They have different materials to work with. Some of their materials are not found on this planet.

PRESIDENT: What do you mean, like iron or elements?

ADVISER #4: Yes, Mr. President. We found many metals and other things that are not found on this planet. Maybe they have more than 104 elements or maybe they are different than ours.

PRESIDENT: The hostile ones or the Ebens?

ADVISER #4: Mr. President that goes for each species although the Ebens do have similar elements as those found on Earth. But the Trantaloids have strange materials ... nothing like those found on Earth. These aliens can imitate humans. They can look like blond humans. However, they are not blond, but ugly-looking insects.

PRESIDENT: Insects, did you say that?

ADVISER #4: Yes, do you have a photograph?

The CARETAKER: Yes, hold on.

WM CASEY: They are pretty nasty looking.

PRESIDENT: Well, they would stand out.

ADVISER #4: No, Mr. President, as I said they can imitate looking like humans.

PRESIDENT: How in the world do they do that? It took a lot of makeup to make me look good in the movies. (loud laughter heard)

ADVISER #4: Well, Mr. President, I can assure you they don't use makeup, at least not like we would. They have the ability to change their bodies. As I said before, they are 1,000 years ahead of us in technology and probably every other science.

PRESIDENT: They can be killed?

ADVISER #4: Yes, they are just flesh and blood, like a human body. They can be killed. But their spaceships have a force field around them. They can be shot down, but it takes some doing on our part.

WM CASEY: Mr. President, we have to use a small-style nuclear missile to shoot them down, but we haven't actually done that yet. We have experimented in Nevada on the captured craft we have of theirs.

PRESIDENT: My God, I hope we haven't used atomic missiles. What does that mean?! I have to give that order!

ADVISER #1: Excuse me, but Mr. President, no, we haven't used any nuclear missiles to shoot down any alien flying craft. I think Adviser #4 and the Director mean that if we had to shoot one down, for instance... if a group of them attacked us.

PRESIDENT: Is that likely?

ADVISER #1: No, I don't think so.

PRESIDENT: Can we intercept their radio transmissions? Do we know their language?

ADVISER #1: We know or we can recognize their language, which is entirely different than the Ebens. They use a very high-band radio system. But they have different frequencies and it is difficult for NSA to track them.

PRESIDENT: Maybe we should call Captain Kirk?! (loud laughter) Oh, a little humor is good in any situation! (loud laughter)

ADVISER #1: OK, Mr. President, I'll call Scotty! (more laughter)

PRESIDENT: Yeah, maybe Gene Roddenberry knows!

ADVISER #1: Our air defenses are as best prepared as we can be against any form of an attack by this group.

PRESIDENT: How do we do that? I mean, our pilots. Do they know?

ADVISER #1: Not exactly. But we have a system to cover any threat.

PRESIDENT: A war plan?

ADVISER #1: Like I said earlier, yes, Mr. President, we do have war plans just for this event or possible event.

PRESIDENT: OK. Well, I think that is enough for one day. Bill, set something up for tomorrow to finish this.

WM CASEY: OK, Mr. President. I'll get with ADVISER #2 and Michael Deaver.

PRESIDENT: I want to thank everyone for a very thorough briefing. I was educated beyond belief. I will have a different attitude every time I look up in the sky. [3]

3/27/81 In the Oval Office of the White House

Evens is summoned to the White House, where President Ronald Reagan greets him as he enters the Oval Office. After the two men are seated and the small talk is out of the way, President Reagan says, "General, I understand that you are the man who is responsible for keeping the UFO matter secret."

"Yes, Mr. President. I am."

The President says, "Well, I have asked you to come here in order so that I could ask a favor from you, General."

Evens is startled by this and says, "I am at your service, Sir."

Reagan says, "MJ-12 has advised me against this, but I believe that an effort should be undertaken in order to begin acclimating the general public to the presence of extraterrestrials. I feel that the public should be properly informed in order to be able to deal with alien related problems, should the need arise. However, this is not possible, since it would be contrary to your objectives. I guess that what I am asking is that you will overlook certain breaches in security with regard to extraterrestrial visitation."

Evens thinks about this for a while, winks one eye at the President, and says, "I'm sorry, Mr. President. I must do my job to the best of my ability."

The President smiles, shakes Evens' hand, and says, "I understand completely, General. I am very glad to have met you. Thank you very much for coming."

"It has been my pleasure, Mr. President."

4/9/81 At the Hotel Daniels in New York City

Evens is present for a trap that has been set for "The Observer."

Several NSA assets are in place to track and monitor the activities of this person just as soon as he becomes exposed. Based upon known past traits of "The Observer," an agent was able to make contact with this person. He was told that a sealed envelope, containing secret information, would be hidden in a private telephone booth in the lobby of this hotel today.

There are several agents, with hidden cameras, located at various places in and around the hotel. They are also equipped with radios, guns, and cans of an invisible aerosol spray. When "The Observer" has been identified, the agents will spray a fine mist of invisible radio-active particles on his clothes so that he can be tracked. The envelope is also covered with the particles and is constantly monitored for any movement.

Evens is also listening in on the radio conversations of the agents through an earphone in his ear. He is very tense. This is the second time that he has been on one of these field operations, but this time, someone else is in charge. Evens is only there as an observer and he hopes that everything goes well. Just then, he hears through the earphone, "All Alphas, all Alphas, this is Papa. We have movement of the package."

"Papa, this is Alpha 8. I have him spotted. He is a male, Caucasian, adult dressed in a brown hat, white overcoat, and dark blue pants. He has a beard and brown hair. He is heading for the elevators."

"Roger, Alpha 8".

Evens walks toward the elevators. He sees the person in the white overcoat and tries not to give himself away.

"Papa, this is Alpha 2. The subject has been painted."

"Roger, Alpha 2."

The subject walks into an elevator car along with several other people heading to the upper floors. Evens also walks into the car just before the doors close.

"Papa, this is Alpha 5. The subject has entered elevator 2 heading upwards."

"Roger, Alpha 5. Alpha 1, be ready for him."

"This is Alpha 1. Roger."

At floor two, the doors open and several people get out. Evens quickly moves next to the subject, motions for him to be quiet, and hands him a note. The subject reads, "THIS IS A TRAP. THE ENVELOPE AND YOUR CLOTHES ARE BEING TRACKED. QUICKLY CHANGE INTO THE CLOTHES IN THE BAG NEXT TO YOU AND ESCAPE. DON'T TALK. CALL ME AT (212) 836-4461. A FRIEND."

The person looks at Evens in horror for a moment. Then, the subject quickly peels off the fake beard, takes off the hat, revealing long brown hair, and strips off the outer clothing.

Evens is pleasantly surprised to see a beautiful woman before him dressed only in a bra and panties. She quickly puts on the clothes from the bag next to her. She leaves her previous clothes on the floor along with the envelope. The other passengers are watching all of this in great surprise.

On the twenty-third floor, "The Observer" smiles at Evens, exits the elevator car, and runs off to the right.

Evens stuffs the clothes and envelope into the bag and also exits the car, carrying the bag of clothes with him. He walks to the left and speaks into his microphone, "Papa, this is Echo. I am with the subject on the twenty-third floor."

"Roger Echo."

Evens walks around on the floor for a few minutes and then walks down the stairs to the next floor.

"Echo, This is Papa. We now show the subject on the twenty-second floor."

"Papa, this is Echo. The subject has changed clothes. I have recovered the subject's clothes and the envelope, which was left behind. I followed, but lost the subject on the 22nd floor."

"Echo, what is the subject's description?"

"Papa, the subject is wearing brown pants and a light brown jacket. The subject is female."

"All Alphas, this is Papa. Be on the lookout for a female, wearing brown pants and a light brown jacket."

4/10/81 At an Apartment in New York City

The telephone rings and Evens answers it with, "Hello?"

"Thank you for helping me yesterday."

Evens smiles to himself and says, "It was my pleasure."

"Who was trying to trap me?"

Evens decides to be truthful with this lady and says, "Agents of the National Security Agency."

"Oh? Do you know who sent them?"

Evens smiles and says, "Yes, I do. I did." There is a long pause at the other end of the line. Evens says, "My name is Tom Evens. It is my job to keep the subject of UFOs secret and I have been watching your activities with great interest. You have been giving me a lot of trouble. It was my plan to have you followed so that you could be silenced, permanently. But, I have had a change of heart."

"Well, that's good to know."

Evens says, "I have decided that the public should know about what is happening, in regard to UFOs, and I'd like your help in getting the word out."

"Well, I don't know if you are speaking the truth. But, I'm willing to listen. My name is Linda Davis."

There is silence over the telephone as Evens realizes that she is the wife of the escaped scientist from the Dulce Base that he had apprehended. He knows that she would hate him if she knew who he was, but it was too late now to stop so he says, "Very well, Linda. It's nice to meet you. What do you say to having lunch with me tomorrow at noon at the restaurant 'Adams' here in New York City?"

"That sounds fine with me. I still don't know if I should be grateful, fearful, or angry. But, I'll be there tomorrow."

Evens says, "Perhaps you should be a little of everything. I'll see you tomorrow. Good bye."

4/11/81 At the Restaurant Adams in New York

Evens is sitting at a table in the rear of the restaurant, drinking a beer. He sees a waiter coming towards him with a pretty lady following behind. She is dressed in a red feminine business suit and skirt that shows off her shapely body. Her soft blond hair rests on her narrow shoulders. He admires her beauty and strength of character and she is drawn to his strong eyes and set jaw. Evens stands and remembers how beautiful she looked in her underwear.

She holds out her hand and says, "Tom, I'm Linda. I believe that I owe you a debt of gratitude."

They shake hands and Evens says, "Yes. Well, I'm sorry to have caused you such trouble."

"It was really quite exciting."

They sit and order lunch from the menus. Linda orders red wine to drink with lunch. After the waiter leaves, she asks, "Could I see your identification, please?"

Evens says, "Here. This is my badge from the agency" and passes it over to her.

Linda looks at it and says, "The National Security Agency, huh? Is that something like the Central Intelligence Agency?"

She passes it back to Evens, who says, "Yeah. Something like that."

Evens takes a sip of beer and says, "You don't remember me, do you."

Linda takes a closer look at his face, thinks about it, and says, "You! You took my husband from me. You told me that he would be safe and now he is dead. All that I was told was that he had a heart attack. What did you do to him? Tell me."

Evens squirms in his seat as he says, "Your husband didn't suffer a heart attack. He committed suicide when he used his teeth to have the truth drugs that we were slowly giving to him flow freely into his vein. I feel terrible about that. I never meant to harm him. I'm really very sorry."

Linda wipes away the tears from her eyes and asks, "So, where does that leave us now?"

Evens says, "I would like to help you to expose what the government is doing about the aliens that are here from other worlds. It is my job at the National Security Agency to prevent this information from being disclosed, but I can help you by providing proof of the government's involvement, if you will let me."

Linda says, "It was my husband's last wish that I reveal what is going on with regard to the alien presence here. As a journalist, I have been trying to honor his wish ever since you took him from me. Unfortunately, I found that the editors of major news outlets want nothing to do with stories about UFOs."

Evens says, "I'm sorry about that, but we pretty well keep the mass media from reporting anything about UFOs. However, 'The Observer' was still able to get the story reported in newspapers about the Baker's Creek Falls shoot-out with a UFO. You are very resourceful."

Linda says, "Well, I do have my contacts."

Evens smiles and says, "Yes, you have been most troublesome to me. In May of 1980, you caused another story to be reported. This time it was about Judy Doraty and her son being abducted by a UFO near Cimarron, New Mexico. That story described their accounts of being taken to an underground base and witnessing a calf being mutilated and having the body parts thrown into a large vat along with human body parts. Then, you were responsible for the newspapers reporting on the Cash-Landrum case, which occurred in December of 1980. That was where the two women received severe radiation poisoning during an encounter with a U.S. disk that was escorted away by 23 military helicopters. The disk that harmed the two women was a Project Redlight asset. Did you think that nobody would care about what you were doing?"

Linda shifts around in her seat and says, "Yeah, I knew that I was taking a risk when I exposed those things. But, I just couldn't sit by and allow these things to go unreported. I was honoring the memory of my husband by letting people know what was happening. Okay, where does that leave us now?"

Evens passes a thick envelope across to Linda and says, "I think you'll find this to be of interest to you."

Linda takes the envelope and says, "Well, with you on my side, I suppose that I am perfectly safe in exposing this stuff."

"Oh, I wouldn't go so far as to say that. I'll do what I can to protect you. But there are a lot of bad people out there who will not appreciate your efforts one bit."

"So I guess that what you are saying is that I should be scared."

"You should be VERY scared. Here. Take this."

Linda takes a small package from Evens and asks, "What is it?"

"It's a secure radiotelephone unit. Not even the military has this yet. It's supposed to be completely secure. We will be able to reach each other at any time with this. I will help you any way that I can. Good luck. You'll need it."

"Gee, thanks."

4/14/81 In a Conference Room at the N.S.A.

Evens is present for a report of what happened with the failed mission in the hotel. He and the other agents involved with the mission are seated around a large table.

The leader of the field operation, whose call sign was Papa, is giving the briefing at a podium in the front of the room. The leader's name is Ron Hansen. He states, "This is a briefing, regarding the field operation of 9 April, 1981. The information presented here is the result of an analysis of witness statements, forensic, photographic, audio and video evidence. First, I will present the known facts of this case. Then, I will detail the facts that remain unsolved. Finally, I will present an analysis of what went wrong and how these mistakes may be avoided in the future."

A photograph of Linda Davis, as she looked when she entered the hotel, is displayed on a large viewing screen. Mr. Hansen says, "First, the known facts. We know that an adult Caucasian entered the Hotel Daniels at 10:16 hours in the morning of 9 April 1981. This individual appeared to be a male, approximately 25 years of age, five feet-four inches tall, and about 130 pounds."

A photograph of Linda Davis leaving the telephone booth is now displayed on the screen. Mr. Hansen states, "We also know that a marked envelope was taken from a concealed location at the same time that this person left the scene. Because the envelope's movements, which were electronically monitored, coincide with the subject's movements, it can be assumed that this person took the envelope, and can thereby be identified as 'The Observer'."

Another photograph is displayed on the screen. This one, taken outside of an elevator, from above the doors, shows Linda Davis entering the car, followed by Evens. Hansen says, "The subject walked directly to a waiting elevator car, with General Evens following him into the car. There were twelve other people in that elevator car at the same time."

The next picture, taken above the elevator car, shows eight people exiting the car. "The elevator traveled to the second floor and eight people exited the car. The elevator then continued upwards. The four other people in the elevator at this time corroborate General Evens' testimony. They all state that the subject looked at a piece of paper and immediately changed clothes with other clothes that were in a bag next to him. He said nothing to anyone. But, it appears that the subject was actually female."

The next picture shows Linda Davis exiting the elevator and walking to the right. Mr. Hansen says, "The elevator stopped on the twenty-third floor and this subject exited the car and walked away toward the right."

Another picture is displayed, showing Evens exiting the car toward the left. "General Evens also exited the car, a short time later. But, he walked to the left. Why did you do that General?"

Evens says, "When I saw that the subject was leaving, I noticed that she did not take the envelope or her other clothes with her. I did not want this evidence to disappear. So, I put the envelope and the subject's clothes in the bag and took it with me. But, while retrieving the clothes, I failed to notice the direction that the subject traveled in. By the time that I exited the car, the subject had disappeared. I simply chose the wrong direction to look in."

Hansen says, "Several minutes passed before you reported the subject as missing. Why didn't you report this right away along with the subject's new identifying features?"

"I did report that the subject was on the 23rd floor just as soon as we got off the elevator. I then became very busy attempting to determine where the subject had gone. It was not until I heard your message about the subject's movements that I thought about reporting what had happened."

Another photograph is displayed on the screen. It shows the hotel lobby with Linda Davis leaving, wearing her new clothes and long brown hair. Hansen states, "General Evens, and the other witnesses have identified this as the person that they saw exit the elevator. Well, at least we now know what she looks like.

"Forensic evidence, on the clothes that were left behind, indicates that the subject recently purchased the clothes at a Robinson's store in New York City. Stray hairs, found in the coat, indicate that the subject's true hair color is blond and not brown. This suggests that the subject colored her hair as a disguise. No prints or other identifying evidence were obtained. Now, I would like to cover the mysteries that are still unsolved. First of all, I'd like to ask you a question, General. You were only present at the operation as an observer. As it turns out, it was fortunate that you were able to follow the subject into the elevator. But, I'd like to know why you got involved?"

Evens says, "This person really upset me. I just wanted to get close enough to see what 'The Observer' really looked like."

Hansen says, "Well, I guess you did. But, there are many puzzling facts in this case. First of all, what do you suppose the subject was reading in the elevator?"

"I don't know. Maybe she was checking a list of things that she needed to do."

"Do you think that she was onto us?"

"It is possible that I may have given the operation away when she saw that I was looking at her. Or perhaps, she was just being careful."

"Okay, but I can't figure out where the bag of clothes came from. No one who entered the elevator was carrying a bag like that."

"I don't know where it came from either. The first time that I noticed it was when the subject was taking clothes from it."

"Could she have had an accomplice?" "I don't think so. I never saw her make eye contact with anyone else."

Hansen shouts, "Damn it!"

2/15/82 At a Parking Garage in Washington, D.C.

Evens and Linda Davis secretly meet in Linda's car.

Linda says, "Thank you, Tom, for meeting with me."

"It's no problem at all. I wanted to congratulate you. It seems that 'The Observer' has been very busy."

"Well, thank you, Tom. I thought you might have read the stories in the press about the UFO landing in Rendlesham Forest, near the Royal Air Force Base in Bentwaters, England. The memo that you gave me with the packet of documents was very useful. It was written by Colonel Charles J. Halt on January 13th, 1981, and described three small aliens walking up to the Wing Commander, General Gordon Williams. I did some investigative work and found the memo to be accurate." [4]

Evens says, "I also understand that 'The Observer' had something to do with the Denver Post article on June 21st 1981, exposing the 'Chip Implants that replace ID cards'."

"That's right. Again, your information about identification implants being developed in 1979 at Los Alamos National Labs, proved to be accurate. That packet, that you gave me, also contained some very interesting top-secret documents. Do you realize that I could be sent to prison for just being in possession of those things?" [5]

"Yes, I do."

Linda says, "Well, that's comforting. There are a total of 16 different documents, dating from June of 1947 until November 12th, 1963. That covers a time frame beginning one month before the Roswell incident and ending just ten days before President Kennedy was assassinated. And, they all deal with the government's involvement with UFOs and extraterrestrials." [6]

"Okay. Now that that has been established, what do you intend on doing with all of it?"

"Well, the documents all look genuine. But, there is no way to verify their authenticity. Let me just go over some of these documents with you. In June of 1947, Dr. J. Robert Oppenheimer and Professor Albert Einstein wrote a document, entitled, 'Relationships with Inhabitants of Celestial Bodies' where they describe various scenarios of interaction with extraterrestrials. But, if they wrote this a month before the first UFO crashed near Roswell, New Mexico, how did they know about the existence of extraterrestrials?" [7]

"Well, there had been numerous sightings of UFOs prior to that time and those scientists just surmised that they were from other worlds."

Linda considers this and says, "Okay. That makes sense. The next document is a copy of military orders which confirms the fact that the Army sent out a special team to investigate the UFO crash on the fourth of July, 1947. Then, there is a Presidential Directive, from Harry Truman to Lt. General Twining, dated five days later, ordering him to appraise unidentified objects being kept at White Sands Proving Grounds. It seems that Truman was also concerned about the reactions of some of the people involved with the project and wanted Twining to investigate their concerns. [8]

"Next, we have an Intelligence Assessment Report by the Interplanetary Phenomenon Unit which summarizes what happened with the recovery of the crashed disc and five dead alien bodies."

Evens says, "Yes, I can vouch for the accuracy of that report because I was part of the team that recovered everything."

"Well then, maybe you can explain the mention about a body at another crash site, not far away, that had been dissected as you would a frog. It also says that animal parts were discovered inside the recovered craft."

"Yes, I saw what was termed as animal parts inside the craft, myself. They were actually from the pilot of a downed military aircraft. The aliens were involved in mutilating people and taking what parts they wanted when the crash occurred." [9] [10]

Linda says, "I see. The next document was General Twining's Air Accident Report on the Flying Disc Aircraft, detailing the advanced technology that they discovered inside the craft. There was also another document, entitled, 'Mission Assessment of Recovered Lenticular Aerodyne Object' which corroborated the other reports. Then, there was a memorandum from President Truman, to the Secretary of Defense, authorizing Admiral Forrestal to establish the group known as the Majestic Twelve. The First Annual Report of the Majestic Twelve was very interesting. It described their purpose, conclusions, and problems associated with exploiting alien technology. These problems related to nuclear weapons, biological warfare, genetics, pharmaceuticals, new materials, future rockets, nuclear propulsion, intelligence, foreign policy, national security, constitutional issues, psychological reactions, the cold war, and government policy of control and denial. [11] [12] [13] [14]

"I must say, for a government that denies the existence of extraterrestrials, it was quite a shock for me to see a Majestic-12 Group Special Operations Manual entitled, 'Extraterrestrial Entities and Technology Recovery and Disposal' written in proper military fashion. It covered recovery operations, handling instructions, extraterrestrial entities, and UFO identification. And finally, we have the two Memorandums from President Kennedy. The first one is dated June 28, 1961 and is addressed to the Director of the CIA. It is a request for a briefing of MJ-12 Intelligence Operations as they relate to Cold War Psychological Warfare Plans. The second one is dated November 12th, 1963 and it is also addressed to the Director of the CIA. It is a request for a classification review of all UFO intelligence files affecting National Security." [15] [16] [17] [18]

Evens says, "Yep. That just about covers it. Now, what I'd like to know is what you're going to do next."

Linda thinks about this for a few seconds and says, "I think that the best way for us to reach the most people is with a televised documentary special. I know a cable television producer that I can approach with this. I'm going to have a little talk with him about the possibility of putting together a documentary release about UFOs, extraterrestrial life, and government involvement. That should do it."

Evens gets a concerned look on his face and says, "Okay. But, be very careful."

2/23/82 Evens' Office at the N.S.A.

General Evens greets Mr. Hansen, the man who ran the operation to identify "The Observer".

Mr. Hansen says, "Thank you for seeing me on such short notice. But, I thought that you'd like to know that we have a lead on the elusive 'Observer'."

"Well, that is good news. Tell me about it."

"It seems that someone contacted a television producer in order to get them to do a documentary about UFOs. Well, the producer called the Pentagon for verification of the existence of the Majestic-12 group that this person had told him about and the call was routed to me. I told him that Majestic-12 did exist and found out the next time that he was going to meet with this person who turns out to be a woman. We'll be waiting for her."

Evens acts pleased and says, "Well, that was quick thinking on your part. Very good. Let me know when you've identified her. Don't worry. I won't interfere with your operation this time. I've learned my lesson."

"Very well. I'll let you know." After Mr. Hansen leaves the office, Evens says to himself, *That idiot! How could she have been so dumb to have revealed the existence of Majestic-12 and not expect anyone to verify the existence of it? Well, I guess I'd better warn her. I'll call her tonight, after work.*

2/23/82 At Evens' House in Baltimore, MD

Evens has just punched in the number for Linda Davis' secure radio communications unit. Tom hears five rings in his unit before Linda finally answers, saying, "Hello".

"Hello, Linda. It's Tom here. It seems that you have made contact with that TV producer, haven't you?"

"Yes, that's right. How did you know?"

"Because, you idiot, he called the Pentagon, to ask for verification of Majestic-12 which you told him about."

"Oh. Did you get the call?"

"No. But the man who is in charge of finding you did. He is setting up a trap for you when you next meet with that producer. Why did you reveal top secret information to him? Didn't you think that he would check on it?"

"No, I didn't think he would. But, I had to show proof of what I was attempting to expose in order to get him to produce the documentary."

Evens asks, "What? You showed him the documents?"

"Yes. I had no choice."

"Please tell me that you did not leave any of the documents with him."

"Yes, I did. He said that he needed to research the subject. Don't worry. He promised that he would never reveal his source."

"You idiot! Now, you have killed us both. Every copy of every classified document is written slightly different from every other one. That is so they can trace where any leaks are coming from. If they get hold of those documents, it will only be a matter of time before they trace them back to me. I think that it would be a good idea for you to pay that producer a surprise visit, tell him that you have changed your mind about doing the documentary at this time, and get those documents back from him as soon as possible."

"Yes, I think you're right. I'll do it the first thing tomorrow. I'm sorry Tom. I didn't mean for this to backfire the way that it has."

Evens calms down a bit and says, "Your apology is accepted. But, I would appreciate it if you were a little more careful in the future."

"Don't worry. I will. Thanks, Tom, for saving my life once again. I owe you."

"You can repay me by making people aware of what is going on regarding extraterrestrials and not getting yourself and me killed in the process."

"I will, Tom. Thanks."

2/27/82 In Evens' Office at the N.S.A.

Evens welcomes Mr. Hansen into his office, saying, "Have a seat and tell me who 'The Observer' really is."

Hansen sits down and says, "I'm sorry to tell you this. But, I still do not know. She canceled their previously scheduled meeting. I tapped the producer's telephones, just in case 'The Observer' might call. But, she never did. So, I had a little talk with the producer myself. He told me that she unexpectedly contacted him in person and said that she had changed her mind about having the documentary produced. It would appear that 'The Observer' either had second thoughts about the venture or someone tipped her off about the setup. He wouldn't tell me who this person was. But, considering the daring behavior of this lady in the past, I doubt that she would start acting scared now. So, that leaves us with the possibility that someone from the inside is providing her with assistance."

Evens ponders what he has heard so far and says, "Yes, it certainly does seem that way. Do you know who that might be?"

"Not at this time. However, we may have a lead to pursue. In another tapped conversation, the producer stated that he had copies of some classified documents, which the lady gave to him and then retrieved from him at their second meeting. It appears that he has hidden the copies and concealed their whereabouts. We have made three attempts to covertly retrieve the documents from his home and office. But, we have not yet been successful. Sooner or later, though, he will make a mistake and reveal their location."

"Well, thank you, Mr. Hansen. Keep up the good work."

12/5/83 At a Parking Garage in Washington, D.C.

General Evens and Linda Davis are meeting secretly in Linda's car once again. Evens says, "You might want to look into a discovery at the University Hospital Medical Center in San Diego. They claim that brain transmitters were found in the X-rays of a skull. Here. Look at this."

Evens hands Linda a secret internal Pentagon document, dated Dec. 1, 1983, that describes in detail the military's directions for calling out the troops in case of some unspecified emergency. The document lists exceptions to the Posse Comitatus Act, the federal law that prohibits the military from operating in the United States. Evens says, "That document gives, as it's authority for such actions, 'the inherent legal right of the United States Government to ensure the preservation of public order...by force, if necessary.' This is a claim that the Supreme Court had dismissed when President Truman tried to use it to justify taking over steel mills in the early 1950's. There is evidence that new Army divisions, like those at Fort Lewis in Washington, will have a dual foreign and domestic role. Another planned division will be located at Fort Ord, California."

Then, Evens tells Linda about how, in 1980, the Federal Emergency Management Agency was granted special powers under standby legislation, in a Bill entitled, the "Defense Resources Act". He hands Linda some papers and says, "This bill would suspend the Bill of Rights, abolish free enterprise, eliminate privately owned property, and generally clamp the American people in a totalitarian vise."

Linda reads through the bill and discovers that Section 202 allows the President to instantly confiscate any real estate or personal property "that shall be deemed necessary for national defense purposes." Section 501 authorizes the takeover of any industry that the White House specifies. Section 1213 outlaws all strikes. The standby legislation also includes "Censorship of Communications", which allows the president, whenever he "shall deem that the public safety demands it", to censor "communications by mail, cable, radio, television, or other means of transmission." This really makes Linda angry. [19]

5/22/88 In Evens' Office at the N.S.A.

General Evens leans back in his comfortable chair, behind his desk, and thinks about all that he and Linda Davis has accomplished together over the years. The movie "V" was presented to the public in 1984, portraying reptilian aliens who fed on human flesh, stored humans for food, etc. The movie, "The Adventures of Buckaroo Banzai in the Eighth Dimension" was also released that same year. In Nov. of 1985, NBC had broadcast a program about "black unmarked helicopters, secret projects, and bad money". In 1986, a book entitled, "Sky Crash" by Jenny Randles, was first published. Also in 1986, "UFO Crash at Aztec", by Steinman and Stevens, was published and a movie entitled "The Aurora Encounter" was released.

In 1987, the "Dulce Papers" were first released. On February 15th, the San Jose 'Mercury' reported on the Pentagon "black budget" programs. They also made sure that President Reagan's remarks, in an address to the United Nations on September 21st, where he voiced his thoughts about aliens threatening the Earth, was reported in the press. On October 11, the Las Vegas Review Journal reported a story on Area 51/Dreamland in Nevada. Information has also been released regarding an incident where, on Nov. 27th, US Army Rangers apparently bungled an attempt to enter a joint US/alien facility in New Mexico.

Other efforts, which are in the works for 1988, include the release of the Strecher Memorandum about AIDS. In August, "The Matrix", a detailed manual by Valdemar Valerian, will be released about extraterrestrials. The publication, "NASA Techbriefs" will show a photo of an EBE with no caption or explanation. Also in 1988, Bo Gritz will distribute his book, "Betrayal of a Nation" regarding the CIA and Delta forces in drug deals. Information in that book will expose how the intelligence agencies are distributing illegal drugs to finance alien-related projects.

Evens also intends to release information about an antimatter weapon, that has been developed at Los Alamos, NM, and is intended to be used as a weapon of last resort if "the Greys cannot be pried away from the planet". Evens knows that the number of Greys on Earth is now estimated to be at 20 million. He is also attempting to have information released on Project Excalibur. This project is involved with developing a warhead that will penetrate 1000 meters of earth and then detonate. This is a very useful weapon for destroying underground bases. [20]

Just then, Evens is shaken from his thoughts by the buzz of his intercom. His secretary says that an individual, by the name of Stan Edwards, is on the telephone and asks to speak with the General. Evens reaches for the telephone and says, "Hello, Stan. It's really good to hear from you. How is retirement treating you?"

"It's good to hear your voice, as well, Tom. Retirement is fine. The kids are grown and out on their own. They're doing fine. My ex-wife and I have gotten back together and we're doing alright."

"That's great, Stan. Listen. I did a lot of soul searching and I thought a lot about what you told me just before you left. I want you to know that you would be real proud of me at how I have handled this job since then."

Stan says, "That's really good to hear, Tom. But, that's why I am calling you. The CIA has been contacting everyone who was ever employed by them that has ever had anything to do with the alien problem. They asked me a lot of questions. They are trying to find out who is revealing all of the information regarding extraterrestrials to the media. They asked me a lot of questions about you, as well. What they asked gives me the impression that they know about you having an association with someone known as 'The Observer'. I think that someone is out to get you and I thought that you should know."

Evens says, "Thanks, Stan, for calling. You have been a good friend. Good-bye."

"Good-bye, Tom. Good luck."

Evens hangs up the telephone and quickly leaves the building.

Captured

7/14/88 At an Apartment in Yelm, WA

Tom Evens has been in hiding for almost two months, ever since he received Stan's telephone call. He had been ready to leave the NSA, at a moment's notice, for many years.

Also, because he was involved with finding people at the agency, he knew exactly how to hide and never be found. He is living in a small town in Washington State. It is very nice there, this time of year. The people are very nice to him there. He rented an apartment and joined the Senior Citizens Center. At the age of 63, Evens quickly blended in with the community.

But now, it is mid summer with mild temperatures, and everything is in full bloom. The town was built in the middle of a beautiful forest and there are evergreen trees everywhere. He could find it very easy to spend the rest of his life here, but he has just read a newspaper article that could prevent that from happening.

The article states that Linda Davis has been indicted for disclosing government secrets. She has been released on bail, but she faces stiff penalties if she is found guilty in a court of law.

He is concerned that she will probably spend the rest of her life in prison for revealing information that he gave to her. He wants to help her disappear just as he has done, but he also knows that this could be a trap to capture him. So, he sits down and writes a letter that is addressed to the people of Earth. Once he has finished the letter, he makes certain that it will be discovered by the proper people in the event of his untimely demise. Then, he begins to make plans for Linda's escape.

7/30/88 At a Parking Lot in a Maryland Suburb

Linda Davis has just finished her grocery shopping and is returning to her car when she hears a familiar voice say, "Hello Linda."

Linda turns around and is surprised to see Evens standing nearby. She then says, "Who are you and what do you want?" Her eyes move left and right to convey the fact that there are government agents following her.

Evens says, "I'm sorry, ma'am. I thought you were someone else" and he starts to leave the area. Just then, three black sedans screech to a halt and men jump out of the cars with pistols drawn.

One of them shouts, "You! Stop where you are and put your hands in the air. Now!"

Evens does as he is told. After he is handcuffed, he is shoved into a sedan and it quickly departs the area.

Linda is placed in another vehicle with agents and it also departs, leaving Linda's groceries behind in a cart.

7/30/88 In the Interrogation Section of the N.S.A.

Linda has been taken to a room with a desk, some chairs and a video camera in the corner of the ceiling. She is left there alone with the door locked. She sits at the desk and waits.

A man enters the room and sits across from Linda. He says, "Hello. My name is Ron Hansen. I have wanted to meet you for a long time. You see, I have been investigating the activities of someone who identifies herself as the 'Observer'."

Linda does not even blink. He says, "We know that it was you who gave classified documents to a television producer in New York. We recovered those documents, and the producer cooperated with us by identifying you as the one who gave them to him." He drops the documents on the table for effect and says, "We have everything we need to put you away for a very long time. All we are asking is for you to be forthcoming about this case and you will be free to go with all charges against you dropped."

Linda smiles and says, "Certainly Mr. Hansen, I would be happy to cooperate with you."

Hansen leans back in his chair and says, "Thank you. That would be greatly appreciated. First of all, I would like to know who gave you the classified documents."

Linda states, "I don't know. I received them in the mail with no return address and a postmark from the Washington DC area."

"Do you still have the envelope?"

"No."

"Okay, after giving the documents to the producer, why didn't you meet him again as planned in a follow-up meeting?"

"I simply became frightened about doing a documentary on this subject and decided not to continue with the project."

Hansen says, "You know, we first attempted to identify you when you picked up an envelope at the Daniels Hotel in New York. You eluded a very elaborate operation there. How did you do it?"

"I was wearing different clothes as a disguise underneath my outer garments, which I took off in an elevator."

"But, witnesses say that you stripped and dressed in clothes from a bag after reading a note."

"The note was my list of things to do. I was going to put my outer clothing in the bag, but I ran out of time. I am sure that others thought that I was taking off all of my clothes, but I had other clothes on underneath."

"Okay. But, why didn't you take the envelope with you?"

"It must have slipped out of my pocket, and I didn't notice it."

Hansen thinks about this for a few seconds, then he passes a form to her and says, "Thank you Miss Davis. You have been most helpful. Please sign this non-disclosure agreement and you will be free to go."

Linda asks, "What are you asking me to agree to?"

"You must never divulge anything about the other man apprehended along with you today, the existence of this case or anything that you have seen or heard here today. If you do, I can assure you that you will regret it."

Linda reads the form, signs it, and passes it back to Hansen, who says "Thank you, Miss Davis. A gentleman will be here momentarily to escort you to where you were picked up and all charges will be dropped against you. Good day to you."

Hansen exits the room and says to a man in the corridor, "Go ahead and take her back to where she was apprehended."

The man asks, "Why? We have enough on her to put her away for life."

"She will not cause anymore trouble and we don't need her testimony against Evens. We only needed her to get Evens and we have all we need against him. Besides, we do not need this case exposed in a public trial especially after President Reagan's speech to the United Nations on September 21st of last year where he shared his thoughts of how humanity would be united if aliens were threatening the Earth."

The man agrees with him and enters the room.

Hansen then enters another room, similar to the previous one, where Evens is sitting and says, "Hello General. It has been a long time."

"Hello Mr. Hansen. I might have known that you would be behind all of this."

"You should never have gotten me involved with finding the 'Observer'. She told us everything about her efforts as the 'Observer' and how you supplied her with these secret documents." Hansen drops the documents on the table.

Evens leans back and says, "Really? That's news to me."

"How do you explain this copy of a classified document, which you signed for, ending up in the possession of a television producer who identified Miss Davis as the one who gave it to him?"

Evens acts surprised and says, "I don't know."

Hansen smiles and says, "Well General, I'd like to say that you will be able to tell your story in a public trial, but that is not going to happen. There is someone who wants to meet you. Come with me, please."

Evens is escorted into a waiting black sedan that leaves the facility.

7/30/88 In a Forest Clearing

They drive to a secluded meadow in the beautiful forest nearby.

Actually, Tom thinks that this would not be such a bad place to die if it were not for the two men guarding him in the limousine. He thinks they are very strange looking in their black suits, dark sunglasses, and eerie manner. There is just something about them that gives Tom the creeps. It is something akin to fear.

Suddenly, there is a great disturbance outside with everything being blown about as if they were in the eye of a hurricane. The two men drag Tom from the car and throw him to the ground. He looks upwards to see a large V-shaped craft slowly descending. It is about 100 feet across. Landing gear is extended and the craft lands heavily nearby, but it still has a humming sensation to it. Tom notices that the ship has wads of fine material on its hull and landing gear that look similar to spider's webs. There is also an insignia of a winged serpent on the side of the craft.

Just then, a hatch opens and a ramp is extended to the ground. There is a smelly kind of humid fog that comes from within the craft, indicating that the interior atmosphere is warm, damp and humid. There is also a kind of orange glow emanating from within the ship. Tom then sees two tall Reptilian humanoid soldiers walk outside of the craft and stand on each side of the hatchway with weapons in hand.

They stand about eight feet tall with slender, but muscular builds. Their foreheads slope downwards and they have elongated heads. The ears are small, pointed flat, and appear to be sculpted into their heads. They have rough, scaly skin with a dark greenish color and glowing red eyes that are catlike and large. Their twin nostrils are at the end of a short stubby muzzle. Their mouths are wide and frog-like with no protruding lips. The arms are long and bony, and the hands are webbed with five fingers. The neck is bony with perceptible notches down to the spine. Their legs are bent forward at the knees, and their feet are long and encased in a kind of heel-less boot. [1]

Evens is amazed that the men with him are not surprised by these beings as he is. He then watches as another humanoid being emerges from the hatchway. He is albino-white with a face shaped like a lizard and red eyes with vertical slit pupils. He is wearing a long robe that covers his body. The two men force Evens to kneel and bow his head in the presence of this being.

The albino entity speaks in a loud and reverberating voice saying, "You are accused of betraying our trust in keeping the extraterrestrial presence here secret. How do you respond to this accusation?"

Evens takes a big gulp and says, "The accusation is true. I have exposed the alien presence in order for humanity to decide for themselves, how best to deal with this situation."

The entity shouts, "Your species is too primitive and is incapable of making rational decisions regarding their own welfare. They need us to guide and protect them" [2]

Tom raises his head defiantly and responds with "You mean, dominate and enslave them, don't you? Sir, humanity can only evolve by having the freedom to learn from their mistakes and that cannot happen if they become your slaves that worship and live only to serve you. Mankind here is far more powerful than you will ever know. They will unite against your plans to turn them into your slaves and defeat you. Once they understand how you have taken over all of the world's leadership positions in order to control humanity under a one-world government, they will rebel. And, your use of the Greys to create millions of human-looking hybrids to help control the masses will also fail."

Tom is shocked to see the albino's robe pulled back to expose his reptilian body with huge outstretched wings like a bat. The entity makes a loud and terrifying sound and shouts, "How dare you speak to me this way! You will obey me and stop revealing our presence!"

Tom feels that he has nothing to lose by saying, "No Sir, I will not do that. I feel sorry for you and the way that you cannot overcome your own slavery for the need to dominate others."

The albino cannot believe the impertinence of this lowly creature and shouts, "How dare you talk to me this way? You will become my finest meal!"

"That is fine with me because I don't want to live here anymore with you here. I hope that you choke on my bones!"

Just then, Tom sees a bright light coming from behind him and hears the albino yell, "No!" He looks behind him and sees a disk that was not there before. A hand reaches out from the craft and pulls him inside.

7/30/88 On Board a Pleiadian Spacecraft

Evens feels disoriented and then notices that he is standing in front of three highly evolved human beings. They are wearing a peculiar gray colored coverall suit that is very pliant and light. The suit is close fitting to their bodies, extremely durable, and the material resembles the skin of an elephant. Around their necks, there is a ring, which evidently serves for the mounting of a helmet.

One of the three is a very attractive woman with blond hair, blue eyes, and a slim figure. She appears to be a normal female human being at about five feet tall. There is nothing that would indicate super abilities, pretentiousness, or spirituality about her, although she is obviously very intelligent. She walks quite normally for a woman, yet somewhat stronger, more confident, and graceful without being particularly dainty or trying to make any special impression. [3]

A man, in the middle of the three, stands about five and a half feet tall. He exudes great love and friendliness. He appears to be about 70 years old with gray in his shoulder length hair. He looks at Tom attentively and has a roguish smile in the features of this old man. [4]

The third person is a man with a beard, mustache, and long brown hair. He appears to be about 50 years old and has a stern look on his face. He has a slender, but physically fit body. He is strong, confident, and has a no-nonsense attitude about him. [5]

Tom asks, "Am I dead?" He is told by the elderly man, "No. We are from the Pleiades cluster of stars. We have been watching what has been going on and have brought you on board our spacecraft when you said that you no longer wanted to live on Earth anymore. If you approve, we will take you to our home planet of Erra where you will live in peace."

Evens blinks his eyes in disbelief at what he has just heard. He then smiles and says, "Yes. I would like that very much. I would also like to thank you for saving my life."

The old man smiles and says, "You are most welcome. My name is Patier. My title is Yahway and I am the commander of a large mother ship. The woman piloting this scout craft is my daughter, Solmay."

The woman turns from the control panel, smiles at Tom and says, "It is a pleasure to meet you."

Tom also smiles and says, "And I am very delighted to meet you as well."

Patier then gestures to the other man and says, "I would like to introduce you to Queitel. He is our station leader for this region of space."

Queitel holds out his hand and says, "It is nice to finally meet you. We have been monitoring your activities for a long time and we appreciate all that you have done to enlighten mankind about the alien presence on Earth."

The two men shake hands. Then Tom looks down and says, "I only wish that I could have done more." He then looks up and asks, "If you are in charge of what happens in this region of space, why aren't you doing anything to save the people of Earth from the alien threats to their freedom and self-determination? How can you allow such suffering to continue there? Don't you care?"

Queitel says, "We care very much about what happens on your planet. We do everything that we can do to prevent malevolent alien influences from harming humanity without causing a conflict that could erupt into war. We must adhere to inter-galactic laws and agreements, which allow for our concealed presence here as well as the presence of other races. Humanity is at risk simply because it is unaware and unwilling to accept the existence of other intelligent races in the universe that are present here. We contact those who are ready for contact, such as yourself, and provide intuitive assistance to help them enlighten humanity about the challenges they face. You have done well. The letter that you left behind for the people of Earth will do much to inspire them to see the truth before them and respond accordingly. We cannot directly interfere unless humanity asks for our help. Even then, we cannot control what humanity does on Earth. It is entirely up to the people whether they will become the slaves of a foreign race that does not appreciate them or earn the right to be free and independent from outside influences." [6]

Tom nods and says, "I understand. I only wish that I could have done more. Now, I am an old man near the end of my life."

Solmay says, "I do not understand what you mean. You are only 63 years of age. On our planet, we live to be about a thousand years old. You are not even at the minimal age where matrimony is considered yet. You have a very long life yet ahead of you, my friend."

Tom looks up to the ceiling and says, "Oh God, give me strength!" Everyone bursts into laughter. Tom then asks, "Does this mean that I will become young again?

Patier says, "Unfortunately, we do not have the ability to reverse the aging process. However, you will find that your body will continue to age at a much slower rate. I am 725 years of age and I expect to live to be 1,000 years old. You will find that we live in a very healthy and stress-free environment with no diseases. Our air is clean, unpolluted, and has a higher oxygen content to it. Your body will become strong, healthy, and invigorated."

"That sounds good to me", says Tom. He thinks for a minute and then says, "I just feel terrible about leaving the Earth and humanity in the situation that it is in. Don't get me wrong. I am very grateful to you for rescuing me from certain death. I just feel as though I am turning my back on humanity. I was wondering if it may be possible for me to return to the Earth at some later time so that I can help the people to overcome their plight. Also, there is a very special lady there that I would like to see again."

Patier smiles and says, "Yes. That is possible, if that is what you want to do."

Tom has a big smile on his face as he says, "Great! That's perfect. Now, where are we, and where are we going?"

Evens' Letter

To the People of Earth:

My name is Major General Tom Evens.

If you are reading this letter, it is because I am no longer able to personally convey what I believe to be critically important information for the survival of mankind as the preeminent race on Earth. In my many years of military service, I have learned many things, which I seek to share with you now. Without this information, I believe that humanity is destined to fall into slavery for masters that are neither respectful of our rights, nor appreciative of anything we do.

Ladies and Gentlemen, we are not alone in the universe. There are a wide range of life forms in our galaxy. Your government and military leaders are aware of more that 57 different extraterrestrial races that have visited this planet. They have kept this information from you for over forty years in order to preserve the secrets that they have discovered and to hide their involvement in criminal conspiracies involving alien races who seek to take over the world. You have been deceived and intimidated about the UFO phenomenon so that the powers that be can continue to gain ever more wealth, influence, and power. [1]

Our first use of atomic bombs sent out shock waves into space that resulted in a veritable traffic jam of spacecraft that came here in order to scrutinize humanity before we destroyed the planet. Different societies exist in the universe at every conceivable level of development and in a wide range of life forms. The universe is not a heavenly place. It is a difficult and competitive environment where all races must deal with the rigors of physical life involving survival, hardship, competition, and deprivation.

The need for resources have become great and many worlds have outstripped their own resources to where they have become barren and unproductive. So, Earth is viewed with great interest because it is rich in mineral and biological resources, it is strategically located, and accessible to many civilizations. Because of this, we are at risk of losing everything, and we are being kept in ignorance of the dangers that we face.

The Army recovered an alien craft that crashed near Roswell, New Mexico on the fourth of July, 1947 along with five dead bodies and one live alien being. As a result of this, the United States has implemented many policies that still affect us today. Since then, all recovered alien spacecraft have been examined at a secret base known as DREAMLAND, in Nevada, which stands for Data REpository And Maintenance Land. Communications have been established with many alien races and an independent group within the government, known as Majestic-12, has been in charge of everything having to do with extraterrestrial contacts and technology exploitation. These people report to no one and have supreme authority over all black projects.

The United States Government entered into a secret agreement with an alien race with large heads and big black eyes known as the Greys. They were allowed to have secret underground bases on U.S. soil, they were permitted to abduct American citizens, and they were promised that we would not interfere with their activities in exchange for advanced technology. At the same time, our leaders decided to reject the peaceful offers of help from other benevolent races because they would not share their advanced weaponry with us.

Today, the abduction and manipulation of people is out of control. The aliens are in the process of creating hundreds of thousands of human-looking hybrid beings to influence and control humanity so that we will become their slaves under a unified New World Order controlled by aliens. To make matters worse, our financial, military and government leaders throughout the world are under the control of a malevolent reptilian race of beings who seek to dominate the world from above while the Greys control us from below. This intelligent reptilian race has lived in ancient cavern city complexes deep underground far longer than mankind has existed on Earth and they believe themselves to be the rightful rulers of this planet.

Fortunately, the people of this planet cannot be conquered forcefully by other alien races. Our world exists in a region of space that is governed by rules of conduct where societies take legal action against one another should those rules be violated. This means that the people of Earth cannot become a part of an association with other worlds unless humanity visibly demonstrates that it agrees to it and welcomes it. So, advanced alien nations have become powerful in influencing the mental environment of other worlds.

Many planets have joined together in Federations with economic, political, and military strength for mutual trade and defense. However, there are also parts of the universe where great empires exist, which are usually centered in one world or region by one race. It is the Draconian Empire of reptilian beings that live deep within the Earth. Their hybrid race, which can appear human, has dominated humanity's political and economic affairs throughout our history.

Collectives are another type of association that have no single home planet and are composed of a group of dissimilar planets with many different races. They are joined together either through conquest or persuasion. They function with a hive mentality and are rigidly controlled with no personal freedom, insight or creativity. They rely on structure, codes of conduct, and their ability to manipulate the thoughts of others who they influence.

It is a Collective of Greys from the Orion Constellation who are on Earth now because they need our resources and they view Earth as a prize, the best among many. They seek to have humanity believe that they will save us from our own destruction. So, they have taken a long time and are very subtle in their influence with humanity. They want us to become a part of them so that they can become even stronger.

They have devoted an enormous amount of time and energy in gaining our allegiance by bonding with humanity through interbreeding, and in establishing a deep and pervasive association. In order for them to gain control over us, they must have us welcome them, want what they have to offer, and believe that we need their help in order to satisfy the rules of conduct that are placed upon them. [2]

Humanity is under siege. Our isolation is over and we will never have it again. We must realize that other intelligent and technically advanced races do exist in the universe and not all of them are here for benevolent purposes. This is the greatest event in human history as well as the greatest threat to human freedom and independence. However, this is also the greatest opportunity for all of mankind to unite and cooperate for the benefit of all. This may not be a tragedy for us, but we will emerge into a greater community of life forms in the universe whether we are prepared or not. It is now inevitable.

Intervention is occurring without the agreement or consent of the population. Our fundamental rights are being violated on a massive scale. Many people are taken against their will repeatedly. The abduction of people by the Greys is not being done for the benefit for mankind. However, many people have acquiesced and now serve as emissaries and intermediaries. Others serve as resources for the alien genetics program, and many others are taken and never seen again.

If something is not done, humanity will give away our world freely, openly, and with very few questions. We can either acquiesce or stand for freedom. The only thing that is going to save humanity is humanity itself. We have everything we need to be successful. But, we are grossly unprepared to deal with other intelligent life forms in the universe to the point that the situation has become rather desperate. Awareness is the first thing. We must all recognize the reality of what we are facing. We must have an objective understanding about the alien life that is here and in the Universe. Our lack of comprehension could truly be tragic.

We must be mentally strong and not open our hearts and minds completely to the aliens. Resist the intervention through awareness, advocacy, and understanding. Become aware of the visitors, but do not yield. Regain your inner authority. Become a power to be reckoned with in regard to any who would trespass or deny your fundamental rights. Become aware of the mental manipulations that are taking place. Choose who and what is influencing your thinking. Learn to determine with discernment and objectivity what others and the world is telling you. [3]

The Greys are persuading people to become acquiescent and less able to discern more and more every day. People are giving up control for direction, counsel, and preservation. They are giving away the authority over their lives and are willing to have their lives completely controlled for a promise of greater alien technology. The peace that is being offered to mankind is the same peace that exists in prisons because everyone will be completely controlled and unable to resist.

With each passing day, opportunities fade as more people are captured and their awareness is manipulated. Although there are not many aliens here, their job is being made easy because of human ignorance and acquiescence. If we are to be strong and self-determined, than we must be able to think independently and consider things deeply, rather than just accepting whatever we are told. This is no time to be ambivalent, complacent, or distrustful. We are vulnerable because we are divided and unaware of life beyond our planet and we have no defense against outside influences.

Even knowledgeable people are being demoralized, discouraged, made to feel weak, helpless, hopeless, and impotent in the face of beings with enormous power. They feel as though they have no possibility of resisting. These feelings are not just a lack of self-trust, but are a manipulation of their minds. We must realize this and deal with it by finding insulation and freedom from the torment with Knowledge. Counteract a wishful and hopeful view of things, which is susceptible to persuasion and manipulation. We must see with clear and sober eyes without hope and fear. Do not give over your mind, heart, and the world for the promise of peace, power, and equality. We will succumb either due to persuasion or by being discouraged from resisting. So, we must not lose faith.

This is the most important problem in the world today. This is not a future prospect, but an immediate challenge. If people cannot respond, then the world will be given away and recklessness brings a heavy price. So long as we are still free to know, to respond, and speak out, then we must do so. We must be willing to establish freedom for every human being on Earth and defend it, if necessary, or domination will certainly occur. To survive, humanity must unite and be willing to protect the world from alien interventions. We must be strong and independent from alien influences and "Freedom" must be our rallying cry.

We must oppose the violation of alien craft in our skies and not let any foreign race upon our soil without permission from the population. Obviously, this permission was never asked for and it was never granted. That is why this is an intervention and not a visitation. It is being forced upon us. We have the power to resist the alien influences for human allegiance. But, we need awareness, discernment, and inner conviction. This must be given priority. There is still time. It can be stopped, but ignorance, greed, hostility, and naivete will undermine our strength. Freedom is a difficult thing to achieve and to maintain.

A movement must arise to demonstrate our displeasure with our uninvited guests, provide awareness of the situation, and an understanding of what we must do to secure our freedom and well-being. We must have a public outcry to oppose the abductions and interbreeding that is taking place. If we resist then it must stop. If we do not have a strong public voice of resistance then it will appear that the intervention is welcomed.

We must be self-sufficient, united, and very discreet. The more self-sufficiency is sustained, the stronger and more independent we will become. The depletion of essential resources causes extreme vulnerability and powerlessness. We must regenerate our resources in order to prevent dependency.

If we are successful in defending our right to be the preeminent race on Earth and can live in freedom, then we will be able to meet other benevolent races in the universe. In the meantime, there is great work to be done and everyone has the possibility to do this work. [4]

In order for humanity to extricate itself from the covert and sinister alliance between our governments and the Greys, which has occurred without the knowledge and consent of the population, the people must regain control over their leaders. Our government has been usurped. Very wealthy and powerful entities are conspiring, behind the scenes, to strip this country of its independence so that they can rule a One-World Government. They are constantly working to erode our personal rights and make the United States interdependent with other countries. It is vital that this gradual erosion of our individual rights and national sovereignty be actively resisted as much as possible.

I am conveying this information so that you will understand the plans that are currently being implemented by extraterrestrial societies to conquer the Earth and turn all of humanity into slaves.

It was previously assumed that each alien society was acting independently of each other for control of Earth's resources. However, people that have been abducted by Grey entities have reported seeing a Reptilian species on board the alien craft. This indicates that these two societies are cooperating with each other.

Obviously, any alien society that seeks to control the surface of Earth must also contend with the Reptilian race that exists underground. The Reptilians have always sought to dominate humanity overtly by controlling our political and economic leaders, but they have never succeeded because there were always rogue groups that refused to cooperate with the dictates of their leaders.

By allowing the Greys to use their influence to convince humanity to merge with their Collective community, both races will be able to do whatever they want and take whatever they desire from this planet. As a result, thousands of people from all over the world are being repeatedly abducted by the Greys in order to create hybrid slaves that can pass as human beings so that they can manipulate and influence humanity into becoming a part of their Collective community.

It is also known that the Reptilians plan to stage an attack by malevolent aliens as a pretext to create a One-World Government that will supposedly save the world with their hybrids in complete control of the planet. Once humanity has been processed into willing slaves, the Reptilians and Greys will then be able to show themselves in public and do whatever they want to do.

In addition, several groups of extraterrestrials wish to establish themselves as Gods or religious leaders in order to influence religious values among mankind because this would be fundamental acquiescence and submission. It would be heralded as a great advancement for humanity with a new unification, equanimity, and spirit over instincts. Extraterrestrials are seeking to convince our religious leaders and contact those who are sensitive, receptive, and cooperative. They try to pacify and reeducate through religious persuasion by using our identification with Jesus and his promise to return.

A second coming is being prepared now. This Jesus will project images of angels, demons, or whatever is desired in order to engender followers and encourage alienation or destruction of the non-believers. There will be a ferocity of religious beliefs expressed in violent ways against those who disagree in the name of God. The people that are believers will be valued as useful, and the others will be discarded. [5]

If we should fail in opposing the intervention, we will be subordinated to powers from beyond our world and the Earth will be stripped of its resources. Humanity will be corralled into work groups, and rebels will be destroyed. We will be managed by hybrids that are bred to lead us into a New World Order where freedom would no longer exist.

We would suffer under a rule that would be harsh and exacting. Religions and societies may be preserved, but we would lose a great deal. We are facing a vast global occupation. One day, you could wake up and find that you are no longer free and that you have no recourse. Every person on Earth would become a slave, doing endless, back-breaking work until their dying days for an alien race that neither appreciates your efforts nor cares if you live or die.

Think about yourself living with no home, possessions, or contact with any of your loved ones. What good is it then to hear a child's laughter when children will soon be laboring like everyone else? This would be the end of times. What would time matter to anyone if there was never any time off to enjoy life? Why would you care what day it is if there are no days off? Every day would be the same as every other day.

The aliens will have all of your property and possessions to do with as they see fit while you are corralled into work camps. You will be forced to deliver all of our resources and when they have taken everything of value and left our planet barren, we will have our very means of survival stolen from us and we will be left bereft. It has happened before on many other worlds. Do you care that it could happen here?

It is easy to become overwhelmed by such information and lose all hope for the future of humanity. It is normal to want to respond emotionally with anger, fear, and acquiescence. This is exactly what the conspirators want. Cool heads must prevail. It is necessary to rise above primitive and primal instincts and respond intellectually with love in your heart for all mankind.

We are not alone in our struggle to be free. Humanity has allies, and they can be of immense help, if we will only use our inner knowledge to pay attention to them. They have had to battle the same forces on many other worlds and they know how we can prevail. [6]

The tall Blonds from Procyon have a benign attitude toward humanity, except for their strong disapproval of our inhumanity to each other. This strong disapproval is further intensified by the fact that our government has made a secret alliance with their hereditary enemies, in order to obtain even more destructive weapon systems than those already in existence. Our government is not interested in negotiating with the Procyonians, as they would not provide our government with weapon systems.

However, because the Greys have invaded the home planet of the Blond humans from Procyon, just as they are attempting to invade Earth, it could be beneficial to heed the advice of a Procyonian by the name of Khyla. He has stated, "It is impossible for you to fight the Greys on a military level. Their technology is too far in advance of yours. It would be like bows and arrows versus machine guns. However, this time around, you would be the ones with the bows and arrows. They can use electromagnetics to axis-switch this planet or take it out of orbit.

Active resistance would be suicidal due to their technological advantage, foolhardy rather than courageous. It is necessary to fight in another manner, through passive resistance. At this stage, one thing you can do is to provide the public with as much information as possible. This will make it more difficult for the collaborators and Greys in disguise within the government to continue to work against humanity in favor of the Greys. Tell the public how to put their minds into a state that the Greys cannot penetrate, by focusing the mind on powerful imagery, different for each individual.

The only way to victory is through the strength of your consciousness. When genetic or other manipulations are being performed on the abductees, the Greys expect them to cringe in fear, and derive a second-hand high from the intensity of the emotions expressed. If instead of cringing in fear, an abductee can put his or her mind elsewhere, focusing attention on dynamic protective imagery of a religious or mystical nature, it decreases the gratification that the Greys are getting from their second-hand high, and it confuses them. Center the consciousness on something so different from what they expect that it puzzles them.

The degree of protection given by such imagery depends largely on the intensity and endurance of the single-pointed attention. So it is best to choose whatever figure you genuinely feel spontaneous admiration for, which makes your heart sing and makes you feel at one with the infinite. That will always work, and it is all you can do for now.

The intelligence of terrestrial humanity has now evolved to the point where it has a choice in the matter. By understanding the long-term hive-mind strategy of the Greys, individual humans who attain multi-dimensional awareness, can circumvent and short-circuit it. If enough individual humans do this, and refrain from quarreling over petty differences, and unite together to liberate the planet, the Greys will be obliged to seek elsewhere in the cosmos for a slave species they can genetically manipulate.

No matter what the physical situation may be, it is essential to send an SOS telepathic message to the higher powers protective of humanity without becoming entangled in negative emotions such as fear, rage or hatred. Negative emotions not only diminish the effectiveness of one's SOS message to the higher powers in the universe, they are the type of response that the Greys are used to evoking and are expert at manipulating.

If you combat the Greys with hatred in your heart, you become like them, and further entangled with them, instead of free from them. A difficulty with the viewpoint of many of the adherents of organized religions is that they tend to perceive the Greys as demons, and therefore to hate them. Although to some extent this analogy is valid, hatred is a form of attachment, a negative emotion they know well how to use to bind you to them.

What I want to get across to you is that the ultimate evil, which underlies all the negativity in the cosmos, finds expression in the form of psychological complacency. It leads an individual to adhere to a group philosophy rather than to think things through for oneself.

Those who feel safe and comfortable in a belief system, merely because many others adhere to it, and who get together to form an arrogant, self-righteous group that is convinced that it has a monopoly on the truth, are doomed to fail. Those who are ready to persecute, kill or stifle anyone who challenges that group's philosophy, have formed an alliance with the ultimate evil, whether they know it or not.

As soon as you become involved in a belief system that you are a "chosen" special group, who are as lords over the common folk because of your secret knowledge, you are on your way to a fall. That type of attitude plants the seed of destruction in any society or culture, leaving it vulnerable to overthrow by those oppressed within its boundaries, as well as by outside forces. All cultures that have elite groups at odds with each other, and with the population at large, sooner or later collapse from either internal or external pressures.

A healthy organism does not encapsulate portions of itself off that cease to interchange freely with other portions of its body. This type of condition is a prelude to cancer, whether it occurs in an individual or in a society. The only chance of retaining your freedom is for the awareness of this principle to penetrate the consciousness of humanity. It is a pearl of wisdom treasured by those who have attained the ability to travel through time.

I have seen civilizations rise and fall, begin again only to die again, over and over and over. It isn't only a problem of this planet. It's a problem that must be faced by all civilizations in the course of their development, no matter where they may be located in the cosmos. Everyone wants that slightly larger piece of the pie than their neighbor for themselves, and eventually this tendency always culminates in choking them.

Sooner or later this will be the undoing of the Greys as well, thereby enabling us to return in triumph from our exile in the corridors of time. The Greys do not see and are incapable of understanding their own fundamental error: that the very weakness they seize upon in humanity is their own inherent weakness, the blind spot that inevitably seals their doom.

Minerals evolve into plants, plants into animals, animals into humans, and humans into angelic energy-forms. But to try to force a rock, when it is in the state of being a rock, to perform like a plant is utterly futile. To try to change the arrogant mentality of a self-righteous government official or fanatical star person is as futile as trying to make a rock perform like a plant, unless the individual has matured to the point of being ripe for major change.

That is what a traveler through time learns: nothing in this cosmos can ever be forced. Everything happens and unfolds as it should, even when you are confronted with the idiocy that has brought about the potential end of your species as you know it. It is a challenge to be faced, just as Paul Revere and Thomas Paine and John Paul Jones faced the challenges of their time. May it bring out the best in you!" [7]

Sincerely,

Major General Tom Evens, U.S. Army

Appendices

Maurice Osborn
August 2004, UK

Appendix A — References

The following is a list of reference materials that are the source for information that is used within this book. This list is comprised of reference numbers and description fields. The reference number field refers to a sequence of numbers, which appear between square brackets within each chapter. These bracketed numbers are located at the end of information that was derived from other sources wherever it appears within each chapter.

The description field contains information about the source of the material that is located in the book, as indicated by the reference number. This information includes the title of the source material, author, publisher, date of publication, heading, and location of the material within the source.

When the reader comes across a statement with a bracketed number that he or she would like to know the source of, they must take notice of what chapter it is located in and the reference number within brackets. Then, the reader can look at Appendix A and find the listing of reference numbers for the associated chapter. Next, he or she can look through the sequence of numbers in the listing for the appropriate reference number. Finally, the information in the corresponding description field provides a complete description of where the statement was derived.

Chapter 1 – First Contact

1   "White Sands Missile Range." VIVA New Mexico!
         http://www.vivanewmexico.com/sw.wsmr.html (accessed June 14, 2009).

2   "Interplanetary Phenomenon Unit Summary, Intelligence Assessment, part 5, page 3." Majestic
         Documents.com: Evidence We Are Not Alone. http://www.majesticdocuments.com/
         (accessed June 14, 2009).

3   "Majestic Twelve Project 1st Annual Report, January 31, 1948, Page 9, ANNEX A, part 11."
         Majestic Documents.com: Evidence We Are Not Alone.
         http://www.majesticdocuments.com/ (accessed June 14, 2009).

4   "Interplanetary Phenomenon Unit Summary, Intelligence Assessment, part 2, page 2." Majestic
         Documents.com: Evidence We Are Not Alone. http://www.majesticdocuments.com/
         (accessed June 14, 2009).

5   "Interplanetary Phenomenon Unit Summary, Intelligence Assessment, part 6, page 3." Majestic
         Documents.com: Evidence We Are Not Alone. http://www.majesticdocuments.com/
         (accessed June 14, 2009).

6   "Top Secret Orders for A Team to depart, July 4, 1947." Majestic Documents.com: Evidence
         We Are Not Alone. http://www.majesticdocuments.com/ (accessed June 14, 2009).

7   "Mission Assessment of Recovered Lenticular Aerodyne, part 7, page 3." Majestic
         Documents.com: Evidence We Are Not Alone. http://www.majesticdocuments.com/
         (accessed June 14, 2009).

8   "Majestic-12 Group Special Operations Manual Extraterrestrial Entities and Technology
         Recovery and Disposal, Chapter 3, Recovery Operations, Section I Security, pages 8
         and 9." Majestic Documents.com: Evidence We Are Not Alone.
         http://www.majesticdocuments.com/ (accessed June 14, 2009).

9   "Interplanetary Phenomenon Unit Summary, Intelligence Assessment, part 5, page 3." Majestic
         Documents.com: Evidence We Are Not Alone. http://www.majesticdocuments.com/
         (accessed June 14, 2009).

10   Berlitz, Charles, and William L. Moore. *The Roswell Incident*. New York: MJF Books, 1997.
         Witnesses Speak - the Town Remembers, pages 77 and 78

11   Dolan, Richard M. *UFOs and the National Security State Chronology of a Coverup, 1941-
         1973*. Boston: Hampton Roads Company, 2002.
         Pages 49 and 50

12   Berlitz, Charles, and William L. Moore. *The Roswell Incident*. New York: MJF Books, 1997.
         The AAF Confronts a Crashed UFO and Dead Extraterrestrials, pages 54 and 55

13   Hesemann, Michael, Philip Mantle, and Bob Shell. *Beyond Roswell The Alien Autopsy Film, Area 51, & the U.S. Government Coverup of Ufos.* Boston: Marlowe & Company, 1998.
        Chapter 4 "Not From This Earth", pages 43 and 44

14   "Majestic Twelve Project 1st Annual Report, January 31, 1948, Page 9, ANNEX A, part 12." Majestic Documents.com: Evidence We Are Not Alone. http://www.majesticdocuments.com/ (accessed June 14, 2009).

15   "Interplanetary Phenomenon Unit Summary, Intelligence Assessment, part 12, page 6." Majestic Documents.com: Evidence We Are Not Alone. http://www.majesticdocuments.com (accessed June 14, 2009).

16   "Interplanetary Phenomenon Unit Summary, Intelligence Assessment, part 3, page 2." Majestic Documents.com: Evidence We Are Not Alone. http://www.majesticdocuments.com/ (accessed June 14, 2009).

17   "Interplanetary Phenomenon Unit Summary, Intelligence Assessment, part 6, page 3." Majestic Documents.com: Evidence We Are Not Alone. http://www.majesticdocuments.com (accessed June 14, 2009).

18   Burton, Bren. "Open Minds Forum Seinu Disclosure - The 'TC Group'" Openminds.org. http://www.openminds.org (accessed June 14, 2009).
        Originally passed to the OM Research Team in March 2006

19   "Majestic Twelve Project 1st Annual Report, January 31, 1948, Page 8, ANNEX A, part 7." Majestic Documents.com: Evidence We Are Not Alone. http://www.majesticdocuments.com/ (accessed June 14, 2009).

20   "Majestic Twelve Project 1st Annual Report, Page 9, ANNEX A, part 8." Majestic Documents.com: Evidence We Are Not Alone. http://www.majesticdocuments.com/ (accessed June 14, 2009).

21   "Interplanetary Phenomenon Unit Summary, Intelligence Assessment, parts 9, page 5." Majestic Documents.com: Evidence We Are Not Alone. http://www.majesticdocuments.com/ (accessed June 14, 2009).

22   Berlitz, Charles, and William L. Moore. *The Roswell Incident.* New York: MJF Books, 1997.
        Witnesses Speak - the Town Remembers, page 77

23   Berlitz, Charles, and William L. Moore. *The Roswell Incident.* New York: MJF Books, 1997.
        Witnesses Speak - the Town Remembers, pages 65 and 66

Chapter 2 – Recovery

1   "(Release 1)." Serpo.org - The Zeta Reticuli Exchange Program.
         http://www.serpo.org/release1.php (accessed June 19, 2009).

2   Berlitz, Charles, and William L. Moore. *The Roswell Incident*. New York: MJF Books, 1997.
         Witnesses Speak - the Town Remembers, pages 55 and 57

3   "Mission Assessment of Recovered Lenticular Aerodyne, Part 2, Technical Evaluation."
         Majestic Documents.com: Evidence We Are Not Alone.
         http://www.majesticdocuments.com/ (accessed June 18, 2009).

4   "Interplanetary Phenomenon Unit Summary, Intelligence Assessment, part 4 on page 2."
         Majestic Documents.com: Evidence We Are Not Alone.
         http://www.majesticdocuments.com/ (accessed June 18, 2009).

5   "Air Accident Report on Flying Disc Aircraft Stored at White Sands Proving Ground, New
         Mexico, page 2." Majestic Documents.com: Evidence We Are Not Alone.
         http://www.majesticdocuments.com (accessed June 18, 2009).

6   "Interplanetary Phenomenon Unit Summary, Intelligence Assessment, part 12, page 6."
         Majestic Documents.com: Evidence We Are Not Alone.
         http://www.majesticdocuments.com/ (accessed June 18, 2009).

7   "Majestic Twelve Project 1st Annual Report, Page 9, ANNEX A, part 10." Majestic
         Documents.com: Evidence We Are Not Alone. http://www.majesticdocuments.com/
         (accessed June 18, 2009).

8   "Interplanetary Phenomenon Unit Summary, Intelligence Assessment, part 6, page 4."
         Majestic Documents.com: Evidence We Are Not Alone.
         http://www.majesticdocuments.com/ (accessed June 18, 2009).

9   "Air Accident Report on Flying Disc Aircraft Stored at White Sands Proving Ground, New
         Mexico, Section 2." Majestic Documents.com: Evidence We Are Not Alone.
         http://www.majesticdocuments.com/ (accessed June 18, 2009).

10   Berlitz, Charles, and William L. Moore. *The Roswell Incident*. New York: MJF Books, 1997.
         Witnesses Speak - the Town Remembers, pages 77 and 78

11   Dolan, Richard M. *UFOs and the National Security State Chronology of a Coverup, 1941-
         1973*. Boston: Hampton Roads Company, 2002.
         Roswell, Roswell!, page 50

12   Berlitz, Charles, and William L. Moore. *The Roswell Incident*. New York: MJF Books, 1997.
         Witnesses Speak - the Town Remembers, page 65

13   Berlitz, Charles, and William L. Moore. *The Roswell Incident*. New York: MJF Books, 1997.
         Witnesses Speak - the Town Remembers, pages 62 and 63

14 Berlitz, Charles, and William L. Moore. *The Roswell Incident*. New York: MJF Books, 1997.
Witnesses Speak - the Town Remembers, page 63

15 Berlitz, Charles, and William L. Moore. *The Roswell Incident*. New York: MJF Books, 1997.
Witnesses Speak - the Town Remembers, pages 64 through 67

16 Dolan, Richard M. *UFOs and the National Security State Chronology of a Coverup, 1941-1973*. Boston: Hampton Roads Company, 2002.
Roswell, Roswell! Page 51

17 "Interplanetary Phenomenon Unit Summary, Intelligence Assessment, part 7, page 4."
Majestic Documents.com: Evidence We Are Not Alone.
http://www.majesticdocuments.com/ (accessed June 18, 2009).

18 "Interplanetary Phenomenon Unit Summary, Intelligence Assessment, part 8, page 4."
Majestic Documents.com: Evidence We Are Not Alone.
http://www.majesticdocuments.com/ (accessed June 18, 2009).

19 "Interplanetary Phenomenon Unit Summary, Intelligence Assessment, part 9, page 5."
Majestic Documents.com: Evidence We Are Not Alone.
http://www.majesticdocuments.com/ (accessed June 18, 2009).

20 Berlitz, Charles, and William L. Moore. *The Roswell Incident*. New York: MJF Books, 1997.
Witnesses Speak - The Town Remembers, page 70

Chapter 3 – Crisis Management

1	Berlitz, Charles, and William L. Moore. *The Roswell Incident*. New York: MJF Books, 1997.
		The AAF Confronts a Crashed UFO, pages 22 and 23

2	Dolan, Richard M. *UFOs and the National Security State Chronology of a Coverup, 1941-1973*. Boston: Hampton Roads Company, 2002.
		Roswell, Roswell! Page 52

3	Berlitz, Charles, and William L. Moore. *The Roswell Incident*. New York: MJF Books, 1997.
		Witnesses Speak - the Town Remembers, pages 73 and 74

4	Berlitz, Charles, and William L. Moore. *The Roswell Incident*. New York: MJF Books, 1997.
		Witnesses Speak - the Town Remembers, page 67

5	Dolan, Richard M. *UFOs and the National Security State Chronology of a Coverup, 1941-1973*. Boston: Hampton Roads Company, 2002.
		The Muroc Sighting, page 68

6	"Directive to Lieutenant General Twining, Harry S. Truman, July 9, 1947." Majestic Documents.com: Evidence We Are Not Alone. http://www.majesticdocuments.com/ (accessed June 18, 2009).

7	Berlitz, Charles, and William L. Moore. *The Roswell Incident*. New York: MJF Books, 1997.
		The AAF Confronts a Crashed UFO and Dead Extraterrestrials, page 28

8	Berlitz, Charles, and William L. Moore. *The Roswell Incident*. New York: MJF Books, 1997.
		The AAF Confronts a Crashed UFO, pages 30 through 34

9	Dolan, Richard M. *UFOs and the National Security State Chronology of a Coverup, 1941-1973*. Boston: Hampton Roads Company, 2002.
		The Floodgates Open, pages 47 and 48

10	Berlitz, Charles, and William L. Moore. *The Roswell Incident*. New York: MJF Books, 1997.
		Witnesses Speak - the Town Remembers, pages 67 through 69

11	"Interplanetary Phenomenon Unit Summary, Intelligence Assessment, part 8, page 4." Majestic Documents.com: Evidence We Are Not Alone. http://www.majesticdocuments.com/ (accessed June 18, 2009).

12	"Interplanetary Phenomenon Unit Summary, Intelligence Assessment, part 9, page 5." Majestic Documents.com: Evidence We Are Not Alone. http://www.majesticdocuments.com/ (accessed June 18, 2009).

13	"Interplanetary Phenomenon Unit Summary, Intelligence Assessment, part 11, page 6." Majestic Documents.com: Evidence We Are Not Alone. http://www.majesticdocuments.com/ (accessed June 18, 2009).

14   "Majestic Twelve Project 1st Annual Report, January 31, 1948, Page 10, ANNEX A, part 8, 9, 10 and 13, page 10." Majestic Documents.com: Evidence We Are Not Alone. http://www.majesticdocuments.com/ (accessed June 18, 2009).

15   "Interplanetary Phenomenon Unit Summary, Intelligence Assessment, part 4, page 2." Majestic Documents.com: Evidence We Are Not Alone. http://www.majesticdocuments.com/ (accessed June 18, 2009).

16   Marrs, Jim. *Alien Agenda The Untold Story of the Extraterrestrials Among Us*. Westport: Pub Overstock Unlimited Inc, 1997.
The Road to Recovery, page 96 [17]

17   Berlitz, Charles, and William L. Moore. *The Roswell Incident*. New York: MJF Books, 1997.
Witnesses Speak - the Town Remembers, pages 74 and 76
18   Marrs, Jim. *Alien Agenda The Untold Story of the Extraterrestrials Among Us*. Westport: Pub Overstock Unlimited Inc, 1997.
The Road to Recovery, page 96

Chapter 4 – Discovery

1   Marrs, Jim. *Alien Agenda The Untold Story of the Extraterrestrials Among Us*. Westport: Pub
         Overstock Unlimited Inc, 1997.
         The Road to Recovery, page 100

2   "Air Accident Report on Flying Disc Aircraft Stored at White Sands Proving Ground, New
         Mexico, by Lt. General Nathan Twining, July 15, 1947." Majestic Documents.com:
         Evidence We Are Not Alone. http://www.majesticdocuments.com/ (accessed June 18,
         2009).

3   "Interplanetary Phenomenon Unit Summary, Intelligence Assessment, part 11, page 6."
         Majestic Documents.com: Evidence We Are Not Alone.
         http://www.majesticdocuments.com/ (accessed June 18, 2009).

4   "Briefing Document: Operation Majestic 12, Prepared for President-elect Dwight D.
         Eisenhower, November 18, 1952, page A-4." Majestic Documents.com: Evidence We
         Are Not Alone. http://www.majesticdocuments.com/ (accessed June 18, 2009).

5   Hesemann, Michael, Philip Mantle, and Bob Shell. *Beyond Roswell The Alien Autopsy Film,
         Area 51, & the U.S. Government Coverup of Ufos*. Boston: Marlowe & Company,
         1998.

6   "Interplanetary Phenomenon Unit Summary, Intelligence Assessment, part 10, page 5."
         Majestic Documents.com: Evidence We Are Not Alone.
         http://www.majesticdocuments.com/ (accessed June 18, 2009).

7   Marrs, Jim. *Alien Agenda The Untold Story of the Extraterrestrials Among Us*. Westport: Pub
         Overstock Unlimited Inc, 1997.
         The Road to Recovery, page 99

8   "Memorandum for the Military Assessment of the Joint Intelligence Committee, by the Central
         Intelligence Group, Sept.19, 1947." Majestic Documents.com: Evidence We Are Not
         Alone. http://www.majesticdocuments.com/ (accessed June 18, 2009).

9   "Memorandum for the Secretary of Defense, by President Truman, September 24, 1947."
         Majestic Documents.com: Evidence We Are Not Alone.
         http://www.majesticdocuments.com/ (accessed June 18, 2009).

10   "Briefing Document: Operation Majestic 12, Prepared for President-elect Dwight D.
         Eisenhower, November 18, 1952." Majestic Documents.com: Evidence We Are Not
         Alone. http://www.majesticdocuments.com/ (accessed June 18, 2009).

11   "Majestic Twelve Project 1st Annual Report, January 31, 1948, Page 9, ANNEX A, part 15,
         page 10." Majestic Documents.com: Evidence We Are Not Alone.
         http://www.majesticdocuments.com/ (accessed June 18, 2009).

12   Marrs, Jim. *Alien Agenda The Untold Story of the Extraterrestrials Among Us*. Westport: Pub
         Overstock Unlimited Inc, 1997.
         The Road to Recovery, page 99

13   "Majestic Twelve Project 1st Annual Report, January 31, 1948, Page 10, ANNEX B, part 1,
          page 11." Majestic Documents.com: Evidence We Are Not Alone.
          http://www.majesticdocuments.com/ (accessed June 18, 2009).

14   Marrs, Jim. *Alien Agenda The Untold Story of the Extraterrestrials Among Us*. Westport: Pub
          Overstock Unlimited Inc, 1997.
          The Road to Recovery, pages 108 through 110

15   "Briefing Document: Operation Majestic 12, Prepared for President-elect Dwight D.
          Eisenhower, November 18, 1952, page A-2." Majestic Documents.com: Evidence We
          Are Not Alone. http://www.majesticdocuments.com/ (accessed June 18, 2009).

16   "Briefing Document: Operation Majestic 12, Prepared for President-elect Dwight D.
          Eisenhower, November 18, 1952, page A-4." Majestic Documents.com: Evidence We
          Are Not Alone. http://www.majesticdocuments.com/ (accessed June 18, 2009).

17   "Briefing Document: Operation Majestic 12, Prepared for President-elect Dwight D.
          Eisenhower, November 18, 1952, page A-4." Majestic Documents.com: Evidence We
          Are Not Alone. http://www.majesticdocuments.com/ (accessed June 18, 2009).

18   Marrs, Jim. *Alien Agenda The Untold Story of the Extraterrestrials Among Us*. Westport: Pub
          Overstock Unlimited Inc, 1997.
          The Road to Recovery, page 101

19   "Briefing Document: Operation Majestic 12, Prepared for President-elect Dwight D.
          Eisenhower, November 18, 1952, page A-5." Majestic Documents.com: Evidence We
          Are Not Alone. http://www.majesticdocuments.com/ (accessed June 18, 2009).

20   Randle, Kevin D. *Project Blue Book Exposed*. New York: Marlowe, 1997.
          Appendix B: The Blue Book "Unidentifieds", pages 210 through 213

21   Dolan, Richard M. *UFOs and the National Security State Chronology of a Coverup, 1941-
          1973*. Boston: Hampton Roads Company, 2002.
          Crescendo, pages 44 and 45

22   Randle, Kevin D. *Project Blue Book Exposed*. New York: Marlowe, 1997.
          "In The Beginning...", pages 7 through 13.

23   "Briefing Document: Operation Majestic 12, Prepared for President-elect Dwight D.
          Eisenhower, November 18, 1952, page A-5." Majestic Documents.com: Evidence We
          Are Not Alone. http://www.majesticdocuments.com/ (accessed June 18, 2009).

Chapter 5 – Disinformation

1   Valerian, Valdamar. *Matrix II: The Abduction and Manipulation of Humans using Advanced Technology.* Leading Edge Research Group, 1990.
Aliens and the Government, pages 4 and 5

2   Gritz, James "Bo" *Called to Serve.* Sandy Valley, NV: Lazarus Company, 1991.
The Politics of Heroin Revisited, pages 334 and 335

3   Valerian, Valdamar. *Matrix II: The Abduction and Manipulation of Humans using Advanced Technology.* Leading Edge Research Group.
An Interview With John Lear, page 261

4   Dolan, Richard M. *UFOs and the National Security State Chronology of a Coverup, 1941-1973.*
Boston: Hampton Roads Company, 2002.
The Death of James Forrestal, pages 120 and 121

5   Bamford, James. *Puzzle palace a report on America's most secret agency.* Boston: Houghton Mifflin, 1982.
Chapter 6. 'Targets', pages 243 and 244

6   "(Release 1)." Serpo.org - The Zeta Reticuli Exchange Program.
http://www.serpo.org/release1.php (accessed June 19, 2009).

7   Marrs, Jim. *Alien Agenda The Untold Story of the Extraterrestrials Among Us.* Westport: Pub Overstock Unlimited Inc, 1997.
The Greatest UFO?, page 25

8   Dolan, Richard M. *UFOs and the National Security State Chronology of a Coverup, 1941-1973.*
Boston: Hampton Roads Company, 2002.
Grudge's Report, page 124

9   Randle, Kevin D. *Project Blue Book Exposed.* New York: Marlowe, 1997.
"In The Beginning...", pages 13 and 14

10   Marrs, Jim. *Alien Agenda The Untold Story of the Extraterrestrials Among Us.* Westport: Pub Overstock Unlimited Inc, 1997.
The Road to Recovery, pages 112 and 113

11   "(Release 27a)." Serpo.org - The Zeta Reticuli Exchange Program.
http://www.serpo.org/release27a.php (accessed June 19, 2009).

12   "Open Minds Forum Seinu Disclosure - The 'TC Group' by Bren Burton, Originally passed to the OM Research Team in March 2006." Openminds.org. http://www.openminds.org (accessed June 19, 2009).

13   Randle, Kevin D. *Project Blue Book Exposed.* New York: Marlowe, 1997.
"In The Beginning...", page 14

14   Marrs, Jim. *Alien Agenda The Untold Story of the Extraterrestrials Among Us*. Westport: Pub Overstock Unlimited Inc, 1997.
Plausible Deniability, pages 126 and 127

15   Valerian, Valdamar. *Matrix II: The Abduction and Manipulation of Humans using Advanced Technology*. Leading Edge Research Group, 1990.
Chronology 1951, page 406

16   Bamford, James. *Puzzle palace a report on America's most secret agency*. Boston: Houghton Mifflin, 1982.
Chapter 3. Anatomy

17   Randle, Kevin D. *Project Blue Book Exposed*. New York: Marlowe, 1997.
"In The Beginning...", page 15

18   Dolan, Richard M. *UFOs and the National Security State Chronology of a Coverup, 1941-1973*. Boston: Hampton Roads Company, 2002.
The Washington DC Sightings, pages 171 through 175

19   Marrs, Jim. *Alien Agenda The Untold Story of the Extraterrestrials Among Us*. Westport: Pub Overstock Unlimited Inc, 1997.
Plausible Deniability, pages 129 and 130

20   Randle, Kevin D. *Project Blue Book Exposed*. New York: Marlowe, 1997.
"In The Beginning...", page 15

21   "(Release 8)." Serpo.org - The Zeta Reticuli Exchange Program.
http://www.serpo.org/release8.php (accessed June 19, 2009).

22   Marrs, Jim. *Alien Agenda The Untold Story of the Extraterrestrials Among Us*. Westport: Pub Overstock Unlimited Inc, 1997.
The Road to Recovery, pages 107 through 110

23   "Briefing Document: Operation Majestic 12, Prepared for President-elect Dwight D. Eisenhower, November 18, 1952, page A-5." Majestic Documents.com: Evidence We Are Not Alone. http://www.majesticdocuments.com/ (accessed June 19, 2009).

24   Marrs, Jim. *Alien Agenda The Untold Story of the Extraterrestrials Among Us*. Westport: Pub Overstock Unlimited Inc, 1997.
Plausible Deniability, pages 132 through 135

25   Randle, Kevin D. *Project Blue Book Exposed*. New York: Marlowe, 1997.
"In The Beginning...", pages 15 through 20

26   Marrs, Jim. *Alien Agenda The Untold Story of the Extraterrestrials Among Us*. Westport: Pub Overstock Unlimited Inc, 1997. Plausible Deniability, page 136

Chapter 6 – Formal Contact

1   Marrs, Jim. *Alien Agenda The Untold Story of the Extraterrestrials Among Us*. Westport: Pub
         Overstock Unlimited Inc, 1997.
         Plausible Deniability, page 137

2   Marrs, Jim. *Alien Agenda The Untold Story of the Extraterrestrials Among Us*. Westport: Pub
         Overstock Unlimited Inc, 1997.
         The Road to Recovery, page 114

3   "(Release 8)." Serpo.org - The Zeta Reticuli Exchange Program.
         http://www.serpo.org/release8.php (accessed June 21, 2009).

4   Valerian, Valdamar. *Matrix II the Abduction and Manipulation of Humans Using Advanced
         Technology*. Yelm, WA: Leading Edge Research Group, 1990.
         Conversations With An Alien Species, pages 332 through 335

5   Valerian, Valdamar. *Matrix II the Abduction and Manipulation of Humans Using Advanced
         Technology*. Yelm, WA: Leading Edge Research Group, 1990.
         'Channeling, UFOs and the Positive/Negative Realms Beyond This World',page
         355A1

6   Osborn, Maurice. *The Essence of the Notes*. Ramona, CA: Maurice Osborn, 2007.
         Chapter 4 'PLEJAREN', pages 87 through 101

7   Valerian, Valdamar. *Matrix II the Abduction and Manipulation of Humans Using Advanced
         Technology*. Yelm, WA: Leading Edge Research Group, 1990.
         Chronology 1953, page 408

8   Valerian, Valdamar. *Matrix II the Abduction and Manipulation of Humans Using Advanced
         Technology*. Yelm, WA: Leading Edge Research Group, 1990.
         from Top Secret/Apotheosis, Nexus Seven, 1989, page 12

9   Valerian, Valdamar. *Matrix II the Abduction and Manipulation of Humans Using Advanced
         Technology*. Yelm, WA: Leading Edge Research Group, 1990.
         Aliens and the Government, page 3

10   Wilson, Richard K., and Sylvan Burns. *The U.S. Government and Extraterrestrial Entities*.
         Regarding Aliens and the Government, 1989 N.A.R, The Secret Treaty

11   Valerian, Valdamar. *Matrix II the Abduction and Manipulation of Humans Using Advanced
         Technology*. Yelm, WA: Leading Edge Research Group, 1990.
         Chronology 1953, page 407

12   Valerian, Valdamar. *Matrix II the Abduction and Manipulation of Humans Using Advanced
         Technology*. Yelm, WA: Leading Edge Research Group, 1990.
         Primary Physical Characteristics of the Grey Entities, page 81

13   Valerian, Valdamar. *Matrix II the Abduction and Manipulation of Humans Using Advanced Technology*. Yelm, WA: Leading Edge Research Group, 1990.
Alien Species (Service to Self), pages 102 and 103

14   Valerian, Valdamar. *Matrix II the Abduction and Manipulation of Humans Using Advanced Technology*. Yelm, WA: Leading Edge Research Group, 1990.
Orion Grey Type 1 and Type 2, pages 51D and 51E

15   Graebe, M. J. "Insectoids." Universe Magazine, January 1998.

Chapter 7 – Aftermath

1   Allen, Gary. *NONE DARE CALL IT CONSPIRACY*. Seal Beach, CA: Concord P, 1971.
        Chapter 5, Establishing The Establishment, pages 93 through 96

2   Valerian, Valdamar. *Matrix II the Abduction and Manipulation of Humans Using Advanced Technology*. Yelm, WA: Leading Edge Research Group, 1990.
        The UFO Cover-up, pages 242 and 243

3   Valerian, Valdamar. *Matrix II the Abduction and Manipulation of Humans Using Advanced Technology*. Yelm, WA: Leading Edge Research Group, 1990.
        Chronology 1955, page 409

4   Valerian, Valdamar. *Matrix II the Abduction and Manipulation of Humans Using Advanced Technology*. Yelm, WA: Leading Edge Research Group, 1990.
        Aliens and the Government, page 4

5   Valerian, Valdamar. *Matrix II the Abduction and Manipulation of Humans Using Advanced Technology*. Yelm, WA: Leading Edge Research Group, 1990.
        The Sirians, page 51A

6   Valerian, Valdamar. *Matrix II the Abduction and Manipulation of Humans Using Advanced Technology*. Yelm, WA: Leading Edge Research Group, 1990.
        Conflict for Control, page 98

7   Valerian, Valdamar. *Matrix II the Abduction and Manipulation of Humans Using Advanced Technology*. Yelm, WA: Leading Edge Research Group, 1990.
        The Sirian Males, page 51A4

8   Valerian, Valdamar. *Matrix II the Abduction and Manipulation of Humans Using Advanced Technology*. Yelm, WA: Leading Edge Research Group, 1990.
        Sirian Female, page 51B

9   Valerian, Valdamar. *Matrix II the Abduction and Manipulation of Humans Using Advanced Technology*. Yelm, WA: Leading Edge Research Group, 1990.
        The Reptilians, pages 96 and 97

10   Valerian, Valdamar. *Matrix II the Abduction and Manipulation of Humans Using Advanced Technology*. Yelm, WA: Leading Edge Research Group, 1990.
        The Greys and the Reptilians, pages 89 and 90

11   Valeria, Valdamar. *Matrix II the Abduction and Manipulation of Humans Using Advanced Technology*. Yelm, WA: Leading Edge Research Group, 1990.
        Grudge 13 Report, pages 65 and 66

12   Valerian, Valdamar. *Matrix II the Abduction and Manipulation of Humans Using Advanced Technology*. Yelm, WA: Leading Edge Research Group, 1990.
        Chronology 1957, pages 409 and 410

13   Valerian, Valdamar. *Matrix II the Abduction and Manipulation of Humans Using Advanced Technology*. Yelm, WA: Leading Edge Research Group, 1990.
Chronology 1957, page 410

14   Valerian, Valdamar. *Matrix II the Abduction and Manipulation of Humans Using Advanced Technology*. Yelm, WA: Leading Edge Research Group, 1990.
Questions and Answers from Robert Lazar, pages 280 through 291

Chapter 8 – Insiders

1   Allen, Gary. *NONE DARE CALL IT CONSPIRACY*. Seal Beach, CA: Concord P, 1971.
        page 81, Chapter 5, Establishing The Establishment

2   Marrs, Jim. *Alien Agenda The Untold Story of the Extraterrestrials Among Us*. Westport: Pub
        Overstock Unlimited Inc, 1997.
        Pass the Buck, pages 390 through 394

3   Marrs, Jim. *Crossfire: the Plot that Killed Kennedy*. New York: Carroll and Graf, 1989.
        "Kennedy and Oilmen", page 277

4   Marrs, Jim. *Crossfire: the Plot that Killed Kennedy*. New York: Carroll and Graf, 1989.
        "The Military- Industrial Complex", page 303

5   Valerian, Valdamar. *Matrix II the Abduction and Manipulation of Humans Using Advanced
        Technology*. Yelm, WA: Leading Edge Research Group, 1990.
        Chronology 1961, page 411

6   Valerian, Valdamar. *Matrix II the Abduction and Manipulation of Humans Using Advanced
        Technology*. Yelm, WA: Leading Edge Research Group, 1990.
        Chronology 1961, page 412

7   Dolan, Richard M. *UFOs and the National Security State Chronology of a Coverup, 1941-
        1973*. Boston: Hampton Roads Company, 2002.
        The Hill Abduction Case, pages 335 and 344

8   Marrs, Jim. *Crossfire: the Plot that Killed Kennedy*. New York: Carroll and Graf, 1989.
        "The Military- Industrial Complex", page 302

9   Marrs, Jim. *Crossfire: the Plot that Killed Kennedy*. New York: Carroll and Graf, 1989.
        "The Military- Industrial Complex", page 304.

10   Marrs, Jim. *Crossfire: the Plot that Killed Kennedy*. New York: Carroll and Graf, 1989.
        "Lucky Goes To War", pages 162 and 163

11   Marrs, Jim. *Crossfire: the Plot that Killed Kennedy*. New York: Carroll and Graf, 1989.
        "Carlos Marcello", pages 164 and 165

12   Valerian, Valdamar. *Matrix II the Abduction and Manipulation of Humans Using Advanced
        Technology*. Yelm, WA: Leading Edge Research Group, 1990.
        Chronology 1987, page 424

13   Valeria, Valdamar. *Matrix II the Abduction and Manipulation of Humans Using Advanced
        Technology*. Yelm, WA: Leading Edge Research Group, 1990.
        Aliens and the Government, pages 1 through 3

14   Valerian, Valdamar. *Matrix II the Abduction and Manipulation of Humans Using Advanced Technology*. Yelm, WA: Leading Edge Research Group, 1990.
An Interview With John Lear, page 258

15   Marrs, Jim. *Alien Agenda The Untold Story of the Extraterrestrials Among Us*. Westport: Pub Overstock Unlimited Inc, 1997.
The Road to Recovery, pages 101 through 107

Chapter 9 – Coup d'Etat

1   "(Release 8)." Serpo.org - The Zeta Reticuli Exchange Program.
            http://www.serpo.org/release8.php (accessed June 22, 2009).

2   Marrs, Jim. *Crossfire: the Plot that Killed Kennedy*. New York: Carroll and Graf, 1989.
            "All The Way With LBJ", page 295

3   Marrs, Jim. *Crossfire: the Plot that Killed Kennedy*. New York: Carroll and Graf, 1989.
            "The Military- Industrial Complex", pages 302 and 303

4   Marrs, Jim. *Crossfire: the Plot that Killed Kennedy*. New York: Carroll and Graf, 1989.
            "The Military- Industrial Complex", page 305

5   Marrs, Jim. *Crossfire: the Plot that Killed Kennedy*. New York: Carroll and Graf, 1989.
            "Kennedy and Vietnam", page 306

6   Marrs, Jim. *Crossfire: the Plot that Killed Kennedy*. New York: Carroll and Graf, 1989.
            "A Killing On Wall Street", pages 275 and 276

7   Marrs, Jim. *Crossfire: the Plot that Killed Kennedy*. New York: Carroll and Graf, 1989.
            "Momo and His Girlfriends", pages 176 and 177

8   "(Release 8, Release 5)." Serpo.org - The Zeta Reticuli Exchange Program.
            http://www.serpo.org/release8.php (accessed June 22, 2009).

9   "(Release 1)." Serpo.org - The Zeta Reticuli Exchange Program.
            http://www.serpo.org/release1.php (accessed June 22, 2009).

10   "(Release 27a)." Serpo.org - The Zeta Reticuli Exchange Program.
            http://www.serpo.org/release27a.php (accessed June 22, 2009).

11   "(Release 10)." Serpo.org - The Zeta Reticuli Exchange Program.
            http://www.serpo.org/release10.php (accessed June 22, 2009).

12   "(Release 8)." Serpo.org - The Zeta Reticuli Exchange Program.
            http://www.serpo.org/release8.php (accessed June 22, 2009).

13   "(Release 11)." Serpo.org - The Zeta Reticuli Exchange Program.
            http://www.serpo.org/release11.php (accessed June 22, 2009).

14   Valerian, Valdamar. *Matrix II the Abduction and Manipulation of Humans Using Advanced
            Technology*. Yelm, WA: Leading Edge Research Group, 1990.
            The Grudge Thirteen Report, page 62

15   Marick, Lawrence. *The Killing of the Messenger, the Death of JFK*. Cambridge, MS.

16   Marrs, Jim. *Crossfire: the Plot that Killed Kennedy*. New York: Carroll and Graf, 1989.
            "Dealey Plaza", pages 9 through 89

17   Gritz, James "Bo" *Called to Serve*. Sandy Valley, NV: Lazarus Company, 1991.
Chapter 23 'Profiles in Conspiracy', pages 502-526

18   Marrs, Jim. *Crossfire: the Plot that Killed Kennedy*. New York: Carroll and Graf, 1989.
"The Motorcade", page 13

19   Valerian, Valdamar. *Matrix II the Abduction and Manipulation of Humans Using Advanced Technology*. Yelm, WA: Leading Edge Research Group, 1990.
RHIC-EDOM File, page 307

19   Marrs, Jim. *Crossfire: the Plot that Killed Kennedy*. New York: Carroll and Graf, 1989.
Part III: Aftermath", pages 313 through 493

20   Valerian, Valdamar. *Matrix II the Abduction and Manipulation of Humans Using Advanced Technology*. Yelm, WA: Leading Edge Research Group, 1990.
Interview With A CIA Employee, page 310B

Chapter 10 – The Exchange

1   "(Release 9)." Serpo.org - The Zeta Reticuli Exchange Program.
             http://www.serpo.org/release9.php (accessed June 22, 2009).

2   "(Release 18)." Serpo.org - The Zeta Reticuli Exchange Program.
             http://www.serpo.org/release18.php (accessed June 22, 2009).

3   "(Release 9)." Serpo.org - The Zeta Reticuli Exchange Program.
             http://www.serpo.org/release9.php (accessed June 22, 2009).

4   "(Release 11)." Serpo.org - The Zeta Reticuli Exchange Program.
             http://www.serpo.org/release11.php (accessed June 22, 2009).

5   "(Release 12)." Serpo.org - The Zeta Reticuli Exchange Program.
             http://www.serpo.org/release12.php (accessed June 22, 2009).

6   "(Release13)." Serpo.org - The Zeta Reticuli Exchange Program.
             http://www.serpo.org/ (accessed June 22, 2009).

7   "(Release 13b)." Serpo.org - The Zeta Reticuli Exchange Program.
             http://www.serpo.org/release13b.php (accessed June 22, 2009).

8   "(Release 2)." Serpo.org - The Zeta Reticuli Exchange Program.
             http://www.serpo.org/release2.php (accessed June 22, 2009).

9   "(Release 3)." Serpo.org - The Zeta Reticuli Exchange Program.
             http://www.serpo.org/release3.php (accessed June 22, 2009).

10   "(Release 7)." Serpo.org - The Zeta Reticuli Exchange Program.
             http://www.serpo.org/release7.php (accessed June 22, 2009).

11   "(Release 7a)." Serpo.org - The Zeta Reticuli Exchange Program.
             http://www.serpo.org/release7a.php (accessed June 22, 2009).

12   "(Release 10)." Serpo.org - The Zeta Reticuli Exchange Program.
             http://www.serpo.org/release10.php (accessed June 22, 2009).

13   "(Release 4)." Serpo.org - The Zeta Reticuli Exchange Program.
             http://www.serpo.org/release4.php (accessed June 22, 2009).

14   "(Release 6)." Serpo.org - The Zeta Reticuli Exchange Program.
             http://www.serpo.org/release6.php (accessed June 22, 2009).

15   "(Release 5)." Serpo.org - The Zeta Reticuli Exchange Program.
             http://www.serpo.org/release5.php (accessed June 22, 2009).

16   "(Release 16)." Serpo.org - The Zeta Reticuli Exchange Program.
             http://www.serpo.org/release16.php (accessed June 22, 2009).

17   "(Release 10)." Serpo.org - The Zeta Reticuli Exchange Program.
          http://www.serpo.org/release10.php (accessed June 22, 2009).

18   "(Release 6)." Serpo.org - The Zeta Reticuli Exchange Program.
          http://www.serpo.org/release6.php (accessed June 22, 2009).

Chapter 11 – National Security

1   Bamford, James. *Puzzle palace a report on America's most secret agency.* Harmondsworth, Middlesex: Penguin Books, 1983. Chapter 3. Anatomy, pages 60 through 62

2   Valerian, Valdamar. *Matrix II the Abduction and Manipulation of Humans Using Advanced Technology.* Yelm, WA: Leading Edge Research Group, 1990. The Primary Objectives of MJ-12, page 8

3   Valerian, Valdamar. *Matrix II the Abduction and Manipulation of Humans Using Advanced Technology.* Yelm, WA: Leading Edge Research Group, 1990. Chronology 1966, page 414

4   Valerian, Valdamar. *Matrix II the Abduction and Manipulation of Humans Using Advanced Technology.* Yelm, WA: Leading Edge Research Group, 1990. Chronology 1966, page 414

5   Valerian, Valdamar. *Matrix II the Abduction and Manipulation of Humans Using Advanced Technology.* Yelm, WA: Leading Edge Research Group, 1990. Chronology 1967, page 414

6   Dolan, Richard M. *UFOs and the National Security State Chronology of a Coverup, 1941-1973.* Boston: Hampton Roads Company, 2002. James McDonald, an Outstanding Nuisance, page 399

7   Dolan, Richard M. *UFOs and the National Security State Chronology of a Coverup, 1941-1973.* Boston: Hampton Roads Company, 2002. The Schirmer Abduction Case, page 437

8   Valerian, Valdamar. *Matrix II the Abduction and Manipulation of Humans Using Advanced Technology.* Yelm, WA: Leading Edge Research Group, 1990. Chronology 1968, page 415

9   Dolan, Richard M. *UFOs and the National Security State Chronology of a Coverup, 1941-1973.* Boston: Hampton Roads Company, 2002. Leaks from Boulder, page 436

10   Valerian, Valdamar. *Matrix II the Abduction and Manipulation of Humans Using Advanced Technology.* Yelm, WA: Leading Edge Research Group, 1990. Chronology 1969, page 415

11   Dolan, Richard M. *UFOs and the National Security State Chronology of a Coverup, 1941-1973.* Boston: Hampton Roads Company, 2002. The Condon Report, 449 through 456

12   Dolan, Richard M. *UFOs and the National Security State Chronology of a Coverup, 1941-1973*. Boston: Hampton Roads Company, 2002.
The End of Project Blue Book, page 460

13   Marrs, Jim. *Alien Agenda The Untold Story of the Extraterrestrials Among Us*. Westport: Pub Overstock Unlimited Inc, 1997.
The Road to Recovery, page 113

14   Valerian, Valdamar. *Matrix II the Abduction and Manipulation of Humans Using Advanced Technology*. Yelm, WA: Leading Edge Research Group, 1990.
Chronology 1969, page 415

15   Dolan, Richard M. *UFOs and the National Security State Chronology of a Coverup, 1941-1973*. Boston: Hampton Roads Company, 2002.
McDonald Rips Blue Book and Manzel, page 421

16   Valerian, Valdamar. *Matrix II the Abduction and Manipulation of Humans Using Advanced Technology*. Yelm, WA: Leading Edge Research Group, 1990.
Chronology 1971, page 416

17   Dolan, Richard M. *UFOs and the National Security State Chronology of a Coverup, 1941-1973*. Boston: Hampton Roads Company, 2002.
The Death of James McDonald, pages 478 through 480

18   Marrs, Jim. *Alien Agenda The Untold Story of the Extraterrestrials Among Us*. Westport: Pub Overstock Unlimited Inc, 1997.
The Greatest UFO?, page 16

19   Valerian, Valdamar. *Matrix II the Abduction and Manipulation of Humans Using Advanced Technology*. Yelm, WA: Leading Edge Research Group, 1990.
Chronology 1969, page 415

20   Marrs, Jim. *Alien Agenda The Untold Story of the Extraterrestrials Among Us*. Westport: Pub Overstock Unlimited Inc, 1997.
The Greatest UFO?, page 16

21   Valerian, Valdamar. *Matrix II the Abduction and Manipulation of Humans Using Advanced Technology*. Yelm, WA: Leading Edge Research Group, 1990.
Chronology 1969, page 415

22   Marrs, Jim. *Alien Agenda The Untold Story of the Extraterrestrials Among Us*. Westport: Pub Overstock Unlimited Inc, 1997.
The Greatest UFO?, pages 5 through 7

23   Marrs, Jim. *Alien Agenda The Untold Story of the Extraterrestrials Among Us*. Westport: Pub Overstock Unlimited Inc, 1997.
The Greatest UFO?, page 24

24   Valerian, Valdamar. *Matrix II the Abduction and Manipulation of Humans Using Advanced Technology*. Yelm, WA: Leading Edge Research Group, 1990. Chronology 1973, page 417

25   Dolan, Richard M. *UFOs and the National Security State Chronology of a Coverup, 1941-1973*. Boston: Hampton Roads Company, 2002. An Animal Mutilation, page 432

26   Walton, Travis. *Fire in the Sky The Walton Experience*. Boston: Marlowe & Company, 1997.

27   BBC's Southern Television Station. November 26, 1977.

28   Valerian, Valdamar. *Matrix II the Abduction and Manipulation of Humans Using Advanced Technology*. Yelm, WA: Leading Edge Research Group, 1990. Chronology 1977, page 418

29   Valerian, Valdamar. *Matrix II the Abduction and Manipulation of Humans Using Advanced Technology*. Yelm, WA: Leading Edge Research Group, 1990. Chronology 1978, page 419

30   Read, J. L. "Simple Truth." *Simple Truth*, January 1, 1991.

31   "(Release 18)." Serpo.org - The Zeta Reticuli Exchange Program. http://www.serpo.org/release18.php (accessed June 24, 2009).

32   "(Release 5)." Serpo.org - The Zeta Reticuli Exchange Program. http://www.serpo.org/release5.php (accessed June 24, 2009).

Chapter 12 – Confrontation

1   Valerian, Valdamar. *Matrix II the Abduction and Manipulation of Humans Using Advanced Technology*. Yelm, WA: Leading Edge Research Group, 1990. The Origin of the Dulce Papers, page 188

2   Valerian, Valdamar. *Matrix II the Abduction and Manipulation of Humans Using Advanced Technology*. Yelm, WA: Leading Edge Research Group, 1990. Dulce Base, pages 195 through 197

3   Valerian, Valdamar. *Matrix II the Abduction and Manipulation of Humans Using Advanced Technology*. Yelm, WA: Leading Edge Research Group, 1990. Dulce Base, page 200

4   Valerian, Valdamar. *Matrix II the Abduction and Manipulation of Humans Using Advanced Technology*. Yelm, WA: Leading Edge Research Group, 1990. Inculcation Devices and Electronic Manipulation of the Mind, page 328

5   Valerian, Valdamar. *Matrix II the Abduction and Manipulation of Humans Using Advanced Technology*. Yelm, WA: Leading Edge Research Group, 1990. Details On Reichian Programming, page 324C

6   Valerian, Valdamar. *Matrix II the Abduction and Manipulation of Humans Using Advanced Technology*. Yelm, WA: Leading Edge Research Group, 1990. Implant Technology, page 320

7   Valerian, Valdamar. *Matrix II the Abduction and Manipulation of Humans Using Advanced Technology*. Yelm, WA: Leading Edge Research Group, 1990. Walk-ins, pages 134 and 135

8   Valerian, Valdamar. *Matrix II the Abduction and Manipulation of Humans Using Advanced Technology*. Yelm, WA: Leading Edge Research Group, 1990. Replacement of Humans, pages 378 through 382

9   Valerian, Valdamar. *Matrix II the Abduction and Manipulation of Humans Using Advanced Technology*. Yelm, WA: Leading Edge Research Group, 1990. Dulce Base, pages 200 and 211

10   Valerian, Valdamar. *Matrix II the Abduction and Manipulation of Humans Using Advanced Technology*. Yelm, WA: Leading Edge Research Group, 1990. A Tentative Taxonomy of Extra-Terrestrial Humanoids, page 60G1

11   Valerian, Valdamar. *Matrix II the Abduction and Manipulation of Humans Using Advanced Technology*. Yelm, WA: Leading Edge Research Group, 1990. An Interview With John Lear, page 263

Chapter 13 – Personal Contacts

1   Valerian, Valdamar. *Matrix II the Abduction and Manipulation of Humans Using Advanced Technology*. Yelm, WA: Leading Edge Research Group, 1990.
A Tentative Taxonomy of Extra-Terrestrial Humanoids, page 60C1

2   Valerian, Valdamar. *Matrix II the Abduction and Manipulation of Humans Using Advanced Technology*. Yelm, WA: Leading Edge Research Group, 1990.
A Tentative Taxonomy of Extra-Terrestrial Humanoids, page 60H2

3   Valeria, Valdamar. *Matrix II the Abduction and Manipulation of Humans Using Advanced Technology*. Yelm, WA: Leading Edge Research Group, 1990.
A Tentative Taxonomy of Extra-Terrestrial Humanoids, pages 60A1 through 60U2

4   Osborn, Maurice. "Alien Abduction Resistance." Webs - Make a free website, get free hosting. http://www.freewebs.com/mauriceosborn (accessed June 24, 2009).
Chapter 3, Initial Perception Techniques, Page 15

5   Valerian, Valdamar. *Matrix II the Abduction and Manipulation of Humans Using Advanced Technology*. Yelm, WA: Leading Edge Research Group, 1990.
"The Greys", pages 52 through 60

6   Osborn Maurice. "Beware of the Grays." Webs - Make a free website, get free hosting. http://www.freewebs.com/mauriceosborn (accessed June 24, 2009).
Section 6.2 Controlling Human Subjects, click ?Beware Grays? option

7   Osborn, Maurice. "Alien Abduction Resistance." Webs - Make a free website, get free hosting. http://www.freewebs.com/mauriceosborn (accessed June 24, 2009).
Chapter 4. Techniques While Paralyzed

8   Osborn, Maurice. "Beware of the Grays." Webs - Make a free website, get free hosting. http://www.freewebs.com/mauriceosborn (accessed June 24, 2009).
Section 6.4 Extrauterine Gestational Units

9   Osborn, Maurice. "Beware of the Grays." Webs - Make a free website, get free hosting. http://www.freewebs.com/mauriceosborn (accessed June 24, 2009).
Section 4.1 Alien Species

10   Osborn, Maurice. "Beware of the Grays." Webs - Make a free website, get free hosting. http://www.freewebs.com/mauriceosborn (accessed June 24, 2009).
Section 5.4 Toddlers and Young Children

11   Jacobs, David M. *The THREAT Revealing the Secret Alien Agenda*. New York: Simon & Schuster, 1999.

12   Summers, Marshall Vian. *The Allies of Humanity Book Two, Human Unity, Freedom & The Hidden Reality of Contact*. New York: New Knowledge Library, 2005.

Chapter 14 – Acclimation

1   Valerian, Valdamar. *Matrix II the Abduction and Manipulation of Humans Using Advanced Technology.* Yelm, WA: Leading Edge Research Group, 1990. Chronology 1979, page 420

2   Valerian, Valdamar. *Matrix II the Abduction and Manipulation of Humans Using Advanced Technology.* Yelm, WA: Leading Edge Research Group, 1990. Chronology 1980, page 421

3   "Release 27a President Reagan ET Briefing." Serpo.org - The Zeta Reticuli Exchange Program. http://www.serpo.org/release27a.php (accessed June 24, 2009).

4   Valeria, Valdamar. *Matrix II the Abduction and Manipulation of Humans Using Advanced Technology.* Yelm, WA: Leading Edge Research Group, 1990. Chronology 1981, pages 421 and 422

5   Valerian, Valdamar. *Matrix II the Abduction and Manipulation of Humans Using Advanced Technology.* Yelm, WA: Leading Edge Research Group, 1990. Chronology 1979, page 421

6   Marrs, Jim. *Alien Agenda The Untold Story of the Extraterrestrials Among Us.* Westport: Pub Overstock Unlimited Inc, 1997. The Road to Recovery, pages 107 through 116

7   Oppenheim, Robert, and Albert Einstein. "Relationships with Inhabitants of Celestial Bodies." Majestic Documents.com: Evidence We Are Not Alone. http://www.majesticdocuments.com/ (accessed June 24, 2009).

8   "Top Secret Orders for A Team to Depart." Majestic Documents.com: Evidence We Are Not Alone. http://www.majesticdocuments.com/ (accessed June 24, 2009).

9   Truman, Harry S. "Presidential Directive to Lt. General Twining." Majestic Documents.com: Evidence We Are Not Alone. http://www.majesticdocuments.com/ (accessed June 24, 2009).

10   Interplanetary Phenomenon Unit. "Intelligence Assessment Report." Majestic Documents.com: Evidence We Are Not Alone. http://www.majesticdocuments.com/ (accessed June 24, 2009).

11   Twining, General. "Air Accident Report on Flying Disc Aircraft." Majestic Documents.com: Evidence We Are Not Alone. http://www.majesticdocuments.com/ (accessed June 24, 2009).

12   "Mission Assessment of Recovered Lenticular Aerodyne." Majestic Documents.com: Evidence We Are Not Alone. http://www.majesticdocuments.com/ (accessed June 24, 2009).

13   Truman, Harry S. "Memorandum for the Secretary of Defense." Majestic
      Documents.com: Evidence We Are Not Alone.
      http://www.majesticdocuments.com/ (accessed June 24, 2009).

14   "Majestic Twelve Project First Annual Report." Majestic Documents.com: Evidence
      We Are Not Alone. http://www.majesticdocuments.com/ (accessed
      June 24, 2009).

15   Majestic Twelve Group. "Extraterrestrial Entities and Techonology Recovery and
      Disposal Special Operations Manual." Majestic Documents.com: Evidence
      We Are Not Alone. http://www.majesticdocuments.com/ (accessed
      June 24, 2009).

16   Kennedy, John F. "Memorandum to the Director of the CIA." Majestic
      Documents.com: Evidence We Are Not Alone.
      http://www.majesticdocuments.com/ (accessed June 24, 2009).

17   Kennedy, John F. "Memorandum to the Director of the CIA." Majestic
      Documents.com: Evidence We Are Not Alone.
      http://www.majesticdocuments.com/ (accessed June 24, 2009).

18   Marrs, Jim. *Alien Agenda The Untold Story of the Extraterrestrials Among Us*.
      Westport: Pub Overstock Unlimited Inc, 1997.
      The Road to Recovery, pages 116 and 117

19   Valerian, Valdamar. *Matrix II the Abduction and Manipulation of Humans Using
      Advanced Technology*. Yelm, WA: Leading Edge Research Group, 1990.
      Chronology 1983, pages 422 and 423

20   Valerian, Valdamar. *Matrix II the Abduction and Manipulation of Humans Using
      Advanced Technology*. Yelm, WA: Leading Edge Research Group, 1990.
      Chronology 1984 through 1988, pages 423 through 427

Chapter 15 – Captured

1   Riley, Martin L., C-Qua T. Wann, and O-Qua T. Wann. *The Coming of Tan Past, Present and Future of Humanity, Extraterrestrial Attention, Environmental Catastrophe.* Studio City: Historicity Productions, 1995.
The Targ Terror May 1988, pages 129 through 131

2   Valerian, Valdamar. *Matrix II the Abduction and Manipulation of Humans Using Advanced Technology.* Yelm, WA: Leading Edge Research Group, 1990.
Psycho-Social Study of Human Conflict Reveals Alien Influence on Humans, page 374B

3   Osborn, Maurice. *The Essence of the Notes.* Ramona, CA: Maurice Osborn, 2007.
Section 4.3.1 Semjase , pages 115 through 120

4   Osborn, Maurice. *The Essence of the Notes.* Ramona, CA: Maurice Osborn, 2007.
Section 4.3.3 Ptaah, pages 122 through124

5   Osborn, Maurice. *The Essence of the Notes.* Ramona, CA: Maurice Osborn, 2007.
4.3.2 Quetzal, pages 121 and122

6   Osborn, Maurice. *The Essence of the Notes.* Ramona, CA: Maurice Osborn, 2007.
Section 6.2 Malevolent Aliens , pages 197 through 200

Chapter 16 – Evens' Letter

1   Osborn, Maurice. *The Essence of the Notes*. Ramona, CA: Maurice Osborn, 2007.
        Chapter 6 Extraterrestrials, pages 197 through 200

2   Summers, Marshall Vian. *The Allies of Humanity Book Two, Human Unity, Freedom & The
                Hidden Reality of Contact*. New York: New Knowledge Library, 2005.
                pages 3, 10, 15, 25 through 30

3   Summers, Marshall Vian. *Allies of humanity*. Boulder, CO: Society for the Greater
                Community Way of Knowledge, 2001.
                Fifth Briefing: Threshold: A New Promise For Humanity, page 69

4   *Understanding the Intervention audio tape*. By Marshall Vian Summers.

5   Summers, Marshall Vian. *Allies of humanity*. Boulder, CO: Society for the Greater
                Community Way of Knowledge, 2001.
                'Manipulation of Religious Traditions and Beliefs', pages 51 through 68

6   Summers, Marshall Vian. *Allies of humanity*. Boulder, CO: Society for the Greater
                Community Way of Knowledge, 2001.
                "Manipulation of Religious Traditions and Beliefs?, pages 66 and 67

7   Valerian, Valdamar. *Matrix II the Abduction and Manipulation of Humans Using
                Advanced Technology*. Yelm, WA: Leading Edge Research Group, 1990.
                A Tentative Taxonomy of Extra-Terrestrial Humanoids, pages 60C1 through 60P1

Appendix B — The Sagan Continuation Project

www.Yowusa.com/scp

Introduction by Marshall Masters

Since 2003, it has been my pleasure to admire Maurice's accomplishments as a fellow author and searcher for the truth. Our relationship started with his analysis of the August 15, 2002 Crabwood England crop circle, which featured an extraterrestrial holding a data disc. Shortly after it was reported, an anonymous author rushed a translation to the web via the Earthfiles.-com web site. I was suspicious of it.

Keep in mind, that before starting my publishing business, I'd been a contract professional in the computer industry for over 2 decades. My client list included notable names, such as AT&T, HP, Lockheed Martin, Oracle and Sun Microsystems.

In an interview on the Coast to Coast AM radio show with George Noory I subsequently stated that I believed the translation to be inaccurate. Maurice listened to the interview, contacted me the next day and asked me to review his translation of the binary message in the disc. I shared it with my fellow yowusa.com co-founders, and our exhaustive analysis proved his translation to be flawless.

Here is Maurice's translation of the binary encoded message in the disc as we published on yowusa.com:

Beware the bearers of FALSE gifts & their BROKEN PROMISES. Much PAIN but still time. BELIEVE. There is GOOD out there. We oppose DECEPTION. COnduit CLOSING,

As you'll note, the sub-title for this book is the first sentence of Maurice's translation. It is only fitting, as this translation launched our relationship, and the next time we would work together would be in 2004.

Maurice decided to go to create a crop circle to answer the 2002 message and asked me to craft an answer, which he then translated into the binary code for his response formation. I did, and here it is:

We WELCOME all who RESPECT our FREE WILL. If you CHOOSE to HELP, then help us to help ourselves. There is GOOD HERE too. WE LOOK for a reply,

Sure enough, Maurice went to England and made his crop circle. I was so inspired by his dedication that I founded the Sagan Continuation Project in honor of astronomer and author Carl Sagan. (www.yowusa.com/scp)

Drawing on my experience with a commercial satellite project at Lockheed Martin, I knew I how to beam this message into space, thousands of times each day, using Earth's vast network of communication satellites and that's what we've been doing since 2004.

After 2004, our paths occasionally crisscrossed with enlightening results and the occasional bump. With Maurice, there is always something new to learn and share, and his excitement for adventure is contagious. This is what motivated me to publish Alien Security.

—Marshall Masters

The Sagan Continuation Project

Sending Contact Messages via the Internet for Free

www.Yowusa.com/scp
ounded September 2003
Marshall Masters, Founder

The mission of the all-volunteer Sagan Continuation Project (SCP) is to continue the outbound contact efforts of astronomer Carl E. Sagan by using the Internet to repetitively beam a reply message into space via our immense network of communication satellites.

The 29-word outbound Internet SCP contact message was composed by computer consultant and SCP founder, Marshall Masters.

The SCP contact message is designed to use the lingua digital of the World Wide Web as the communication medium via communication signals radiating into space, beyond the many communication satellites presently serving the Internet.

Help Make Contact By Using The Internet for Free

To participate in this free, all-volunteer program, simply include the SCP contact message in your E-mail and web pages:

We WELCOME all who RESPECT our FREE WILL. If you CHOOSE to HELP, then help us to help ourselves. There is GOOD HERE too. WE LOOK for a reply,

If you have your own web site or personal home web page, you can also send this message without displaying it by including it as a non-display comment line in the header section of your HTML pages as shown in the example below:

```
<HTML>
<HEAD>
<!We WELCOME all who RESPECT our
FREE WILL. If you CHOOSE to HELP,
then help us to help ourselves. There
is GOOD HERE too. WE LOOK for a
reply,>
</HEAD>
```

If you wish, also please feel free to use the Sagan Continuation Project logo. When your E-mails and web pages are sent through the Internet, this message will be broadcast into space as it is being bounced off our orbiting satellites. The logo can be found at http://www.y-owusa.com/scp/scp_logo.jpg.

The more who choose to participate, the more often the digital pattern message will be transmitted into space, and the more likely this recurring transmission pattern will be recognized beyond our world.

This Is Not a First Contact, Because First Contact Has Been Made
THIS IS OUR REPLY TO THEIR ANSWER

On the afternoon of November 16, 1974, astronomer Carl Sagan sent the first digital outbound contact message into space using the Arecibo telescope, the world's largest single-dish radio telescope. Sagan, who also crafted the 1975 Viking and 1977 Voyager contact message used a symbolic picture 23 characters wide by 73 long to form the 1974 Arecibo contact message.

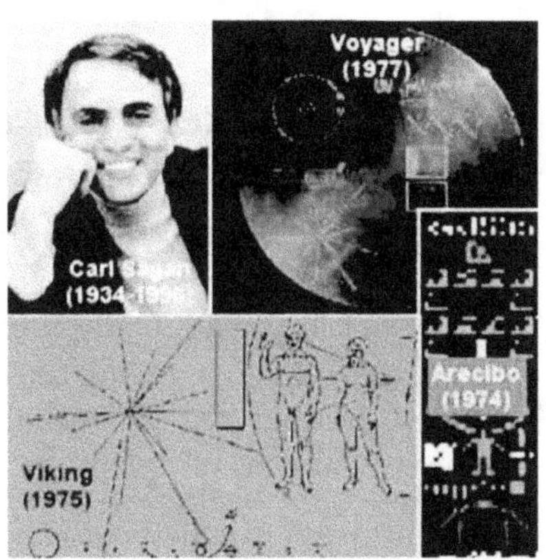

In 2001, a reply to Sagan's 1974 Arecibo contact message appeared in a field adjacent to the Chilbolton Radio Telescope in Hampshire, England.

Crop Circle Connector

Chilbolton Radio Telescope Near Wherwell, Hampshire, England

Reported Sunday August 19, 2001

YOWUSA.COM Articles

August 25, 2001: Is The US Militarization of Space Behind The Chilbolton Crop Circles? (http://www.yowusa.com/et/2001/et-2001-08a/1.shtml)

August 31, 2001:Dr. Eltjo Haselhoff – Chilbolton Crop Circles A 'Quantum Leap' In Design (http://www.yowusa.com/et/2001/et-2001-08b/1.shtml)

This formation created a great swirl of controversy in 2001, which resulted in a floating parade of hoaxers and debunkers on our television sets and web sites, telling us that this formation was anything but genuine.

This left a cloud of doubt over the 2001 Chilbolton Reply to Sagan's 1974 Arecibo contact message, as many wondered if the 2001 Chilbolton formation was a matter of idle speculation or fact.

Or more to the point, are we still equivocating because the truth frightens us? If so, what is that truth, and what will it take for us to see it?

Lighting Strikes Twice — A Second Reply To Sagan's 1974 Arecibo Contact Message Appears in 2002

There is an old saying that lighting never strikes twice. However, scientific studies have clearly shown that it can and does. In a similar vein, a second reply was received here on Earth to Carl Sagan's 1974 Arecibo contact message in a crop circle formation that that appeared in Crabwood England on August 15, 2002.

In terms of sophistication and message content, the Crabwood formation remains the most important crop circle formation ever witnessed on Earth.

Further, the glyph of the binary disc in the formation uses the exact same binary coding sequence used by Carl Sagan's 1974 Arecibo and 1977 Voyager contact messages.

Within hours after this formation appeared, a translation of the message by 2 anonymous authors was published by the Earthfiles.com web site, and it proved to be a clear disinformation fraud designed to negate the true significance of this formation with unnecessary controversy.

During his 3-hour interview with Coast To Coast AM host George Noory in May 2003, YOWUSA.COM publisher and SCP founder Marshall Masters, explained that Earthfiles.com site was cleverly duped by disinformation operatives who cashed in the confidences they'd acquired from the site owner through the sharing of truthful (but not sensitive) information. When this formation appeared, they capitalized on this trust and were able to use the Earthfiles.com site owner as unwitting (but all too eager) broadcaster of this highly successful disinformation ploy.

Is this speculation? Consider this; the Earthfiles.com site owner has yet to reveal the names of these anonymous authors. Also, consider this; as a former member of an armed forces information office, Marshall Masters was taught early on that the difference between good disinformation and bad disinformation is that good disinformation always gets the benefit of the doubt. To this day, these 2 anonymous Earthfiles.com authors and their disinformation ploy continue to receive the benefit of the doubt.

That being said, it is fair to point out that YOWUSA.COM was also eager to publish an accurate translation of the message contained in the 2002 Crabwood formation.

YOWUSA.COM, August 18, 2002
Crabwood Formation Offers Clear Evidence of Contact Event

Upon close examination of the Crabwood formation, it becomes readily apparent that the four aspects of workable protocol are offered: Data structure, error checking, send complete and receive confirmation.

With the Crabwood formation, this elaborate setup scheme is most likely not used. Rather, it appears that the data is presented quickly and simply where the binary ones and zeros represent the actual black and white pixels used to form the image of the alien.

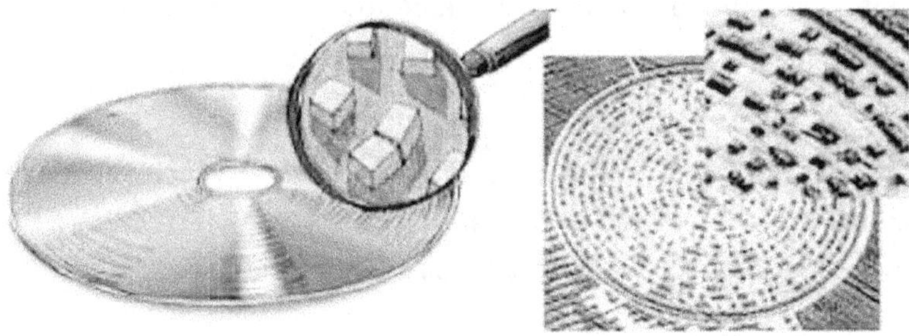

It is important to note that a final determination requires much better imagery and aggressive analysis. This is why we are making our plea that the formation not be plowed-under until it can be properly photographed.

However, in the summer of 2003, an accurate translation of the message was deciphered by computer software developer and crop circle researcher Maurice Osborn.

YOWUSA.COM, 03-May-2003, 03-July-2003
Are Extraterrestrials at Odds With
Crop Circle Messages?

Using the binary numerical representation method embedded in the 1974 Arecibo message created by Drake and Sagan, Osborn performed a careful analysis of the 2002 Chilbolton glyph and translated it using ASCII code as follows:

"Beware the bearers of FALSE gifts & their BROKEN PROMISES. Much PAIN but still time. BELIEVE. There is GOOD out there. We oppose DECEPTION. COnduit CLOSING,"

In the context of this project, the significance of the formation is that it uses a combination of the binary coding system transmitted into space by Carl Sagan in 1974 and the ASCII lingua digital of the Internet to convey the message on the disc.

Contact Is Now Undeniable

In 1974, Carl Sagan transmitted a contact message into space and this message has been replied to twice in the fields of England August 2001 and August 2002.

Inspired by the fact that these 2 replies to Sagan's 1974 contact message are real, Maurice Osborn traveled to England in August of 2004 to create a contact message using a man-made crop circle and the message you beamed into space the very moment you accessed this web page:

We WELCOME all who RESPECT our FREE WILL. If you CHOOSE to HELP, then help us to help ourselves. There is GOOD HERE too. WE LOOK for a reply,

Maurice has also completed a video detailing exactly how he planned to create his crop circle in England in August, 2004, using the sophisticated computer program he wrote and shares freely with others.

If you still have any doubts that the 2002 Crabwood formation is genuine, you need to watch Maurice's video that details the process of using his computer program to make a crop circle. After viewing it, you'll see that it would be impossible for debunkers or hoaxers to recreate the 2002 Crabwood formation in a single evening, let alone a single month!

To Find Knowledge, You Must Be Willing To Leap Over Your Beliefs

Most of humankind is unable to accept the possibility that we are not alone and that contact has been made because our cosmic view is limited by our own Earth-centric orthodoxies. Our monotheistic religious orthodoxies tell us that we were created by a non-corporeal God, while our funding-driven scientific orthodoxies tell us that we evolved from subordinate corporeal creatures.

As with all things, the truth usually lies somewhere in the middle, and that truth could be revealed to us through species-to-species contact with one extraterrestrial race or more. A prospect that terrifies most of us, but why? It is because down deep inside each of us is something we know, sense or avoid. Perhaps is it is we, who are the aliens!

If we are truly are committed to finding the real truth of this matter, then let us go forward with Carl Sagan's insightful advice in mind:

"We wish to find the truth, no matter where it lies. But to find the truth we need imagination and skepticism both. We will not be afraid to speculate, but we will be careful to distinguish speculation from fact."

When waiting for results, let us remember that Carl Sagan sent the first digital outbound message in 1974, and it was not answered until 2001, so patience and determination are going to be the keys to success, but you never know unless you try.

Your call to duty, should you accept it, is to include the SCP contact message within your E-mails and web pages at no cost to you.

We WELCOME all who RESPECT our FREE WILL. If you CHOOSE to HELP, then help us to help ourselves. There is GOOD HERE too. WE LOOK for a reply,

Do you feel that you might be taking this too seriously and you're now tempted to bury your head in the ignorant sands of scorn? If so, keep in mind that crop circle researcher Maurice Osborn went above and beyond the call of duty to build a crop circle in the fields of England in 2004, using the SCP contact message at his own expense!

For you, this step is free and only requires a modicum of effort, so please take action today by broadcasting your first SCP contact message into space with your E-mail and web pages.

Battle Book
Reports

Share Free Printable eDocs
battle.AlienSecurity.info

Marshall Masters
Ken Keyes, Jr.
H. Michael Sweeney

Battle Book Report 1 — Doing the Tell

By Marshall Masters

The binary ASCII code contained within the Crabwood England formation that appeared on August 15, 2002 was faithfully decoded by Maurice Osborn and therein, we find the three key works that sum up what we can do today to take back our planet. We too must say, "We oppose DECEPTION."

The question then become against whom and how? The answer is what I call, "doing the tell."

Civility in an Earlier Time

When the Internet first became popular in the mid-1990s, the World Wide Web was a far more civil place than it is today. Back then, it was new, exciting and courtesy was more the rule than the exception. Then over the years, hate language and rabid attacks began to spread.

The result is that public forums such as chat rooms, message boards and comments on video share and audio share sites are often polluted with rancid anonymous hate attacks.

Consequently, we find it increasingly difficult to find a civil, constructive dialog anywhere on the World Wide Web, unless we're into gardening and knitting.

The disinformation attacks on UFOlogy and crop circles sites have grown to pandemic proportions. The result is that when researchers gather, the dominant topic is often how to cope with the increasing flood of virulent hate speech aimed at them.

Many falsely assume that all of these attacks are the work of cranks, naughty teens and other such "run-by fruiters." This is not so and if you think it is, you've been duped.

Granted, it is foolish to assume there is a snake under every rock, however snakes do live under rocks and so do cockroaches.

Turning Over the Rocks

Since I first began writing on Earth changes and other alternative science issues back in 1999, I've seen a huge increase in organized disinformation attacks and I've documented it with several lengthy articles on the yowusa.com web site.

This is because since 2007, I began to see a PTB-financed army of disinformation operatives running a good portion of attacks on our topic areas of 2012 and Planet X. No doubt, they had honed their skills in the area of UFOlogy. Nonetheless, this new trend was unlike anything we'd ever seen in our genre, dating back to 1999 when we first started publishing.

To help put this in context, in 2003 there was well-documented Planet X / Nibiru scare and we published against it, with an exclusive interview with noted author, Zecharia Sitchin.

The scare was largely triggered by Mark Hazlewood's book Blindsided, and it fueled a panic that needlessly scared a lot of good people. Nonetheless, at no point during that entire episode was there any evidence of an funded and organized disinformation operation. It was truly, an organic and natural event.

However, that changed after we broke the story, *South Pole Telescope (SPT) — America's New Planet X Tracker* on yowusa.com back in April 2006 (spt.aliensecurity.info).

After that, we began seeing new kinds of attack personal attacks on us an upon our site. Attacks that were far more sophisticated and aggressive than anything we'd seen during the period of 1999 through the first half of 2006.

The attacks grew in steady progression and just ignored them until in 2008, the trickle turned into a flood after we published an article titled, *First Two Planet X SPT Leaked Image Videos by NibiruShock2012 Now Seen as Highly Credible,* in April 2008 (ns2012.aliensecurity.info).

We reported that in February, and then again, in March 2008, an anonymous whistle blower using the name of NibiruShock2012 posted two disclose videos on YouTube. They both contained leaked images of Planet X taken from the SPT observatory in Antarctica.

What struck us during our analysis was not so much the images, which were genuine though unverifiable. Rather, it was the sudden and massive number of disinformation attacks waged against this YouTube account. In the course of investigation, we further determined that the original owner had been hacked or compromised and that an impostor had begun destroying the credibility of the first two disclosure videos.

Once we published those findings, a class-5 hurricane strength storm of disinformation attacks slammed into us. We'd obviously hit a nerve.

I backed off the story a bit, because I knew I was an information-killing field I did not fully understand at the time. That's not to say I threw in the towel. Rather, it was just the opposite. Like it or not (and frankly I didn't like it), I knew it would be a long haul battle for truth so I decided to do two things.

First, create a database by documenting the attacks. The second was up armor as they say in the Military, except I used the law of attraction that's so well explained in the popular video, *The Secret*. I used their method to let the universe know I needed some help with these disinformation attacks and it came!

The law of attraction started working for us when an email from a yowusa.com reader popped up. It was one of those mysteriously helpful ones that come from a throwaway address we get from time to time and this one was a gem. It contained a simple message. I read this, and then it gave me two links to the disinformation articles by H. Michael Sweeney of Clackamas, OR.

In 2001, Mr. Sweeney published two groundbreaking articles on disinformation and they are included in the appendices of this book:

- *Battle Book Report #3: Twenty-Five Ways to Suppress Truth*
  (25.aliensecurity.info)

- *Battle Book Report #4: The 8 Traits of a Disinformationalist*
  (8.aliensecurity.info)

Bam, wow, zowie... holy disinformation Bat Man. It was like finding a Chilton Auto Repair Manual on your doorstep. You know, after having scattered much of the engine in your mother's Chevy across the garage floor only to find yourself fresh out of ideas. Except now, you could put it together and look darn clever in the process.

What Mr. Sweeney did for us was to open our eyes to the overall patterns. We used his two articles as analysis criteria for a constructive evaluation of the disinformation attack database we've created. The results were most constructive to say the least. The first thing we saw was that we were not up against individual disinformation operatives, but rather, entire teams of disinformation operatives.

Disinformation Wolf Packs

I refer to these disinformation teams as disinformation wolf packs, because they hunt and attack in precisely the manner as the Nazi U-Boat submarines the terrorized the North Atlantic during WWII. The wolf pack concept was conceived and commanded by Admiral Karl Doenitz, who later commanded the entire Nazi navy in the final years of WWII.

The only difference here is that while everyone knew who was behind the U-Boat wolf packs of WWII, the masterminds behind these present day disinformation wolf packs stay in the shadows as do their operatives. A fact that makes them even more insidious than Nazis. That took me back to the law of attraction. I needed information that would help me to profile these operatives. Again, the universe came crashing through and this time, it came in the form of two published authors, Philip Gardiner and Marshall Vian Summers. Both well-acquainted with these disinformation wolf packs and their modus operandi.

I recorded them separately for two different Cut to the Chase (yowusa.com/radio) interviews and then realized that they were talking about the same thing, but from two very different, yet complimentary points of view.

The result was my August 2008 interview, *Terrestrial and Extraterrestrial Disinformation — Propaganda Experts Philip Gardiner and Marshall Vian Summers* (disinfo.aliensecurity.info).

I usually leave my radio interview shows up for a matter of days or weeks depending on popularity and then archive them so that folks can access them with paid subscriptions. However, I've kept this interview up on the site since day one and free to the public so be sure to listen to it.

The real gem for me in all of this was my lengthy conversation with Philip Gardiner who is renowned for his books on secret societies. In our chat, he revealed to me that he actually worked as a disinformation and propaganda for the British government.

When I noted that we had traced most of the disinformation attacks back to the UK, he agreed and then he shared with me the information I needed to profile these rancid hate mongers of disinformation.

Remember that snakes live under rocks and so do cockroaches. In this case, the latter have more in common with disinformation operatives than the former.

3-D Cockroaches

Based on what I learned, I now refer to these disinformation operatives as "3-D cockroaches." The term is not mean to be pejorative or diminutive as cockroaches are very survival species with a better track record than our own.

Rather, the term s "3-D cockroaches" aptly simply describes the nature of these disinformation operatives and their modus operandi. Simply put, they defame, distract, destroy and always do their best work in the dark. (In other words, they're always anonymous.)

As a rule, nearly 90% of their attacks originate from Microsoft email addresses and the principal basing area is the UK for the attacks we've seen. Most of the remainder we've seen comes out of Australia and America. Aside from that, what else do we know about them?

3-D Cockroach Profile

The 3-D cockroaches are not bright, witty and entertaining people. Rather, they usually have the mindset of a petty retail clerk who works for a borderline psychopath. Are they low paid thugs? No way. In fact, their bosses must compete with the serious kinds of money these people can ear working for a collection agencies and the such.

Think of it. Is being a disinformation something an intelligent, sensitive and artistic person would want to do for a living? Frankly, I think they'd rather take a blind leap into the exciting world of fast food, than to trash decent people for a living.

However, the key thing to remember about these 3-D cockroaches is that they have mortgages too, and every morning they show up to work to do the same thing, day in and day out, to pay them.

That is, to defame those trying to bring valuable knowledge to the public and their methods are dry and predictable. Their preferred first assault begins with a vicious, hit-and-run slander and libel campaign.

Once the contributing individual or individuals are muffled with shock from the personal attacks, the cockroaches move on to the second stage where they distract forum members away from the subject at hand. Usually by injecting unrelated, hackneyed and unsolvable conspiracy theories such as 9-11, TWA 800, Nazi whatever.

Then with the original message muffled and the members scattered with distraction, they begin using acrimony and intrigue to divide the forum and thereby destroy it. This is not free speech. This is free hate speech.

What you need to remember is that rank and file 3-D cockroaches are predictable and while you cannot insult them, you can frustrate them. If you're blocking their attempts to corrupt a legitimate dialog, you're impinging on their ability to pay their mortgages. It's not much, but use it nonetheless and never get personal.

Judge Not, Lest Ye Be Suckered In

To view these 3-D cockroaches in human terms, such as "how could you do this to people?" is self-deluding and naïve. This is because they see us no differently than hungry fingerlings crowded into a plastic tub at some aquaculture fish farm. Ergo, set aside your judgment of them and focus solely on their behavior. Do this, and you'll understand their true goal.

The goal, or PTB-mandate if you will, of these 3-D cockroaches is to prevent open and intelligent dialogs from evolving into any form of awareness, which in turn could potentially challenge the interest of the monsters who sign their paychecks.

Ergo, paying their mortgages is a function of keeping the good guys disoriented so the bad guys are free to rape and pillage at will. Classic conquer and divide stuff and the yearly bonuses have not doubt been lavish for those working the UFOlogy genre.

Yet, are they always successful? When disinformation attacks go unchallenged, you betcha. This is one reason why the Internet is littered with abandoned message boards, blogs and so forth.

However, when their attacks are properly challenged, it's like switching on a big bright kitchen light, and then watching the roaches beat feet for the cracks in the baseboards. It's not hard to do, if you know where the collective light switch is.

We Can Oppose Deception!

If enough of us come together to "oppose DECEPTION," we can actually make the roaches beat feet for the cracks in the baseboards, at will. Best of all, the sooner the public debate reaches an awareness critical mass level, the sooner we can overwhelm these manipulative exploiters altogether.

The first thing to understand is that using our noodles, is how we fight them. Not by nuking them. Besides, using weapons of mass destruction against advanced malevolent races (no matter how bad-ass we think we are) is about as smart as bringing a dull, rusty penknife to a gun fight.

On the other hand, by interfering with their ability to destroy that, which truly threatens them, we can and will prevail. So what threatens them? Awareness. To them, human awareness is the mother of all Energizer bunnies from hell.

All you need do is to weed the garden and let the awareness blossom on its own. After that, The Hundredth Monkey phenomenon described in Battle Book Report #2, will eventually kick in. Get enough humans to jump up upon an awareness bandwagon and the rest as they say, is history.

Proof of this comes from the steady and consistent messages sent to us from the benign races. That if we take the high road by claiming sovereignty over our own world in a peaceful manner, something really powerful can happen.

We'll enable benign races to more actively help us to help ourselves. Remember. It's not their fight. It's our world and our fight and you know what that means.

The Fight for Free Will Starts with You

If you want to become a soldier for human free will, making history is simple. It is something I call "doing the tell."

You publicly tell the disinformation operatives who are working to destroy any possibility of widespread awareness via the Internet that their ploys are obvious, via the forums they are working to destroy.

Protection Lurking

Thing of the comic heroes of our youth such as Zorro, Superman, Spiderman and so on. Do they get involved with the day-to-day, yadda-yadda of life. No. They only jump to take out the bad guys and then disappear in a heartfelt cloud of thanks. You can do it too. I call it protection lurking.

Like a comic book superhero, you lurk in forums where you see folks bringing something more to the picnic than ants, and silently monitor the dialog. When you spot a 3-D cockroach making a run on someone, jump in and take him out.

It is advisable not to join the conversation on these dialogs though you may be sorely tempted to do so. This is because when post comments relative to the dialog itself, the cockroach can use these to attack you.

Without these opportunities, all he can do is to trash you for calling him out, which only drives nails in his coffin. Ergo, if he does go after you this way, you can drag him into a fight he'll never win. However, you need to know how he'll come at you and how you'll go at him. This is where Mr. Sweeney excels.

Using the Disinformation Playbook

Once you understand disinformation wolf pack tactics and strategy, their attacks become like pornography. You'll immediately know them when you see them. Likewise, you'll know how to easily sort out the cranks, naughty teens and the such as well. Ignore the run-by-fruiters, and focus on the cockroaches. Do that, and the jerks will usually know when to back off the hate rhetoric.

However, regardless of who is using hate rhetoric, by thinking like a PTB-financed disinformation operative you got the advantage. As I explained earlier, the two articles published in 2001 by H. Michael Sweeney of Clackamas, OR are the best counter-disinformation available and are included in the appendices of this book:

- *Battle Book Report #3: Twenty-Five Ways to Suppress Truth (25.aliensecurity.info)*

- *Battle Book Report #4: The 8 Traits of a Disinformationalist (8.aliensecurity.info)*

In his brilliant articles, Mr. Sweeney not only shows you how to spot the rancid attacks of these 3-D cockroaches, and how to expertly counter them. Please feel free to make photocopies of them as well as any other page in this book for personal use. Or to share with a friend. Spread the power of knowledge and go thump a bully!

Do it as Sweeney shows you how, and you'll make the roaches run for the baseboards every time. On the other hand, if you're thinking that your smarter than the average bear...

Avoid the Gutter

If you think fighting fire-with-fire with equally rancid verbiage is worth a try, then know this. Insults and personal attacks may be somewhat effective against cranks or naughty teens, but with disinformation operatives, you're born dead. Hate speech is their specialty and they own the gutter.

Jump into that gutter with them, and they'll slash you to doll rags with verbal razors. It's not personal. They'll just see you as a some kind of naïve boy scout or girl scout who needs to be date-raped out of a targeted forum. Remember, hate speech is their world, and they own the gutter. Never, never, never forget it.

Always take the high road when doing the tell and do Sweeney's way. You'll prevail every time, and more so when you're part of an independent, covert free will team. Then you can more effectively and rapidly prevent the 3-D cockroaches from destroying constructive on-line forums.

Form a Free Will Team

To enhance your effectiveness, collaborate with trustworthy, like-minded friends by forming a free will team. As you all get better at it, the more fun it becomes for all concerned.

This might sound odd, but over time, your free will team will develop tactics to lay traps for the cockroaches so that you can steal their thunder and other such nifty stuff.

Likewise, do not be hesitant to use their own disinformation tactics against them. There is no "fair fight" here so holding one hand behind your back is plain stupid. They always use anonymous, throw-away Microsoft email accounts and lots of them. So should you.

If you give a cockroach your real name, all you're doing is painting a slander and libel bull's-eye on your forehead. Do what they do. Pick random names out of the phone book and use the street addresses of vacant lots, out of service telephone numbers, and so forth. After you shut down a disinformation operation on a particular forum, drop the anonymous alias or restrict it to the forum you're monitoring. Above all else, but never use it elsewhere.

In essence, you need to think like a sniper. In your zone of fire are all these petty retail clerks and they're incapable of conducing a convincing moral dialog beyond their second or third post.

You can also hone your skills with other resources such as *Sun Tzu's Art of War.* The Web is well-dotted with free copies, and Sun Tzu's strategies can be more fun than a season pass to Disneyland, if you apply them wisely.

Free Will Team Dynamics

When putting your team together, keep it small. Three to five team members is usually best. A good rule of thumb is that if you can count all the bodies on one hand, you've got a team If it takes two or more hands, you haven't' got a team. You've got a self-imploding bureau-cracy.

Likewise, if you've got empire-building aspirations, you're sailing towards the breakers. Any team that is consistently led by the same person will fall into predictable patterns. When this happens, your team will eventually be profiled by a smarter-than-average 3-D cock-roach. Then he'll turn the tables on you with a carefully planned ambush.

His goal will be to throw a serious wrench into the dynamics of your team. One that causes the team's morale to plummet as your leadership comes into question. Consequently, if you cannot adapt quickly enough with an effective counter-move, your team will partially or completely evaporate.

Thankfully, there are three simple ways to shield your team from this kind of vulnerability.

1. Always let the mission decide the leader, on case-by-case basis.

2. Always share the credit.

3. Always look for creative new ways to do the tell so the cockroaches can never profile you.

In essence, use the old Saddam Hussein strategy. Never spend two nights in the same house. You'll have more fun doing it than Saddam did.

Taking the First Step

To start things off after you've finished reading this book and the appendices, sit down with pen and paper and create a call sign for yourself such as the character from popular movie you identify with. Then write our your own personal My Doing the Tell Mission Goals, and store them someplace safe.

Be sure to write down your goals straight from the gut. This will give you the most honest reflections of what is really in your heart. After these initial feelings pass, we tend to become ego-driven or political so the first take is almost always, the best.

Then tell someone you know and trust about this book and suggest the possibility of them joining with you, assuming this is something of interest to them. Then while they're reading the book, you can follow up on the other materials discussed in this book.

Assuming they've finished reading the book with our goals and want to join the team, then they'll do the same and so on, until the team is fully formed.

Above all else, have fun with this. Corny jokes, cold drinks and pizza are known to have an empowering effect, so frequent mass quantities are advisable.

So there it is. After you reading this book, it will be your time to choose. You'll either move out as a soldier for free will, or you'll move aside. Either way, you'll have the truth and the choice to with it as you will. Go get some.—*Marshall Masters*

Battle Book Report 2 —The Hundredth Monkey

Yowusa.com, August 5, 2008
Share Free Printable eDoc
100.AlienSecurity.info

100th Monkey by Ken Keyes, Jr.
Article Source: wowzone.com

Companion Article to Cut to the Chase Interview #91:Terrestrial and Extraterrestrial Disinformation — Propaganda Experts Philip Gardiner and Marshall Vian Summers (http://yowusa.com/radio/cttc/2008/cttc-0808-91/1.shtml)

Foreword by Marshall Masters

The principal goal of disinformation is to subjugate a people, a nation or even an entire world for that matter. Elusive world elites with their own agendas practice it artfully. They use it to shield their service-to-self ambitions from any semblance of honest transparency - which is the case with all evil aims in the incubating phase. Nonetheless, we sense this

great evil, but the force of their disinformation is so overwhelming that we feel powerless to do anything about it.

Consequently, righteous alarmists brand us as "sheeple" and advocate that we rise up in furious masses to follow them to victory. Sounds great, but don't hold your breath waiting for a "Million Man Anti-disinformation March" on Washington this month. This is not improbable, but it won't come about by their leadership. This is because, while activist warnings create awareness, their incitements do little more than to generate heated web gossip.

The reason these alarmists are failing is that they offer the "usual suspects" approach, which is a far cry from being an inspiring, grass-roots strategy that inspires us to act as individuals. Simply put, it is a way for each of us to simply acquire knowledge, act upon it and then share it with one other, and they in turn do the same. Being the 100th monkey in a chain of spiritual awareness, is much easier than leading an army.

This is where The Hundredth Monkey by Ken Keyes, Jr. offers us a brilliant insight into how simple it can be, to trigger a noble, global service-to-others grass roots rebellion against self-serving elites and their disinformation minions.—Marshall Masters

The Hundredth Monkey
By Ken Keyes, Jr.

THE FOLLOWING WAS TRANSCRIBED FROM A BOOK WITH COPYRIGHT INFORMATION AS FOLLOWS: LIBRARY OF CONGRESS CATALOG NO. 81-70978 / ISBN 0-942024-01-X.

This book is not copyrighted. You are asked to reproduce it in whole or in part, to distribute it with or without charge, in as many languages as possible, to as many people as possible. The rapid alerting of all humankind to nuclear realities is supremely urgent. If we are wiped out by nuclear destruction in the next few years, how important are the things we are doing today?

Author's Dedication

This book is dedicated to the Dinosaurs, who mutely warn us that a species that cannot adapt to changing conditions will become extinct.

Author's Foreword

Two events converged on me this summer. They supplemented each other and gave me the inspiration and added push I needed. They made me respond to the urgency I had felt brewing in me for some time to express my concern about the worldwide danger of nuclear weapons.

The first event was my viewing the videotape "The Last Epidemic," taken at a symposium held in November, 1980 on the unacceptability of nuclear weapons for human health. I was deeply impressed by the physicians and scientists who brought their knowledge and eloquence to that meeting. Their stature and level of experience, insight and courage left no doubt in my mind that my priorities had to be rearranged. I had to add my voice and speak out now!

The second experience was my exposure to the Hundredth Monkey Phenomenon, which I learned about in talks by Marilyn Ferguson and Carl Rogers. This phenomenon shows that when enough of us are aware of something, all of us become aware of it.

That concept confirmed my own intuitive trust in the basic tenet of my work — that the appreciation and love we have for ourselves and others creates an expanding energy field that becomes a growing power in the world. This radical new support gives me the counterbalance of hope to offset the doomsday story of nuclear destruction.

There is no need to feel helpless or get paralyzed by hopelessness. We know we have the power to make changes if we can join together and raise our voices in unison. There is more power in numbers that we ever hoped to dream about! I call for us to let our numbers grow exponentially as we all take it on ourselves to spread these messages.

We are the bearers of a new vision. We can dispel the old destructive myths and replace them with the life-enriching truths that are essential to continued life on our planet.

St. Mary, Kentucky

Ken Keyes, Jr.

December, 1981

The Hundredth Monkey

I appreciate your letting me share the drama of our megaton madness with you.

This book does not deal with petty matters.

It tells how to operate our lives — and our world.

It tells us how to stay alive!

The mess we've brought upon ourselves is a most perilous and challenging one.

The broad picture pieced together here will show you the immensity of the nuclear dangers, the futility of any defense or protection, the power of the new awareness and your role in the unfolding drama.

There is a phenomenon I'd like to tell you about.

In it may lie our only hope of a future for our species.

Here is the story of the Hundredth Monkey:

The Japanese monkey, Macaca Fuscata, has been observed in the wild for a period of over 30 years.

In 1952, on the island of Koshima, scientists were providing monkeys with sweet potatoes dropped in the sand. The monkeys liked the taste of the raw sweet potatoes, but they found the dirt unpleasant.

An 18-month-old female named Imo found she could solve the problem in a nearby stream. She taught this trick to her mother. Her playmates also learned this new way and they taught their mothers, too.

This cultural innovation was gradually picked up by various monkeys before the eyes of the scientists.

Between 1952 and 1958, all the young monkeys learned to wash the sandy sweet potatoes to make them more palatable.

Only the adults who imitated their children learned this social improvement. Other adults kept eating the dirty sweet potatoes.

Then something startling took place. In the autumn of 1958, a certain number of Koshima monkeys were washing sweet potatoes — the exact number is not known.

Let us suppose that when the sun rose one morning there were 99 monkeys on Koshima Island who had learned to wash their sweet potatoes.

Let's further suppose that later that morning, the hundredth monkey learned to wash potatoes.

Then it Happened!

By that evening almost everyone in the tribe was washing sweet potatoes before eating them.

The added energy of this hundredth monkey somehow created an ideological breakthrough!

But notice.

A most surprising thing observed by these scientists was that the habit of washing sweet potatoes then jumped over the sea —

Colonies of monkeys on other islands and the mainland troop of monkeys at Takasakiyama began washing their sweet potatoes!*

(*Lifetide by Lyall Watson, pp. 147-148. Bantam Books 1980. This book gives other fascinating details.)

Thus, when a certain critical number achieves an awareness, this new awareness may be communicated from mind to mind.

Although the exact number may very, the Hundredth Monkey Phenomenon means that when only a limited number of people know of a new way, it may remain the consciousness property of these people.

But there is a point at which if only one more person tunes-in to a new awareness, a field is strengthened so that this awareness is picked up by almost everyone!

Your awareness is needed in saving the world from nuclear war.

You may be the "Hundredth Monkey" . . .

You may furnish the added consciousness energy to create the shared awareness of the urgent necessity to rapidly achieve a nuclear-free world.

"If I knew then what I know now, I never would have helped to develop the bomb," spoke George Kistiakowsky, an adviser to President Eisenhower who worked on the Manhattan Project.

Let's look at the almost incredible nuclear monster we have created in the last forty years on planet Earth . . .

Herbert Scoville, Jr., former deputy for research of the Central Intelligence Agency warns,

The unfortunate situation is that today we are moving—sliding downhill—toward the probability or the likelihood that a nuclear conflict will actually break out—and that somebody will use one of these nuclear weapons in a conflict or perhaps even by accident.

The only result of a substantial nuclear exchange would be a hollow victory in which the "winners' would be no better off than the losers.

An all-out nuclear war could make our planet uninhabitable for a million years!

A nuclear war can end the way we live.

It cannot be won — it can only be lost.

Winning equals losing.

The word "war" is too mild to apply to this nuclear craziness.

Carl Sagan at the Conference on the Long-Term Biological Consequences of Nuclear War stated:

We have an excellent chance that if Nation A attacks Nation B with an effective first strike, counter-force only, then Nation A has thereby committed suicide, even if Nation B has not lifted a finger to retaliate.*

(*The Cold and the Dark by Paul R. Ehrlich, Carl Sagan, Donald Kennedy, Walter Orr Roberts, p. 33. W. W. Norton and Co., 1984.)

Suppose you and your family are rafting down an unexplored river.

Most of your attention is on steering the raft away from the rocks and keeping it off the banks so that it will not get damaged or stranded.

Several miles downstream unknown to you lies a huge waterfall that will fling you and your family on the rocks below.

It is easy to miss the significance of certain signals that are coming to you.

You have noticed a distant, rumbling background sound. But what does it mean? You can see a mist in the air ahead of you. There's nothing alarming that seems to call for your immediate attention.

And, besides, you are so busy guiding the raft and keeping it off the rocks that you don't want to think or anything else right now.

Maybe the rumbling will go away . . . .

But the distant rumbling is getting louder.

We can ignore it — or we can use our intelligent minds to inform us of the dangers we must avoid.

What are the signs and the scientific data that are so easy for us to ignore — but which are giving us a clear warning of a certain catastrophe that lies ahead if we remain on our present course?*

(*In 1954, actors John Wayne, Susan Hayward, Agnes Moorehead and producer Dick Powell filmed "The Conqueror" on the sandy dunes outside St. George, Utah. We had previously conducted a number of atomic bomb tests in Nevada about 150 miles away. For three months, the filmmakers were breathing the dust laced with radioactive plutonium fallout. Twenty-five years later John Wayne, Susan Hayward, Agnes Moorehead and Dick Powell had all died of cancer. Of the "220 people in the cast and crew, ninety-one had contracted cancer by late 1980, and half of the cancer victims had died of the disease." From Killing Our Own by Harvey Wasserman and Norman Solomon, p. 81, Dell Publishing Company, Inc., 1982. Also see The Day We Bombed Utah: America's Most Lethal Secret by John G. Fuller, New American Library, 1984. This book documents the way the government has repeatedly lied to us and withheld documents — even in court proceedings under oath.)

In 1970, a pediatrician in Grand Junction, Colorado, noticed an increase in cleft palate, cleft lip and other birth defects.

The homes of these people had been built with waste rock and sand from a uranium refining operation!

The University of Colorado Medical Center obtained federal funds to investigate this.

But these funds were cut off a year later.

Why?

Navajo Indians who went down into uranium mines in Arizona have died — and are right now dying — of lung cancer, previously rare among Navajos.

In a recent study, Dr. Gerald Buker pointed out that the risk factor of lung cancer among Navajo uranium miners increases by at least 85%!

Robert Minogue and Karl Goller of the Nuclear Regulatory Commission jointly wrote on September 11, 1978:

The evidence mounts that, within the range of exposure levels encountered by radiation workers, there is no threshold, i.e., a level that can be assumed as safe in an absolute sense . . . . any amount of radiation has a finite probability of inducing a health effect, e.g., cancer.*

(*Shut Down, p. 72. The Book Publishing Co., 156 Drakes Lane, Summertown, TN 38483. 1979. In the nuclear honeymoon decades of the forties and fifties, the harmful effects of nuclear radiation on human health were underestimated by as much as ten thousand times! Ibid, p. 167.)

Nuclear submarine workers at Portsmouth, New Hampshire, are developing cancer at a rate that is double the expected incidence.

Dr. Helen Caldicott, author of Nuclear Madness, was invited to speak to a meeting of these workers, but only four men appeared.

They told her that the Navy had threatened them with the loss of their jobs if they came to hear her talk.

Are jobs more important than life itself?

In November, 1980, a group of physicians and scientists held a symposium at the University of California in Berkeley. At this symposium Dr. Kosta Tsipis, Professor of Physics, Massachusetts Institute of Technology, stated,

. . . our earth is surrounded by a thin layer or ozone. Ozone is a particular isotope of oxygen that has the lovely property of absorbing much of the ultraviolet rays of the sun. The ultraviolet rays of the sun are the ones that cause skin burns. When you go to the beach and you get sunburned, that's what does it. In addition, the ultraviolet rays of the sun blind eyes that are exposed to them for any period of time. The very fact that we can exist on this earth—that there is a fauna, animals with eyes on this earth—is based on the existence of the ozone layer that filters out most of the ultraviolet rays of the sun and therefore allows us to survive.

What happens when a nuclear weapon explodes is that a very large number of nitrogen oxides are generated by the radiation that flies out from the explosion. As a matter of fact, a one- megaton weapon will generate 10 molecules of nitrogen oxides. These molecules are lifted up together with the fireball, and reach (for a one-megaton weapon) the altitude of say 50, 60, 70 thousand feet, where the ozone is. At that point, these molecules will start eating up the ozone— literally—taking it away from circulation . . . for long periods of time. It is a very complex photochemical process, but we know that it occurs . . . . The National Academy of Sciences felt quite sure to state that if you have exploded . . . in a very short period of time 50% of the weapons that will be available in the arsenals of the Soviet Union and the United

States by 1985, this simultaneous explosion will create enough nitrogen oxides to take out 50 to 70% of the ozone layer above the northern hemisphere and 30 to 40% of the ozone layer in the southern hemisphere, because we assume that all of these explosions will take place in the northern hemisphere . . .

The latest word out of the scientific laboratories is that a 20% depletion of the ozone layer will allow enough ultraviolet light to come to earth that it will blind all unprotected eyes. Now, we can all wear glasses, but the animals and the birds will not wear glasses, and they will all be blinded and they will all eventually die. And this is the largest-scale ecological catastrophe that one can imagine—that all the fauna on the earth will be blinded and eventually die.

I can think of nothing else that is a more massive ecological dislocation — to use a mild word. The entire ecosystem will collapse. Because if we don't have insects, for example, to pollinate the flowers, we won't have fruit . . . . The whole thing collapses, and that is what will happen, most probably, if only 50% of the weapons in the arsenals of the two superpowers in 1985 were to be exploded within a few days in a nuclear war.

If you're within a few miles of a nuclear detonation, you'll be incinerated on the spot!

And if you survive the blast, what does the future promise?

The silent but deadly radiation, either directly or from fallout, in a dose of 400 rems could kill you within two weeks.

Your hair would fall out, your skin would be covered with large ulcers, you would vomit and experience diarrhea and you would die of infection or massive bleeding as your white blood cells and platelets stopped working.

If you have less exposure to this deadly radioactivity, you may develop leukemia in five years.

Hiroshima survivors were thirty times more likely to have this fatal disease than the unexpected population!*

(*Between 1945 and 1963 several hundred thousand soldiers were marched through areas where the Nevada atomic weapons tests were conducted. The rate of leukemia among these men had been 400 times the national average! Shut Down, p. 165, The Book Publishing Co., 1979.)

A smaller amount of exposure sets you up for cancer in twelve or more years.

Even a tiny invisible particle of plutonium is so radioactive that it can cause cancer or alter your genes so that your children may be deformed at birth!

Plutonium has been called "thalidomide forever."

(*Dr. John Gofman is the co-discoverer of uranium-233 and a leading medical researcher. In his 908-page book Radiation and Human Health (Sierra Club Books, San Francisco, 1981) he tells exactly how radiation produces cancer, leukemia and birth defects. This book enables you to estimate diminished life-expectancy from various radiation exposures. It evaluates the genetic consequences to future generations of our current radiation exposures.)

Uranium, mined from the earth, is converted by a processing facility or a nuclear power plant into plutonium, strontium-90 and many other dangerous radioactive poisons.

Plutonium is used in making high-yield nuclear bombs. It has a half-life of 24,400 years and is poisonous for at least a half-million years.

Dr. Helen Caldicott writes:

As a physician, I contend that nuclear technology threatens life on our planet with extinction. If present trends continue, the air we breathe, the food we eat, and the water we drink will soon be contaminated with enough radioactive pollutants to pose a potential health hazard far greater than any plague humanity has ever experienced. Unknowingly exposed to these radioactive poisons, some of us may be developing cancer right now. Others may be passing damaged genes, the basic chemical units that transmit hereditary characteristics, to future generations. And more of us will inevitably be affected unless we bring about a drastic reversal of our government's pronuclear policies.*

(*Nuclear Madness by Dr. Helen Caldicott, p. 1. Bantam Books, 1980. Copyright 1978, 1980 by Helen M. Caldicott.)

We are about to drown in nuclear sewage. We now have about one hundred million gallons of dangerous radioactive effluents that no one knows what to do with. And it's globally increasing at a catastrophic rate.

There is no way to safely dispose of this extremely dangerous, corrosive, radioactive garbage in leak-proof containers that will be continuously protected by competent guards free from war, earthquakes, floods and tornadoes for hundreds of thousands of years!

What right have we to burden future generations with this ever-increasing threat to their well-being?

We conducted over 70 nuclear bomb tests around the Marshall Islands between 1946 and 1963.

Each mushroom cloud scattered trillions of plutonium atoms throughout the world!*

(*By 1970 natives of the Marshall Islands were suffering from increased incidence of cancer, retarded growth and miscarriages.)

Let's suppose just one particle of plutonium landed in a forest near you.

It could rest on a limb of a tree, be stirred up in the air and inhaled by a bird.

This single plutonium particle could create a radiation-induced disease in the bird, which would die prematurely.

Suppose the dead bird decomposes in a field and when driving by, you breathe dust that contains this invisible bit of plutonium.

This particle of human-made plutonium could ruin the genetic regulating mechanism in one of your cells that prevents wild cancerous growths.

Your body could then begin producing cancer cells . . . .

It's a matter of probability and risk — not certainty.

And this same deadly plutonium atom could escape from your remains and be recycled with bad news consequences for the next half-million years!

"All of us, particularly the inhabitants of the northern hemisphere, carry some plutonium in our lungs and other organs," according to Dr. John T. Edsell, Professor of Biochemistry at Harvard.*

(*Dr. John Gofman estimates that, because of the damage to part of their clearance mechanism, the lungs of cigarette smokers "might be a hundred times more sensitive to the effects of plutonium.")

The Savannah River nuclear plant, according to Dr. Carl Johnson of the Medical School of the University of Colorado, may have already polluted 1,000 square miles of Georgia and South Carolina with plutonium.*

(*"And as late as 1979, radio-iodine was measured in vegetation in nearby Columbia, Georgia, at a concentration that corresponds to a human thyroid dose of 24,000 millirems per year — 320 times the amount permitted by the Environmental Protection Agency (EPA). High levels of tritium, which the plant releases routinely, have also been detected in the Savannah River and in local milk and vegetation . . . Dr. Karl Z. Morgan, former director of the Health Physics Laboratory at Oak Ridge National Laboratories in Tennessee, notes that in 1969 the flesh of a deer taken from the plant site was discovered to have the equivalent of the 2,250 millirems per year of cesium, or 90 times the EPA limit for a human." "Nuclear County," by Zachary Sklar, Geo., Vol. 3, p. 32, August 1981.)

A 1975 study found that more than 10,000 pounds of this deadly chemical are thinly dispersed in the earth's atmosphere.

Your precious body is probably already carrying this hidden handmaiden of genetic ruin and death.*

(*Radioactive atoms are already in our food chain. The United States Department of Agriculture in Food, The Yearbook of Agriculture 1959, p. 118, reported that strontium-90 from the United States and Russian atomic bomb tests had scattered radioactive strontium- 90 over the entire earth. It was first detected in animal bones, dairy products and soil in 1953. It is now in the bodies of all human beings regardless of their age or where they live. The Bulletin of the Atomic Scientists, Vol. XVII, No. 3, p. 44, March 1962, stated that children growing up in the United States have about 6 to 8 times more strontium-90 in their bones than their parents.)

Let's make sure that we don't get additional doses!!#!

We've already trapped ourselves in a small degree of irreversible nuclear damage.

To avoid further harm to ourselves and our children, the people of the world must somehow avoid further nuclear insanity.*

(*A leakage on September 11, 1957, and again on May 11, 1969, in the AEC Rocky Flats plutonium plant released plutonium near Denver, Colorado. There has been a 24% increase in cancer in men and a 10% increase in women in the portion of the Denver metropolitan area nearest to the Rocky Flats plutonium processing plant.)

One million tons of TNT is known as a megaton. A grand total of over three megatons of non nuclear explosives were used in World War II from 1941 to 1945.

Today, nuclear bombs up to 20 megatons each are poised for action.

Only one of these could destroy a large city and make the land dangerous for eons!

Dr. Bernard Feld, professor, MIT, and the editor-in-chief of the Bulletin of the Atomic Scientists said,

Sometimes later in this decade, military plans which are being seriously discussed now by the military establishments on both sides would lead to . . . an immediate exchange . . . in a nuclear war of something between 10,000 and 20,000 megatons each.

The fallout in the United States would be total. That is to say, there would be no areas, really, that could escape. There would be lethal fallout covering the entire United States and essentially the entire Soviet Union. Worldwide this would lead to something . . . somewhere in the region of, let's say, 20 radiation units per capita everywhere on earth.

And this I would regard as a situation, which we would all have to consider to be absolutely intolerable.

And, therefore, it seems to me that we have no choice in the direction in which we have to move. The problem that faces us is not whether nuclear disarmament is feasible, but how we can go about convincing our leaders. And, presumably, they will be convinced when all the people, or at least a majority of the people, of our countries are convinced of the unacceptability of the current course of events in which missile is piled on top of missile, in which weapon is piled on top of weapon, and in which doctrines concerning their use are being proliferated not only in the insane superpowers but in other so-called civilized countries as well.

How are we going to convince ourselves that this is an intolerable direction, stop where we are, turn it around and eventually reduce these stockpiles . . . ?

David Hoffman points out, "In a nuclear war, the best defense is not to have an offense."*

(*David Hoffman is the co-founder of "Interhelp," a think tank focusing on practical ways to get us out of our nuclear predicament.)

War no longer functions for settling disputes between nations.

War itself must be abolished in the twentieth century — just as slavery was eliminated during the nineteenth century.

Our survival demands new ways for operating our civilization!

A single conventional bomb can blow up the reactor rods that fuel a power plant.

If Europe had nuclear power plants during World War II, our bombs could have devastated the continent and made it uninhabitable for thousands of years by radioactive pollution of the air, food and water.*

(*A 1964 Atomic Energy Commission study showed that a serious nuclear accident could kill 45,000 people, injure 100,000 and contaminate "an area the size of Pennsylvania.")

Any nuclear reactors anywhere make us vulnerable to aggression and fanaticism by politicians and terrorists — even if they don't have access to nuclear bombs.

When we even maintain a supply of nuclear bombs as a "deterrent," we are dangerously perpetuating the illusion that our safety and security lie in nuclear materials.

Such a consciousness makes inevitable the competitive stockpiling and future use of these materials.

And the passions of many military and political leaders and terrorists are such that sooner or later they will unleash every bit of destructiveness they can get their hands on!

A nuclear war could blow enough fine dust into our stratosphere to filter out sunlight and create a nuclear winter that could freeze out most human and animal life on the planet.

Here is a report of the conference "The World After a Nuclear War" in Washington, D.C., November, 1983:

Well over a hundred scientists working independently in countries such as the United States, Germany and the Soviet Union presented a grim consensus that was summed up by Stanford University Ecologist, Paul Ehrlich, "The two to three billion who are at least able to stand up after the last weapon goes off are going to be—at least in the Northern Hemisphere —starving to death in a dark, smoggy world." The World Health Organization has concluded that a major nuclear war between the United States and the Soviet Union could leave 1.1 billion dead from immediate nuclear effects of the blast, fireball and radiation. Another 1.1 billion would be injured. Since medical facilities would be almost wiped out, most of the injured will die. The ultimate toll within a few months is estimated by this study to be more than 2 billion people or roughly half the world's population.

But will the survivors be much better off? Ehrlich points out that even at noon, the earth will be almost dark because of the millions of tons of dirt and debris that the nuclear explosions will throw into the sky. He points out that rampaging forest and city fires may burn 50% to 60% of the United States and send huge amounts of smoke into the sky. It will take many months to settle back to earth. Scientists estimate that temperatures in the plains of North America and the steppes of Central Asia may drop as much as 40C (72F) — it could literally freeze in July.

With our atmosphere enshrouded in nuclear dust carried up into the stratosphere, sunlight would not sustain photosynthesis, according to Joseph Berry, noted plant physiologist, of the Carnegie Institution of Washington.

Several atmospheric chemists pointed out that in some regions the light would fall to as little as 5% to 10% of the former levels. Carl Sagan said that if a little less than half of our nuclear materials are exploded (5,000 megatons), the Midwest would drop 15 to 20 below zero Fahrenheit for months.*

(*Science News, November, 1983. For complete information on this conference, see The Cold and the Dark by Paul R. Ehrlich, Carl Sagan, Donald Kennedy, Walter Orr Roberts. W. W. Norton and Co., Inc., 1984.)

Have you ever felt overconfident?

Have you ever felt like taking a chance just to see how it comes out?

Have you ever felt so angry that you were determined to hurt someone even if you hurt yourself, too?

Have you ever felt so depressed, so discouraged, that you just didn't give a damn?

Have you ever felt like kicking over a game you couldn't win?*

(*People close to Nixon in his last days in office reportedly deactivated the signal mechanism that our President can use to hurl our nuclear holocaust at Russia and destroy the world.)

The United States and Russia have enough military hardware to destroy every city on earth seven times!

And other nations are scrambling to acquire this dreadful suicidal power!*

(*The U.S., Russia, France, Great Britain, Italy and West Germany are selling nuclear and conventional arms to other countries at the rate of over $350 million per day! It's sad to note that our economies and our diplomacy are developing a dependency on our roles as merchants of death.)

Why do we have to live under these perilous conditions?

Eventually, every large or small country on this planet could have a supply of deadly nuclear bombs.

Nuclear bombs are not that difficult to make . . . .

Eight thousand pounds of plutonium and uranium are now missing from U.S. facilities, according to the Nuclear Regulatory Commission!

The insane arms race is almost out of control.

Nuclear war by design or by accident is possible and imminent!

It Could Happen Any Minute!

"Nuclear war," according to Roger Fisher, Professor of Law at Harvard, "is not a solution. It is worse than any problem it might 'solve.'"

An all-out nuclear war between the U.S. and Russia could kill hundreds of millions of people and subject the survivors to radiation sicknesses — and cause countless mutations of the genetic blueprints of our species.*

(*If our nuclear insanity continues, our descendants may be so mutated that they cannot even be classified as members of our species, Homo sapiens.)

"Nuclear weapons aren't weapons — they're an obscenity," said Dr. Marvin Goldberger, President, California Institute of Technology.

According to Dr. Herbert L. Abrams of the Harvard Medical School, the corpses produced by a nuclear war between Russia and the United States if laid end to end would reach from the earth to the moon.

Could any worthwhile human desire however right, good or needed be actually achieved by this sacrifice of the human race?

Rear Admiral Gene R. LaRocque, United States Navy (retired), suggests that a nuclear war may be started by mechanical mishaps and electronic and personnel errors:

> . . . one of our strategic submarines, the George Washington, ran right into a Japanese ship just a few months ago and sank it! That's one of our best missile submarines! . . . We've lost two of our nuclear attack submarines that sank in the ocean and we don't know why to this day — the Scorpion and the Thresher. And earlier this year one of our missiles was accidentally fired from Arkansas because a mechanic dropped a wrench . . .

We've had several incidents where nuclear weapons have literally fallen out of airplanes, literally just fallen through the bomb bays. Probably the most interesting one is the one that fell out of a strategic bomber in the Carolinas some years ago . . . . landed in Carolina in a swamp, and they looked all over for that nuclear weapon. We haven't found it yet . . . .*

(*The Defense Department bought the land, put a fence around it, and now it's a nuclear safety area! From a talk given on October 31, 1981 at a Los Angeles symposium organized by Physicians for Social Responsibility and the Council for a Livable World.)

Daniel Ellsberg, who was an assistant to former Secretary of Defense McNamara, reminds us of an accident in 1961 when an Air Force plane carrying a 24-megaton bomb crashed in North Carolina.

On crash impact five of the six interlocking safety mechanisms on the bomb failed!

Only one switch kept the bomb from unleashing the equivalent of 1,000 Nagasaki-type explosions!*

(*From Survival newsletter, Sept.-Nov. 1981, published by Southern California Alliance for Survival.)

We've been lucky so far!

A Russian airplane carrying a nuclear weapon crashed in the Sea of Japan.

U.S. submarines carrying nuclear missiles have collided with Russian ships.

By mistake, we dropped on Spain four plutonium bombs, which fortunately did not explode.

Oops — so sorry!

The failure of a 46 computer part has produced a false signal that Russian missiles were on the way.

On November 9, 1979, a reportedly fail-safe computer responded to a war games tape by turning on all American early warning systems around the world!

On June 3 and again on June 6, 1980, computer errors in our warning system began a rapid chain of events that could have ruined the planet.

You and I may have been only minutes from nuclear death when these technical errors were spotted!!!*

(*Military folks will protest that, while true, the above are unfair statements. They haven't blown us apart yet, have they?)

What if an error is not detected within minutes?

Up until the last half of this century, civil defense was usually protective against ordinary bombs.

With less than thirty minutes warning of a missile attack, we can forget it!

The fire storm of a nuclear missile will turn most underground shelters into crematoriums, anyway.

Today Protective Measures are Ineffective, and Ultimately Futile.

Nuclear bombs are so hopelessly devastating that at the November, 1980 Conference of the Physicians for Social Responsibility, Dr. H. Jack Geiger said,

> It is my belief that any physician who even takes part in so-called emergency medical disaster planning—specifically to meet the problem of nuclear attack—is committing a profoundly unethical act. He is deluding himself or herself, colleagues, and by implication the public at large, into the false belief that mechanisms of survival in any meaningful social sense are possible.

Albert Einstein warned:

"We must never relax our efforts to arouse in the people of the world, and especially in their governments, an awareness of the unprecedented disaster which they are absolutely certain to bring on themselves unless there is a fundamental change in their attitudes toward one another as well as in their concept of the future.

"The unleashed power of the atom has changed everything except our way of thinking."

Nothing is worth playing Russian roulette with the journey of Homo sapiens.

As you and I live out our lives and set up the way for future generations, let us resolve to avoid nuclear destruction.

Why let ourselves be wiped out by not responding to the clear signs of future catastrophe?*

(*See The Fate of the Earth by Jonathan Schell. Alfred A Knopf, Inc., 1982. It places the issue in a large perspective with a brilliant analysis of the forces at play. The Fate of the Earth is an important guide at this crucial time.)

Carl Sagan, professor of astronomy at Cornell University and creator of the "Cosmos" series, said:

What a waste it would be after 4 billion tortuous years of evolution if the dominant organism contrived its own self-destruction. We are the first species to have devised the means. There is no issue more important than the avoidance of nuclear war. It is incredible for any thinking person not to be concerned with this issue. No species is guaranteed tenured life on this planet. We are privileged to be alive and to think. We have the privilege to affect the future.

Since nuclear missiles fly both ways, neither the United States nor Russia can make itself more secure by making the other less secure.

Nuclear weapons can no longer provide us with security.

Our choice is clear:

A non-nuclear future or none at all!

Our life on the planet is more important than money or military power!

Do we have to be such fanatics that we destroy the world by squabbling over conflicting ideas?

Is a "cerebral itch" more important than life itself?

Is human destiny a hectic trip from Adam to Atom?

All around us we're getting messages loud and clear:

The danger of the annihilation of human civilization should not be made the subject of theoretical arguments, but be used as a basis for creating a common awareness of the alarming situation the world is facing today and of the need for exercising the political will to search for acceptable solutions.

Report of the Secretary-General Of the United Nations*

(*"General and Complete Disarmament, Comprehensive Study on Nuclear Weapons," (A/35/392, page 151, September 12, 1980.)

And again:

The overwhelming priority to do away with nuclear arms has not penetrated the collective consciousness or conscience of the general public . . . . Nuclear arms must not just be limited; they must be eliminated. – Rev. Maurice McCrackin, Community Church of Cincinnati

Rear Admiral LaRocque warns us:

It's very important for all of us today to realize that the Soviet Union is not the enemy. Nuclear war is the enemy. We're going to have to learn to live with the Russians or we and the Russians are going to die at about the same time.

So urgent is the situation that we must shortcut through our usual ways of thinking.

Humanity and world peace must be given priority above everything else.

As individuals we must act affirmatively and stop supporting the drift toward nuclear holocaust.

Dale Bridenbaugh, Richard Hubbard and Gregory Minor took their stand and resigned from highly paying positions as nuclear engineers at General Electric on February 2, 1976.

They told the Joint Committee on Atomic Energy:

When we first joined the General Electric Nuclear Energy Division, we were very excited about the idea of this new technology—atomic power—and the promise of a virtually limitless source of safe, clean and economic energy for this and future generations. But now . . . the promise is still unfulfilled. The nuclear industry has developed to become an industry of narrow specialists, each promoting and refining a fragment of the technology, with little comprehension of the total impact on our world system . . . . We [resigned] because we could no longer justify devoting our life energies to the continued development and expansion of nuclear fission power — a system we believe to be so dangerous that it now threatens the very existence of life on this planet.

The problem of nuclear poisoning of the planet can only be solved by educating the people on earth about the nuclear facts of life.

The people of the Soviet Union, the United States and all other countries can be made aware of the nuclear peril —

When the people of this earth know the facts, they will not want to live poised on the brink of nuclear annihilation!

("Mankind must put an end to war or war will put an end to mankind." John F. Kennedy.)

"The war planning process of the past has become totally obsolete. ATTACK IS NOW SUICIDE," said Thomas J. Watson, Jr., former Ambassador to the Soviet Union and President of IBM. Watson warns us against:

". . . the illusion that we cannot sign treaties with the Russians because they systematically violate them.

Let us be clear about this: there are major differences between our two countries. Soviet values are diametrically opposed to ours. Contention between us on a global scale is a fact of life. Suspicion is the keynote of our relations.

But having said that, let me add this: on the evidence, the Soviets do keep agreements provided each side has an interest in the other's keeping the agreement, and provided each side can verify compliance for itself."*

(*Keynote address at Harvard's 330th commencement on June 4, 1981.)

In 1958 a Russian nuclear installation exploded at Kyshtym. Radioactive clouds devastated the countryside for hundreds of miles. This area of the Ural Mountains is now a wasteland that cannot be safely inhabited for millennia.

It's interesting to note the U.S. Government hid this CIA report for almost 20 years.

It only came to light in 1977 under the Freedom of Information Act.

Continue reading on page 2...

In 1981 George Kennan, former Ambassador to Moscow, and one of our foremost authorities on Russia, called for immediate, across-the-board 50% reductions in all kinds of nuclear arms as a first step by both sides. He pointed out:

We have gone on piling weapon upon weapon, missile upon missile, new levels of destructiveness upon old ones, helplessly, almost involuntarily, like victims of some sort of hypnotism, like men in a dream, like lemmings heading for the sea.

And the result is that today we have achieved—we and the Russians together—in the creation of these devices and their means of delivery, levels of redundancy of such grotesque dimensions as to defy rational understanding. What a confession of intellectual poverty it would be, what a bankruptcy of intelligent statesmanship, if we had to admit that such blind, senseless acts of destruction were the best we could do!

Dr. Jim Muller of the Harvard Medical School reports that:

In March, 1981 at a conference held by the International Physicians for the Prevention of Nuclear War, Dr. Yevgeni I. Chazov, Deputy Minister of Health of the U.S.S.R. and cardiologist to Chairman Brezhnev and other Kremlin leaders, revealed that he had spent 35 minutes on national Soviet television discussing the medical consequences of nuclear war. The conference itself was covered in detail by Pravda, with a circulation of over 10 million,

Izvestia, over 8 million, and so on. Statements about the impossibility of surviving nuclear war and appeals to world leaders to prevent it were printed intact.*

(*In June, 1982, Dr. Muller, with Dr. Bernard Lown and Dr. John Pastore, appeared on Soviet television with Dr. Chazov and two other Russian physicians. Dr. Chazov said, "We have come here openly and honestly to tell the people about our movement, whose main objective is the preservation of life on earth." They discussed such topics as the effects of a one-megaton bomb on a city, medical care for the victims and the long-term effects of radiation fallout. The one-hour telecast was seen by an estimated 100 million Russians and it was not censored.)

Dwight D. Eisenhower, who served as a five-star general in World War II and who also served as President of the United States, could speak as ". . . one who has witnessed the horror and the lingering sadness of war — as one who knows that another war could utterly destroy this civilization which has been so slowly built over thousands of years . . ."

In 1953, Eisenhower said, "Every gun that is made, every warship launched, every rocket fired, signifies in a final sense a theft from those who hunger and are not fed — those who are cold and not clothed.

"This world in arms is not spending money alone — it is spending the sweat of its laborers, the genius of its scientists, the hopes of its children."

By 1959, this general and statesman said,

"I like to believe that people in the long run are going to do more to promote peace than are governments.

"Indeed, I think that people want peace so much that, one of these days, governments had better get out of their way and let them have it."

The Council for a Livable World has pointed out that military expenditures of themselves are destructive to human life — even if the weapons they stockpile are never used.*

(*The Council for a Livable World was founded in 1962 by the eminent nuclear physicist Dr. Leo Szilard to combat the menace of nuclear war and strengthen national security through rational arms control.)

The people of Earth are now spending one million dollars per minute on armaments!

Once we stop preparing to blast each other apart, we will find that we can easily solve all the world's hunger, water and shelter problems.*

(*More than $18 billion in arms sales were made to Third World countries in 1980 — up from $8 billion in 1975. Let them eat — guns?)

What can you and I do about the biggest problem our world has ever faced?

In case you are feeling that there is nothing you can do about the increasing nuclear menace that hangs over our heads, remember the story of the Hundredth Monkey.

You may be the Hundredth Monkey!

Your own awareness and action can be the added energy needed to make the difference between life and death for you, your family — and all of us.

Dr. Caldicott reminds us,

The power of an aroused public is unbeatable. Vietnam and Watergate proved that. It must be demonstrated again. It is not yet too late, for while there is life there is hope. There is no cause for pessimism, for already I have seen great obstacles surmounted. Nor need we be afraid, for I have seen democracy work.*

(*Nuclear Madness by Dr. Helen Caldicott, p. 93. Bantam Books, 1980. Copyright 1978, 1980 by Helen M. Caldicott.)

Mass Action is Effective.

Eighty thousand people in June, 1977 marched in Australia demanding that uranium be left in the ground where it belongs.

This protest was successful!

In Germany, after experiencing nuclear protests, West German Chancellor Helmut Schmidt said, "One cannot simply force nuclear energy down people's throats."

A Time magazine poll showed that 76% of the voters in the U.S. support a nuclear freeze.

Statewide votes in Massachusetts, Michigan, Montana, New Jersey, North Dakota, Oregon, Rhode Island, California, Wisconsin and the District of Columbia have called for immediate negotiations for a verifiable freeze in the production, testing and deployment of all nuclear weapons, missiles and delivery systems.

In Massachusetts voters backed a proposal that would require a referendum before any nuclear waste site or power plant can be established.

The United Nations organization with its worldwide offices will help if requested:

Once there is an initiative from a region, the countries and regional organizations concerned should be able, upon their request and in the manner they wish, to draw to the fullest extent on the resources and possibilities of the United Nations system.*

(*Report of the Secretary-General of the United Nations, "General and Complete Disarmament, Study on All the Aspects of Regional Disarmament." [Page 64, A/35/416, October 8, 1980])

Here's some good news.

In June, 1981 a Gallup poll asked Americans, "Do you think that the United States should or should not meet with the Soviet Union this year to try to reach agreement on nuclear disarmament?"

Eighty percent said we should meet, thirteen percent said we should not, with seven percent undecided.*

(*Nuclear War: What's in It For You? by Ground Zero is an excellent book that will increase your nuclear awareness. Pocket Books.)

In addition to mass action, we must alter the separating mental habits that created the nuclear problem from the start.

Let's examine the change in consciousness that must take place for four billion of us to get along together on planet Earth.

How we think and feel has got us into this nuclear problem,

The way to our survival lies in altering how we think and feel.

We must use the power of our collective consciousness as we learn to focus on peace — and human togetherness.

The men and women of the nuclear nations must be willing to give up their PLUTONIUM SECURITY BLANKETS.

Instead we must REALLY be willing to REALLY listen so we can REALLY understand what's REALLY bothering us.

We must get behind emotional rigidity, intellectual jargon and logic-tight compartments of the mind.

We must realize that there are no simple right answers.

We must stop risking the survival of our planet by demanding that we always get our way. If we always get our way, there is no real negotiation.

Together we must develop effective understandings based on both sides working together to create mutually acceptable solutions that we can all live with.

It's our separate-self mental habits that are the cause of our survival predicament.

The bomb is not the real problem — it's only an effect of our attitudes.

Our mental habits of understanding events in an "us-vs.-them" perception rather than an "us-and-them" insight are creating a devastating mental, emotional and moral separateness in our minds.

If the human race can't learn to get along with itself, it will soon exterminate itself.

A group of our top scientists working in the Manhattan Project during World War II developed the atomic bomb from textbook theory to Hiroshima in only four years!

What would happen if an equally dedicated group backed by our nation's resources worked together to create a world consciousness of our common humanity and a unity of our human hearts and minds that would make all armaments useless?

Any problem created by the human mind can be solved by the human mind.

What's stopping us?

If you had a highly contagious, often fatal, disease, you would care enough about other people to try to avoid transmitting it.

Could the expectations and demands that make you feel hatred, alienation and a "me-vs.-them" separateness be considered a disease?

Such emotion-backed demands are more deadly to the survival of the human race than all contagious diseases added together!

Remember this the next time your mind makes you experience hatred and hardheartedness.

If we want humankind to survive into the next century, we can no longer afford to transmit the deadly disease of hatred, non-caring and forcefully getting one's was that lead to murder, assassination and ultimately to nuclear destruction.

Increasingly our minds have put great energy into three forms of separateness that make us create thoughts and actions that result in a lethal threat to our continued life on planet Earth!*

(*See No Boundary by Ken Wilber. Center Publications, 1979. This is a discussion of how our minds create division and separateness.)

First, your mind is divided against itself.

You have become self-conscious, self-downing, self-critical, and in too many ways have lost your deeper levels of appreciating yourself.

Have you sometimes noticed that when you're feeling most separate from someone else, behind it all your mind is just not feeling good about you?

Secondly, your mind has become divided against your own body.

Your thinking has obstructed the free flow of your feelings. Your mental activity constantly crowds out your experiencing the aliveness of your body.

You have neglected your body and instead put your energy into activities involving pride, prestige and that ever-seductive "success" that have not brought you happiness or peace of mind.

Thirdly, just as your mind has become divided against itself and against the body that houses it, it has also increasingly alienated itself from your four billion cousins that are here and now sharing the planet with you.

You have lost the bond with Mother Earth herself and all her creatures — and forgotten how we all depend on each other.

In too many situations we automatically experience people as "them" — not "us."

These jungle-type habits of mind are dangerous to our species.

In the millions of years in which our ancestors were surviving in the jungles, it was important for their minds to create an instant "self-vs.-other" perception.

For animals eat other animals and no species can survive if all of its members are eaten up.

This instant perception of "otherness" is basic to survival for animals in the jungle.

We can learn a more effective way to make our lives work.

We are still creating a "jungle" of our civilized lives by continuing the operation of our "us-vs.-them" mental habits.

We're all in this together!

"Love alone," wrote Teilhard de Chardin, "is capable of uniting living beings in such a way as to complete and fulfill them, for it alone takes them and joins them by what is deepest in themselves."

Understanding, Cooperation and Love are the Keys to Human Survival!

The problem I find in trying to go from the separate-self to the consciousness of my unified-self is that my ego operates under the illusory programming that in order to like or love you, I must like or love everything you do or say.

I identify you with your thoughts or your actions.

I lose sight of the fact that your thoughts and actions just reflect your life experiences and your training.

I may crystallize my mind against what you do or say and fail to notice your good intentions . . . that usually are just like mine!

Even if you drop a bomb on me your purpose is to settle arguments — and create peace!

These are good intentions — just like mine!

You just need a more effective way to realize your positive intentions!

A stereo set is not the record it plays.

If a record is scratchy, we don't throw out the stereo set. All we have to do is change the record.

We don't have to reject a human being because we don't like his or her programming.

We can just make it clear that we like the person — but we don't like a particular action.

And our thoughts and actions can change because they're not us — in our essence.

I have the direct experience that in my essence I am something apart from the mental habits that spin out my personality and the current soap opera of my life.

Thus I can dislike a person's behavior and still feel that this is a human being who like me is just trying to make life work using the programming we picked up when we were young.

Your thoughts and actions are only a set of mental habits in a state of flux as you evolve from stage to stage of your life's growth.

All of us have done mean, sloppy and uncaring things that we wish we hadn't done.

I always hope that you won't identify me with the things that I've done that were unskillful responses to life situations.

The mind can be trained to nurture a "me-and-you" consciousness in which patience and understanding will compassionately harmonize the flow of our activities so that we all want to help each other work things out.

We can develop an awareness that things aren't problem-free for me until they're problem-free for you!

This applies equally to relationships between individuals or between countries.

When I create my experience of you I may forget that you are not your thoughts or actions.

I don't know you from inside — as I experience myself.

I may forget that in every important way you are like me.

You have a human heart that feels pain and warmth, sadness and happiness.

In your essence and in your intentions you are basically good — just like me!

And my ego is often too ready to treat as important all the differences that my mind notices: lifestyle, skin color, social status, educational background, our differing ideas and opinions and on and on.

When I continually magnify these outward signs, I create the experience that you are really different from me.

It's time we begin to realize that you and I are far more alike than we are different.

We are all fellow beings traveling the road of life together.

We don't live in isolation.

We are all interconnected.

We all live in one world.

We are affected by a lack of harmony of any type anywhere on the planet — even if we're not consciously aware of it.

We are not separate.

What we say and do can affect the well-being of all of us.

We know that our health may be affected if we live among diseased people.

What we are beginning to learn is that our peace of mind may be affected if we live among disturbed people.

Our happiness may be affected if we live among unhappy people.

Our love may be affected if we live among clashing, unloving people.

And even the future of our species is in doubt with various nations stockpiling nuclear devices designed to destroy each other.

The nuclear nations today have created more than 50,000 nuclear devices — in an expression of the consciousness of the separate-self.

These dangerous toys enable some children of Earth pompously playing the roles of military and political leaders, to kill fellow humans in other nations.*

(*See Missile Envy by Helen Caldicott, William Morrow and Co., Inc., 1984.)

We pay a horrendous price for this separate-self — this "me-vs.-you" jungle-type consciousness.

No matter what illusions may dominate our minds, nuclear devices are suicidal for our species.

Any perception that our lives are an "us-vs.-them" matter is an illusion and can only create alienation, unhappiness — and perhaps death.

If our species is to survive, it must replace the illusions of separateness with the emotional experiences of acceptance, cooperation and togetherness.

Instead of "you vs. me" it must become "you and me" — on this planet together.

However much our ideas and ideologies may clash, we must remember that nothing is more important for survival and for happiness in life than feelings of understanding and commonness of human purpose.

All of the nations of earth are acting like spoiled children who are fighting over marbles.

Children forget that their happiness comes not from possession of the marbles, but from the fun of playing together — and from creating the great adventure of life together.

We can learn to keep our squabbles within bounds.

We must learn to disagree without throwing each other out of our hearts — and thus create rock-like hatreds.

We can become skillful at changing the desire systems in our minds.

Whatever we expect to get by creating hatred and separateness even if "justified" is always purchased at far too great a price.

Human love—our heart-to-heart love—is more valuable than anything else.

If we have this, we have enough.

Without this love in our hearts, nothing else will be enough!

Kierkegaard said, ". . . to love human beings is still the only thing worth living

for — without that love, you really do not live."

Let's not ruin our future because of anything that happened in the past.

Let us challenge our present approaches and rethink old assumptions.

Would you want your children to die because your mind is not flexible enough to forgive?*

(*Bernard Benson in The Peace Book [Bantam Books, 1982] gives a sensitive new angle by letting a child ask the pertinent questions and give practical solutions. Philip Noel Baker[Co-chairman of the World Disarmament Campaign and winner of the Nobel Peace Prize] said, "Everyone who wants to live should read this book." It has been translated to Russian and the author was interviewed by children on TV in Moscow.)

From the point of view of our complex desire systems, life will always seem "imperfect."

We Win Some and We Lose Some

Can we expand our hearts so that we do not hate even the proponents of nuclear power?

Can we learn to feel love and compassion for the people involved in perpetuating nuclear technology even when they're unable or unwilling to understand the reasons for our concern?

Always remember that feelings of anger and hatred and separateness are our only problem.

Let's not try to save the world by increasing the problem!

The next step in our growth as individuals and as a species requires that our minds experience the planetary urgency of letting go of separating mental habits and demands that close our hearts to other people.

We are challenged by our destiny to increase our ability to create with many people the enjoyable experiences of acceptance and cooperation.

Individual and species survival means increasing our tolerance, our patience and our own understanding so that we do not continue to drive ourselves crazy when people or situations are not the way we want them to be.

We can no longer afford to create separateness and alienation if we want to get the most from our lives.

We can still want what we want. We can think it's only fair or right to get it.

We can still put gentle energy into trying to change things.

But we must learn not to throw people out of our hearts.

We tear each other apart too easily . . .

We're all like kids, taking our disagreements and our differences too seriously!

When will we learn that it is only our emotion-backed demands that make us create the internal experience of unhappiness?

Our egos and rational minds are so good at making us feel and think that the problem of human separateness lies in the outside world — and not inside ourselves!

With practice, this mental skill of inner flexibility will make us even more effective and powerful.

It takes a strong person to be able to lovingly but directly communicate what he or she wants to someone who disagrees — and acts hostile.

You will increase your skill in helping the world when you learn to be mentally flexible.

This means being able to constantly blend back into creating an experience of life as a whole with appreciation, cooperativeness and love for the people around you — even when they oppose you.

We haven't yet become effective at operating our minds and our emotions to create that subtle blend of both head and heart that lets us use our treasure chest of inner wisdom.

This wisdom is kept tightly locked up when our egos and minds run off the tapes that continually create the illusion of separateness.

Only by opening our minds and hearts will we find the rich, intuitive wisdom that always lies within every human being — even if it isn't used.

The conflicting energies in our world are so great today that perhaps we need the "millionth monkey" to project the energy of wholeness and cooperation — of friendship and love, of sharing life on this planet together.

Whatever That Critical Number is, You are Needed to Save Our Civilization.

You are essential!

It may be that without you, it will not happen and our species will hurtle itself into partial or complete destruction.

How do we play the game of saving the world?

To begin with, you probably can't help others understand unless you have a grasp of the scope of the nuclear wipeout we all face.

One of the most readable and fascinating books on this subject is Killing Our Own by Harvey Wasserman and Norman Solomon. This book tells about the countless human deaths already caused by the Hiroshima and Nagasaki bombs, the Nevada bomb tests, the tests in the Pacific Islands, uranium mining, exposure in nuclear industries, and the near meltdown of the Three-Mile Island nuclear power plant.

Above all, be creative — and energetic.

Since the future of both you and your family is at stake, turn on the immense resources of your mind.

Find the ways in which you can flow your energy into increasing worldwide awareness that the nuclear bomb mentality must be eliminated.

The strength of our species lies not in sharp fangs or piercing claws.

It lies in our ability to use our minds to cooperate with each other as we play the games of life.

The same powerful minds that created nuclear bombs and intercontinental missiles can also learn how to create human unity and cooperativeness.

We can save the world from people-made disaster — when we set the goal high and add our determination and our persistence.

Appoint yourself as a roving Ambassador of the State of Loving and Caring.

Will you accept your share of the responsibility for creating the Hundredth Monkey energy that will change the consciousness of the entire planet?

We can tilt the scales to eliminate the awesome threat of nuclear catastrophe and environmental ruin.

Be informed, hopeful and energetic.

Be vigilant with your thoughts of peace and love.

Sense your power to lift the mood of despair.

Let your enthusiasm seep in and penetrate the collective consciousness!

Meet with people, talk with people, share with people.

Find and support organizations that channel our energy into survival.

Write to your senators and representatives and other politicians.

Let them know what you want them to do.*

(*John Kenneth Galbraith of Harvard University, at the October 31, 1981 symposium of the Physicians for Social Responsibility, told the 2,700 participants, "Nothing is more needed in Washington than a rebuke to those who are not pressing actively and energetically for arms control." You can get the voting records of congressmen on specific issues by writing the U.S. Senate, Capitol Building, Washington, D.C. 20510 and the U.S. House of Representatives, Capitol Building, Washington, D.C. 20515.)

Most of the things you are now doing in your life will become meaningless or nonexistent if we are hit by nuclear catastrophe!

Take a new look at your priorities . . .

This does not necessarily mean leaving your work or your present lifestyle.

It means giving an increasing energy and priority to expanding your own awareness, to communicating with other people who are now asleep, and to withdrawing energy from all thoughts and actions which create human alienation, separateness, destruction and death.*

(*Green ribbons were worn as a reminder of the children being killed in Atlanta. Yellow ribbons were worn as a reminder that our citizens were being held as hostages in Iran. There is a worldwide energy to wear blue ribbons symbolizing that everyone on earth is a hostage to the ever-present threat of nuclear annihilation. You may wish to buy a roll of blue ribbon and a package of safety pins and pass out these symbols of protest to your friends — and wear one yourself. Thousands of people in Europe are wearing leaves as Friends of the Peace Book by Bernard Benson.)

Do not wait until others around you are opening their hearts.

Instead, begin doing things now that are so desperately needed for the conscious unfolding of your life — and the survival of our species.

Your dedication to saving our lives and the planet Earth will bring your own life to a level of satisfaction and well-being that you may never otherwise achieve.

You will become increasingly happier as you learn to love more.

And you will begin to discover the miracle of your full potential as a human being.

Your life will gain meaning and purpose.

Your energy can tip the scales when you add it to thousands of others' — merging, slowly raising our collective consciousness to the point of power when it makes the all-important difference!

This survival energy spreads far beyond those involved and touches every life on Earth!

The change in you is already taking place!

You now know the immensity of the dangers, the futility of "safety" measures, and the need for action right now using the power of our new awareness.

The Hundredth Monkey Phenomenon points out our responsibility and our power.

It is up to every one of us to change the myths that say we have to depend on nuclear energy for power and defense.

We can no longer believe that the safeguards are adequate — or that we are helpless to change the national policies of the governments of our world.

We will replace the myths with knowledge.

Our persistence will relentlessly channel our positive thoughts toward peace and a harmonizing world.

And that starts right here—in my heart and yours—right now!

In this short book I can only give you a glimpse of the miracle of life you can experience . . .

This rapture of life is your birthright to create and enjoy.

This book can only hope to inspire you to take the next steps in your own development — for your sake and the survival of our species.

This is the most pressing problem we face today.

Everything else in our civilization is of secondary significance.

It is worthy of your full attention as an intelligent, caring, wise and wonderful person.

We can begin to lose the game of life when we play nuclear war games.

Like children our egos and minds create the illusion that the ideas in our heads and our desires for "marbles" are more important than feelings of human togetherness in our hearts.

We cannot afford to play such enthusiastic games with loaded nuclear pistols any more!

The Marbles Just Aren't Worth It!

Author's End Note

Many Thanks to:

Britta Zetterberg and Penny Keyes for their wealth of helpful suggestions for improving this book.

Battle Book Report 3 — Twenty-Five Ways to Suppress Truth

Yowusa.com, August 5, 2008
Share Free Printable eDoc
25.AlienSecurity.info

Twenty-Five Ways to Suppress Truth
H. Michael Sweeney, June 2001
PO Box 1941, Clackamas, OR 97015 USA

Companion Article to Cut to the Chase Interview #91:Terrestrial and Extraterrestrial Disinformation — Propaganda Experts Philip Gardiner and Marshall Vian Summers.

Foreword by Marshall Masters

In early 2008, we began to analyze Planet X / Nibiru South Pole Telescope (SPT) leak videos by YouTube users, such as NibiruShock2012.

Some of these videos, particularly the first two by NibiruShock2012, triggered massive, well-organized disinformation attacks. When we began documenting these disinformation attacks, we became the target of equally brutal attacks, which continue to this day. How-

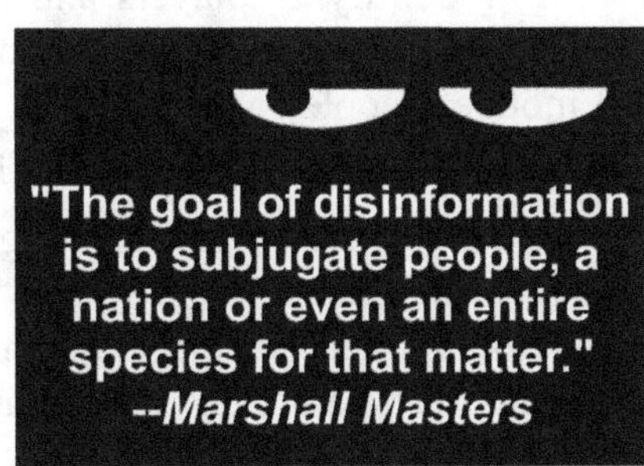

ever, if the goal of these attacks was to diminish our popularity, the exact opposite proved to be true.

As a consequence of these well-funded and highly-organized wolf pack disinformation attacks on us, our visibility on the web has skyrocketed. Consequently, we've seen dramatic increases in visitor traffic to yowusa.com and similar increases in new subscriptions and book sales. As the old saying goes, we "fell into a bucket of manure and came up smelling like roses."

In the process, we took careful note of the tactics formerly and currently used against us and then found a wonderfully insightful disinformation article by H. Michael Sweeney. As we read it, we were amazed at how predictable these tactics can be. The knowledge Mr. Sweeney gives you is invaluable, and it will empower you in ways you could not have previously imagined.—Marshall Masters

The Rules of Disinformation

H. Michael Sweeney

Built upon Thirteen Techniques for Truth Suppression by David Martin, the following may be useful to the initiate in the world of dealing with veiled and half-truth, lies, and suppression of truth when serious crimes are studied in public forums. This, sadly, includes every day news media, one of the worst offenders with respect to being a source of disinformation. Where the crime involves a conspiracy, or a conspiracy to cover up the crime, there will invariably be a disinformation campaign launched against those seeking to uncover and expose the truth and/or the conspiracy.

There are specific tactics, which disinfo artists tend to apply, as revealed here. Also included with this material are seven common traits of the disinfo artist, which may also prove useful in identifying players and motives. The more a particular party fits the traits and is guilty of following the rules, the more likely they are a professional disinfo artist with a vested motive. People can be bought, threatened, or blackmailed into providing disinformation, so even "good guys" can be suspect in many cases.

A rational person participating as one interested in the truth will evaluate that chain of evidence and conclude either that the links are solid and conclusive, that one or more links are weak and need further development before conclusion can be arrived at, or that one or more links can be broken, usually invalidating (but not necessarily so, if parallel links already exist or can be found, or if a particular link was merely supportive, but not in itself key) the argument. The game is played by raising issues which either strengthen or weaken (preferably to the point of breaking) these links. It is the job of a disinfo artist to interfere with these evaluation... to at least make people think the links are weak or broken when, in truth, they are not... or to propose alternative solutions leading away from the truth. Often, by simply impeding and slowing down the process through disinformation tactics, a level of victory is assured because apathy increases with time and rhetoric.

It would seem true in almost every instance, that if one cannot break the chain of evidence for a given solution, revelation of truth has won out. If the chain is broken either a new link must be forged, or a whole new chain developed, or the solution is invalid an a new one must be found... but truth still wins out. There is no shame in being the creator or supporter of a failed solution, chain, or link, if done with honesty in search of the truth. This is the rational approach. While it is understandable that a person can become emotionally involved with a particular side of a given issue, it is really unimportant who wins, as long as truth wins. But the disinfo artist will seek to emotionalize and chastise any failure (real or false claims thereof), and will seek by means of intimidation to prevent discussion in general.

It is the disinfo artist and those who may pull their strings (those who stand to suffer should the crime be solved) who MUST seek to prevent rational and complete examination of any chain of evidence that would hang them. Since fact and truth seldom fall on their own, they must be overcome with lies and deceit. Those who are professional in the art of lies and deceit, such as the intelligence community and the professional criminal (often the same people or at least working together), tend to apply fairly well defined and observable tools in this process. However, the public at large is not well armed against such weapons, and is often easily led astray by these time-proven tactics. Remarkably, not even media and law enforcement have NOT BEEN TRAINED to deal with these issues. For the most part, only the players themselves understand the rules of the game.

This why concepts from the film, Wag-The-Dog, actually work. If you saw that movie, know that there is at least one real-world counterpart to Al Pacino's character. For CIA, it is Mark Richards, who was called in to orchestrate the media response to Waco on behalf of Janet Reno. Mark Richards is the acknowledged High Priest of Disinformation. His appointment was extremely appropriate, since the CIA was VERY present at Waco from the very beginning of the cult to the very end of their days - just as it was at the People's Temple in Jonestown. Richards purpose in life is damage control.

For such disinformationalists, the overall aim is to avoid discussing links in the chain of evidence which cannot be broken by truth, but at all times, to use clever deceptions or lies to make select links seem weaker than they are, create the illusion of a break, or better still, cause any who are considering the chain to be distracted in any number of ways, including the method of questioning the credentials of the presenter. Please understand that fact is fact, regardless of the source. Likewise, truth is truth, regardless of the source. This is why criminals are allowed to testify against other criminals. Where a motive to lie may truly exist, only actual evidence that the testimony itself IS a lie renders it completely invalid. Were a known 'liar's' testimony to stand on its own without supporting fact, it might certainly be of questionable value, but if the testimony (argument) is based on verifiable or otherwise demonstrable facts, it matters not who does the presenting or what their motives are, or if they have lied in the past or even if motivated to lie in this instance -- the facts or links would and should stand or fall on their own merit and their part in the matter will merely be supportive.

Moreover, particularly with respects to public forums such as newspaper letters to the editor, and Internet chat and news groups, the disinfo type has a very important role. In these forums, the principal topics of discussion are generally attempts by individuals to cause other persons to become interested in their own particular position, idea or solution -- very much in development at the time. People often use such mediums as a sounding board and in hopes of pollination to better form their ideas. Where such ideas are critical of government or powerful, vested groups (especially if their criminality is the topic), the disinfo artist has yet another role -- the role of nipping it in the bud. They also seek to stage the concept, the presenter, and any supporters as less than credible should any possible future confrontation in more public forums result due to their early successes. You can often spot the disinfo types at work here by the unique application of "higher standards" of discussion than necessarily warranted. They will demand that those presenting arguments or concepts back everything up with the same level of expertise as a professor, researcher or investigative writer. Anything less renders any discussion meaningless and unworthy in their opinion, and anyone who disagrees is obviously stupid -- and they generally put it in exactly those terms.

So, as you read any such discussions, particularly so in Internet news groups (NG), decide for yourself when a rational argument is being applied and when disinformation, psyops (psychological warfare operations) or trickery is the tool. Accuse those guilty of the later freely. They (both those deliberately seeking to lead you astray, and those who are simply foolish or misguided thinkers) generally run for cover when thus illuminated, or -- put in other terms, they put up or shut up (a perfectly acceptable outcome either way, since truth is the goal.)

Here are the twenty-five methods and seven traits, some of which don't apply directly to NG application. Each contains a simple example in the form of actual (some paraphrased for simplicity) from NG comments on commonly known historical events, and a proper response. Accusations should not be overused -- reserve for repeat offenders and those who use multiple tactics. Responses should avoid falling into emotional traps or informational sidetracks, unless it is feared that some observers will be easily dissuaded by the trickery.

Twenty-Five Rules of Disinformation

The first rule and last five (or six, depending on situation) rules are generally not directly within the ability of the traditional disinfo artist to apply. These rules are generally used more directly by those at the leadership, key players or planning level of the criminal conspiracy or conspiracy to cover up.

1. *Hear no evil, see no evil, speak no evil.*

Regardless of what you know, don't discuss it -- especially if you are a public figure, news anchor, etc. If it's not reported, it didn't happen, and you never have to deal with the issues.

Example: Media was present in the courtroom (Hunt vs. Liberty Lobby) when CIA agent Marita Lorenz 'confession' testimony regarding CIA direct participation in the planning and assassination of John Kennedy was revealed. All media reported was that E. Howard Hunt lost his libel case against Liberty Lobby (Liberty Lobby's newspaper, The Spotlight, had reported Hunt was in Dallas that day and were sued for the story). See Mark Lane's remarkable book, Plausible Denial, for the full confessional transcript.

Proper response: There is no possible response unless you are aware of the material and can make it public yourself.. In any such attempt, be certain to target any known silent party as likely complicit in a cover up. In this case, it would be the entire Time-Warner Media Group, among others. This author is relatively certain that reporters were hand-picked to cover this case from among those having intelligence community ties.

2. *Become incredulous and indignant.*

Avoid discussing key issues and instead focus on side issues, which can be used to show the topic as being critical of some otherwise sacrosanct group or theme. This is also known as the 'How dare you!' gambit.

Example: 'How dare you suggest that the Branch Davidians were murdered! The FBI and BATF are made up of America's finest and best trained law enforcement, operate under the strictest of legal requirements, and are under the finest leadership the President could want to appoint.'

Proper response: You are avoiding the Waco issue with disinformation tactics. Your high opinion of FBI is not founded in fact. All you need do is examine Ruby Ridge and any number of other examples, and you will see a pattern of abuse of power that demands attention to charges against FBI/BATF at Waco. Why do you refuse to address the issues with disinformation tactics (rule 2 - become incredulous and indignant)?

3. *Create rumor mongers.*

Avoid discussing issues by describing all charges, regardless of venue or evidence, as mere rumors and wild accusations. Other derogatory terms mutually exclusive of truth may work as well. This method which works especially well with a silent press, because the only way the public can learn of the facts is through such 'arguable rumors'. If you can associate the material with the Internet, use this fact to certify it a 'wild rumor' from a 'bunch of kids on the Internet', which can have no basis in fact.

Example: You can't prove his material was legitimately from French Intelligence. Pierre Salinger had a chance to show his 'proof' that flight 800 was brought down by friendly fire, and he didn't. All he really had was the same old baseless rumor that's been floating around the Internet for months.'

Proper response: You are avoiding the issue with disinformation tactics. The Internet charge reported widely is based on a single FBI interview statement to media and a similar statement by a Congressman, neither of which had actually seen Pierre's document. As the FBI is being accused in participating in a cover up of this matter and Pierre claims his material is not Internet sourced, it is natural that FBI would have reason to paint his material in a negative light. For you to assume the FBI to have no bias in the face of Salinger's credentials and unchanged stance suggests you are biased. At the best you can say the matter is in question. Further, to imply that material found on Internet is worthless is not founded. At best you may say it must be considered carefully before accepting it, which will require addressing the actual issues. Why do you refuse to address these issues with disinformation tactics (rule 3 - create rumor mongers)?

4. *Use a straw man.*

Find or create a seeming element of your opponent's argument that you can easily knock down to make yourself look good and the opponent to look bad. Either make up an issue you may safely imply exists based on your interpretation of the opponent/opponent's arguments/situation, or select the weakest aspect of the weakest charges. Amplify their significance and destroy them in a way that appears to debunk all the charges, real and fabricated alike, while actually avoiding discussion of the real issues.

Example: When trying to defeat reports by the Times of London that spy-sat images reveal an object racing towards and striking flight 800, a straw man is used. The disinformationalist, later identified as having worked for Naval Intelligence, simply stated: 'If these images exist, the public has not seen them. Why? They don't exist, and never did. You have no evidence and thus, your entire case falls flat.'

Proper response: 'You are avoiding the issue with disinformation tactics. You imply deceit and deliberately establish an impossible and unwarranted test. It is perfectly natural that the public has not seen them, nor will they for some considerable time, if ever. To produce them would violate national security with respect to intelligence gathering capabilities and limitations, and you should know this. Why do you refuse to address the issues with such disinformation tactics (rule 4 - use a straw man)?'

5. *Sidetrack opponents with name calling and ridicule.*

This is also known as the primary 'attack the messenger' ploy, though other methods qualify as variants of that approach. Associate opponents with unpopular titles such as 'kooks', 'right-wing', 'liberal', 'left-wing', 'terrorists', 'conspiracy buffs', 'radicals', 'militia', 'racists', 'religious fanatics', 'sexual deviates', and so forth. This makes others shrink from support out of fear of gaining the same label, and you avoid dealing with issues.

Example: 'You believe what you read in the Spotlight? The Publisher, Willis De-Carto, is a well-known right-wing racist. I guess we know your politics -- does your Bible have a swastika on it? That certainly explains why you support this wild-eyed, right-wing conspiracy theory.'

Proper response: 'You are avoiding the issue with disinformation tactics. Your imply guilt by association and attack truth on the basis of the messenger. The Spotlight is well known Populist media source, responsible for releasing facts and stories well before mainstream media will discuss the issues through their veil of silence. Willis DeCarto has successfully handled lawsuits regarding slanderous statements such as yours. Your undemonstrated charges against the messenger have nothing to do with the facts or the issues, and fly in the face of reason. Why do you refuse to address the issues by use of such disinformation tactics (rule 5 - sidetrack opponents with name calling and ridicule)?'

6. *Hit and Run.*

In any public forum, make a brief attack of your opponent or the opponent position and then scamper off before an answer can be fielded, or simply ignore any answer. This works extremely well in Internet and letters-to-the-editor environments where a steady stream of new identities can be called upon without having to explain criticism reasoning -- simply make an accusation or other attack, never discussing issues, and never answering any subsequent response, for that would dignify the opponent's viewpoint.

Example: 'This stuff is garbage. Where do you conspiracy lunatics come up with this crap? I hope you all get run over by black helicopters.' Notice it even has a farewell sound to it, so it won't seem curious if the author is never heard from again.

Proper response: 'You are avoiding the issue with disinformation tactics. Your comments or opinions fail to offer any meaningful dialog or information, and are worthless except to pander to emotionalism, and in fact, reveal you to be emotionally insecure with these matters. If you do not like reading 'this crap', why do you frequent this NG, which is clearly for the purpose of such discussion? Why do you refuse to address the issues by use of such disinformation tactics (rule 6 - hit and run)?'

7. *Question motives.*

Twist or amplify any fact, which could be taken to imply that the opponent operates out of a hidden personal agenda or other bias. This avoids discussing issues and forces the accuser on the defensive.

Example: 'With the talk-show circuit and the book deal, it looks like you can make a pretty good living spreading lies.'

Proper response: 'You are avoiding the issue with disinformation tactics. Your imply guilt as a means of attacking the messenger or his credentials, but cowardly fail to offer any concrete evidence that this is so. If you think what has been presented are 'lies', why not simply so illustrate? Why do you refuse to address the issues by use of such disinformation tactics (rule 6 - question motives)?'

8. *Invoke authority.*

Claim for yourself or associate yourself with authority and present your argument with enough 'jargon' and 'minutia' to illustrate you are 'one who knows', and simply say it isn't so without discussing issues or demonstrating concretely why or citing sources.

Example: 'You obviously know nothing about either the politics or strategic considerations, much less the technicals of the SR-71. Incidentally, for those who might care, that sleek plane is started with a pair of souped up big-block V-8's (originally, Buick 454 C.I.D. with dual 450 CFM Holly Carbs and a full-race Isky cams -- for 850 combined BHP @ 6,500 RPM) using a dragster-style clutch with direct-drive shaft. Anyway, I can tell you with confidence that no Blackbird has ever been flown by Korean nationals nor have they ever been trained to fly it, and have certainly never overflown the Republic of China in a SR or even launched a drone from it that flew over China. I'm not authorized to discuss if there have been overflights by American pilots.'

Proper response: 'You are avoiding the issue with disinformation tactics. Your imply your own authority and expertise but fail to provide credentials, and you also fail to address issues and cite sources. You simply cite 'Jane's-like' information to make us think you know what you are talking about. Why do you refuse to address the issues by use of such disinformation tactics (rule 8 - invoke authority)?'

9. *Play Dumb.*

No matter what evidence or logical argument is offered, avoid discussing issues except with denials they have any credibility, make any sense, provide any proof, contain or make a point, have logic, or support a conclusion. Mix well for maximum effect.

Example: 'Nothing you say makes any sense. Your logic is idiotic. Your facts nonexistent. Better go back to the drawing board and try again.'

Proper response: 'You are avoiding the issue with disinformation tactics. You evade the issues with your own form of nonsense while others, perhaps more intelligent than you pretend to be, have no trouble with the material. Why do you refuse to address the issues by use of such disinformation tactics (rule 9 - play dumb)?'

10. Associate opponent charges with old news.

A derivative of the straw man -- usually, in any large-scale matter of high visibility, someone will make charges early on which can be or were already easily dealt with - a kind of investment for the future should the matter not be so easily contained.) Where it can be foreseen, have your own side raise a straw man issue and have it dealt with early on as part of the initial contingency plans. Subsequent charges, regardless of validity or new ground uncovered, can usually then be associated with the original charge and dismissed as simply being a rehash without need to address current issues -- so much the better where the opponent is or was involved with the original source.

Example: 'Flight 553's crash was pilot error, according to the NTSB findings. Digging up new witnesses who say the CIA brought it down at a selected spot and were waiting for it with 50 agents won't revive that old dead horse buried by NTSB more than twenty years ago.'

Proper response: 'You are avoiding the issue with disinformation tactics. You ignore the issues and imply they are old charges as if new information is irrelevant to truth. Why do you refuse to address the issues by use of such disinformation tactics (rule 10 - associate charges with old news)?'

11. Establish and rely upon fall-back positions.

Using a minor matter or element of the facts, take the 'high road' and 'confess' with candor that some innocent mistake, in hindsight, was made -- but that opponents have seized on the opportunity to blow it all out of proportion and imply greater criminalities which, 'just isn't so.' Others can reinforce this on your behalf, later, and even publicly 'call for an end to the nonsense' because you have already 'done the right thing.' Done properly, this can garner sympathy and respect for 'coming clean' and 'owning up' to your mistakes without addressing more serious issues.

Example: 'Reno admitted in hindsight she should have taken more time to question the data provided by subordinates on the deadliness of CS-4 and the likely Davidian response to its use, but she was so concerned about the children that she elected, in what she now believes was a sad and terrible mistake, to order the tear gas be used.'

Proper response: 'You are avoiding the issue with disinformation tactics. Your evade the true issue by focusing on a side issue in an attempt to evoke sympathy.

Perhaps you did not know that CIA Public Relations expert Mark Richards was called in to help Janet Reno with the Waco aftermath response? How warm and fuzzy it makes us feel, so much so that we are to ignore more important matters being discussed. Why do you refuse to address the issues by use of such disinformation tactics (rule 11 - establish and rely upon fall-back positions)?'

12. Enigmas have no solution.

Drawing upon the overall umbrella of events surrounding the crime and the multitude of players and events, paint the entire affair as too complex to solve. This causes those otherwise following the matter to begin to loose interest more quickly without having to address the actual issues.

Example: 'I don't see how you can claim Vince Foster was murdered since you can't prove a motive. Before you could do that, you would have to completely solve the whole controversy over everything that went on in the White House and in Arkansas, and even then, you would have to know a heck of a lot more about what went on within the NSA, the Travel Office, and the secret Grand Jury, and on, and on, and on. It's hopeless. Give it up.'

Proper response: 'You are avoiding the issue with disinformation tactics. You completely evade issues and attempt to prevent others from daring to attempt it by making it a much bigger mountain than necessary. You eat an elephant one bite at a time. Why do you refuse to address the issues by use of such disinformation tactics (rule 12 - enigmas have no solution)?'

13. Alice in Wonderland Logic.

Avoid discussion of the issues by reasoning backwards or with an apparent deductive logic, which forbears any actual material fact.

Example: 'The news media operates in a fiercely competitive market where stories are gold. This means they dig, dig, dig for the story -- often doing a better job than law enforcement. If there was any evidence that BATF had prior knowledge of the Oklahoma City bombing, they would surely have uncovered it and reported it. They haven't reported it, so there can't have been any prior knowledge. Put up or shut up.'

Proper response: 'You are avoiding the issue with disinformation tactics. Your backwards logic does not work here. Did the media report that the CIA killed Kennedy when they knew it? No, despite their presence at a courtroom testimony 'confession' by CIA operative Marita Lorenz in a libel trial between E. Howard Hunt and Liberty Lobby, they only told us the trial verdict. THAT would have been the biggest story of the Century, but they didn't print it, did they? Why do you refuse to address the issues by use of such disinformation tactics (rule 13 - Alice in Wonderland logic)?'

14. Demand complete solutions.

Avoid the issues by requiring opponents to solve the crime at hand completely, a ploy which works best with issues qualifying for rule 10.

Example: 'Since you know so much, if James Earl Ray is as innocent as you claim, who really killed Martin Luther King, how was it planned and executed, how did they frame Ray and fool the FBI, and why?'

Proper response: You are avoiding the issue with disinformation tactics. It is not necessary to completely resolve any full matter in order to examine any relative attached issue. Discussion of any evidence of Ray's innocence can stand alone to serve truth, and any alternative solution to the crime, while it may bolster that truth, can also stand alone. Why do you refuse to address the issues by use of such disinformation tactics (rule 14 - demand complete solutions)?

15. Fit the facts to alternate conclusions.

This requires creative thinking unless the crime was planned with contingency conclusions in place.

Example: 'The cargo door failed on Flight 800 and caused a catastrophic breakup which ruptured the fuel tank and caused it to explode.'

Proper response: The best definitive example of avoiding issues by this technique is, perhaps, Arlan Specter's Magic Bullet from the Warren Report. This was eloquently defeated in court but media blindly accepted it without challenge. Thus rewarded, disinformationalists do not shrink from its application, even though today, thanks in part to the movie, JFK, most Americans do now understand it was fabricated nonsense. Thus the defense that works best may actually be to cite the Magic Bullet.

'You are avoiding the issue with disinformation tactics. Your imaginative twisting of facts rivals that of Arlan Specter's Magic Bullet in the Warren Report. We all know why the impossible magic bullet was invented. You invent a cargo door problem when there has been not one shred of evidence from the crash investigation to support it, and in fact, actual photos of the cargo door hinges and locks disprove you. Why do you refuse to address the issues by use of such disinformation tactics (rule 15 - fit facts to an alternate conclusion)?'

16. Vanish evidence and witnesses.

If it does not exist, it is not fact, and you won't have to address the issue.

Example: 'You can't say Paisley is still alive... that his death was faked and the list of CIA agents found on his boat deliberately placed there to support a purge at CIA. You have no proof. Why can't you accept the Police reports?' This is a good ploy, since the dental records and autopsy report showing his body was two inches too long and the teeth weren't his were lost right after his wife demanded inquiry, and since his body was cremated before she could view it -- all that remains are the Police Reports. Handy.

Proper response: There is no suitable response to actual vanished materials or persons, unless you can shed light on the matter, particularly if you can tie the event to a cover up other criminality. However, with respect to dialog where it is used against the discussion, you can respond... 'You are avoiding the issue with disinformation tactics. The best you can say is that the matter is in contention ONLY because of highly suspicious matters such as the simultaneous and mysterious vanishing of three sets of evidence. The suspicious nature itself tends to support the primary allegation. Why do you refuse to address the remaining issues by use of such disinformation tactics (rule 16 - vanish evidence and witnesses)?'

17. Change the subject.

Usually in connection with one of the other ploys listed here, find a way to side-track the discussion with abrasive or controversial comments in hopes of turning attention to a new, more manageable topic. This works especially well with companions who can 'argue' with you over the new topic and polarize the discussion arena in order to avoid discussing more key issues.

Example: 'There were no CIA drugs and was no drug money laundering through Mena, Arkansas, and certainly, there was no Bill Clinton knowledge of it because it simply didn't happen. This is merely an attempt by his opponents to put Clinton off balance and at a disadvantage in the election: Dole is such a weak candidate with nothing to offer that they are desperate to come up with something to swing the polls. Dole simply has no real platform.' Assistant's response. 'You idiot! Dole has the clearest vision of what's wrong with Government since McGovern. Clinton is only interested in raping the economy, the environment and every woman he can get his hands on...' One naturally feels compelled, regardless of party of choice, to jump in defensively on that one...

Proper response: 'You are both avoiding the issue with disinformation tactics. You evade discussion of the issues by attempting to sidetrack us with an emotional response to a new topic -- a trap that we will not fall into willingly. If you truly believe such political rhetoric, please drop out of this discussion, as it is not germane, and take it to one of the more appropriate politics NGs. Why do you refuse to address the issues by use of such disinformation tactics (rule 17- change the subject)?'

18. Emotionalize, Antagonize, and Goad Opponents.

If you can't do anything else, chide and taunt your opponents and draw them into emotional responses that will tend to make them look foolish and overly motivated, and generally render their material somewhat less coherent. Not only will you avoid discussing the issues in the first instance, but even if their emotional response addresses the issue, you can further avoid the issues by then focusing on how 'sensitive they are to criticism.'

Example: 'You are such an idiot to think that possible -- or are you such a paranoid conspiracy buff that you think the 'gubment' is cooking your pea-brained skull with microwaves, which is the only justification you might have for dreaming up this drivel.' After a drawing an emotional response: 'Ohhh... I do seem to have touched a sensitive nerve. Tsk, tsk. What's the matter? The truth too hot for you to handle? Perhaps you should stop relying on the Psychic Friends Network and see a psychiatrist for some real professional help...'

Proper response: 'You are avoiding the issue with disinformation tactics. You attempt to draw me into an emotional response without discussion of the issues. If you have something useful to contribute that defeats my argument, let's hear it -- preferably without snide and unwarranted personal attacks, if you can manage to avoid sinking so low. Your useless rhetoric serves no purpose here if that is all you can manage. Why do you refuse to address the issues by use of such disinformation tactics (rule 18 - emotionalize, antagonize, and goad opponents)?'

19. Ignore facts presented, demand impossible proofs.

This is perhaps a variant of the 'play dumb' rule. Regardless of what material may be presented by an opponent in public forums, claim the material irrelevant and demand proof that is impossible for the opponent to come by (it may exist, but not be at his disposal, or it may be something which is known to be safely destroyed or withheld, such as a murder weapon.) In order to completely avoid discussing issues, it may be required that you to categorically deny and be critical of media or books as valid sources, deny that witnesses are acceptable, or even deny that statements made by government or other authorities have any meaning or relevance.

Example: 'All he's done is to quote the liberal media and a bunch of witnesses who aren't qualified. Where's his proof? Show me wreckage from flight 800 that shows a missile hit it!'

Proper response: 'You are avoiding the issue with disinformation tactics. You presume for us not to accept Don Phillips, reporter for the Washington Post, Al Baker, Craig Gordon or Liam Pleven, reporters for Newsday, Matthew Purdy or Matthew L. Wald, Don Van Natta Jr., reporters for the New York Times, or Pat Milton, wire reporter for the Associated Press -- as being able to tell us anything useful about the facts in this matter. Neither would you allow us to accept Robert E. Francis, Vice Chairman of the NTSB, Joseph Cantamessa Jr., Special Agent In Charge of the New York Office of the F.B.I., Dr. Charles Wetli, Suffolk County Medical Examiner, the Pathologist examining the bodies, nor unnamed Navy divers, crash investigators, or other cited officials, including Boeing Aircraft representatives a part of the crash investigative team -- as a qualified party in this matter, and thus, dismisses this material out of hand. Good logic, -- about as good as saying 150 eye witnesses aren't qualified. Then you demand us to produce evidence that you know is not accessible to us, evidence held by FBI, whom we accuse of cover up. Thus, only YOU are qualified to tell us what to believe? Witnesses be damned? Radar tracks be damned? Satellite tracks be damned? Reporters be damned? Photographs be damned? Government statements be damned? Is there a pattern here?. Why do you refuse to address the issues by use of such disinformation tactics (rule 19 - ignore proof presented, demand impossible proofs)?'

20. False evidence.

Whenever possible, introduce new facts or clues designed and manufactured to conflict with opponent presentations -- as useful tools to neutralize sensitive issues or impede resolution. This works best when the crime was designed with contingencies for the purpose, and the facts cannot be easily separated from the fabrications.

Example: Jack Ruby warned the Warren Commission that the white Russian separatists, the Solidarists, were involved in the assassination. This was a handy 'confession', since Jack and Earl were both on the same team in terms of the cover up, and since it is now known that Jack worked directly with CIA in the assassination (see below.)

Proper response: This one can be difficult to respond to unless you see it clearly, such as in the following example, where more is known today than earlier in time... 'You are avoiding the issue with disinformation tactics. Your information is known to have been designed to side track this issue. As revealed by CIA operative Marita Lorenz under oath offered in court in E. Howard Hunt vs. Liberty Lobby, CIA operatives E. Howard Hunt, James McCord, and others, met with Jack Ruby in Dallas the night before the assassination of JFK to distribute guns and money. Clearly, Ruby was a co-conspirator whose 'Solidarist confession' was meant to sidetrack any serious investigation of the murder AWAY from CIA. Why do you refuse to address the issues by use of such disinformation tactics (rule 20 - false evidence)?'

21. Call a Grand Jury, Special Prosecutor, or other empowered investigative body.

Subvert the (process) to your benefit and effectively neutralize all sensitive issues without open discussion. Once convened, the evidence and testimony are required to be secret when properly handled. For instance, if you own the prosecuting attorney, it can insure a Grand Jury hears no useful evidence and that the evidence is sealed an unavailable to subsequent investigators. Once a favorable verdict is achieved, the matter can be considered officially closed. Usually, this technique is applied to find the guilty innocent, but it can also be used to obtain charges when seeking to frame a victim.

Example: According to one OK bombing Federal Grand Juror who violated the law to speak the truth, jurors were, contrary to law, denied the power of subpoena of witness of their choosing, denied the power of asking witnesses questions of their choosing, and relegated to hearing only evidence prosecution wished them to hear, evidence which clearly seemed fraudulent and intended to paint conclusions other than facts actually suggested.

Proper response: There is usually no adequate response to this tactic except to complain loudly at any sign of its application, particularly with respect to any possible cover up. This happened locally in Oklahoma, and as a result, a new Grand Jury has been called to rehear evidence that government officials knew in advance that the bombing was going to take place, and a number of new facts which indicate it was impossible for Timothy McVeigh to have done the deed without access to extremely advanced explosive devices such as available ONLY to the military or intelligence community, such as CIA's METC technology. Media has refused to cover the new Oklahoma Grand Jury process, by they way.

22. Manufacture a new truth.

Create your own expert(s), group(s), author(s), leader(s) or influence existing ones willing to forge new ground via scientific, investigative or social research or testimony which concludes favorably. In this way, if you must actually address issues, you can do so authoritatively.

Example: The False Memory Syndrome Foundation and American Family Foundation and American and Canadian Psychiatric Associations fall into this category, as their founding members and/or leadership include key persons associated with CIA Mind Control research. Read The Professional Paranoid or Psychic Dictatorship in the U.S.A. by Alex Constantine for more information. Not so curious, then, that (in a perhaps oversimplified explanation here) these organizations focus on, by means of their own "research findings", that there is no such thing as Mind Control.

Proper response: Unless you are in a position to be well versed in the topic and know of the background and relationships involved in the opponent organization, you are not well equipped to fight this tactic.

23. Create bigger distractions.

If the above does not seem to be working to distract from sensitive issues, or to prevent unwanted media coverage of unstoppable events such as trials, create bigger news stories (or treat them as such) to distract the multitudes.

Example: To distract the public over the progress of a WTC bombing trial that seems to be uncovering nasty ties to the intelligence community, have an endless discussion of skaters whacking other skaters on the knee. To distract the public over the progress of the Waco trials that have the potential to reveal government sponsored murder, have an O.J. summer. To distract the public over an ever disintegrating Mc-Veigh trial situation and the danger of exposing government involvements, come up with something else (Flight 800?) to talk about -- or, keeping in the sports theme, how about sports fans shooting referees and players during a game and the focusing on the whole gun control thing?

Proper response: The best you can do is attempt to keep public debate and interest in the true issues alive and point out that the 'news flap' or other evasive tactic serves the interests of your opponents.

24. Silence critics.

If the above methods do not prevail, consider removing opponents from circulation by some definitive solution so that the need to address issues is removed entirely. This can be by their death, arrest and detention, blackmail or destruction of their character by release of blackmail information, or merely by destroying them financially, emotionally, or severely damaging their health.

Example: As experienced by certain proponents of friendly fire theories with respect to flight 800 -- send in FBI agents to intimidate and threaten that if they persisted further they would be subject to charges of aiding and abetting Iranian terrorists, of failing to register as a foreign agents, or any other trumped up charges. If this doesn't work, you can always plant drugs and bust them.

Proper response: You have three defensive alternatives if you think yourself potential victim of this ploy. One is to stand and fight regardless. Another is to create for yourself an insurance policy that will point to your opponents in the event of any unpleasantness, a matter which requires superior intelligence information on your opponents and great care in execution to avoid dangerous pitfalls (see The Professional Paranoid by this author for suggestions on how this might be done). The last alternative is to cave in or run (same thing.)

25. Vanish.

If you are a key holder of secrets or otherwise overly illuminated and you think the heat is getting too hot, to avoid the issues, vacate the kitchen.

Example: Do a Robert Vesco and retire to the Caribbean. If you don't, somebody in your organization may choose to vanish you the way of Vince Foster or Ron Brown.

Proper response: You will likely not have a means to attack this method, except to focus on the vanishing in hopes of uncovering it was by foul play or deceit as part of a deliberate cover up.

Author's Note: There are other ways to attack truth, but these listed are the most common, and others are likely derivatives of these.

Battle Book Report 4 — The 8 Traits of a Disinformationalist

Yowusa.com, August 5, 2008
Share Free Printable eDoc
8.AlienSecurity.info

The 8 Traits of a Disinformationalist
H. Michael Sweeney, June 2001
PO Box 1941, Clackamas, OR 97015 USA

Companion Article to Cut to the Chase Interview #91:Terrestrial and Extraterrestrial Disinformation — Propaganda Experts Philip Gardiner and Marshall Vian Summers

Foreword by Marshall Masters

In this article by H. Michael Sweeney switches his attention from the specific tactics used by disinformation operatives, to a close examination of their eight most common traits. When you combine this behavioral examination with the tactical analysis he offers in Twenty-Five Ways To Suppress Truth (Page 1 of 2), you have a bottom up strategic view of disinformation at the behavioral and tactical level.

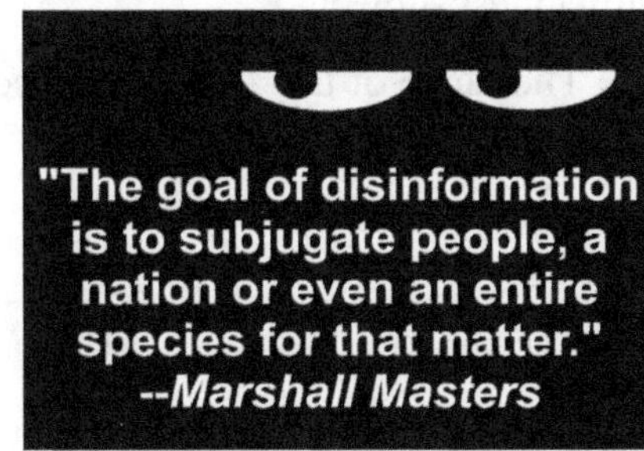

However, the key to a top down strategic view of disinformation at the behavioral and tactical level, actually comes to us from the book Power vs. Force: The Hidden Determinants of Human Behavior by David R. Hawkins.

When we frame the behavioral and tactical aspects of Sweeney's articles with relevant principles explained in Power vs. Force we quickly realize following disinformation top down truths:

Force is aspriritual, and motivates via service-to-self.

Power is spiritual and inspires service-to-others.

Dark masters such as Adolf Hitler always use force.

Spiritual masters like Mahatma Gandhi had true power.

Ergo, disinformation is about force — not power.

These truths explain why disinformation operatives are repetitious — and not clever. This is because they can only exercise the economic and political force given them by their dark masters. This simple truth is apparent in the predictability of their tactics.

This is not to understate the efficacy of their force, which is considerable. However, this force does have a permanent, built-in Achilles Heel, in that it is susceptible to high order, spiritual energy.

As a result of the ongoing disinformation attacks on us, we've observed is that disinformation force, Achilles Heel can unexpectedly trigger blowbacks for the perpetrators. This explains why the ongoing disinformation attacks on yowusa.com are producing net losses for the attackers.

For a more in-depth understanding, we turn to Power vs. Force. This is because it gives us what could be called a consciousness energy scale. By employing this scale, it is then a simple matter to obtain a global sense of clarity as to the exact nature of this disinformation Achilles Heel.

In doing the research for his book, Hawkins developed the following energy scale through extensive kinesiological testing (the study of the mechanics of body movements in human test subjects.)

The range of this logarithmic scale is 20 to 1000, where any results below 20 are deemed to be totally destructive to humanity.

Energy Level	Attitude / Emotion	Comments
20	Guilt	Dark Masters and Disinformation Operatives
50	Apathy	
75	Grief	
100	Fear	
125	Desire	
150	Anger	
175	Pride	
200	Courage	Intellectual Seekers of Truth
250	Neutrality	
310	Willingness	
350	Acceptance	
400	Reason	
500	Love	Spiritual Masters
540	Joy	
600	Peace	
700-1000	Enlightenment	

After comparing the energy levels in this scale against the various disinformation attacks waged against us, the unexpected contra-effective nature of these attacks became self-evident.

What we found is that the dark masters and their disinformation operatives can only operate in the sub-200 range. They understand the above-200 range enough to know that this is not their kill zone. They understand it at one level, but cannot experience it directly.

It is important to note that while the dark masters and their disinformation operatives cannot directly experience the emotions and attitudes above the 200 level, they are highly conversant in the language and logic.

Therefore, they use this language to seduce intended victims into a sub-200 emotion or attitude. Once the victim does, it is a simple matter for them to set the disinformation grapple hooks into their victims and then methodically and predictably grind away at both their sense-of-self, and self determination. Fortunately for us, were not seduced in this matter. The result is that we learned a valuable lesson entirely by accident.

The disinformation attacks, we experienced after we began releasing our South Pole Telescope analysis videos was unlike anything we've seen since the site was first launched in 1999. Until this year, these attacks were almost always the result of hit-and-run cranks and crackpots, who enjoy spamming us with vulgar and ignorant hate mail, and other attacks as well.

However, this disinformation attacks that started this year are stunning in their scope and force. They are clearly well-funded and benign carried out by a large wolf pack team, of highly organized disinformation operatives.

We admit, it is bothersome, but we are resolved not to view them as personal affronts and to respond as such. Rather, we keep our focus on noble research and by this simple act, we've negated the truly harmful aspects of this attack. In fact, we have actually benefited from them vis-a-vis increased Internet visibility that has attracted larger numbers of new, like-minded seekers of the truth to our site.

The reason for this is best summed up by an old Texas saying. "Anyone will stop to watch a dog fight," and this is a key component of disinformation attacks. Operatives rely on lazy readers to give their attacks just enough attention to slime the victim before they surf on.

In our case, the blow-back came when those who stopped to watch this dog fight realized that the possibility that they too, could have a dog in this fight. Consequently they've come to read our site and appreciate that noble and consistent way we pursue truths, wherever they may lead.

On the flip side, did all those who came to watch this disinformation dog fight draw the same conclusion? Regrettably no. In fact, we continue to get a small but steady stream of nasty letters from those seduced into a sub-200 level emotion or attitude. However, what we find most notable is their numbers. They are a small minority, whereas the larger majority continues to operate in the above-200 levels.

We attribute this phenomena is evident to the evolutionary nature of Planet X / Nibiru and 2012 awareness itself. While it may not translate into other areas of human interest in a similar manner, the fact that those who are truly aware operate at levels above those of the dark masters and their disinformation operatives remains.

The bottom line with disinformation is that if you remain resolved to stay focused in the above-200 range, you can moderate most of the damage, they cause. Further, by learning and recognizing their tactics, you can further turn these attack to your favor in much the same way the martial arts teach a small person how to defeat a larger opponent through a skilful use of leverage. The question then becomes, where are the leverage points?

Here is where the Sweeney article, The 8 Traits of a Disinformationalist a is of great value, because it essentially identifies behavioral leverage points so that leverage can best be applied.—*Marshall Masters*

Eight Traits of the Disinformationalist

H. Michael Sweeney, June 2001

It is the disinfo artist and those who may pull their strings (those who stand to suffer should the crime be solved) who MUST seek to prevent rational and complete examination of any chain of evidence that would hang them. Since fact and truth seldom fall on their own, they must be overcome with lies and deceit.

Those who are professional in the art of lies and deceit, such as the intelligence community and the professional criminal (often the same people or at least working together), tend to apply fairly well defined and observable tools in this process. However, the public at large is not well armed against such weapons, and is often easily led astray by these time-proven tactics.

1. Avoidance

They never actually discuss issues head-on or provide constructive input, generally avoiding citation of references or credentials. Rather, they merely imply this, that, and the other. Virtually everything about their presentation implies their authority and expert knowledge in the matter without any further justification for credibility.

2. Selectivity

They tend to pick and choose opponents carefully, either applying the hit-and-run approach against mere commentators supportive of opponents, or focusing heavier attacks on key opponents who are known to directly address issues. Should a commentator become argumentative with any success, the focus will shift to include the commentator as well.

3. Coincidental

They tend to surface suddenly and somewhat coincidentally with a new controversial topic with no clear prior record of participation in general discussions in the particular public arena involved. They likewise tend to vanish once the topic is no longer of general concern. They were likely directed or elected to be there for a reason, and vanish with the reason.

4. Teamwork

They tend to operate in self-congratulatory and complementary packs or teams. Of course, this can happen naturally in any public forum, but there will likely be an on-going pattern of frequent exchanges of this sort where professionals are involved. Sometimes one of the players will infiltrate the opponent camp to become a source for straw man or other tactics designed to dilute opponent presentation strength.

5. Anti-conspiratorial

They almost always have disdain for 'conspiracy theorists' and, usually, for those who in any way believe JFK was not killed by LHO. Ask yourself why, if they hold such disdain for conspiracy theorists, they focus on defending a single topic discussed in a NG focusing on conspiracies. One might think they would either be trying to make fools of everyone on every topic, or simply ignore the group they hold in such disdain. Or, one might more rightly conclude they have an ulterior motive for their actions in going out of their way to focus as they do.

6. Artificial Emotions

An odd kind of 'artificial' emotionalism and an unusually thick skin -- an ability to persevere and persist even in the face of overwhelming criticism and unacceptance. This likely stems from intelligence community training that, no matter how condemning the evidence, deny everything, and never become emotionally involved or reactive. The net result for a disinfo artist is that emotions can seem artificial. Most people, if responding in anger, for instance, will express their animosity throughout their rebuttal.

But disinfo types usually have trouble maintaining the 'image' and are hot and cold with respect to pretended emotions and their usually more calm or unemotional communications style. It's just a job, and they often seem unable to 'act their role in character' as well in a communications medium as they might be able in a real face-to-face conversation/confrontation.

You might have outright rage and indignation one moment, ho-hum the next, and more anger later -- an emotional yo-yo. With respect to being thick-skinned, no amount of criticism will deter them from doing their job, and they will generally continue their old disinfo patterns without any adjustments to criticisms of how obvious it is that they play that game -- where a more rational individual who truly cares what others think might seek to improve their communications style, substance, and so forth, or simply give up.

7. Inconsistent

There is also a tendency to make mistakes which betray their true self/motives. This may stem from not really knowing their topic, or it may be somewhat 'Freudian', so to speak, in that perhaps they really root for the side of truth deep within.

I have noted that often, they will simply cite contradictory information that neutralizes itself and the author. For instance, one such player claimed to be a Navy pilot, but blamed his poor communicating skills (spelling, grammar, incoherent style) on having only a grade-school education. I'm not aware of too many Navy pilots who don't have a college degree. Another claimed no knowledge of a particular topic/situation but later claimed first-hand knowledge of it.

8. Time Constant

There are three ways this can be seen to work, especially when the government or other empowered player is involved in a cover up operation:

Any NG posting by a targeted proponent for truth can result in an immediate response. The government and other empowered players can afford to pay people to sit there and watch for an opportunity to do some damage. Since disinfo in a NG only works if the reader sees it – fast response is called for, or the visitor may be swayed towards truth.

When dealing in more direct ways with a disinformationalist, such as email, delay is called for – there will usually be a minimum of a 48-72 hour delay. This allows a sit-down team discussion on response strategy for best effect, and even enough time to 'get permission' or instruction from a formal chain of command.

In the NG example 1 above, it will often also be seen that bigger guns are drawn and fired after the same 48-72 hours delay – the team approach in play. This is especially true when the targeted truth seeker or their comments are considered more important with respect to potential to reveal truth. Thus, a serious truth sayer will be attacked twice for the same sin.

Remarkably, not even media and law enforcement have not been trained to deal with these issues. For the most part, only the players themselves understand the rules of the game.